W9-BVG-874

Burdens of Proof
in Modern Discourse

Burdens of Proof

in Modern Discourse

Richard H. Gaskins

Yale University Press
New Haven and London

Designed by James J. Johnson.
Set in Ehrhardt Roman types by Tseng
Information Systems.

Printed in the United States of America by
Vail-Ballou Press, Binghamton, New York.

*Library of Congress Cataloging-in-Publication
Data*
Gaskins, Richard H.
    Burdens of proof in modern discourse /
Richard H. Gaskins.
        p.   cm.
    Includes bibliographical references and
    index.
    ISBN 0-300-05716-4 (cloth)
    ISBN 0-300-06306-7 (pbk.)
    1. Law—Methodology.   2. Burden of
proof.   3. Forensic orations.   4. Law—
United States—Methodology.   5. Burden of
proof—United States.   I. Title.
K213.G37   1993
340.1—dc20   92–23823

A catalogue record for this book is available
from the British Library.

The paper in this book meets the guidelines
for permanence and durability of the
Committee on Production Guidelines for
Book Longevity of the Council on Library
Resources.

10 9 8 7 6 5 4 3 2

For Elizabeth

It made one think of
the prisons of the spirit men create for themselves
and for others—so overpowering,
so much part of the way things appear to have to be,
and then, abruptly, with a little shift,
so insubstantial.

—V. S. NAIPAUL

Contents

Contents

Chapter 3. Institutionalizing the Challenge to Authority:
Justice through Correct Procedure   75

Chapter 4. Antinomies of Interpretation:
Critical Perspectives on Burden-Shifting   103

Part II. Philosophical Presumptions

Chapter 5. The Erosion of Scientific Authority   141

Chapter 6. The Rise of Ethical Authority   169

Preface

This is a book about patterns of reasoning. It is concerned with modes of thinking found throughout public discourse, including the arenas of law, politics, and academic and professional disciplines, as well as everyday life. It tells the story of a powerful strategy—the *argument-from-ignorance*—that plays a crucial but largely unheralded role in public debate, reflecting certain endemic features of modern culture. I plan to give this form of argument a thorough investigation and to trace its contemporary influence in constitutional law, scientific investigation, and moral philosophy and in wider public discourse modeled on each of these sources of intellectual authority. In the absence of any established tradition for discussing arguments-from-ignorance, I shall be testing a variety of analytical tools taken from the disciplines of rhetoric, law, organizational theory, artificial intelligence, and philosophy.

Although these chapters are meant to be critical as well as descriptive, this is a story without any villains. All of us, as we direct our discourse toward a modern public, know the powerful constraints that influence our own argument strategies. We are painfully aware of the uncertainties and ambiguities that lie beneath the foundations of our most central principles. We have all had the uneasy feeling of pursuing a line of thought far enough to see it shift suddenly onto unexpected levels, confounding our sense of order and desire for consistency. We know that competing schools of thought emerge within every discipline and for every public problem; we observe them struggling for dominance, moving in and out of fashion. And we cannot miss the adversarial overtones that increasingly turn discussions into futile contests of public assertion in which there can be no real winners.

Whatever their source, these frustrations are a common experience for anyone seeking to clarify public issues and to promote broader understanding and agreement. The lawyer may seem utterly confident in advancing the most enlightened arguments in court, but he or she knows that the leading precedents can always be interpreted in opposing ways. The scientist may report significant findings after long and careful experimentation, but the results are always provisional and must be heavily qualified in practical applications. Even philosophers (despite their more assertive tone in recent years) must hedge their broad principles with subtle qualifiers and assumptions. These are examples of the weighty rhetorical burdens known to everyone engaged in public discourse—intellectually, professionally, and personally.

By calling attention to the hidden role of arguments-from-ignorance, I hope to clarify the reasons for these pervasive burdens and thereby to ease some of the frustrations. There are certain risks in this whole enterprise, however, that must be faced at the outset. Since I shall be focusing on many popular arguments at their point of greatest vulnerability, my analysis can easily be read as relentless criticism, concerned only with exposing the flaws in prevailing orthodoxies. Despite my intentions, readers may come away with the sense that a favorite argument has been distorted or unfairly dismissed. There is perhaps not enough consolation in the fact that I shall identify the same rhetorical strategies on opposing sides of current controversies. In today's adversarial rhetorical environment, this kind of analysis can always be seen as lending comfort to the enemy.

The reader who is willing to endure some of these reactions, however, can expect to find more than a series of exposés in the chapters that follow. The path of criticism, while complex, is carefully designed to reach constructive ends. I firmly believe we can find new ways to strengthen our capacities for common discourse, and I assume this goal is shared by all whose arguments come under scrutiny here—and by my readers, too, on whose scrutiny I, in turn, must depend.

The most daunting feature of modern argument, for those who apply reasoning to political, academic, and everyday settings, may be its overwhelming sense of limitations. Principles are always getting stretched too thin under new applications; and all of us know, at some level, that we ignore those limits at our peril. But nor do we want to abandon the entire field of discourse—to end up talking only to ourselves. In the long run, a better understanding of defensive strategies can moderate our sense of vulnerability, even if it breaks the rhetoric of our immediate campaign.

We should not expect to cure all maladies of public discourse, however. Even if the argument-from-ignorance gains new recognition as an important but neglected symptom, there are many other factors (social, cultural, economic) that will guide our future state of rhetorical health. Nonetheless, the emphasis here on cognitive argument patterns suggests that we can improve our rhetorical future: we can cope therapeutically with the nagging sense that our basic principles have been overworked, and we can eventually find more productive ways to handle the fundamental differences that emerge in public debate. These will remain our goals throughout the study.

The argument-from-ignorance is widely distributed across the rhetorical landscape. Its general pattern is an affirmative inference from the lack of knowledge. In order to work as an argument, it requires some kind of decision rule (usually unstated) about how the parties to a discussion should proceed in the face of uncertainty or indeterminacy.

There are two distinct fields in which such rules are routinely formulated. In the legal system, courts apply formal rules assigning the *burden of proof,* which determines the winner whenever available evidence cannot resolve a particular case. In computer technology and artificial intelligence, programmers construct *default rules* to guide computation through the potentially infinite by-ways of unstructured communication. In this study, I shall assume the presence of similar parameters across a wide range of practical and academic discourse: in public and private organizations, in scientific and ethical communities, and in political and cultural groups—for all of whom rational discussion is constrained by fugitive rules and procedures.

My approach overlaps with many current scholarly investigations of paradigms, conceptual frameworks, and foundational presumptions. But in contrast to most of these studies, the focus on arguments-from-ignorance draws together both strategic and conceptual elements. Rather than strengthening modern skeptical tendencies, my analysis of boundary assumptions has the potential to reunite adversarial camps in an organic community of discourse. Throughout this text, I shall challenge the common assumption that human ignorance invariably imposes an adversarial burden on public debate.

The text divides into two main parts, representing complementary ways of approaching arguments-from-ignorance. Part I draws on jurisprudential analogies and seeks to clarify broader patterns of human reasoning in terms of judicial practice. A careful analysis of the judicial process reveals important *dialectical* aspects of modern discourse, including the subtle deployment of strategic presumptions and burdens of proof. This special sense of *dialectic* becomes the unifying theme of Part 1.

In clarifying the jurisprudential and rhetorical functions of dialectic, I will demonstrate its pivotal role in constitutional litigation over the past three decades. Supreme Court activism during this period may be understood as both cause and effect of a growing adversarial spirit found across political and academic debate. For our purposes, determining the order of causation is less important than tracing the simultaneous expansion of judicial institutional authority and the rhetorical power of arguments-from-ignorance. Exploiting both ends of the jurisprudential analogy, Part 1 connects these trends to issues of logic as well as contemporary culture.

The second part approaches the same set of issues from a philosophical direction. It focuses on conceptual dichotomies, or *antinomies,* as the breeding ground for contemporary arguments-from-ignorance. In particular, the opposition between scientific and ethical authority seems to have played a dominant role in shaping the conflicts of modern discourse. It has fostered a contemporary drama in which scientific reason comes under periodic scrutiny from a purportedly higher normative tribunal. As part of their adversarial confrontation in the twentieth century, both science and ethics have increasingly modeled themselves on judicial proceedings—a trend reflected in their strategic use of arguments-from-ignorance, as well as in their penchant for courtlike structures.

The use of legal concepts, constitutional history, and judicial metaphors creates an especially rich opportunity to explore current rhetorical conditions. The legal system provides the clearest example of the arguments-from-ignorance that increasingly dominate public discourse. Courts allocate the burden of proof—in technical terms, the *risk of non-persuasion*—with an instructive variety of implicit and explicit techniques. In recent years, the volatility of proof burdens has brought courts into the center of many public controversies. Today, court procedures reflect the assurance and authority that flow from the institutional power to shift burdens of proof.

In a culture that casts profound suspicion on all other forms of authority, judicial power assumes unique importance. It is the institutionalized expression of our dominant rhetorical ideal: the authority to determine who shall bear the burden of ignorance in a society where traditional and scientific forms of argument have long been stretched beyond capacity. In response to social crises, procedures modeled on judicial practice intrude into the domains of traditional authority (reborn in the adversarial discipline of applied ethics) and scientific method. On both sides of this great modern divide between values and facts, the widening gap between legitimacy and evidence yields an endless cycle of intellectual crises. What we desperately want—but can never find—is a kind of authority from which there is no appeal, whose final determinations can lay claim to full legitimacy.

In recent decades, the fact that judicial institutions have at least approached this ideal explains the increasing power of judicial symbols. The constitutional trends discussed in the first part of this study illustrate the more subtle strategies of academic and political argument to be covered in later chapters. The growing litigiousness of our society, the adversarial style in public debate, and the expansion of judicial procedures in institutional life are all reflections of the themes discussed below. Authority modeled on legal procedures becomes the natural response to a distinctive form of ignorance: the indeterminacy that accompanies our expanding scientific capacities and shifting normative ambitions. The argument-from-ignorance is now an inescapable component of modern discourse, for which jurisprudential models provide the most concrete form of expression.

No chronicle of arguments-from-ignorance can ignore the cultural climate in which such arguments have flourished. This book will offer no immediate correctives for the dysfunctions of modern discourse: neither philosophical manifestoes nor blueprints for cultural reform. (The ground is already covered with both kinds of remedies.) Instead, I will suggest alternatives to the dichotomies that supply the primary energy to our adversarial culture. Above all, this book will challenge the common practice of interpreting conceptual dualisms as irresolvable, just as legal adversaries interpret their respective interests as mutually exclusive. The durable Kantian technique of consigning dichotomies to separate worlds, linked only by an inscrutable transcendental connection, has now spread far beyond the field of professional philosophy. In the final chapter, I will consider some rhetorical alternatives.

The process of shifting the burden of proof, paradoxically, provides an important bridge across the adversarial gaps in public debate. These shifts define specific paths that generally fall from notice once they have been crossed. But proof burdens continue to ply these secret paths in all the sudden and revolutionary shifts that characterize modern thought. Reconstructing the strategic context of arguments shows us not only how opinions diverge, but also how they reestablish contact, however briefly, on the path toward sudden reversals. Instead of viewing each shift from only the one-sided perspective of its latest journey, we can focus on the reversible procedures that define its circuitous past—and future. Strategic shifts in modern argument constitute a hidden network for reconnecting adversarial positions. Each shift in the burden of proof becomes a conceptual fulcrum, a publicly accessible point of repose for the unity of divergent ideas.

Using principles from Hegel's dialectical logic, we can ultimately reconstruct

xvii

all philosophical dichotomies as contextually interrelated. On this reading, the argument-from-ignorance loses its stultifying force—not by being exposed and banished, but by being forced to travel through a continuous cycle of determinate shifts. Whether this approach offers any consolation for the sorrows of modern discourse depends, in the end, on whether current participants are ready to surrender their power (short lived though it may be) to crush their foes with all the force of a transcendental court of last resort.

The act of reading a book shares the many challenges set by our examination of public discourse. To borrow the jurisprudential analogy, the reader's response is a kind of judicial exercise: while the reader occupies the judge's seat, the author tries to arrange the evidence in an appealing manner. Sometimes, of course, books are deliberately organized as confrontations of two or more positions (the ever-popular symposia), where each side can be cross-examined by another. In single-author works, the writer usually decides to play the role of prosecutor, or defense attorney, or perhaps some combination. It all depends on whose ideas are being put on trial.

Like any skilled advocate, the author projects an argument that transcends the adversarial context of the dispute. Truth and justice are brought into miraculous harmony with the interests of today's client. This is fairly easy for individual authors who conduct their own cross-examination. In such cases, the reader needs to be all the more vigilant to see through adversarial tricks in the interests of assuring that justice is finally done.

But readers also assume certain responsibilities. In weighing the evidence and passing judgment, they preside over an elaborate dialectical procedure, much of which remains implicit in the acquired habits of practical judgment. The very criteria of judgment have to be selected, interpreted, and applied to new situations. Informal rules of evidence are taken from past experience and used to screen out irrelevancies. Above all, the reader has to determine the standard of proof to be demanded and assign the risk of non-persuasion. If the standard selected is proof beyond a reasonable doubt and if that burden falls on the author, then the reader's final judgment is virtually inevitable. When the result is formalized as a book review, of course, the judgment can always be reversed on appeal to another group of readers; they too will be operating with a particular set of dialectical tools.

Rather than pursue this adversarial ritual, I hope to elicit a different kind of response from readers of these chapters. You and I have an opportunity to explore together the whole strategic framework of public discourse, which must include the dialectical burdens that are usually left to silent negotiation between author and reader. The special demands of this enterprise here require us to suspend the habitual forms of adversarial discourse. If we lay aside our partisan interests in the specific arguments surveyed in this book, perhaps we can find common ground in discovering the strategic practices that are tacitly shared by opposing sides.

My purpose in examining the constitutional jurisprudence of the Warren Court, for example, is not to take any final position on its legitimacy, which remains one of the most heavily debated questions in legal scholarship. Readers are free to pass whatever judgments they wish on this issue; but we may still agree that the Warren Court displayed exemplary skill in the art of shifting burdens of proof. So, also, have the critics of the Warren Court shown their own mastery of dialectical procedure: the "neutral" critics of judicial activism, the radical critics of liberal "formalism," and the libertarian critics of progressive reform. The analysis below is meant to draw attention to a set of practices shared by all competing factions in many of today's most vocal rhetorical disputes. The point will instantly be lost, however, if the reader mistakes my analysis for a conventional attack on one or more of these particular positions.

We need to find new ways to address more openly the strategic context of modern argument. If successful, we can possibly moderate the adversarial strife that has become an inhibiting feature of public discourse. I have tried to find the most basic concepts for analyzing this elusive context, approaching the general topic from both jurisprudential and philosophical directions. I realize, of course, that no author can ultimately shed the risk of non-persuasion. But nor can the reader escape responsibilities that come with evaluating that risk, the responsibilities of reaching judgment in the face of indeterminate and conflicting evidence. At this level, our roles converge; in public discourse we are all authors and readers, and together we must look for ways to share our burdens more fruitfully.

Burdens of Proof
in Modern Discourse

Introduction

Arguing from Ignorance

In his correspondence from 1702, the philosopher Leibniz offers the following preface to his proof for the existence of God:

> For every being ought to be judged possible until the contrary is proved, until it is shown that it is not possible at all.
>
> This is what is called *presumption*, which is incomparably more than a simple *supposition*, since most suppositions ought not to be admitted unless they are proved, but everything that has presumption for it ought to pass for true until it is refuted.
>
> Therefore the existence of God has presumption for it in virtue of this argument, since it needs nothing besides its possibility. And possibility is always presumed and ought to be held for true until the impossibility is proved.
>
> So this argument has the force to shift the burden of proof to the opponent, or to make the opponent responsible for the proof. And as that impossibility will never be proved, the existence of God ought to be held for true.[1]

Today we take a skeptical view of Leibniz's effort to stack the argument in his favor. We are more likely to heed the sober warning from that champion of Enlightenment values, Sigmund Freud: "Ignorance is ignorance," Freud declared in his famous study of religious belief, "and no right to believe anything can be derived from it."[2] We know nothing whatsoever about higher beings and the afterlife, he went on to say, and thus we should refrain from using our ignorance as an excuse for dealing in illusions of salvation—however comforting they might seem.

But just how much—or how little—are we entitled to infer from the lack of information? If our ignorance of religious matters is as profound as Freud believed, how can he presume to dictate such strong prohibitions? His effort to censor our fantasy life reflects, in this instance, the traditional caution of scientific method: that we suspend judgment pending the accumulation of evidence sufficient to support our inferences. In effect, the onus is placed on all positive assertions to prove themselves before a tribunal where the very right to make an assertion is ultimately determined. In this unusual court, it appears, statements are deemed guilty until proven innocent.

And yet, this is really not the kind of case where an accretion of evidence could make much difference. By hypothesis, we are confronted by *systematic* ignorance, or the utter lack of knowledge competent to be introduced before the tribunal of modern science. Freud's judgment thus flows from a predetermined structure of decision—above all from his critical assignment of the burden of proof. One of the characteristic social tasks of judicial proceedings is to allocate that burden in legal cases where relevant evidence is found to be absent. In this respect, the metaphorical tribunal of science follows the procedures of its legal counterpart.

Faced with Freud's argument, a determined adversary will try to challenge the residual authority of science and its confident placement of proof burdens. After all, if we are ignorant of the afterlife, why should that count against belief? Perhaps it demonstrates instead the poverty of our science and the danger of lodging final authority in scientific experts. On appeal to a different kind of court—one in which the whole scientific enterprise is compelled to prove its exclusive jurisdiction over truth claims—Freud's argument might easily be reversed.[3]

Our jurisprudential analogy suggests the tacit structure of an increasingly common style of public argument: "I am right, because you cannot prove that I am wrong." In more subtle formulations, the argument-from-ignorance has become a commonplace of modern reasoning. It is found in great abundance in public argument, in philosophical speculation, and throughout academic discussion. There is, however, no automatic reason to dismiss the argument-from-ignorance as an outcast or fallacy. It is not some massive rhetorical plot, nor should its users be assigned base motives. It is exploited equally by deconstructionists and by neo-Aristotelians, by austere formalists and by practical reasoners, by cautious scientists and by adventurous mystics.

The chapters below will suggest that we have to acknowledge this argument pattern as an inescapable feature of contemporary discourse. Its widespread use is a natural consequence of modern pluralism—cultural, political, and epistemological. It is also a rhetorical index to some of the deepest inhibitions in current public debate: our increasing insecurity in resting arguments on fundamental principles, on disciplinary foundations, or on some political notion of the common good. Most of us deeply regret these conceptual barriers, but there is no simple way to make them disappear. There may, however, be ways to reduce the polarizing tendencies of public debate, which arise as each side seeks to impose the entire burden of ignorance on its opponent.

Exactly who ought to pay the price of deep-seated uncertainty? In the current rhetorical climate, shifting the burden of proof to our opponents becomes an irresistible argument strategy. It tends to harden and exaggerate the differences between speakers on opposite sides of an issue. The debate over substance turns into a battle for the tacit authority to dismiss an opponent's entire case. Each side declares, "I win, because you have not produced sufficient evidence to prove your point." Reduced to its simplest form, this argument can scarcely disguise its paradoxical claim to authority. The speaker is not simply expressing a personal opinion, but also assumes the roles of judge and jury. Something in the premises allows our inference to be managed like a lawsuit, in which the other side bears a preassigned burden of proof. When pushed in this direction, public debate becomes increasingly juridical in structure and adversarial in tone.

The Risk of Non-Persuasion

The burden of proof is a ubiquitous device whose wider influence on litigation has been curiously ignored by legal commentators. It generally blends into the background of legal procedure, like the default settings in computer programs with which it has some striking parallels. As part of the tacit framework within which the drama of adjudication unfolds, the burden of proof is often viewed by lawyers as little more than basic stage directions: it determines which party to a legal dispute has the obligation to speak first, or which one must step forward with special forms of evidence.

In recent decades, a more elusive dimension of the burden of proof has begun to play a larger role in the legal drama. The *risk of non-persuasion* is the lawyer's technical term for the chance that arguments presented before judge and jury will fail to support any relevant inference: whether guilt or innocence in crimi-

3

nal cases, or the presence or absence of liability in civil cases. The reasons for non-persuasion can be many, ranging from the lack of evidentiary facts to the mysteries of jury psychology, and to the inherent ambiguities of legal standards. Non-persuasion can even be calibrated according to degrees, as in the criminal trial requirement of proof beyond a reasonable doubt.

The burden of proof compensates for the many uncertainties of litigation, allowing the judicial system to reach determinate outcomes in the absence of relevant information. It is, in short, the law's response to ignorance, a decision rule for drawing inferences from the lack of knowledge. In the first three chapters of this book, I shall explore recent legal applications of this principle, including its creative role in the Supreme Court's sudden turn to judicial activism during the Warren era.

But the larger concern is to treat the risk of non-persuasion as the focal point for a much wider rhetorical function, as illustrated in the pair of arguments from Leibniz and Freud. Although seldom acknowledged by its accustomed users— indeed, it is rarely formalized outside of actual legal settings—the burden of proof turns out to be a vital component of modern argument. Sudden and dramatic shifts in rhetorical burdens signal the inevitable cyclical changes that affect most fields of discourse: the paradigm shifts in scientific theory, the alternating styles of ethical argument, and the proverbial pendulum swings in public opinion.

The Varieties of Ignorance

Everyday legal proceedings are supposed to reach definite conclusions about individual entitlements and responsibilities, notwithstanding any limits of information. Courts are routinely expected to meet this need, even when vitally relevant information is either too costly or simply unavailable. Moreover, judges often reject potential evidence that ordinary observers might otherwise consider, based on the assumption that it could not be weighed fairly by a neutral party. Thus the courts deliberately make themselves ignorant of self-serving statements, of third-hand accounts of what witnesses may have said, and of the layperson's conjectures on technical matters. Formal legal rules about the burden of proof compensate for precisely these occasions of routine or *practical* ignorance. The same rules also apply in cases where scientific or other expert opinion appears divided, as frequently happens, for example, with health and safety issues in environmental lawsuits. In such inquiries, ignorance is not merely practical but reaches into the domain of accessible theories.

The language of proof could misleadingly suggest that factual evidence alone marks the difference between ignorance and knowledge in public discussion. In legal proceedings, as in wider rhetorical contexts, however, the basic norms or rules for weighing evidence often contribute more fundamentally to the condition of ignorance. These rules are the reigning presumptions used by the legal system to interpret and to draw conclusions from factual evidence. When uncertainty arises about the meaning or legitimacy of these presumptions, a more profound level of ignorance casts its shadow over the strategic course of argument. This source of ignorance is not merely informational, but largely consensual or *cultural* in origin.

Many legal standards are notoriously vague but must nonetheless be applied to complex cases. Civil rights laws, for example, condemn the practice of discrimination, but they do not tell us exactly what it is. Is there employment discrimination, for example, when a company's hiring and promotion policies—although neutral on their face—have a disparate impact on people of different races or genders? Or does discrimination require some conscious intention by employers to single out particular groups for lesser treatment? The legal standards themselves do not tell us which it is, and under these conditions it makes a crucial difference where the burden of proof rests. Must you bear the burden of showing that I am violating the amorphous terms of such laws, or must I prove that I am not violating them?[4]

Finally, in addition to practical and consensual indeterminacies, we can identify an even more fundamental level of public ignorance. This distinctive notion is ultimately derived from philosophical theories about hidden, or *transcendental*, layers of possible knowledge. Despite the elusive role of transcendental ignorance in common areas of public discourse, its influence on contemporary legal and moral reasoning has become impossible to ignore. Academic theories have helped fix the presumptions of transcendental reasoning in the public mind, as our social institutions search for professional guidance in coping with the cultural indeterminacies I have just described.

The central assumptions of transcendental philosophy would initially seem too abstruse and improbable to attract even limited public acceptance. As commonly applied to the duality of facts and values, for example, transcendental theory projects a realm of potential knowledge (the realm of values) while denying that human beings have direct sensory access to it. The philosophical underpinnings of this position are ancient, but in modern thought they are associated with the influence of Immanuel Kant and with periodic revivals of Kantian thinking. In each of their historical appearances, Kantian postulates secure the claims of factual knowledge (identified with the evolving procedures of natural science) while investing human capacities with esoteric powers to comprehend values, including moral and political values.

The resulting ambiguities in knowledge labeled "transcendental" have been understood in divergent ways by partisans of Kantian thinking. A transcendental interpretation of values can support either their unqualified assertion or their skeptical dismissal. Like an international treaty open to opposing interpretations, this fragile arrangement offers a working substitute for real consensus. We now rely heavily on this conception of knowledge (or ignorance) to nurture opposing tendencies in our dichotomous culture. The result, however, is perpetual adversarial strife as each side mounts an unanswerable critique of its counterpart. Public discourse has been deeply marked by presumptive distinctions between facts and values. Along with other important dualisms, they are the legacy of transcendental reasoning pioneered by influential neo-Kantian movements at the end of the nineteenth century.

During the past two decades, a strong revival of public interest in ethical dilemmas and legal rights bears the unmistakable sign of this neo-Kantian dichotomy—drawn into service, this time, as a protest against the dominance of science and technology in modern society. Unable to supplant natural scientific thinking as the primary interpreter of everyday life, transcendental value theory attempts to carve out a purely ethical space, a moral sanctuary, or a private sphere of individual choice—all defined primarily by the exclusion of science-based knowledge.

In public discourse, the potential scope for such transcendental domains depends on the ability of proponents to seize command of the burden of proof. Rather than establishing their claims by appeals to empirical evidence (the method favored by natural science), guardians of the moral sphere are left with indirect arguments, for which the bedrock premise is the alleged inability of science to *dis*prove moral claims.

The conflict over religion, cited at the beginning of this introduction, illustrates this recurring shift in presumptions. Freud's verdict on religious belief, despite its uncompromising finality, invites a skeptical response to the presumptive authority of scientific procedure. This rejoinder follows a complex strategy that has once more elevated itself into an elegant and influential discipline. But all such burden-shifting foundations retain an inescapable adversarial dimension, leaving the way open for harshly skeptical counter-theories to score periodic victories.

The Challenge to Authority

As long as the burden of proof blends into the background of judicial rules and the conventions of everyday discourse, its presence is easy to ignore. But sudden shifts in the burden of proof from one party to the other, whether in lawsuits or in wider rhetorical practice, can be far-reaching—even revolutionary. The early chapters below will explore these shifts and some of the complex reasons for their occurrence. In general terms, burden-shifting indicates a challenge to established presumptions—those elusive default settings that surround any rule-based procedure.

In the United States during the 1960s, the Supreme Court provided a virtual laboratory demonstration of such methods in its far-reaching extension of the due process clause of the Constitution. At least for a brief period, the federal courts seemed to offer certain litigants a powerful forum for challenging the presumptions of authority and competence enjoyed by public agencies and officials and by a number of nominally private actors. A wide assortment of challengers—criminal defendants, welfare recipients, school children, along with others afflicted by modern bureaucratic forces—found the courts willing to impose new and formidable proof burdens on public and private decision-makers. The due process episode highlights an important rhetorical idiom behind contemporary challenges to authority, in which the challenger's assumptions remain hidden behind a facade of judgelike neutrality.

Throughout this book I will interpret recent events in the American legal system as symptoms of more elusive rhetorical trends in public discourse. There is no need to infer strict relations of cause and effect between the legal system and broader cultural trends; it is enough to suggest that the judicial process institutionalizes steps that remain largely implicit in other fields of argument and thus provides an important key for understanding essentially parallel strategies. The field of artificial intelligence, along with other recent efforts to construct models of informal reasoning, has begun to explore similar patterns under the rubric of "default reasoning." But the legal system remains a unique model of public discourse, shaped by the need to resolve all disputes according to rules of universal application. By contrast, systems of artificial reasoning consider hypothetical problems that can ignore social expectations for finality and legitimacy in decision-making.

The Rhetorical Significance of Legal Proceedings

Court battles provide endless fascination for both popular and professional audiences. The spectacle of combat is perhaps most lavishly staged in criminal proceedings, which may rise to the level of high social drama, especially when interpreted through press commentary. Sometimes the attorneys steal the show with ingenious tactical maneuvers and tableaux of moral outrage. Excesses of adversary partisanship are commonly excused (and often encouraged) so long as they serve the higher cause of justice. At other times, judges dominate the proceedings through heroic displays of disciplined neutrality—cutting through the deceptions of lawyers, defying the pressure of public opinion, or stifling their own simple emotions to see that justice prevails. What draws us to these postures is the central paradox of judicial proceedings: their promise of transforming the conflict of human interests into neutral justice. This is the miracle we all expect from the courts, whether or not they can actually deliver. It is a goal reaffirmed as much by their alleged judicial failures as by their comparatively rare successes.

Further paradox results from associating this precarious, often flawed institutionalized process with norms of human rationality. Jurisprudential analogies figure heavily in twentieth-century views on human capacities, as philosophers and social critics have searched for flexible models of rationality that range far beyond the formal patterns of deductive logic. Much of the early impetus came from the prestige of scientific method, as it elevated experimental and inductive reasoning to central prominence in the emerging disciplines of both the natural and social sciences. By the end of the nineteenth century, law itself got swept up in this transfer of authority away from formal concepts toward a confident encounter with facts. This more pragmatic view of the judicial system was signaled by the famous jurist Oliver Wendell Holmes, Jr., in his epigram declaring that the life of the law has not been logic, but experience.

The challenge for law has been to unite the experimental temper with the hard normative task of producing justice. Notwithstanding their well-documented deficiencies in performance, judicial institutions are often idealized as a paragon of effective practical reason. The jurisprudential analogy thus holds powerful implications for broader areas of moral and political thinking, where our ability to reach rational consensus has been widely questioned. The distinctive rationality of legal proceedings has even found proponents within scientific communities, especially where technical questions touch on important public policy issues.

Such wider implications of judicial procedures were sketched out early by American pragmatism, which treated the cooperative human quest for justice as a more encompassing project that absorbed the scientific search for truth. With their characteristic optimism, the pragmatists anticipated little of the disillusionment that has since tarnished both science and the law as tools for human inquiry. For John Dewey in particular, public political life had the potential to display the highest forms of human intelligence, to which individual cognitive endeavors were properly subordinated. Despite our renewed doubts about existing legal or political institutions as exemplars, what we might call *flexible legality* remains a powerful ideal. Throughout the current century—with its political upheavals and its tendency toward moral ambivalence—those who remain essentially optimistic about human capacities have clung to the model of judicial rationality. Their presumptions have also drawn strength from recent developments in linguistics and artificial intelligence.

But such optimistic borrowings from legal models have also been accompanied by deep skepticism. Generally the skeptical response accepts the legalistic ideal but questions our ability to put it into practice, whether in the judicial process itself or in the larger cooperative processes of social life. The miracle of transforming partisan perspectives into some neutral, unified vision represents a powerful myth—one that we can scarcely live without as we reach the end of this troubled century. Yet there is also great risk involved in tying scientific, logical, and moral truth to this problematic legal paradigm. Above all, it leaves academic disciplines and public debate open to periodic waves of radical and systematic doubt, as merciless critics continually unmask the realities behind every legalistic miracle. By embracing the justice ideal as a model of truth, we have fostered an endless succession of skeptical, relativistic, and nihilistic alternatives to the occasional constructive achievements of legal institutions.

Beyond the Crisis of Authority

Examples discussed in later chapters will raise questions about particular actions taken by legal institutions and also about more traditional claims backed by scientific and moral authority. Along the way, the reader may be tempted to construe these discussions according to the current fashion for limitless critique, sometimes labeled "deconstruction." Indeed, by drawing attention to the rhetorical power of burden-shifting argument strategies, I shall underscore the divergence between text and subtext in the utterances of established authority. The skilled deconstructionist will likely draw ominous conclusions from such gaps, treating them as evidence of manipulation by opaque social or cultural forces.

But I propose to take rhetorical gaps as I find them and will defer making broad inferences about social power, based on selective investigations of rhetorical subtexts. I shall conclude, in fact, that the typical inference pattern of deconstructionism is but one more example of the argument-from-ignorance. By now, nearly everyone knows how to detect unstated presumptions in textual sources—especially in texts whose conclusions are most abhorrent. Although this style of critique comes fully equipped with inhibitions on positive assertions, everyone also understands the hidden thrill of insinuating countercultural conclusions from the unmasking of authority. The familiar conventions of deconstructionism have become a skeptical cliché powerful enough to sustain academic revolts across a range of disciplines and always hinting at sweeping conclusions that can never be directly asserted.

By emphasizing the adversarial structure of modern argument, I mean to show how skeptical styles of critique apply virtually the same rhetoric found in most positive assertions of authority. Indeed, these perennial adversaries are usually bound together in the same antinomy, in which the strongest argument for either side is the danger implied by embracing its opposite. Thus the leading argument for prevailing authority becomes the rejection of nihilism; while the skeptic challenges the precarious construction of new orthodoxies on negative foundations. Infinite gradations are possible leading toward either extreme, but they invariably meet near the middle of a polarized continuum. This pattern seems to repeat itself with startling regularity throughout academic discourse and public debate.

Despite the element of mystery surrounding the shifting of proof burdens in modern discourse, there is no special reason to regard it as inherently illicit. If it strikes the critic as an act of cowardice or weakness, this implies that the more courageous alternative is to rely on real evidence and that anything less is a shameful deception. But an alternative view will emerge as the study advances: that our encounters with presumptions and proof burdens mark the limits of possible evidence. A line of argument has played itself out, and further inquiry will have to rest on new foundations. If we start with an adversarial aim, of course, we can seize this opportunity to declare our own line of argument as the default successor. But soon enough we will reach the limits of that line too, and there we face a choice: whether to continue under the protective cover of our presumptions or to look once again for new foundations. The final chapter will consider whether there can be a coherent logic for weaving these divergent strands into a common pattern. Under such a logic, we might actually find a higher virtue in periodic burden-shifting, provided it were allowed to proceed uninhibited.

Any notion of a discontinuous logic of foundations conflicts with the more common philosophical view that treats the foundations of argument as transcendental. This assumption has recently found its skeptical counterpart in the anti-foundationalist theories of adversarial pragmatists—critics who define their program by total opposition to a metaphysics of presence that few philosophers (of any period) would accept. It is the same old polarity in a new guise: the best argument to be made for either side is that it avoids the absurdity of its antithesis.

Throughout this book, I shall look behind contemporary modes of argument for tacit theories of undecidability or indeterminacy—in short, for postulates of transcendental ignorance. In many cases, these presumptions may arise from

10

human impatience with less extreme forms of ignorance, both practical and cultural. Enduring these lesser degrees of ignorance means tolerating vertiginous levels of ambiguity: an unbearable assignment for many academic and political partisans. Postulating a completely incurable form of ignorance makes it possible to reach the default conclusion much more swiftly. In this way, transcendental strategists hope to structure ignorance along adversarial lines, in which they alone shall play the pivotal roles of judge and jury. From this fateful practice comes the contemporary experience of academic debate without end and political controversy without resolution. Alternating cycles of self-assured affirmation and skeptical critique have thus tended to dominate the rhetorical climate of the late twentieth century.

We cannot escape the risk of non-persuasion that accompanies practical or cultural ignorance, but we can possibly take steps to limit the transcendental burdens. This means giving up the partisan advantage that comes to our own subdiscipline or political movement from manipulating the burden of proof in cases we have declared undecidable. Accordingly, as this book encounters arguments that fall short of their ambitions, I shall try to avoid using these discoveries to infer equally untenable alternative positions. The task is to find examples and patterns of argument that overreach themselves, but in every instance that failure must be understood in specific rather than global terms.

Instead of supporting inferences of radical doubt, my purpose is to investigate particular occasions in which modern judicial, scientific, and moral authority have overstepped their apparent limits. To the extent I can reconstruct the complex chain of burden-shifting arguments by which contemporary discourse has reached its current impasse, my analysis may at least have a therapeutic result.

In addition, I will try to suggest philosophical alternatives to the whole transcendental style of argument. Most contemporary academic disciplines have their roots in the neo-Kantian soil of late nineteenth-century Germany, from which transcendental argumentation drew its richest nourishment. Despite the enormous expansion of academic inquiry since that day, we seem no closer to resolving the adversarial battles that turn one discipline against another and that increasingly engage erstwhile colleagues within single fields. Perhaps it is not too late to mediate these struggles. In the process, we may find more constructive ways to cope with contemporary ignorance in practical affairs, in scientific and cultural life, and in the domain of public values.

11

Part I | Jurisprudential Analogies

We are not final because we are infallible;
but we are infallible only because we are final.

—U.S. SUPREME COURT JUSTICE
ROBERT JACKSON

Chapter 1 | The Burden of Proof: From Rhetoric to Dialectic

Arguments-from-ignorance play a central role in modern discourse, even though they are generally ignored by current theories of formal and practical reasoning. They appear at the margins of conventional argument practice, where our desire for finality and legitimacy extends beyond the force of available evidence and established principles. Rhetorical strategies for allocating the consequences of indeterminacy in public debate remain largely implicit. But they can be discovered by analogy with judicial procedures for assigning presumptions and for shifting burdens of proof. These judicial practices provide an institutionalized model for dialectical functions in modern discourse. The jurisprudential analogy permits us to postulate dialectic as a social process—at once dynamic and conceptual—for managing the elusive default assumptions in contemporary academic and public debate.

Judicial Procedure as a Model of Practical Reasoning

Lawyers raise hard questions about virtually everything, including formal logic. Over the past century, legal critics have repeatedly challenged the popular view that logic is the backbone of judicial decision-making.[1] In exploring other modes of reasoning, however, their attention has wavered between the competing legal ideals of flexibility and legitimacy. On the one hand, courts are expected to adapt established rules to fluid social conditions and must constantly work from a kind of situation-sense that transcends pure deduction. On the other hand, to command respect, their decisions are rhetorically organized as valid inferences from preexisting norms.[2] Given these tensions, it is understandable that lawyers are drawn to flexible models of human reasoning. And legal theorists are still searching for that elusive goal: a logic of practical judgment to underwrite the legitimacy of judicial pronouncements.[3]

In the following chapters I shall explore the fate of this project, which has managed to promote both serene confidence and deep skepticism about judicial decision-making. But let us begin with an intriguing reverse hypothesis: an influential theory of practical reasoning that takes its inspiration from the judicial

process. In his study of argument patterns, Stephen Toulmin used a jurisprudential analogy to ground a practical logic of wide application.[4] His work helped
to spark a resurgence of interest in argumentation theory, which has been called
on to rescue the informal decisions of everyday life from invidious comparisons with strict deductive logic. Numerous applications of Toulmin's model have
been made to political and ethical discourse as well as to fields of professional
expertise, and they have recently been supplemented by technical advances in
computational logic and artificial intelligence.[5]

In view of this special interest in presumptions and proof burdens, it is important to note that Toulmin's theory simply presumed, without critical analysis, the
basic efficacy of the legal process. Using an argument pattern that appears no-
where within his own theory, Toulmin built the very foundations of his practical
logic on a seemingly felicitous analogy. But for many legal theorists, jurisprudential procedure is more often the problem than the solution. They tend to reverse
Toulmin's analogy and to presume the efficacy of practical reasoning in various
domains, including law.[6] Let us therefore detain the lawyer as a skeptical witness
against Toulmin's theory and see where its assumptions run into trouble.

"Logic," says Toulmin, "is concerned with the soundness of the claims we
make—with the solidity of the grounds we produce to support them, the firm-
ness of the backing we provide for them—or, to change the metaphor, with
the sort of *case* we present in defence of our claims."[7] What begins as simply a
metaphor is quickly exchanged by Toulmin for a definitive model or paradigm;
upon reflection, he says, "law-suits are just a special kind of rational dispute, for
which the procedures and rules of argument have hardened into institutions. . . .
A sound argument, a well-grounded or firmly-backed claim, is one which will
stand up to criticism, one for which a case can be presented coming up to the
standard required if it is to deserve a favourable verdict. How many legal terms
find a natural extension here!"[8] More to the point, how few! Toulmin spends an
entire book elaborating a jurisprudential analogy but explores none of the territory of jurisprudence. Like a nineteenth-century European tourist, he took his
preconceptions along with him, and then informed the audience back home that
the natives "think like we do." In borrowing from the judicial process, Toulmin
overlooked virtually all its problematic features.

Toulmin's approach to reasoning can be quickly summarized. In everyday
life, he tells us, inferences are much richer than the process of deduction by
formal syllogisms. He believes that highly substantive, preexisting rules of valid
inference exist everywhere in our ordinary and professional experience, where
they operate much like rules of law in the judicial process. In law, for example, the
statute books contain the rule stipulating that people born in the British colonies

"of suitable parentage shall be entitled to British citizenship." Unless other rules explicitly interfere, this rule may be applied to common data to ground the valid claim that Stephen Toulmin is a British citizen. A parallel use of inference rules or warrants, says Toulmin, can be found in ordinary discourse. For example, we will typically conclude that "Harry cannot have black hair," once he is admitted to have red hair; our (implicit) warrant tells us that "if anything is red, it will not also be black."[9]

Things get a bit more adventurous, Toulmin says, moving from such trivialities into a field like sociology. There empirically established warrants may be invoked, such as the rule that "a Swede can be taken almost certainly not to be a Roman Catholic"—although a conclusion about any particular Swedish national will have to reflect the modal term contained in the warrant.[10] Warrants in the field of ethics are even more complex and are likely to be highly embedded in a system of customary norms. Toulmin's most revealing example comes from that chameleon of upper-class conformity, the fictional Bertie Wooster: "I saw that there would have to be a few preliminary *pourparlers* before I got down to the nub. When relations between a bloke and another bloke are of a strained nature, the second bloke can't charge straight into the topic of wanting to marry the first bloke's niece. Not, that is to say, if he has *a nice sense of what is fitting,* as the Woosters have."[11] Drawing on a series of such carefully crafted examples, Toulmin rests his case for the theory that all knowledge is really warranted belief. He wants to show that valid inference in everyday life is in fact much broader than the traditional philosopher's model of deductive logic. In fields other than formal logic, he says, "a time comes when we have produced in support of our conclusions data and warrants full and strong enough, in the context, for further investigation to be unnecessary—so in this sense non-analytic arguments also can be conclusive."[12]

Toulmin's effort became an important part of a philosophical movement during the 1950s, identified with the Oxford school of analysis. His ambition was shared with his more famous colleagues Ludwig Wittgenstein and J. L. Austin: to lower the pretensions of academic philosophy.[13] By assuming that ordinary discourse was free of such arcane philosophical mysteries as "what is truth?" or "what can we know with absolute certainty?" Oxford analysts thought to put professional philosophy out of business, or at least to cure it of its strange, self-inflicted neuroses. Toulmin's book helped direct this strategy against the prior representatives of British analysis, notably Bertrand Russell and the early Wittgenstein, who had identified true knowledge with technical propositions written in a formal logical style.[14]

Given his specific concern with relations of truth and inference, the para-

17

doxical role of presumptions in Toulmin's own argument is especially significant. In addition to his foundational assumption that ordinary language is somehow exemplary,[15] Toulmin advances the jurisprudential analogy not only as an alternative to formal truth-models and computational analogies, but also in opposition to overtly psychological or sociological theories of human reasoning. This ingenious presumption permitted Oxford analysis to remain balanced on that knife-edge of neutrality between formalism and empiricism, and thus to resist those mathematical logicians and psycho-social reductionists who might question this optimistic vision of mankind's everyday search for truth.[16] Toulmin's analogy, in line with other applications of Oxford philosophy, neatly shifted the burden of proof to anyone daring to challenge the normative status of conventional discourse.

As any common lawyer knows, however, analogies often raise more questions than they resolve. If reasoning in everyday life bears any resemblance to formalized judicial proceedings, a look at everyday operations in the legal system will reveal potential problems with practical reasoning. Toulmin himself anticipates the important questions of where warrants come from and what validates them for proper inference behavior. For decades, critics of legal formalism have raised such issues about the judicial process, based on skeptical assessments of actual judicial decisions.[17] In law, warrants come from the statute books, as Toulmin notes, but that is only the beginning of a complex tale. Statutes may conflict with higher sources of law (constitutions, customs, natural law, divine will). They may also conflict with each other, given the piecemeal pattern of legislation found in most democratic systems. Finally, they are typically formulated on a general level, requiring artful application to concrete cases; thus the judicial decision-maker often contributes to the creation of warrants in putting them to use.

Without pausing over these perennial issues of legal process, Toulmin nevertheless acknowledges that warrants in every specific field of inquiry (law included?) are to be judged by "standards appropriate within that field." "An assurance that a warrant *has worked* is all we can reasonably demand." In general, "The proper course for epistemology . . . [demands] of arguments and claims to knowledge in any field . . . that they shall achieve whatever sort of cogency or well-foundedness can relevantly be asked for in that field." [18] This approach disperses the important questions of authority and validity but scarcely eliminates them. Conflicting notions of "accepted" and "acceptable" rules exist not only in law and all other normative endeavors, but also in the daily conduct of natural and social sciences. Rather than taking his jurisprudential analogy as far as it can go, Toulmin reverts to the convenient Oxford assumptions that substantive problems can be reduced to questions of conventional linguistic usage and that the world is made up of coherent language communities. Within such communities we can—like Bertie Wooster in his world—be expected to know how to behave.[19]

When Toulmin acknowledges the diversity of practice within a single field, he interprets it functionally as a prelude to future consensus. Although it seriously undercuts his declared neutrality on classic philosophical problems, one cannot help detecting here the philosophical premise of scientific realism: within any language community, an initial picture of the world evolves as ideas achieve closer representations of the universe as it truly is. "Our starting-point will be confessedly empirical. . . . We must study the ways of arguing which have established themselves in any sphere, accepting them as historical facts; knowing that they may be superseded, but only as the result of a revolutionary advance in our methods of thought. In some cases these methods will not be further justifiable— at any rate by argument: the fact that they have established themselves in practice may have to be enough for us."[20] Toulmin follows the above quotation with the helpful note that, "In these cases the propriety of our intellectual methods will be what the late R. G. Collingwood called an 'absolute presupposition.'" This revealing comment supports the interpretation that Toulmin's argument rests on the common legal practice of assigning burdens of proof.

Toulmin's genial, optimistic outlook for steady social progress toward diversified rational consensus breaks down entirely in the very field of argument he selects as his paradigm: judicial decision-making. It defeats the law's universalist ambitions to subdivide the formal legal system into increasingly fragmented communities based on separate understandings of appropriate legal rules. Instead of accepting this dispersion, the legal system relies on distinctive procedures for restoring formal unity in cases where parties are known to take sharply opposing views on current rules. Indeed, when the legal way of arguing reaches conclusions, it does so after deliberately inviting polarized interpretations of established rules. An examination of such institutional practices in the judicial system shows important features that shade Toulmin's bucolic portrait of human reasoning.

In addition to administering an adversary system, the judicial process goes well beyond Toulmin's model of argument in handling both facts and rules. For testing facts, the law recognizes a special set of rules surrounding the hearing and weighing of evidence. Moreover, it institutionalizes the very distinction between facts and rules, assigning each realm to separate players in the judicial process. Diversity within the legal structure is commonly controlled by appellate review of lower court decisions and, in the United States, by yet a further process for judicial review of actions taken by other branches of the legal system.

Judicial stewardship over rules (as something distinct from adjudicated facts) is of central importance in understanding how legal procedures preserve unity in the midst of structured diversity. The catalogue of available judicial techniques is vast, including judicial notice of facts, judicial findings on guilt or liability notwithstanding factual evidence, summary judgment on legal claims taken in abstraction from underlying factual issues, judicial instructions to the jury, the treatment of legal presumptions embodied in statutory or judicial rule-structures, and the filling of gaps in prevailing legal rules. Equally important, the existence of an appeals process highlights the element of finality that pervades the entire process. In the United States, the coherence of the legal system is an ongoing creation by appellate courts.

In response to powerful centrifugal pressures within the legal process—most of which Toulmin manages to suppress in his jurisprudential analogy—certain critical devices for preserving unity can be identified. These methods are institutionalized in the legal system, particularly in the judicial procedures enumerated above. Toulmin's analogy prompts speculation on whether such self-corrective devices have counterparts in broader fields of reasoning. After all, according to Toulmin, the judicial comparison is "something more than a mere analogy." As noted above, he believes that "law-suits are just a special kind of rational dispute, for which the procedures and rules of argument have hardened into institutions."[21] Does this mean there is some counterpart to judicial rules of evidence in scientific reasoning, in ethics, or in philosophy? Indeed one might ask the same procedural question about Toulmin's favored realm of ordinary discourse. And in all these areas, as well as in formal logical systems, are there counterparts to the central judicial tasks of maintaining unity and imposing finality?[22]

The most powerful device of this sort is the wholesale management of tacit presumptions. The legal term *burden of proof* captures this loosely connected set of reasoning strategies, which seem to turn up in nearly every field of inquiry. Their common thread is the need to structure vast areas of indeterminacy—in plainer language, ignorance—that confronts organized inquiry, not only in practical endeavors like law, but in scientific investigation, moral reasoning, and philosophical thinking. One may eventually be able to organize these strategies in terms of default logics currently being investigated in artificial intelligence research.[23]

The term burden of proof has been relatively neglected even in legal commentary, and its importance in explaining current judicial practices has yet to be fully appreciated. Both for law and for other fields where it finds application, this concept is a powerful device for maintaining unity within the increasingly fragmented domains of rational inquiry.[24] Skillful advocates in today's legal battles have perfected the art of shifting the burden of proof onto their opponents. But many other fields of inquiry have likewise mastered the tacit strategy of shifting the burden of ignorance onto their critics. The jurisprudential source of this important pattern has recently become evident, as scientific and ethical issues enter more fully into public policy debate.

The Burden of Proof in American Law

Burdens of proof in the legal system resist any simple description. Most legal theorists approach them formally as a distinct body of legal rules, although a few writers may see them more cynically as signs of a hidden power structure behind the legal system. In American law, the burden of proof is narrowly associated with that stage of judicial proceedings where factual evidence is introduced and weighed; and thus it frequently appears as an adornment to the law of evidence. Commentators are chiefly concerned with distinguishing two different burdens faced by litigants: the obligation to produce some kind of evidence to support their case, and the risk that inconclusive findings at trial will count against them. The former is defined as the *burden of going forward*, and the latter as the *risk of non-persuasion*. Once this distinction has been made, however, the burden-of-proof concept fades into the footnotes.[25]

A far more powerful manifestation of legal burdens occurs in the judicial treatment of *presumptions*. Everyone has heard of the presumption of innocence in criminal trials, even though opinions differ widely on what it means and whether it offers much consolation to defendants. The source of this presumption is itself obscure, but it has been celebrated as the golden thread of Anglo-American law, extending back for many centuries.[26] Nonlawyers may be less familiar with the somewhat different burden imposed on plaintiffs in civil trials, where anyone bringing a case into the judicial process is required to prove a claim "by a preponderance of the evidence." In effect, the defendant in civil trials enjoys a presumption of nonliability, unless evidence produced at trial is sufficient to persuade the judge or jury according to this notoriously inexact quantitative standard. Such broad presumptions represent much more than technical adjuncts to the law of evidence. They overlap in significant ways with substantive legal rules and frequently become the central focus of adversarial dispute. Overcoming such presumptions and shifting their burden to the other party are critical strategic goals in many criminal and civil cases.

Yet another type of presumption derives from the American political structure based on the separation of powers. Although the authority of federal courts to review legislative and executive actions was effectively asserted early in the nineteenth century, bitter struggles have continued into the present day on

21

whether federal and state legislation enjoys a *presumption of constitutionality*. After decades of intricate manipulation, this phrase has become virtually meaningless, but the underlying concept figures heavily in contemporary debate over judicial activism.[27] Under Chief Justice Warren in the 1950s and 1960s, the United States Supreme Court began to inject more authority and flexibility into judicial review, while trying to maintain the Court's traditional image as an impartial tribunal. Much of that flexibility came from adjusting the presumption of constitutionality. Since that time, the Court has amply demonstrated how the same methods can be used to reach conservative outcomes, as well as liberal ones.

Apart from muddying the waters of judicial review, presumptions play a further role in the wider legal system. Legislatures and administrative bodies build presumptions into legal standards as a way of structuring the inevitable uncertainties of implementation. It is not enough, for example, for Congress to pass a law protecting the safety of new foods or drugs without also anticipating the many indeterminate issues of enforcement. Factual evidence on matters of product safety is often conflicting or inconclusive, and rules alone cannot say exactly when "safe" is safe enough. By allocating in advance certain procedural and evidentiary burdens among relevant interest groups, legislation favors substantive outcomes that defy the bland and balanced rhetoric one finds in many statutes.[28]

Sometimes legislative presumptions themselves become targets for judicial review and thus are scrutinized through the courts' own presumptive apparatus.[29] In sum, although the narrow term *burden of proof* is found almost exclusively at the trial stage of judicial proceedings, the closely related concept of presumptions figures heavily in the course of judicial appeals and across all three branches of the legal system.

Controversies about proof and metaphors of sensory verification occur at all levels of the judicial hierarchy, frequently masking deeper conflicts over public values. Appeals courts derive conclusions of law from the fact that no evidence in contradiction was introduced at trial, or at least insufficient evidence. In most such cases, the nature and salience of evidence are more important than sheer quantity. To close the gap between quantity and quality of evidence, a structure of presumptions must cut through complex social ambiguities. For example, the defendant in a discrimination suit may have to prove an absence of subjective bias. The opponent of pornography may be forced to demonstrate a strong causal connection between the printed page and social behavior.

The rationale for judicial decisions in such cases can be stated in terms of evidence, but the underlying issue is about presumptions: what conclusions can be drawn from controversial or indeterminate evidence—that is, from ignorance in its many guises? When exactly is evidence good enough to meet the implicit burdens lurking in legal rules? In short, where is the dividing line between proof and ignorance, and what follows from inconclusive data? The institutionalized procedures of law force us to confront these questions rather than treating them as painlessly settled by nature or custom.[30]

The tendency of our legal system to convert issues of public policy into technical regulations of trial evidence reflects an underlying spirit of practical empiricism in Anglo-American law. As William Twining pointed out in his survey of legal evidence theory, this "optimistic, often bland, [empiricist] rationalism" contrasts sharply with the "sceptical tendencies in much recent writing about the judicial process. . . . Hardly a whisper of doubt about the possibility of knowledge, about the validity of induction, or about human capacity to reason darkens the pages" of the major English and American commentators on evidence law up to the current day.[31] The proof procedure to which strategic burdens are attached is a loose composite of empiricist epistemology: it borrows something from Locke's tabula rasa theory, J. S. Mill's rules for induction, and more recent analytical theories of perception and probability.

The traditional process for determining underlying facts in legal disputes emphasizes the immediacy and autonomy of the evidence to be inscribed on the blank tablets of jury or judge. It essentially ignores the more likely possibility that evidence in all forms passes through special cognitive filters, which are easily colored by social, psychological, or dogmatic predispositions.[32] The latter approach suggests the true importance of evidentiary presumptions and burdens, whereas the empiricist has little interest in compensating for the boundaries of cognition. For empiricism, it scarcely matters who must initially "go forward" with the evidence, as long as someone is given an incentive to produce the basic facts. After all, if the underlying truth is really on your side, you have no reason (other than laziness) to avoid taking the risk of non-persuasion.

Traditional legal commentary has been comfortable placing burdens on the party seeking the law's intervention: on the plaintiff in civil cases and on the prosecution in criminal trials.[33] One finds the same presumption of continuity in Mill's inductive logic; until fresh evidence persuades the observer to revise a prior hypothesis about the natural world, that hypothesis is allowed to stand.[34] In practice, however, the law manages to complicate this simple faith, and the Anglo-American legal system is not entirely true to its empiricist spirit.

Twining has carefully traced that spirit through writings of the leading evidence commentators and reformers—Bentham, Thayer, and Wigmore. Bentham was especially critical of the numerous formalities and fictions found in daily judicial practice, which impede the natural flow of evidence by imposing technical restrictions on the admission of hearsay and documentary materials. "Until the late eighteenth century," Twining notes, "evidence doctrine consisted almost entirely of a disconnected potpourri of scattered precedents." It was the proliferation of such seemingly artificial practices that led Bentham to advocate "the abolition of all formal rules," and the adoption of a more " 'natural' system of free proof, based on everyday experience and common-sense reasoning." [35]

The American commentators Thayer and Wigmore (both law professors) shared some of Bentham's impatience with legal artifice but accepted the growth of technical evidence rules under Anglo-American law as a consequence of the jury system, under which excluding irrelevant evidence was viewed as a practical necessity.[36] In Twining's summary, the modern tendency in legal thinking is to follow Thayer's view that the law of evidence is "an essentially negative 'set of regulative and excluding precepts' based on policy, which set certain artificial constraints on what witnesses and what classes of probative facts may be presented to a jury and how certain types of fact may or must be proved." [37] Commenting specifically on burdens of proof, Wigmore defended the diversity of prevailing rules with an appeal to that favorite American reducing agent: experience. "The truth is that there is not and cannot be any one general solvent for all cases. It is merely a question of policy and fairness based on experience in the different situations." [38]

The bifurcation of disputes into distinct issues of facts and law forced courts to distinguish legal procedures for finding the facts from procedures for bringing the facts into contact with legal rules. In both theory and practice, however, this separation differs markedly from the cognitive distinction between perception and judgment. Under Mill's influential logical model, facts in most social situations are really conclusions derived by induction from other facts, and only the most primitive facts are derived from original sensations.[39] In rough conformity with this model, juries are expected not only to observe but to draw inferences, which by their very nature can never reach the level of certainty assigned by classical logic to deductive reasoning.

The heavy psychological element in Mill's logic matches the common judicial theory that fact-finding is really a process of human inference about probabilities. The declaration of legal facts is thus an event reflecting varying degrees of certainty on the part of the inference-maker. With this sort of logic in mind, it makes sense to speak of certainty beyond a reasonable doubt, which is the standard of proof now associated with criminal trials. At least two other standards have been established for other types of cases: proof by a preponderance of the evidence, and (perched somewhere between the first two standards) clear and convincing evidence.[40]

The model of fact-finding as a human process creates certain anomalies within the institutionalized setting of law.[41] In supervising the actions of the jury, courts attempt to manage an arena of complex social behavior and not just isolated acts of individuals making inductive inferences. Legal rules barring the jury from receiving certain kinds of evidence are thus only a small part of the trial courts' responsibilities; more significant contributions are presumptions for structuring possible inferences, mandated standards of proof, and judicially construed burdens of proof. In connection with burdens of proof, courts retain the authority to overrule the inferences of juries; their options include making final judgments notwithstanding the evidence and reversing jury findings because of insufficient evidence.

Even prior to jury action, trial courts are often required to scrutinize the factual allegations of the plaintiff in order to verify their relevance to substantive issues of law. You may want to charge somebody with crude and thoughtless social behavior, but unless the court has reason to think that the defendant violated a legal rule, the facts alleged are irrelevant to any legal dispute. This sort of case can be summarily dismissed prior to trial, and the jury will have no occasion to determine what really happened. Summary judgment and other preemptory actions by trial court judges represent important framework conditions under which our legal system renders its decisions.[42]

Policing these boundary procedures is quite unlike any of the tasks for adjudication that appealed to Stephen Toulmin when he offered his bold analogy for practical reasoning. The jurisprudential functions of trials and appeals suggest important omissions in Toulmin's model of preestablished warrants applied to well-defined data. Toulmin wanted an institutional analogue as simple as the analytic philosopher's model of everyday human judgment. If his legal analogy implies more complex elements, it seems likely that human judgment is itself more complicated than Toulmin allowed.

In the everyday legal system, a concern for correct procedures often dominates the courts' important task of producing statements of fact. Indeed, the language of judicial fact-finding generally avoids the concept of truth, preferring instead to speak of probability and degrees of certainty that fall short of complete demonstration. Institutionalized procedures for discovering facts must be judged by functional criteria and not by the correspondence of their results to some independent measure of truth. Seen in this procedural light, the judicial analogy points to the theory of scientific truth developed early in this century by American pragmatist philosophy.[43]

The pragmatists argued that scientific truth was the evolving product of a properly constituted research community and not the direct mirror of nature. In a similar spirit, the American legal system bases the authority and legitimacy of the judicial process on the integrity of its procedures rather than any privileged access to truth. If objective truth is inaccessible to institutionalized inquiry, judicial procedures for defining facts serve a most vital social function.[44] And if such higher truths elude practical reasoning in general, society must come up with procedural substitutes.

The openly functionalist defense of current law has been proudly summarized in a popular legal textbook on evidence, under the heading "Truth and the Adversary System."

> The lawyer's role as an identifier, selector, and marshaller of evidence is not accidental. That role grows out of our system of dispute resolution. We do not resolve disputes by tying rocks to litigants, throwing them into pools and then giving verdicts according to whether a litigant sinks or swims. Rather, we resolve disputes primarily through settlement or trial. . . .
>
> Because one cannot usually return in a time machine to show a trier of fact "what really happened," investigations do not produce "facts." They produce evidence, from which the trier of fact will resolve the parties' factual dispute(s) by deciding the *probable facts*. . . . We are not cameras, able to observe, absorb and recall all that occurs in our presence. What we observe, remember and state is greatly influenced by such matters as our individual abilities, the nature of our settings, personal biases, expectations, and the skills of attorneys who extract our stories. . . .
>
> Out of necessity, then, our system of justice is content with less-than-complete truth based on admittedly imperfect evidence. That is not to say that ours is a system of injustice, or that trials are inappropriate ways of settling disputes. . . . With objective truth unattainable, and the adversary system in place, one zealously attempts to ferret out and shape evidence so that a factfinder finds to be true facts which trigger a favorable legal result.[45]

Although the adversary system devotes much of its energy to ferreting and shaping, it seems natural that it should also want to influence the basic structural framework for proof, including the all-important allocation of proof burdens. You may, for example, want the jury to find that your client in an accident case endured pain and suffering worth one million dollars in compensation. When it comes to proof, you will much prefer to let the opponent carry the burden of showing that this precise degree of pain did not occur, rather than your proving that it did. Legal issues are nominally about facts, but in practice they are often contests of persuasion concerning indeterminate matters. Where persuasion requires the jury to build complex inferences, influenced as much by group psychology as by inductive reasoning, the risk of non-persuasion becomes a heavy burden indeed. The honorable path for a zealous seeker of favorable legal results

26

is to try to shift that burden to the adversary whenever possible. That way your client wins, unless the opposing party can somehow make an affirmative case for a different version of the facts.

In practice, courts permit these burdens to shift quite freely and have formalized a distinctive set of rules for easing the transition. A well-known example occurs in the field of accident law in cases where the underlying facts may be inaccessible or otherwise difficult to weigh. Suppose a pedestrian is injured by a falling scaffold, but there is no clear evidence to show whether the scaffold-maker or its user did anything negligent. Or suppose an ordinary boiler explodes and injures several workers, but no one can say for sure whether the boiler was improperly designed and built. In cases like these, American courts have increasingly applied the legal rule of *res ipsa loquitur* ("the thing speaks for itself"). Despite its archaic sound, this rule is a twentieth-century invention for rescuing accident claims that might otherwise be thrown out of court for lack of evidence. Most important, it allows such cases to reach the jury, before whom defendants face the dubious task of demonstrating their lack of negligence.[46]

Res ipsa loquitur seems to invite the jury to infer the defendant's negligence, based on the common-sense assumption that scaffolds do not normally fall and boilers do not normally explode, unless someone like the defendant has been negligent. "Thus where a human toe is found in chewing tobacco, or a worm in a bottle of soda it is hard indeed to escape the imputation of negligence somewhere in the process used by the manufacturer or bottler."[47] In a practical sense, this rule turns certain defeat for the plaintiff into probable victory. The change occurs not because anything has been proved, but because the very lack of evidence is made to work against the opposing party.

27

Unlike the more controversial pro-plaintiff doctrine of strict liability, res ipsa loquitur is not a substantive rule imposing liability without fault but only a procedural rule for taking the vexed issue of fault to the jury. Everyone knows, however, that juries like to resolve such murky situations in favor of the suffering plaintiff.[48] Shifting the burden of proof can thus achieve the same result as a new substantive rule, but it stays with the more neutral language of evidence and purports simply to facilitate the jury's duty to draw inferences.

By allowing the jury to pursue a line of inference based more on sympathy than on data, courts might appear to compromise the integrity of inductive proof. One could argue that such cases do not belong in court at all, if no one can offer sufficient evidence for juries to make responsible judgments.[49] No careful scientist responds to the absence of data by leaping to conclusions based on personal preference (at least, not according to standard empiricist theories of science). But the legal system has long foreclosed any such neutral posture by placing the burden of proof initially on plaintiffs. Unlike classic scientific discovery, institutionalized inquiry in law must formulate explicit rules for allocating in advance the consequences of uncertainty in specific cases. If rules like res ipsa loquitur make it possible to transfer some of that burden to defendants, they simply restore symmetry by enabling the courts to change sides.

Fact-finding by induction is borrowed from a scientific epistemology for which the practical consequences of indecision are not nearly so extreme. The judicial obligation to reach conclusions in every case makes it impossible to suspend judgment and to wait for the gradual build-up of evidence. Even with relatively large amounts of evidence in a single trial, the integrity of induction is weakened any time the jury is forced to reach final judgment on specific issues. Instead of a scientific progress report on the long-term accumulation of knowledge, the law requires definitive conclusions on a series of discontinuous issues. The inductive ideal in law has thus been attacked by some commentators as a delusion.

> The delusion lies in our almost complete lack of anything approaching accurate knowledge of where the balance of probabilities lies in many of the situations presented by the cases. Of course some generalizations would command wide, even universal, support. These are the judgments of "common sense." But even here it is not safe to forget how often the science of the morrow makes a fool of the common sense of today. Moreover the area is vast wherein thoughtful people who accept today's common sense would either disagree or refuse to guess on which side of the line the greater probability lies.[50]

The sources of non-persuasion in law are many. In the cases covered by res ipsa loquitur, even the most zealous investigation would produce too little information for the neutral observer to form a judgment of probabilities favoring one side or the other. The plain, everyday facts that might allow these cases to go forward in the traditional manner are simply not available, for a host of practical reasons. But the quotation also contains some glimmerings of the skepticism that Twining found virtually lacking in most legal commentaries on evidence. If juries have trouble when facts are not available, why should they perform any better under the barrage of evidence presented in many modern trials? Should we even talk about factual inference when the jury is required to relate its conclusions to such opaque legal terms as negligence, proximate cause, and all the other jargon of modern accident law? Finally, how can the inductive model of fact-finding be reconciled with the zealous activity of attorneys in screening and manipulating the jury—including the increasing use of simulated trials to rehearse the lawyers' adversarial case?[51]

The traditional lawyer's confidence in the jury's power to make inductive generalizations about everyday events is much like Toulmin's confidence that experts simply know the applicable rules of their discipline. (After all, that is what is meant by "experts.") If for any reason the process of forming customary judgments cannot be properly carried out, as Toulmin concedes, practical inquiry reaches its limits; we run out of valid things to say. But the judicial process has the unique social role of declaring winners and losers in every case, whether or not the conditions for responsible induction are present. Despite Toulmin's advice to remain silent when ordinary judgment fails, the legal process charges forward by means of presumptions and burdens, which have to be allocated in some specific fashion. When individual cases need to be decided here and now, there is no way to emulate the stoicism of science at the frontiers of research, where observers sit back and wait calmly for new data to emerge.

> The courts . . . cannot afford to adopt a scientifically agnostic premise in this field—this would paralyze too much of the law. And in many cases it is neither common nor practically feasible to call on those experts who know as much as anyone about the probabilities in their areas of special competence. The result is a void, so far as accountability to any genuinely scientific standards go; it is a matter of dealer's choice and the court is the dealer.[52]

The doctrine of res ipsa loquitur is only one example of a recurring feature in modern law, where deciding who has the burden of proof becomes more important than settling the underlying facts—facts which may be unavailable or highly volatile. It would always be possible, of course, for the legal system to take a more direct approach and adopt substantive rules in favor of accident victims, regardless of what the evidence says about negligence.[53] But virtually the same result can be achieved by a simple procedural maneuver that appears neutral on its face. And if defendants wax indignant over their new burdens, why don't they just get on with establishing their innocence? Judging from the degree of controversy in actual trials, fending off burdens of proof remains an unceasing goal for zealous advocates.

The judicial practice of adjusting proof burdens soon becomes ritualized in the form of special rules. Any commentary on accident law must now discuss the vast body of rules and precedents on res ipsa loquitur, alongside those on the substantive issues of negligence and proximate cause. In this way the law rapidly formalizes its procedural role, and any expert on the law of accidents can now find a wide selection of preexisting warrants for shifting the burden of proof.[54] But there is still something missing from this new body of rules: that dynamic element of legal procedure that is constantly qualifying old warrants and creating newer ones. Whether this creative force can ever be fully captured in a formal

29

body of rules is perhaps best discussed by reflection on the broader dimensions of human discourse.

Between Logic and Rhetoric

From the nineteenth century to the present, the process of human reasoning has received a level of attention comparable only to the pioneering achievements of classical philosophy. This revival of interest has many roots, but perhaps most important is the hope that an understanding of basic thought patterns can shed more light on practical affairs. As a post-Kantian intellectual trend, the procedural analysis of thinking looks for cognitive patterns of universal significance beyond the subjective habits of individual thinkers. Although the notion that thoughts somehow create the world has been repeatedly dismissed as romantic excess, our capacity to reason undeniably sets cognitive boundaries to the kind of world we can live in. At the margins of that world are the value judgments which are desperately needed but which do not meet either the validation standards of modern science or the canons of formal logic. Current theories of reasoning mark out the extremes of optimism and pessimism about our common desire to live in a world with room for both scientific facts and human values.

Following various paths from the central distinction between pure and practical reason, post-Kantian reflections have tended to identify pairs of incommensurable human capacities, separated by the gulf commonly supposed to exist between thought and action. In its revived form, the study of rhetoric is one of several movements that seek to transcend this gulf, principally by challenging interpretations of thought based on normative paradigms of formal deduction.[55] The alternatives opened up by this "new" rhetoric are limited only by the creativity of modern scholarship, which over the past half-century has carried the message of rhetoric into many fields—especially those of esthetics, ethics, and law.[56]

A parallel movement began even earlier in this century as part of American pragmatism's selection of action and experience as fundamental, social-cum-philosophical, categories.[57] Although it professed hostility to dualisms of all kinds, pragmatism belongs to a specific intellectual reaction against narrow formalism; its main energy was spent in rehabilitating that which transcends formalism, and the unity of both domains was treated more as an ideal goal than as accomplished fact. A similar fate can be identified with a host of modern dualisms, in all of which the second element is a self-appointed corrective to the static formalism of the first: truth and proof, assertion and performance, semantics and pragmatics, certainty and consensus, correspondence and coherence, understanding and explanation, justification and discovery, demonstration and rhetoric, deductive reason and practical reason, and logic and action.

The need to transcend formal models of reasoning is a dominant theme in Chaïm Perelman's widely read essays on argumentation, which have greatly furthered the revival of interest in rhetoric. Perelman's initial investigations in law followed the formalist path laid down by the Viennese positivist Hans Kelsen, for whom the important feature of legal systems was their underlying norm-structure—an essentially deductive edifice whose ultimate source of value descended from a postulated "basic norm." [58] But Perelman became convinced that such constructions required too much abstraction from everyday legal realities, and that they imposed a reductive pattern on the infinitely rich examples of valid reasoning to be found in public life. Reacting against the treatment of law as a formal system of norms, Perelman projected an entirely different model of reasoning, both for law and for the wider forum of public discussion. [59]

As with other critiques of formalism, Perelman's theory is easiest to summarize in negative terms, by its utter rejection of formalistic limits and the consequent desire to rescue flexibility and freedom as values central to public deliberation. In much the same spirit as Toulmin's jurisprudential analogy, Perelman treats legal proceedings as accomplished examples of reasoning patterns found implicitly in other domains. As in law, public dialogue starts with generally accepted norms rather than philosophical first principles. The goal of public discussion is agreement on how those norms apply to new situations—not apodictic demonstration. Along the way, participants in public life use countless techniques of persuasion, skillfully designed to move a potentially universal audience toward a consensus accessible to all reasonable participants.

Over time Perelman embellished this theory at considerable length, producing an organon of argumentation with Aristotelian thoroughness. But his writings are best represented by their numerous programmatic statements, which challenge the normative presumptions of formal reasoning models. At the close of his great treatise, one finds a most passionate statement of Perelman's basic claim:

> Only the existence of an argumentation that is neither compelling nor arbitrary can give meaning to human freedom, a state in which a reasonable choice can be exercised. If freedom was no more than necessary adherence to a previously given natural order, it would exclude all possibility of choice; and if the exercise of freedom were not based on reasons, every choice would be irrational and would be reduced to an arbitrary decision operating in an intellectual void. It is because of the possibility of argumentation which provides reasons, but not compelling reasons, that it is possible to escape the dilemma: adherence to an objectively and universally valid truth, or recourse

to suggestion and violence to secure acceptance for our opinions and decisions. The theory of argumentation will help to develop what a logic of value judgments has tried in vain to provide, namely the justification of the possibility of a human community in the sphere of action when this justification cannot be based on a reality or objective truth.[60]

As a subtle example of argumentation in its own right, based entirely on affirmative inferences from negative assertions, this passage illustrates a central paradox in Perelman's approach. It all boils down to a hypothetical proposition, using an argument form strangely absent from Perelman's own compendium: if formal models of reasoning lead to abhorrent practical results, then the new rhetorical model must be embraced as a valid alternative. One could respond to this eloquent plea by asking whether Perelman's model of rhetoric—in addition to being something useful and inspirational—is also valid, true, correct, or rational. But from Perelman's point of view this question misses the purpose of the whole rhetorical enterprise: to liberate us from all such inaccessible criteria of categorical judgment.

The standards of formal logic and objective truth may have their limited place, says Perelman, but they are insufficient for guiding legal and ethical communities through intricate deliberations over matters great and small. In the legal system and in the larger arena of public discussion, a more flexible standard of validity must prevail: something like reasonableness-in-the-judgment-of-the-conversants is all we have and is therefore all we need. Ironically, the jury is still out (and always will be) on whether this new rhetoric lives up to its own fluid standard of validity. In the eyes of its academic partisans, of course, it has been greeted as a revelation, but other critical communities have been much less enthusiastic.[61]

Behind Perelman's strategy lies the classical insight that formal standards of deductive logic cannot establish themselves as definitive. According to Aristotle, deduction is a relationship among propositions that are ultimately redeemed by methods other than deduction.[62] Logic is a process for transferring universality from one proposition to another, but the process itself cannot be the only source of truth or insight. One cannot, in short, expect formal logic either to prove or to refute the program of the new rhetoric, nor that of any other serious competitor. It thus becomes perfectly safe to challenge the deductivist claim to monopolize the process of valid inference, and to do so by assigning it the impossible burden of refuting its rivals. If that refutation is indeed impossible, nothing stands in the way of embracing the new rhetoric, postulated as a default category.

Of course, rhetoric, too, is in no position to refute directly any universal claims on behalf of formal logic; one could not even formulate such a categorical argument in the rhetorical idiom. But even more important, the new rhetoric has perhaps not even prevailed according to its own rhetorical standards. Some permissive spirit or contingent license is necessary to keep it alive as an option for further deliberation. In short, something like a presumption of validity-until-proven-false haunts Perelman's basic argument.

Perelman's reason for extending this qualified privilege of validity to his own theory of rhetoric appears in his attractive image of human freedom expressed so vividly by the above quotation. Without some kind of presumption in favor of rhetoric, he says, we are left with the dismal choice between rigid authority and chaos—between a rival presumption that reduces all valid reasoning power to static, hegemonic deduction and its skeptical cousin, which denigrates all human reasoning (short of perfect deduction) as a pretentious failure. These are the choices as Perelman has implicitly constructed them.

Perelman's move follows the grand strategy of shifting the burden of proof. Whereas for centuries the onus weighed heavily on would-be challengers to formal logic, Perelman's argument reverses that presumption. Henceforth all challengers of modern rhetoric will be required to demonstrate its inherent flaws, and the mere fact that rhetoric is different from traditional logic will not be counted as an argument. It may be impossible for rhetoric to prove itself affirmatively by rhetorical standards, but it is equally impossible for rhetoric to fail completely by its own generous criteria. Rhetoric thus launches itself as a new field of inquiry, unless its opponents somehow regain the strategic advantage lost by the shift in burden of proof.

It may appear strange that such an important and distinctive argument finds no place in the content of the new rhetoric.[63] There are indeed many references to tacit assumptions as a standard feature of practical arguments—along with the notion of presumptions and defeasible concepts. But Perelman's treatise is slow to draw the relevant analogies with legal procedure and shows little interest in pursuing them.

> The usual characteristic of legal presumptions is the difficulty there is in overcoming them: they are often irrefragable or can be rebutted only by following very precise rules. Sometimes they concern only the burden of proof. Before any audience, this is almost always a function of the accepted presumptions, but the choice of these presumptions is not prescribed, as it is in certain legal situations.[64]

These rather obscure comments appear in the context of "observations regarding special agreements particular to certain audiences," where Perelman concedes the powerful role of tacit presumptions in restricting the judgments of validity made by particular audiences. When confronted by an audience with firmly established presumptions different from those of the speaker, Perelman advises, "it might be to a speaker's advantage" to choose a different audience.[65] Given his desire that public debate should eventually reach a universal audience, it is not surprising that Perelman treats presumptions as isolated parochialisms, rather than as broad cognitive or strategic forces. For him presumptions are simply localized biases or prejudices, characteristic of discrete groups but certainly not binding on the community as a whole.

By contrast, Perelman notes that in "certain legal situations" presumptions are "prescribed" and thus cannot be avoided. In a community defined by the jurisdiction of a legal system, the force of official presumptions is inescapable. It is exactly this preclusive aspect of legal presumptions that Perelman himself wished to invoke on behalf of rhetoric; he obviously wanted hypothetical space for rhetoric as a universal practice and not as some parochial activity based on a mere prejudice. In contrast to Perelman's fictive universal audience, the legal system offers the more complex image of a fragmented universe, held together artificially by the authority of law within a specific territory.

As noted in the last section, the use of presumptions and other proof-structuring devices in law promotes a degree of uniformity that would otherwise be unattainable under standard legal procedures. The techniques available to judges allow the legal system to resist the centrifugal energy of social and cultural diversity, scientific uncertainty, and ethical pluralism. Chapters 2 and 3 present some prominent examples of this extraordinary power at work in the United States Supreme Court, where it has been deployed on such divisive issues as equal treatment and fair procedure. Of course, burdens of proof were present in the legal system well before the Warren Court developed its special brand of activism. The novelty was rather the willingness of the highest court to shift those burdens so freely and thus to stimulate perceptions of a judicial revolution. Where previously the burden of proof had protected the legal status quo, its sudden volatility made it into a potent force subject to adversarial debate. Whoever could control it had the awesome privilege of defining the law's universal scope on major public issues.

The possible stabilizing influence of the burden of proof was defended in one of the first modern texts to champion the return to rhetorical study. Curiously, Bishop Whately's use of the term in his *Elements of Rhetoric* (1827) remains one of the most thorough treatments to date.[66] No doubt more recent writers, including Perelman, have been wary of the openly conservative functions Whately assigned to presumptions and proof burdens.[67] Given their interest in the creative, flexible, and liberating aspects of rhetoric, Whately's treatment turns the wrong direction.

34

It is a point of great importance to decide in each case, at the outset, in your own mind, and clearly to point out to the hearer, as occasion may serve, on which side the *Presumption* lies, and to which belongs the *Burden of Proof.* . . .

A moderate portion of common-sense will enable any one to perceive, and to show, on which side the Presumption lies, when once his attention is called to this question; though, for want of attention, it is often overlooked: and on the determination of this question the whole character of a discussion will often very much depend . . . .

The following are a few of the cases in which it is important, though very easy, to point out where the Presumption lies.

There is a Presumption in favor of every *existing* institution. Many of these (we will suppose, the majority) may be susceptible of alteration for the better; but still the "Burden of proof" lies with him who proposes an alteration; simply, on the ground that since a change is not a good in itself, he who demands a change should show cause for it . . . .

There is a "Presumption" against any thing *paradoxical,* i.e. contrary to the prevailing opinion: it may be true; but the Burden of proof lies with him who maintains it; since men are not be expected to abandon the prevailing belief till some reason is shown.[68]

Whately seems entirely comfortable with—indeed, reassured by—this systematic bias toward existing authority and the status quo in ordinary discourse. Among other consequences, it favors an established religious faith along with compatible secular beliefs. In contemporary rhetoric, however, Perelman and others emphasize the dynamic power of persuasion to overcome differences of starting assumptions and thereby to promote change.[69] The functionalist view that words are stimuli to action presumes that change is always possible and thus imposes yet another burden on the skeptic to prove that persuasion cannot overcome the inertia of received opinion.

In any case, Whately never denied that proof burdens could be met, and in fact he seemed disturbed by how easily religious authority could be actively contested. For contemporary advocates of rhetoric, established beliefs are the necessary starting point for public debate, but none are considered immune from discussion and possible revision. The humanistic values espoused by Perelman predispose him to distinguish between the legal system, where official presumptions are allowed to close off debate, and wider discourse, where nothing is ultimately held sacred.[70] Presumptions and burdens of proof merit little attention in this larger universe because they are presumed to be provisional, defeasible, and fluid. Perelman concedes that particular audiences may sit on their assumptions and not give proper heed to persuasive speakers; but for him there are always other audiences to turn to, if only hypothetical ones. His controversial notion of a "universal audience" serves as a Kantian ideal, holding out the unlimited prospect for new, more accommodating audiences to appear.

Perelman's humanistic idealism is not the only way open to the partisans of rhetoric, as the enormously varied literature aptly shows. Perhaps the major barrier to restoring rhetoric to intellectual respectability has been its history of troubled association with relativism. If truth and logic are superseded by consensus and persuasion, then the price of Perelman's "freedom" could be the utter loss of standards, fixed principles, and other forms of authority.[71]

One reaction to this prospect is to convert rhetoric into a purely descriptive study—the analysis of ways in which persuasion has been successful in the past, generalizations from that analysis, and appropriate technical guidance for future persuaders.[72] Rhetoric may then be considered instrumentally good when used on behalf of social norms already validated by some method other than persuasion. This approach rescues rhetoric from its popular associations with value promiscuity, but it defeats Perelman's liberal mission by placing values under the protection of some authority beyond practical reason.

In the end, most advocates of rhetoric would like to find a path back to the concepts of truth and logic but without abandoning the functional insights of rhetoric as a guide to effective practical action. Some of them have followed the path taken by Aristotle, for whom dialectic provided the link between a formal realm of logical demonstration and a contingent world of rhetoric.[73] The concept of dialectic has its own complexities,[74] which cannot be fully resolved within the limits of Aristotelian logic. But it does provide a useful rubric for summarizing some of the legal strategies discussed in this chapter.

Dialectic represents various structural or procedural constraints on the process of practical reasoning, which allow public discourse to reach concrete results. Even when the outcomes of discussion are considered highly tentative and subject to continual revision, as in Perelman's analysis, they must enter functionally into concrete social situations. There must, in other words, be some degree of finality in practical discussion, which allows the results to play the same role as conclusions in a logical argument.[75]

The legal system offers the most concrete illustration of such constraints. Indeed, the judicial process institutionalizes the dialectical elements implicit in practical reasoning, especially in its multiple techniques for imposing order and finality on disputes that might otherwise remain indeterminate. In the American system, the jury process of identifying facts is also one method for reaching closure on disputed questions and is especially useful when there is no independent way to verify such outcomes against impartial standards of truth. But even more important than the jury is the role of the judge, whose task is to see that disputes are resolved, notwithstanding the infinite range of applicable rules, the plurality of social values about how those rules should be interpreted, and the indeterminacy of many factual issues. The daily function of courts is to resolve disputes, whether or not they can do so with the philosophical clarity of an Aristotle or the empirical fidelity of a Francis Bacon.

Among the many dialectical functions performed by the courts, I have singled out their administration of burdens of proof. By purposely expanding this concept beyond the set of technical rules found under that label in the major textbooks on legal evidence, I mean to include the entire range of practices by which courts gain control over indeterminate questions of fact and value. Such questions pose a continual challenge to the finality and legitimacy of legal decisions, just as they threaten the stability of social conventions and public discourse. By institutionalizing its dialectical procedures, however, the legal system has provided a laboratory for examining the implicit strategies to be found in other areas of factual, normative, and political dispute. Transforming its own dialectical procedures into operating rules has insulated the courts, to some degree, from recent assaults made on other forms of authority. This may explain the current tendency in American society to impose judicial structures on contested issues in environmental policy and medical ethics—fields that require finality on largely undecidable scientific and ethical issues.

Dialectic and the Problem of Authority

The dialectical framework for practical reason occupies an uncharted middle ground between logic and rhetoric. Like rhetoric, it is a body of techniques that cannot be reduced to steps in a deductive argument; it is active rather than demonstrative, socially organized rather than purely intellectual, flexible and creative rather than rigid and apodictic. But unlike rhetoric, dialectic must also support certain attributes associated with formal logic: authority, decidability, and finality. It transports logic into the temporal dimension of practical affairs and thereby embodies the anomaly of self-executing authority, constrained decidability, and provisional finality. Dialectic is not an optional extension of rhetoric, but one of its practical presuppositions. As such it may prove something of an anomaly for the new rhetoric, to the extent it implies restraints on public discourse.

The jurisprudential analogy has been a source of inspiration to partisans of practical reasoning from Aristotle to Perelman.[76] Although the significance of law is invariably found in its ability to unite flexibility and legitimacy, recent theories of rhetoric have seriously neglected the institutionalized dialectic by which law accomplishes this subtle task. More than legal rhetoric, which classical authors long ago mapped out with admirable thoroughness, the dialectical features of the modern judicial system illustrate the tacit strategies at work in major fields of contemporary discourse, both academic and practical.

The dialectical functions of law, always present in the daily operations of judicial bodies, are generally shielded by rhetoric and routine. Eventually everyone learns how to adapt to stable procedural presumptions, to institutionalized burdens of proof, and to predictable judicial oversight of litigation. Dialectical procedures thus harden into explicit rules and become part of the formal rhetoric of judicial practice. What demands attention, however, are the sudden fluctuations in dialectical patterns. When entirely new dialectical practices first appear, the outcomes of legal deliberations start to change, even though the underlying formal rules remain the same. Plaintiffs start winning cases they were previously sure to lose; new de facto procedural powers of litigants begin to put unexpected strain on legal and social institutions; and judicial review of legislation changes its entire character.

In time, these shifts in dialectical practice will themselves become doctrinal rules like res ipsa loquitur, or new judicial principles of evidence or equity, or new constitutional maxims. Before they get woven into the judicial fabric, however, they command universal attention; indeed, they may reveal wider pressures on social institutions far beyond the legal system. Because the law periodically brings its dialectic closer to the surface than other forms of practical reasoning, we are able to focus squarely on the dialectical framework of judicial argument, separate from formal doctrines or specific case outcomes. Thus the emphasis in this study on dynamic proof burdens in recent judicial practice: the adversarial disputes in this forum point to analogous strategies in other fields, which remain largely submerged in implicit dialectical structures.

Behind all the recent judicial management of proof burdens, courts are clearly being asked to assume a more active role in public crises shaped by various social forms of ignorance. It makes little difference whether these crises are assigned to factual uncertainty or the broader indeterminacies of legal rules; courts use the same dialectical techniques for both occasions. The empiricist spirit of American law favors the rhetoric of facts: legal disputes are said to turn on the nature of the evidence, but this is largely a question of idiom. Today the courts wrestle with complex problems for which the appropriate kinds of evidence remain unclear.

In many legal disputes, the search for essential facts encounters practical and procedural limits. Any social process of fact-labeling (like the jury system) further magnifies elements of public uncertainty. Similarly, the unavoidable judicial act of classifying specific legal claims under available (and often conflicting) general rules exposes vast areas of cultural and normative indeterminacy, which the seamless web of rules is always too thin to mask. Finally, the adversarial structure of judicial proceedings virtually guarantees that conflict will accompany the assignment of burdens and any modification of presumptions. For all these reasons, judicial dialectic stands out as a visible model of the dynamic process hidden behind many other forms of public reasoning.

Both within and beyond the field of law, dialectic raises the problematic issue of authority in contemporary discourse. The current legal dialectic alerts us to an historic shift toward a strategy of argument found increasingly in modern reasoning, based on a view of authority as inaccessible, indeterminate, but nonetheless inherently oppressive. In contrast to Aristotelian certitude on scientific and practical matters, it is now common for speakers to invoke authority by elaborate detours through negative lines of inference. Rather than claiming direct authority for one's own position, it seems much safer to expose the limitations of an opponent's rival claim. A poignant example of such indirect arguments appeared in Chaïm Perelman's eloquent plea for his new rhetoric. Throughout public debate, tacit structures of presumption support this idiom of indirect statement, which draws affirmative inferences from the lack of certifiable authority to the contrary.

The conclusions from such indirect inferences are by no means all alike. Just as the majesty of the law can be summoned to find a defendant guilty or innocent, the argument-from-ignorance can yield conclusions that are either deeply skeptical or dogmatically affirmative.[77] We know this from centuries of philosophical debate, in which the premise that the human mind is weak has been used variously to prove that "therefore we can know nothing," and that "thus we know a higher being must exist"—and all points between these extremes. Today, however, many indirect inferences have a more guarded or hypothetical quality, as in Perelman's argument, where rhetoric was justified as a practical necessity, a postulate of default reasoning. Whether or not rhetoric can certify its own truth, Perelman said, we need to have it; and we need it to be powerful enough to validate everyday reasoning. Such arguments-from-ignorance suit the ambivalent, pluralist reasoner, as well as to the skeptical and the credulous.

In public discourse, dialectic governs the essential elements of authority, decidability, and finality in the process of inference. But if dialectic really has the ubiquitous and powerful influence being suggested here, how have dialectical procedures managed to escape careful scrutiny, especially in recent commentaries on rhetoric, argumentation, speech acts, and other forms of modern discourse? In fact, certain aspects have had a most powerful impact on recent academic debates about conceptual schemes, cognitive foundations, and moral principles. Unfortunately, the adversarial mode of these controversies promotes a series of partial views that leave the full dimensions of dialectic hidden behind a polemical screen.

In short, the study of dialectic must dodge serious reflexive hurdles that continually threaten to divert its attention. Most academic interpretations of public discourse, despite sincere efforts to reach "critical" conclusions, are themselves driven by arguments-from-ignorance. The adversarial character of these debates comes from sharply opposed visions of public authority, none of which can be easily reconciled with the interpretive authority asserted by their respective partisans.

Jurisprudential analogies can help preserve some distance from these paradoxes, but they provide no sure guarantees. Toulmin's theory of rule systems, for example, projects a benign view of authority that adheres closely to the depoliticized perspective of Oxford analysis. As in the legal system, any process of rule-following can always be described as a self-sufficient world by those who inhabit it. In such cases, the authority for a rule-based decision is located firmly in the rule itself, and not in some inaccessible realm of eternal correctness. Toulmin's theory of knowledge wants to move the authority for all kinds of knowledge out of the various heavens allegedly postulated by philosophers and into the everyday world. Truth is warranted belief; the validity of our judgments rests entirely with the warrant and does not need further backing from unknown regions that transcend everyday life. All we need to do is get on with the task of cataloguing specific warrants that appear to work in a diverse group of disciplines or professions.

Such an approach to systems of rules has been warmly greeted not only by recent schools of philosophy, but also by social scientists eager to describe complex features of human culture.[78] By anchoring cultural description in a context of rule-governed behavior, social science can dispense with grand theoretical abstractions, while also reducing the infinite detail of social life to manageable levels. The literal existence of rules in the conscious life of ordinary people is unimportant; the social observer simply postulates the immanent rule system that would make coherent sense out of everyday practice.[79] An important stimulus to this approach came from the sensational reception of Noam Chomsky's program to analyze human language as a process of rule-following behavior. And in Europe the development of structural linguistics offered even wider scope for comprehending both language and cultural behavior based on a common structural model.

Considering this enormous outburst of scholarly attention to rule systems, on which several academic generations have now built their reputations, we can understand both the attraction of a jurisprudential analogy and its limitations.

The law seems to offer a working model of a system of rules that requires no further validation beyond the everyday process of generating rule-based decisions. To be sure, rules change, parties disagree, and people are often disappointed by the outcomes of legal procedures; but disputes get settled, and the system itself is able to evolve under a subset of rules devoted to the constitution of its own structure.[80]

Missing from this picture, however, are all the strategic elements identified with judicial dialectic. As G. P. Baker and P. M. S. Hacker have pointed out, the model presumes that rules are self-executing. But "rules are not mysterious Platonic receptacles containing their applications, independently of human volition. There cannot be more in a rule than we put in it, and what we 'put in it' is revealed by our normative practices . . . . What the rule is, what it 'contains,' is wholly determined by the way we use [it]." Baker and Hacker further suggest that the model of rules has been built on a misreading of more than one analogy:

> The idea of a rule determining its applications independently of us seems to have at least two sources. First, that we use a rule as a norm of correctness, and hence are prone to be misled by the partial truth that a rule determines correctness independently of us (as we might think that the Law delivers the verdict independently of judges, since the judge's verdict may be quashed, and he too may be condemned by the Law). Secondly, we misleadingly think of a rule as akin to a mathematical function, and we compound confusion by having a muddled conception of a function. So we conceive of a rule as determining what follows from it (and what conforms with it) in much the same way as we think of a function as determining its value for any possible argument within its domain.[81]

Unfortunately, Baker and Hacker's critique does not move much farther than Toulmin's position, with which it shares deeper similarities.[82] Toulmin is willing to separate the jurisdictions of various rule systems into multiple domains of inquiry. Whenever a question falls outside one of these domains, he concedes that our knowledge has reached its limits; we may be at a loss for words, but then invariably we pick up the pieces and move on to other, more tractable problems.[83] And the same cheerful shrug greets the further problem of knowing to which domain any new problem properly belongs. Toulmin's very fatalism ignores the distinctive dialectical features of judicial argument, where specific judges have the authority to determine these boundary questions. Perplexed judges cannot merely shrug their shoulders and move on to the next jurisdiction, the way Perelman advises his skilled speaker who runs into unreceptive listeners.

Legal systems illustrate the sobering challenge faced by real communities, to which we all belong and (more or less willingly) adapt. The view that indeterminate issues can remain forever unresolved until custom or fate supplies an agreeable solution is a presumption popularized by scientific method as it developed by the end of the nineteenth century. As shifting proof burdens gradually overtake this comfortable nostrum, however, the inescapable dialectical problems of authority, decidability, and finality come into sharper view. The jurisprudential analogy speeds this process along.

How to analyze dialectical issues remains a challenging problem, as the effects of ignoring them become increasingly unacceptable for many academic fields. Clearly one way to register the impact of dialectic is by describing the outward manifestations of authority, using some combination of social and behavioral theory. This strategy was pursued fruitfully by a number of commentators identified with the American legal realist movement, a diverse group of critics who rejected as mythology the idea that the law's legitimacy emanated from a body of formal rules.[84] History and sociology were mobilized to explain how legal rules are actually formed, and contemporary psychology supplied irreverent insights into the noncognitive side of judicial behavior. The quality of such analyses varied greatly, but it has significantly improved with time as better-trained social and behavioral scientists come to explore the rich empirical texture of legal institutions. How people make decisions (judges, lawyers, clients—but also people in other walks of life) has become an especially popular and apparently inexhaustible field of research.[85]

But the descriptive approach to legal dialectic suffers increasingly from its self-imposed abstraction from normative analysis. What can be captured by description is obviously related in some way to the exercise of social power and public authority, of which judicial authority and legal norms are but prominent examples. But the normative implications of dialectic are inescapable if paradoxical: normative analysis forces one dialectically ordered process to pass judgment on another. This reflexive order is familiar in legal settings, where the authority to pronounce final judgment on various parts of the legal system must itself be hierarchically prescribed.

To whatever extent a liberal society grants critical scope to independent citizens and academic specialists, one can expect to find highly diverse normative judgments on contemporary uses of authority. But with no institutional process for ordering these interpretations, such judgments will probably never coalesce.[86] (Even if there were such a process, it too would eventually fall under critical scrutiny.) On any public issue, then, partisans for the status quo can argue forever with outraged critics, leaving the final outcome to conflicting judgments of multiple courts of public and academic opinion.

Normative debate takes an even sharper turn when any single group of critics starts to challenge the whole pluralistic climate in which public and academic discussion has traditionally been conducted. Under the conventions of liberal debate, as multiple normative frameworks compete in the idealized battle of ideas, challengers to the intellectual status quo face an uphill struggle. Even if some communities are able to accept wide differences of opinion, prevailing social and cultural conventions cannot expect to satisfy everyone at once. As norms harden around specific cultural movements, they come to enjoy a presumptive legitimacy that leaves all challengers holding the burden of proof.[87] If somehow that burden can be shifted to the prevailing authorities, however, the prospects for minority viewpoints are immediately and dramatically transformed.

The field of law provides one more concrete example, once again with broader implications for dialectical strategies used in other practical and academic situations. Among legal academics, the critical legal studies movement (CLS) has energetically practiced the strategy of shifting intellectual burdens of proof against defenders of traditional values associated with the American legal system.[88] The precise target is not always specified, and it is often broadly sketched in a variety of jargons imported from abroad. But the common theme of CLS scholarship is an attack on dominant discourses in American society, which are alleged to impose widespread, oppressive stratification in economic and cultural life, despite official rhetoric of tolerance and liberty. The central CLS critique, indeed, is that the neutral posture of the whole political and legal system masks the exercise of de facto power by people variously privileged under the legal, economic, and cultural status quo.

43

This quick summary doubtless leaves out much of the vocabulary and nuance one finds in the abundant CLS literature but will do for our purposes. What is most important is the strategy that launched this vigorous dispute between defenders of mainstream liberal views and their radical critics. The CLS technique of shifting the intellectual burden of proof to the protectors of dominant values is a transparent leveling device. It reduces established authority to the status of petitioner in a fragmented cultural climate, where few petitions are ever granted. Under CLS jurisdiction, the dominant discourse makes a remarkably poor showing when it can no longer presume that the social system lives up to its ideals of formal equality under law, rugged economic individualism, and pluralist democracy.[89] These ideals suddenly look like empty rhetoric, as their defense counsel try to explain to a skeptical courtroom how they can be said to work in a society manifestly burdened with social inequality, economic exploitation, and political fragmentation.

These are still academic battles, of course, in which both sides select their own courtrooms, manipulate presumptions, and declare themselves the winners—day after day. The acrimony of such intellectual encounters is increased by the fact that each side must concentrate its energy on exposing the boundless failures of the other, rather than patiently seeking agreement for affirmative hypotheses advanced in the spirit of Perelman's rhetoric.

Is it mere coincidence that this adversarial style of academic argument has emerged within the field of legal studies? As skilled lawyers, the rhetorical partisans in both camps intuitively grasp the strategy of shifting proof burdens onto their opponents. They are also schooled in the complementary technique of construing all evidence in the manner most favorable to their client—when the interests of winning the case have long displaced any traditional illusions about searching for impartial truth. At the same time, the substantive arguments being used on both sides are highly derivative from other fields. The CLS movement certainly did not invent the radical critique of liberal authority, but it has borrowed most of its arguments and vocabulary from European post-structuralist critics.[90]

The originality of CLS consists rather in exploiting the same dialectical terms that its mentors developed for serving liberal goals a mere generation ago. The generational aspect is particularly intriguing in this debate, which was initiated mainly by the students of legal academics who championed the Supreme Court's creative use of similar burden-shifting strategies in constitutional litigation during the 1960s. The "critical" challenge in legal studies has come from a generation of students trained to approach issues of public policy by manipulating the presumptions of constitutional law. The irony of this generational revolt illustrates an important feature of dialectical strategies involving the burden of proof: their capricious ability to support conclusions that are progressive or skeptical, affirmative or critical, constructive or nihilistic. Arguments-from-ignorance have this protean quality—a fact that, over time, tends to strengthen their affinity for relativistic applications.

As a presupposition of rhetoric, dialectic supplies the framework within which (1) contestable authority is resolved in the form of conclusions, (2) indeterminate questions are rendered decidable, and (3) finality (however provisional) is imposed on practical issues. In contemporary argument, dialectic has become a largely autonomous method or procedure—moving from one context to another—rather than a stable normative tribunal. Like everyday legal procedures, modern argument seems driven by a complex mechanism of strategic reasoning, which both sides must use but dare not call into question. The premier strategy of shifting the burden of proof imitates, to a remarkable degree, the adversarial style of legal reasoning.

For Aristotle, the dialectical conditions for extending the harmony of formal logic into other areas of discourse were not especially controversial. To be sure, the endless academic controversies catalogued in Aristotle's works suggest that, even in his day, philosophical debates could still resist the unitary force of contemporary dialectic, embodied most powerfully in Aristotle's own magisterial effort to create a philosophical synthesis. If we take Aristotle's word, however, it is entirely possible that practical inquiry into natural, legal, and normative subjects in contemporary Athens was conducted within an accepted framework of dialectical procedures.

For us, however, the status of contemporary dialectic—especially outside the legal process—is highly problematic, both in academic pursuits and in practical life.[91] The authority of modern science and moral reasoning has been a significant concern for post-Cartesian philosophy, and today both fields coexist in a fragile neo-Kantian truce introduced at the end of the nineteenth century. Most academic disciplines were formed during this period and remain vulnerable to dialectical tensions, expressed in the professionalization of academic and scientific research, as well as in the continuing fragmentation of disciplines.

The main generic split in modern dialectical procedures derives from the notorious distinction between facts and values, which creates a wide gulf between two broad categories of disciplines. At the end of the twentieth century, similar gaps have appeared within almost every individual field, as the two approaches continue to vie for interpretive dominance. Thus the "hard" sciences have been seriously challenged by a series of historical and sociological critiques, whereas social inquiry and the humanities have sustained enormous pressures to adopt the quantitative and empirical methods of classical science.

The impasse in academic disciplines mirrors a more urgent sense of crisis in public affairs, in which the separation of flexibility and legitimacy is often associated with tumultuous cultural and political events. In contrast to the organic political communities we impute to classical Athens, we have a sense of ourselves as fragmented societies based on unsteady coalitions of factionalized interests.[92] In contrast to an ideal community where widespread consensus is deemed possible on major value issues, an alternative view has developed of a fragile collection of incompatible political ideologies, antagonistic socioeconomic classes, and culturally diverse minorities. The ideal of a single social authority has moved beyond reach; the mere pretense of such unanimity automatically awakens skeptical doubts.[93]

If Bishop Whately were to revise his *Elements of Rhetoric* for a late twentieth-century audience, he would no doubt sadly inform us that, in public debate, the old presumption in favor of "every existing institution" has now been shifted. The burden of proof no longer falls on "him who proposes an alteration," but

45

rather on anyone who dares to suggest that existing institutions are doing their job. Whately's conservative presumption, now blatantly reactionary, has been seriously challenged by its rhetorical counterpart: the increasingly radical presumption of institutional failure.[94] Both parties in this struggle embrace the conceptual postulates of modern ignorance, which supply the grounds for possible inference.

Chapter 2 | Shifting the Presumptions of Social Order: Equality through Nondiscrimination

This chapter is the first in a two-part examination of judicial dialectic in the constitutional decisions of the U.S. Supreme Court. Both chapters 2 and 3 illustrate the powerful social implications of strategically managed burdens of proof, including their tendency to polarize political issues and to undergo sudden reversals.

By perfecting a subtle technique for selectively shifting the presumption of constitutionality, the U.S. Supreme Court under Chief Justice Warren created a powerful tool for judge-led social reform. Although the Court applied its method only in limited contexts, it inspired a generation of legal advocates to redefine social issues as adversarial battles over nondiscrimination. The ensuing struggle between liberal and conservative judges illustrates the volatile effects created by cyclical shifts in burdens and standards of proof, especially in the areas of social welfare, gender equity, and affirmative action.

Judicial Strategies and Public Discourse

In recent decades, the U.S. Supreme Court has become the most prominent public forum for argument strategies based on shifting the burden of proof. This rhetorical style was central to the sudden emergence of constitutional law as a catalyst for progressive reform in the 1960s, with the return of judicial activism during Earl Warren's tenure as Chief Justice. Two guiding themes from this period illustrate the dialectical power of arguments-from-ignorance: the Court's treatment of formal equality as a principle of social reform and its treatment of judicial hearings as a privileged forum for challenging institutional authority. The Warren Court's energy and idealism put new life into the inescapable dialectical functions of judicial procedure. And although the Supreme Court's influence on public policy has now grown more ambiguous, its distinctive techniques of reasoning have remained largely unchanged despite shifts in political ideologies of Court appointees. Indeed, these techniques have influenced dialectical strategies well beyond the formal legal structure.

During the Warren period (1953–69), the Supreme Court experimented with two major doctrinal tools: the constitutional principles of equal protection and procedural due process. The combined results inspired a movement for liberal reform, under the slogan "law as an instrument of social change."[1] "Law" in this instance meant constitutional adjudication, and during the early 1960s a distinctive judicial idiom established itself firmly in the rhetoric of moderate liberal reform. The campaign to alter society through constitutional law—including everything from criminal justice reform to the Equal Rights Amendment (ERA)—helped attract idealistic new recruits to law schools, where their sense of social mission intersected parallel changes in curricula and teaching styles. As they emerged from legal education, even well into the 1970s, many students hoped to enter public-interest legal practice, which at one time drew healthy financial support from both the public and private sectors.[2]

By the early 1980s, changes in Supreme Court membership and more conservative national political trends had dampened much of this spirit. As the federal government imposed severe funding cuts on legal services, the momentum of progressive reform was decisively slowed. Throughout the 1970s, in fact, the confident reform rhetoric of the Warren period took on darker tones as increasingly strident legal challenges seemed powerless to induce substantial changes in either public or private institutions. Some whose sympathies remained with the progressive agenda began to sublimate their energy onto a more philosophical plane, where similar rhetorical strategies could actively continue without practical restraints.[3]

For many others, the Warren Court's distinctive technique for challenging institutional authority, based on the skillful shifting of customary proof burdens, suggested new outlets in political protest and social critique.[4] Freed from the pressures of maintaining a working majority on the Supreme Court, arguments in the judicial mode could expand into a wider challenge to virtually any type of public or private authority. Even the Supreme Court's own decisions have not escaped review in the transcendental tribunals of moral philosophy, political action, and cultural critique, as public controversy over affirmative action and abortion have shown.

Among a small but vocal group of legal academics during the 1980s—those associated with the CLS movement—the strategy underlying constitutional reform took a distinctly radical turn. One of CLS's central accomplishments, indeed, has been a hostile commentary on the moderate reform agenda of the public-interest law movement. Ironically, the same techniques that first inspired the optimistic notion of law as an instrument of social change were turned against the surviving advocates of law-guided reform. Both camps share the common rhetorical strategy of forcing their opponents to bear the strategic burden in a debate that cannot be won on the basis of neutral evidence. Each side, paradoxically, rests its implicit authority on a method that forces others to prove the legitimacy of their actions or theoretical positions, and only after the standard of proof has been set high enough to preclude simple answers. For all the sharp polemics between these two groups, they occupy identical rhetorical ground.

The liberal and radical descendants of Warren Court partisans are not alone in preserving burden-of-proof arguments. The Supreme Court itself, which was sharply divided throughout the 1980s, continued to deploy much the same rhetoric, with the added complication that conservative judges quickly mastered the art of burden-shifting. This dispersion of creative judicial talent is scarcely surprising, given that the method is practiced widely by legal advocates throughout the judicial process. Any well-trained lawyer should be able to paint a portrait of neutral law in tones flattering to his or her client's cause, and it is safe to assume that appellate judges recognize all the pertinent techniques. The basic strategy of burden-shifting remains vital for any judicial faction (of any ideological persuasion) in supporting the posture of judicial neutrality. It also supplies dialectical tools for dismissing competing arguments, as based on either inadequate evidence or unprincipled judicial activism.

Such self-serving arguments may eventually invite public cynicism, even for court opinions that command a solid majority of justices. Most observers, however, are reluctant to conclude that constitutional disputes are nothing more than politics.[5] To be sure, public opinion has frequently opposed specific court decisions in the areas of civil rights, school prayer, abortion, and personal privacy. But the judicial ideal of neutral decision-making remains a vital element in most of these criticisms.[6] On the whole, people prefer to think of their position as consistent with impartial law, whereas their opponents are always trying to exploit some loophole, often in connivance with careless or incompetent judges. Most popular criticisms of judicial outcomes are modeled on those of practicing advocates: even though they may lose a particular case, they remain committed to the broad ideal of legality—if only because they expect to be back in court someday soon.

For the lay public, this ambiguous embrace of constitutional law is much easier to maintain when a majority of the current Supreme Court smiles occasionally on one's own point of view. But alternative institutional supports can be found for the conceit that public policy views overlap with fundamental law. As Robert Bork found out in 1987, when his nomination for a seat on the Court was rejected by the U.S. Senate, even Congress can occasionally manage the symbolism of fundamental law. The entire debate over the Bork nomination

49

drew attention to an important anomaly in American public discourse: we cannot abandon the judicial ideal of neutral law, even as we perfect the techniques for manipulating judicial doctrines and burdens to achieve partisan ends.[7]

Out of the Ashes of Legal Realism: Warren Court Activism

Within a decade of Earl Warren's appointment as Chief Justice, the Supreme Court embarked on a period of judicial activism that defied all the odds of historical and ideological context. In the 1950s, progressive judges and sympathetic legal commentators had only recently declared themselves the winners in a historic battle to limit the practice of judicial review—the power of courts to declare legislative or administrative actions unconstitutional.[8] Through the heroic efforts of justices like Hugo Black, William O. Douglas, Robert Jackson, and Felix Frankfurter, the Court had just managed to rebuild its doctrinal structure around the axiom that courts should use their judicial powers rarely, if ever.

For judges and legal critics during the first postwar decades, the ideal of judicial neutrality became virtually synonymous with the practice of judicial restraint.[9] At least two major influences may account for this view. First, this generation had fully absorbed the teachings of the legal realist movement, which portrayed the judicial process as an inescapably creative enterprise. They therefore assumed that personal and social values were inextricably bound up with the formal rhetoric of judicial decisions.[10] Second, many of them also subscribed to the view that social authority was essentially the product of interest-group debate and thus properly belonged to the legislature.[11]

The realist legacy can be summed up in Holmes's epigram that the life of the law was not mere logic, but "experience." [12] And the political experience of the postwar judges, shaped by the emergence of legislative supremacy during the New Deal, confirmed the belief that legislatures were the dynamic, progressive force in society, whereas the conceptual conservatism of the judiciary made it the natural ally of political reaction. When progressive judges gained control of the Supreme Court in 1937, they immediately adopted a strict *presumption of constitutionality* as a formal doctrinal constraint on their own powers of judicial review.[13]

Given this background, the sudden emergence of the Warren Court's progressive brand of judicial activism was an exceptional event, catching most legal commentators by surprise. Warren's first initiatives centered on civil rights and the battle over desegregating public schools in the South. These cases, in addition to being a significant body of lawmaking, permitted the Court to start flexing the relatively undeveloped equal protection clause of the Fourteenth Amendment. Their supple craftsmanship, which allowed the Court to step gingerly around the old separate but equal doctrine and thus to restore the constitutional power of equal protection in the field of race relations, later proved useful for extending that principle to other legal problems. Eventually legislative distinctions based on gender came under close judicial scrutiny, along with other aspects of public policy impinging on economic welfare.

The second major doctrinal vehicle for the Warren Court—the procedural due process principle—was likewise vetted in a single area before being extended more widely. The Court's initial decisions focused on the conduct of criminal trials, but due process challenges soon spread to almost every aspect of governmental power. That story will be examined in chapter 3.

The complex structure of equality as a legal principle made it a shrewd instrument for judicial activism operating in the shadow of legal realism. In some sense, the entire statutory system is built on implicit judgments about equality and inequality among people, things, and events that fall under public regulation. Legislative classifications designate a vast network of situational equalities, punctuated by judgments of inclusion and exclusion. For its part, the judicial process makes implicit assessments of equality whenever it classifies individual cases under existing legal precedents. In both arenas, the law identifies formal equivalences among diverse people or among disparate events, which may nevertheless be unlike one another in an infinite number of ways. Under legal concepts, people who are treated as a class may share only a single physical characteristic, like race or gender, and disparate events may be treated as equivalent if they potentially serve the same social or cultural function. Unlike pure mathematics, where two conceptual abstractions can share a Platonic unity, in the legal realm the equality of diverse things is always a limited function of perspectives or situations.[14]

The term *formal* is used here to designate those equalities that are actively constructed and recognized by the legal system. Formal equalities are to be contrasted with the vast number of substantive comparisons open to commonsense observers, based on an infinite variety of descriptive, instrumental, and normative criteria. Legal or formal equality is thus a constantly fluctuating set of situational judgments, selected from a much wider field of substantive relationships. From a nonlegal perspective, formal equality always seems highly artificial; it deliberately ignores moments of equality and inequality that may be immensely important for nonlegal purposes. Two people who violate the same criminal law can be equally guilty, for example, despite profound physical or moral differ-

51

ences between them. The boundaries of formal equality are forever changing in response to conflicting social pressures; but they remain boundaries that exclude far more territory than they can directly encompass.[15]

Judgments of formal equality, seen against the richer background of substantive criteria, follow the basic structure of adjudication according to the widely accepted legal realist model. The chief innovation of legal realism, indeed, was to look beyond abstract patterns of legal concepts and to locate legal judgments in a dynamic context of social forces. Two distinct conclusions have generally been drawn from this model. First, the act of judging is itself conditioned by a social context and thus the objectivity of legal decisions premised on formal reasoning can always be questioned. Second, some mode of taking substantive conditions into account is inescapable if judges are to adapt legal principles to changing social circumstances. Judges distort the present world if they cling to legal categories and principles appropriate to some past social reality. The notion of a purely logical or mechanical jurisprudence is thus both inefficient and hypocritical, and in the final analysis impossible.[16]

A further, normative level of the realist critique crossed fatefully with important political controversies at the time of the New Deal. As legal realists canvassed the Supreme Court's record for the first third of the century, they held the Court responsible for blocking vital elements of the progressive legislative agenda. In one especially odious case going back to 1905, for example, the Court had invalidated a New York law regulating working conditions in the baking industry, holding that the law violated the property rights of employers and employees.[17] In this case and many others, the only constitutional authority cited by the Court in defining such rights was the vaguely worded due process clause of the Fourteenth Amendment. With the hindsight of succeeding decades, this tendentious reading of the Constitution became a symbol for judicial reactionism.[18]

In the hands of progressive legal critics, the realist analysis—reflected here in the sharp distinction between formal and substantive judgments—became the basis for dividing governmental power between judicial and legislative branches. When the Court finally made its dramatic doctrinal shift in 1937, a new majority embraced the realist critique and its assumption that matters of substance belonged entirely to the legislature. The courts were admonished to exercise restraint, particularly on occasions when individual decisions seemed to require making creative leaps beyond existing precedent. Although this politically inspired approach to judicial review was originally developed by progressive lawyers, it was later eagerly embraced by conservative critics of the Warren Court—as judicial activism transformed itself into a powerful progressive tool.[19]

Before progressive activism could be launched, however, appellate court judges faced obvious conflicts. Many of them accepted the realist critique, and at least some of them were responsible for building it into the web of constitutional doctrine following the 1937 watershed. As a result, Supreme Court adjudication was harnessed to a method described as plodding, uncreative, and perhaps ultimately untenable. The important substantive insights required for realistic decisions were to be systematically excluded from judicial attention. Under the circumstances, judicial restraint was the only defensible prescription. But even restraint was possibly illusory, since over the long run the failure to revise principles of fundamental law could be just as arbitrary and socially undesirable as overt judicial activism.[20] A delicate resolution of this dilemma enabled the Warren Court to begin its cautious revival of judicial initiative, based on the notion of "reasoned elaboration," or the meticulous observance of formal procedure and the cultivation of judicial craftsmanship.[21]

An engineering metaphor might best capture this paradoxical solution. Although it acknowledged a judicial universe divided into two unbridgeable worlds of form and substance, the Warren Court in the 1950s began to construct something resembling a bridge between them. The base of this bridge was to be firmly anchored in the accessible realm of technical form, but it seemed to lead off into the impenetrable fog of substantive values. The inherent ambiguity of this task meant that critics could variously size up the construction crew—initially led by Chief Justice Warren—as bold heroes, naive or foolhardy adventurers, or sly deceivers. The difference between hero worship and deep skepticism concerning the Court's enterprise seemed to rest on conflicting projections about exactly where the bridge might end up. Much critical attention was given to construction technique nearest the formalist foundation; any cracks or fissures were immediately detected, minutely analyzed, and factored into competing assessments of the larger project. All these prodigious efforts, both constructive and critical, should not obscure the central paradox: the bridge project had been launched with the solemn understanding that it would never touch ground at the other end.

All the anomalies of American pragmatism are wrapped up in this purely technical ideal of judicial performance.[22] Skepticism about the ability of anyone (except perhaps "the people") to discern final values was allowed to mix with honest faith in technical proficiency; the results combined elements of heroism and critique. Judges could act legitimately, under this post-realist theory, through a combination of formalistic virtuosity and perspicuous selection of occasions when the very failure to act would erode existing principles.[23]

This approach allowed most liberal commentators, eventually, to endorse the unanimous decision of the Warren Court in Brown v. Board of Education, along

53

with other civil rights cases of the 1950s.[24] However, as the Warren Court extended the equal protection doctrine into denser fog, the principle of legitimation by good technique showed unmistakable signs of strain. Scholarly opposition to the Court's methods grew rapidly after the legislative reapportionment cases of the 1960s.[25] Finally, the basic doctrinal structure began to crumble a decade later as the Court wavered in extending equal protection principles to state programs in public education and social welfare.

The Judicial Management of Proof: Brown v. Board of Education

The postwar cult of judicial craftsmanship created ideal incentives for the Warren Court to build its activist program on the manipulation of presumptions and proof burdens. As post-realist judges, members of the Court were acutely aware of the conflicting substantive applications that surround all legal principles. At the same time, choosing openly among alternative directions was seen as the quintessential function of legislation, based on progressive institutional theories going back to the turn of the century. And yet, the decision not to adapt legal principles to changing conditions is also a substantive choice, especially in cases where legislative bodies had proved strangely resistant or hostile to change. This dilemma was endemic to the model of realist jurisprudence, and the Warren Court felt it most keenly in controversies surrounding civil rights.[26]

Under the progressive accommodation with realism, courts were entitled to nullify actions taken by either the legislative or administrative branch of government, but only when utterly transparent constitutional rights were at stake— not because the court preferred a different policy.[27] Given the wide latitude in judicial interpretation, however, it makes an enormous difference who bears the burden of proof on constitutional questions: whether it is the government that must show how its actions are constitutional or the challenger that must show how they are not. This choice is critical, since the degree of proof required can be set so high in either case that it is virtually impossible to meet.

Suppose, for example, a legal battle over state regulations on employment conditions in the baking industry, where the key constitutional question comes down to whether such regulations are reasonably designed to protect public health and safety. Any review of underlying facts will produce evidence pointing both ways; the regulations will doubtless appear reasonable in some respects but not in others. In relation to such opaque criteria as *reasonableness,* a burden of proof placed on either party can be made exceedingly difficult to carry.[28] An especially weighty presumption that all legislation is "reasonable" will insulate most laws (whether progressive or conservative in spirit) from constitutional

54

challenge. A shift in presumptions, on the other hand, greatly facilitates constitutional attack.

In the landmark school desegregation decision of 1954, Brown v. Board of Education,[29] the Warren Court managed to turn several important questions of proof against the challenged segregation laws, without yet revealing the full strategy of burden shifting. One year earlier, the Court had postponed its much-awaited decision to pursue (among other topics) an arcane investigation of what the 1868 Congress had originally intended in passing the Fourteenth Amendment with its controversial equal protection clause. But when Earl Warren became Chief Justice in late 1953, the Court was suddenly ready to make its own history.[30] The scholarly inquiry into Congressional intent was quietly laid aside as "inconclusive," with the unstated presumption that the Court was therefore free to use the Fourteenth Amendment as a basis for intervening in contemporary events.[31]

The key breakthrough in the 1950s race discrimination discussions was the rejection of the notorious separate but equal doctrine. The Supreme Court had established this phrase in a famous 1896 case approving segregated public services in the South, provided they could be deemed "equal" by some tangible measure.[32] The 1954 Brown decision did not directly overrule this doctrine but instead raised to an unbearable weight the burden on states to prove that their segregated services were, in truth, equal.

In all four cases converging in the Brown litigation, lower courts had already found that states had equalized their separate school systems or were moving in that direction—assuming as relevant criteria the measures of "buildings, curricula, qualifications and salaries of teachers, and other 'tangible' factors." But Warren responded to these findings with a disarming inference: "Our decision, therefore, cannot turn on merely a comparison of these tangible factors. . . . We must look instead to the effect of segregation itself on public education."[33]

Warren's controversial "therefore" tipped the balance against the school districts, and ultimately against the entire structure of state-enforced segregation. With one strategic logical connective, the Court qualitatively increased the burden of proof for states that were already scrambling to meet the evolving fiscal criteria coming out of the separate but equal doctrine. How could the states possibly show that segregated school systems were equal in all intangible respects? None of them had even attempted to supply this elusive kind of proof at the trial level, and thus Warren could proceed unhindered to his dramatic conclusion that separate school systems were "inherently unequal."[34]

Much has been made of Warren's reference to trial testimony from the Kansas case, which had suggested that segregated schools caused psychologi-

55

cal harm to black children.[35] Although the lower federal court had accepted the essence of this uncontroverted testimony in its list of factual findings, Warren did not even try to use it as a substantive premise; after all, he wanted to conclude that separate was inherently unequal, whether or not future trial courts made similar findings. But the reference provided Warren an opportunity to cite a whole list of empirical studies on segregation, which purportedly agreed with the Kansas court's factual finding. In the time-honored manner of appeals courts, Warren dryly noted that the Kansas finding was not unreasonable, since it was "amply supported by modern authority."[36]

Although some critics accused Warren of tailoring a constitutional principle to fit social science evidence, his argument was in fact much more subtle. Strictly speaking, this part of his decision was extraneous, since the legal outcome of the case was not in any way determined by the offhand factual notation in the Kansas court's opinion.[37] But Warren's reference sent a clear warning to future litigants: that proving the absence of psychological harm resulting from segregation would be a severe task. In effect, Warren announced a new and exacting burden of proof for all states hoping to retain segregation in any form, and he did so without having to vouch for the truth of either the Kansas testimony or the empirical works listed in his famous footnote.

56   Brown v. Board of Education was received by some critics as a brilliant display of post-realist craftsmanship and by others as a serious deviation from judicial restraint.[38] Both views refer to the crafty locutions with which Warren sidesteps the history of the Fourteenth Amendment, the doctrine of separate but equal, and the empirical question of whether segregation affects the psychological development of schoolchildren. These are the key elements in Warren's opinion, but instead of deductive proof Warren gives us a series of apparent evasions— arguments that strangely transcend their formal boundaries. With hindsight, these arguments can be interpreted as Warren's first experiment in the technique of burden-shifting as a form of activism. Everyone who read the opinion— friend and foe alike—knew it represented an important change in the law of race discrimination, but everything was encoded in the rhetoric of judicial formalism.[39] Critical attention soon moved to an important secondary level of judicial decision-making: the tacit manipulation of presumptions and proof standards. At this level, restraint and activism were two sides of the same formalist coin, depending on which side the Court chose to emphasize.

Further evidence for this higher-order strategy comes from the companion case to Brown, Bolling v. Sharpe, which struck down school segregation in the District of Columbia. Since the Fourteenth Amendment and its equal protection language applied only to the states, this case had to be decided under the due process language of the Fifth Amendment. This clause turned out to be a relatively uncluttered legal principle, at least for this case, since it completely avoided the long shadow cast by the separate but equal gloss on the Fourteenth Amendment. With virtually a clean doctrinal slate, the Warren Court reached its conclusion in scarcely more than two pages of large print: "Segregation in public education is *not* reasonably related to any proper governmental objective" and thus must be halted.[40]

But why did Warren place the burden on the District government to prove that its objectives were proper and its methods reasonable? This is, in fact, a complete reversal of the presumption of constitutionality, which the Court had been converting into a mighty fortress ever since 1937. By way of an answer, the Bolling opinion further announced that "Classifications based solely upon race must be scrutinized with particular care, since they are contrary to our traditions and hence constitutionally suspect."[41] This impressive metaphor of heightened scrutiny was destined to become a ritual signal in later Supreme Court decisions, informing us that the presumption of constitutionality was being reversed. Whenever the metaphor appears in later cases, the shoe automatically moves to the other foot: instead of the challenger having to prove that legislation is unreasonable, the burden shifts to the legislature to defend both its purpose and methods.

Bolling v. Sharpe displays no serious judicial inquiry into factual evidence on either point; the Court's eloquent brevity made it brutally plain that no conceivable evidence would be permitted to redeem publicly supported racial segregation. From the viewpoint of Warren's defenders, segregation advocates could no longer hide behind the presumption of constitutionality, although that presumption continued to protect legislative authority in most areas other than race relations.

The Invention of Strict Scrutiny

During the 1960s, the Warren Court started to expand the occasions on which it applied its special standard of judicial review, moving tentatively beyond cases involving race classifications. The hardening disparity in review techniques was reflected in a growing dichotomy in the Court's decisions: cases based on heightened scrutiny (though few in number) invariably overturned legislative actions, whereas cases based on the post-1937 presumption of constitutionality left everything intact. As one commentator summed it up, the Warren Court's new equal protection practice "embraced a rigid two-tier attitude . . . with scrutiny that was 'strict' in theory and fatal in fact . . . [and] with minimal scrutiny in theory and virtually none in fact."[42]

The Warren Court technique was actually much less rigid than most commentators—friend and foe alike—wanted to believe. It was primarily in cases with racial overtones that the Warren Court deployed its burden-shifting strategy under the formal banner of equal protection. After Brown v. Board of Education was decided, no legislative body managed to offer a "reasonable" enough justification for racial disparities in existing laws, no matter whether the issue was public education, public swimming pools, or interracial marriage.[43] In reaching decisions on these and other matters, the Court's basic strategy remained that of invoking the need for careful scrutiny, which could increasingly be anchored in its own prior race discrimination decisions.

This ingenious formalism came back some years later to haunt proponents of affirmative action, according to whom race or gender classifications should be condoned for benign purposes. Whether this contingency ever figured in the Warren Court's calculations is hard to know, but its decisions always managed to stop short of declaring the principle that race classifications as such were always unconstitutional. (To announce such a principle directly, in the 1950s, would have violated the reigning ideals of post-realist craftsmanship.)[44] Even in the late 1960s, the Warren Court was not prepared to say openly whether all future cases involving race would meet the same fate. Its decision striking down prohibitions on interracial marriage, for example, was carefully fortified by assurances that a fundamental interest (marriage) was affected, thereby compounding the harmful impact of unequal treatment accorded to whites and blacks.[45]

Despite such caution, however, the implications of Warren's burden-shifting strategy were quickly grasped by eager constitutional litigators and sympathetic legal commentators, who began to translate a studiously ad hoc practice into hard judicial doctrine.[46] In lower courts and in law review articles during the later 1960s, an elaborate doctrinal theory was thus invented, according to which the federal courts were free to apply *strict scrutiny* in either of two broad kinds of cases: (1) whenever a law or regulation named (or unduly affected) certain vulnerable groups dubbed "suspect classes," or (2) whenever alleged *fundamental interests* were at stake.[47] According to some versions of this formalistic scheme, a secondary doctrine spelled out specific burdens created by strict scrutiny, under which states were required (1) to identify *compelling* purposes behind their laws, (2) to prove that the means selected were closely tailored to those particular purposes, and (3) to show that there were no *less drastic* means that might have been chosen.[48]

This breathtaking formal structure, now commonly identified by textbooks and commentaries with the equal protection jurisprudence of the Warren Court itself, is in fact a kind of legal fantasy constructed retrospectively by progressive advocates of judge-led social change. Ironically, it was first mooted in Supreme

Court opinions by dissenters to the Warren brand of activism in an effort to ridicule what they saw as the artificial, formal presuppositions of that style. The *locus classicus* for the basic doctrine is Justice Harlan's dissent in Shapiro v. Thompson, a welfare-rights case from the waning days of the Warren period.[49]

In this case, Harlan was doubtless responding to virtuoso formalizations that were already appearing in the legal briefs of reform-minded advocates. His major criticism—likewise represented in contemporary legal debate—merely dusted off the old progressive attack on judicial review.[50] Formal legal doctrines, he noted, are susceptible to political abuse by judges, and any creation *ex nihilo* of new doctrines was presumed to be blatantly political. Echoing the skeptical critique embraced by the New Deal generation of legal reformers, Harlan added with heavy irony that "I know of nothing which entitles this Court to pick out particular human activities, characterize them as 'fundamental,' and give them added protection under an unusually stringent equal protection test."[51]

The Shapiro case marks the precise moment when the Warren Court burden-shifting strategy began to unravel.[52] Such techniques are at their strongest when no one draws attention to them; formulating a complete doctrine around the occasions for careful or strict scrutiny thus brought the whole fluid practice into the spotlight. Although the Court managed to strike down the challenged residency requirements for welfare benefits, it was forced to invent a subtle rationale for extending the burden-shifting strategy beyond race discrimination cases. In an argument widely perceived as both ingenious and opportunistic, the Court declared that residency requirements interfered with the constitutional right of interstate travel.

Beneath the formal surface of this case, it appears that as many as four justices were already anticipating the next doctrinal step—the announced litigation goal of welfare-rights advocates—of declaring that all welfare cases should be scrutinized by the stricter standard of judicial review.[53] In technical terms, a near-majority of the Court was prepared to find that welfare laws contained the *suspect classification* of wealth—"suspect" in a sense derived by analogy from the race discrimination cases. With that finding, a weighty burden of proof would immediately have shifted to the states, along with Congress, to defend the ends and means of the entire public welfare system. That doctrinal step, as everyone knew, was likely to promote wide ferment in the nation's welfare structure.[54] In retrospect, it is interesting that Warren himself withheld the crucial vote that could have made the Shapiro case into a monument of social activism. Just two months before he left the Court, he filed one of his rare dissents to this expansive reading of the equal protection clause, arguing that wealth and right to travel interests were only indirectly implicated in welfare-residency laws.[55]

59

For whatever reason, no majority on the Supreme Court emerged to take the critical step toward constitutionalizing public welfare programs and other entitlements—either in Shapiro or in subsequent cases that worked their way through the judicial hierarchy in succeeding years.[56] Instead, a coalition of justices (minus Warren) adopted a cautious approach to strict scrutiny in the Shapiro case, seizing upon the fortuitous notion of a constitutional right to travel. The states could not prove that residency restrictions had not deterred at least some people from moving across state lines. A double negative was thus sufficient to trigger the stricter standard of scrutiny, and thereby to shift the burden onto the states to demonstrate compelling reasons for limiting access to their welfare rolls.[57]

The doctrinally convenient right to travel had no special connection to poverty, but it was an incremental stage in the broader litigation strategy for extending strict scrutiny beyond cases of race discrimination. Had the Supreme Court eventually gone on to declare wealth a suspect classification, the Shapiro opinion might now be interpreted as a cautious, craftsmanlike move toward the future. As it turned out, however, Shapiro is a surviving anomaly, the remains of an arrested political movement: the campaign to harness the Warren Court's powerful burden-shifting strategy.[58] As with odd species left stranded by the course of natural selection, this case reminds us of the bold instrumentalism that encouraged lawyer-reformers to invent a neutral doctrinal structure for advancing a popular political agenda.

It is also important to note how easily the practical advantages of legal doctrines could shift between political adversaries. The formal doctrine of strict scrutiny was able to serve both the long-term hopes of social-reform advocates and the immediate defensive interests of judicial dissenters. For the reformers, a doctrinal lever for burden-shifting would allow judges to carry social change into new fields, assisted by the creativity of movement lawyers in suggesting analogical extensions for a wide range of suspect classes and fundamental interests. All this could be accomplished through the formal interpretation of legal concepts, without requiring the courts to weigh the underlying instrumental motives for expansion.[59] At the same time, however, the Warren Court dissenters hoped that doctrinal recognition would immediately curtail further reform efforts. If future judges could be persuaded to reject new invitations to analogical extension, the formal doctrine would draw a tight limit around the strategy of strict scrutiny, which had scarcely moved much beyond the special consideration given to race classifications.

Still another strategic reason for converting burden-shifting into a formal doctrine emerged after the Supreme Court changed membership in 1969. As President Nixon's appointments began to alter the Court's direction, the doctrinal mechanism became a key defensive weapon for liberal reformers in the ensuing ideological struggle. If the fledgling strict-scrutiny strategy could be preserved as a full-blown doctrine, it could possibly frustrate a more conservative Court's efforts to reverse Warren's achievements. Strict scrutiny was thus welcomed into the neutral body of constitutional doctrines even though its concrete applications were left open to opposing definitions. In a decade of more conservative judges, the strict-scrutiny doctrine could serve as a fortress from which new but isolated victories might eventually be secured.[60] In particular, the growing aspirations of the women's movement included the goal of placing gender on the list of suspect classifications, thereby shifting the burden onto state and federal authorities to defend gender-based legislation.

Using Strategic Burdens: Poverty, Gender, and Affirmative Action

The early years of the Burger Court stirred conservative hopes for shifting back to the pre-Warren presumption of constitutionality. The central irony of this turning point concerns the formal doctrine of strict scrutiny, which was constructed by liberal advocates as a means for expanding the process of burden-shifting. Using the leverage of general concepts like fundamental interest and suspect classification, that doctrine was supposed to catapult the Warren Court technique beyond the field of welfare rights and into the new territory of gender discrimination. Instead the doctrine of strict scrutiny increasingly became a formal barrier to activist judicial review as it fell into the hands of a more conservative judiciary prepared to manipulate burdens of proof for its own selective ends. The expansion of equal protection doctrine was thereby halted at the border between race discrimination and social welfare.

By investing their entire adversarial fortune in the doctrine of strict scrutiny, welfare-rights advocates gambled and lost everything in a remarkably short period of time. Given the win-or-lose nature of burden-shifting strategies, once the Court definitively rejected strict scrutiny for welfare litigants, their claims were condemned to stay in the domain governed by the presumption of constitutionality.[61] Of course, the new Burger Court majority was not so crass as to declare a naked preference for the older standard of review. As skilled judicial craftsmen, they simply invoked ordinary post-realist rhetoric—the legacy of progressive judges prior to the Warren period—to establish a residual presumption in favor of judicial restraint.[62] It then became the dubious task of activist litigators to prove, before a skeptical Court, that they were entitled to the stricter standard of review.

This inevitable argument—which uses proof burdens to assign contested proof burdens—can be found in several opinions from the early 1970s, including the pivotal case of Dandridge v. Williams. In Dandridge, welfare advocates challenged certain rules adopted by the state of Maryland for implementing the federally supported Aid to Families with Dependent Children program (AFDC). Although the suit was really questioning the adequacy of Maryland's benefit levels under AFDC, the precise legal issue had to be narrowed to bring it under the equal protection rubric. Accordingly, plaintiffs attacked that part of the state plan that imposed a cap on total monthly benefits going to any one family, even though the basic formula corollated benefits to the number of children. In urging the Supreme Court to employ strict scrutiny, the plaintiffs wanted to force Maryland to prove that this complex eligibility formula did not discriminate against large families. In effect, they postulated that Maryland was discriminating against the fifth child born into an eligible family, since the cap on total family benefits was mathematically reached after coverage of four children.[63]

Litigators were encouraged to develop such ingenious hypotheses on the assumption that state legislatures would be forced to carry the burden of proof. But the Burger Court rejected this comfortable strategy and allowed the burden to remain with plaintiffs, citing its default duty to apply the presumption of constitutionality to such cases. Justice Stewart's majority opinion noted that there was "no contention that the Maryland regulation is infected with a racially discriminatory purpose or effect such as to make it inherently suspect." And there was no clear violation of fundamental interests already recognized under the Constitution, despite any claim that "the administration of public welfare assistance . . . involves the most basic economic needs of impoverished human beings." Stewart's conclusion, shrewdly worded to convey a tone of Solomonic regret, was the "we can find no basis for applying a [stricter] constitutional standard."[64]

No basis at all? One year before, in the Shapiro case, as many as four other justices were ready to bring all welfare programs into the embrace of strict scrutiny, largely because of the intrinsic importance of welfare aid "upon which may depend the ability of the families to obtain the very means to subsist— food, shelter, and other necessities of life."[65] In the Dandridge case, Stewart invoked the identical premise but then declared (with the backing of a new Court majority) that it provided no basis for invoking strict scrutiny. By thus acknowledging that welfare is something truly fundamental, but not fundamental enough to trigger strict scrutiny, Stewart placed an imposing burden on the advocates of welfare rights, who had hoped to extend the strict-scrutiny doctrine to their advantage. Considering the whole flavor of the Shapiro opinion, Stewart could easily have found some basis for special judicial consideration. Instead he confined Shapiro to a footnote, dismissing it as an isolated case concerned primarily with the "constitutionally protected freedom of interstate travel."[66]

Is wealth a suspect classification? For substantive debate over social-welfare policies, this issue seems entirely too abstract and impractical. But it necessarily became the pivotal question for Supreme Court justices around the time of transition to the Burger Court. A "yes" answer would doubtless have inaugurated a series of federal court challenges to welfare programs, in which nearly any legislative provision might have been invalidated. A "no" answer removed such issues from federal court consideration altogether. Although both sides agreed that federal courts had no official role in dictating specific goals or procedures for public welfare programs, the Supreme Court became a battleground for assigning the inescapable burden of this judicial incapacity. Either the states or the advocates of welfare rights would inherit that incapacity in the form of nearly insurmountable burdens of proof. Once the doctrinal question was squarely posed and firmly settled in the Dandridge case, the welfare-rights litigation strategy was left in complete disarray.

Not surprisingly, Justice Marshall's dissent in the Dandridge case urged the Court not to answer the larger question in strict doctrinal terms. Using standard realist arguments about the artificiality of formal distinctions, Marshall suggested that the Court should adjust its degree of scrutiny according to the extent that each case seemed to impinge on fundamental interests. Under this approach, at least some serious judicial review might be warranted for state welfare programs, especially when there were tangible effects on bedrock economic interests.[67]

Although Marshall's recommendation seems refreshingly direct and less mechanical than Stewart's opinion, its underlying strategy is calculated in similar terms. Marshall's suggestion is the obvious rejoinder of the Court's waning liberal faction; it seems unlikely, for example, that he would have applied the same sliding-scale approach to a case like Brown v. Board of Education. As long as an existing doctrine can serve the strategic interests of a dominant judicial faction, it is treated with the full deference accorded to objective law. But as Court dynamics change and formal doctrine starts to cut the other way, it suddenly becomes artificial, the tool of sly manipulation, the vehicle of judicial usurpation, and ultimately an emblem of the new majority's defective craftsmanship.[68]

Such opportunistic appeals to objective legality may seem completely natural to professional lawyers, especially to those who concentrate on appellate arguments in broad constitutional cases.[69] But for anyone who stands outside the stream of litigation, doctrinal disputes like the battle over strict scrutiny become abstract, surrogate arguments for the substantive debate that courts are unable to conduct more openly, given prevailing attitudes toward judicial review. Although by now it seems plain that doctrinal arguments in the area of equal protection were shaped by the strategic purposes of diverse interest groups, the controversies described above were played out with the utmost sobriety by all participants. The rhetoric of objective law remains irresistible to any faction that sustains the hope, however remote, of commanding a judicial majority.

As the welfare-rights controversy came to an abrupt end, the Burger Court was poised to follow a different path in the area of gender discrimination. By 1973, in response to mounting litigation, the Court came within a single vote of declaring gender a suspect classification.[70] But judicial partisans sought to avoid the polarized battle played out in the welfare-rights cases, and the Court found a rhetorical compromise that allowed the burden of proof in gender cases to shift on a completely ad hoc basis. This practice eventually became known under the curious doctrinal language of *quasi-suspect classifications*.[71] It was, to be sure, a transparent strategic maneuver that preserved a wide middle ground for decision-making. Laws suspected of gender discrimination were officially subjected to an intermediate level of scrutiny, leaving the Court free to manipulate burdens and standards of proof in individual instances.[72]

Although this approach represented a partial victory for progressive advocates, it left the Court's doctrinal structure balanced on a knife-edge between activism and restraint. Some litigation strategists hoped that passage of the Equal Rights Amendment would force the Court to raise gender to the same doctrinal level as race, thereby completing the campaign they feared might be lost in the early years of the Burger Court.[73]

But the formalism of equal rights caused widespread confusion in the political arena, contributing to eventual defeat for the ERA. Supporters were effectively handed the burden of proving that certain politically volatile consequences would not result from the ERA: women in the military, abolition of child support, abortion on demand, unisex bathrooms. Although these controversial results were scarcely necessary theorems from the formal principle of equal treatment, they were also not impossible deductions by a judiciary armed with strict scrutiny. Advocates of the ERA were therefore trapped, and they eventually lost the crucial strategic battle in the court of public opinion.[74]

Some feminist legal critics writing in the 1980s have found an underlying tension between the formal techniques derived from Warren Court activism and the inescapably substantive dimensions of gender inequality.[75] Perhaps it was wise, in the context of widespread racial segregation during the 1950s and 1960s, to pursue social reform through a judicial rule placing an insupportable burden of proof on all forms of differential treatment between blacks and whites. But the same strategy could actually deepen the social and economic disadvantages of women if public policies were forced to ignore relevant substantive differences from men—even if those differences were ultimately the products of cultural stereotypes and prior economic injustice. As Mary Becker has written:

Consider the effect on women of the shift from the traditional maternal preference in child custody disputes. During the sixties judges assumed that it was in the best interest of a child of tender years to give custody to its mother. Many jurisdictions have either eliminated this presumption or replaced it with a presumption in favor of joint custody, thus giving a bargaining chip to fathers in negotiations with mothers. Because mothers seem to want custody much more than fathers, the result of giving this bargaining chip to fathers is that mothers who desperately want custody offer economic concessions to settle the custody issue rather than submitting it to a judge.[76]

Becker makes a similar point about recent judicial trends in child support and alimony payments following divorce, which have drifted toward gender-neutral criteria. In general, she argues, presumptions against differential legal treatment of men and women may only exacerbate social and economic inequalities in the absence of more comprehensive social reforms. Within such broader policies, Becker would include affirmative programs for ensuring truly equal economic opportunities—taking into account the physiological effects of pregnancy and such cultural barriers as the gendered structure of the workplace, stereotyping by supervisors, and the prevalence of sexual harassment. "Formal equality," she concludes, "is not capable of producing enough change in the status quo, and is likely to impose significant costs on those women most in need of change because most unlike men."[77]

Becker's critique bypasses the high ideals of law as an instrument of social change and concentrates on the incomplete, and therefore inadequate, strategies associated with the Warren era. What she calls "formal equality" is the residue from the Warren Court's practice of shifting the presumption of constitutionality while raising the standard of proof so high as to preclude any positive case for maintaining statutory inequalities. As a limited tool developed to nullify laws supporting racial segregation in the 1950s and 1960s, that procedure had a surgical neatness and simplicity. But nullifying laws does not automatically translate into a comprehensive social policy for correcting inequality in all its dimensions.

The troubled public debate in the United States over affirmative action reflects this same critical gap, greatly complicating the pursuit of substantive equality for racial minorities as well as for women. Depending on judicial will, a strong legal presumption against differential treatment can be made to apply with equal force to policies viewed as either hurting or helping specific groups.

This formal symmetry is reinforced by the popular term *reverse discrimination* used chiefly by critics of affirmative action programs that offer special advantages to groups affected by past discrimination.[78] The rhetorical power of such terminology depends mainly on what happens to proof burdens: whether the proponent of affirmative action is left with the task of justifying differential treatment, and whether the standard of proof remains so high as to preclude almost any justification.

Although these controversies spread quickly into public debate, the Supreme Court offered little clarification of the larger issues. When it upheld affirmative action programs and other forms of differential treatment, it justified such measures as remedial steps designed to counteract past discrimination.[79] In many cases, of course, it was impossible to know whether existing disparities of racial treatment were, in fact, products of past discrimination, as judgments on such matters are largely shaped by presumptions and burdens of proof.

It was possible, for example, for courts to defer to legislative findings that past discrimination justified prospective affirmative action. Even without legislative presumptions, courts have frequently been willing to adopt broad remedial measures for past discrimination rather than narrowly targeted responses. And some justices have long favored a presumption that statistical patterns of differential treatment by race are reflections of past discrimination, absent proof to the contrary.[80]

In 1989, however, the Court revived its strained cognitive metaphors for dealing with affirmative action. In striking down a voluntary plan by the city of Richmond, Virginia, which set aside a portion of construction projects for minority contractors, the Supreme Court ruled that strict scrutiny should apply to all racial distinctions, whether "benign" or "invidious" in alleged purpose. For years the Court had avoided any firm position on whether the burden of proof was the same for both kinds of policies. In cutting back on affirmative action, the Court took refuge in strategic ignorance.

> Absent searching judicial inquiry into the justification for such race-based measures, there is simply no way of determining what classifications are "benign" or "remedial" and what classifications are in fact motivated by illegitimate notions of racial inferiority or simple racial politics. Indeed, the purpose of strict scrutiny is to "smoke out" illegitimate uses of race by assuring that the legislative body is pursuing a goal important enough to warrant use of a highly suspect tool. The test also ensures that the means chosen "fit" this compelling goal so closely that there is little or no possibility that the motive for the classification was illegitimate racial prejudice or stereotype.[81]

Thus the burden-shifting technique developed by the Warren Court to challenge racial segregation thirty-five years earlier became the convenient judicial strategy for defeating voluntary affirmative-action programs. It is too soon to know how strictly the Court will scrutinize arguments of state and local governments that still want to defend such programs; Justice O'Connor's majority opinion seems to leave open the possibility that some defendants may succeed. But evidence of any kind is unlikely to persuade at least two justices who believe that "racial neutrality" is a "moral imperative." [82] Indeed, evidence alone was not the central issue for the dissenting judges, who argued for precisely the kind of distinction Justice O'Connor dismissed as impossible to administer.

> Racial classifications "drawn on the presumption that one race is inferior to another or because they put the weight of government behind racial hatred and separatism" warrant the strictest judicial scrutiny because of the very irrelevance of these rationales. By contrast, racial classifications drawn for the purpose of remedying the effects of discrimination that itself was racebased have a highly pertinent basis: the tragic and indelible fact that discrimination against blacks and other racial minorities in this Nation has pervaded our Nation's history and continues to scar our society. [83]

It is difficult to forecast what impact the Richmond case will eventually have on affirmative action programs. Under the guise of constitutional neutrality, the Court has obviously raised significant hurdles for such plans by adopting the judicial presumption that they are invidiously intended. [84]

The practical consequences of these new decisions might well be muted if other public forums besides the courts provided a less adversarial tone for debating civil rights, gender discrimination, and welfare equity. But such problems do not inhabit the kind of arena implied by Aristotle's rhetoric, nor by Perelman's "new rhetoric," nor even by Toulmin's professionalized "fields of knowledge." The highly sensitive issues of inequality have instead been debated under severe rhetorical constraints. The leading federal statutes have borrowed the formal language of constitutional principles, and their implementation has been decisively shaped by judicial assignments of proof burdens.

As perhaps the most important of the federal statutes, Title VII of the 1964 Civil Rights Act bans employment discrimination on the basis of race, sex, and other criteria. [85] The legislative history of this act reveals a background of fractious controversy on whether private employment was an appropriate target of federal regulation, and on how to define the equal opportunity that proponents of the bill hoped to promote. This conflict proved so great, indeed, that key con-

67

cepts in the final version of Title VII had to defer the truly difficult questions to the future course of implementation and court interpretation.[86]

The mark of this legislative stalemate was the selection of the simple term *discrimination* to define employment practices prohibited under the statute. Even by 1964, the Supreme Court's experience in articulating the equal protection language of the Fourteenth Amendment had revealed the difficulty of applying such general terms to the concrete problems of race discrimination. Although a great many specific circumstances were debated at length by Congress, the final statute provided few clues as to how the term *discrimination* ought to be applied to concrete problems.

To take but one example, much attention had been given to private industry's use of testing procedures as a basis for restricting employment and promotion opportunities. Some groups had argued that employment tests were consciously used to discriminate against black employees or at least had the inescapable effect of limiting the growth of black employment. On the other side, representatives of private industry had argued for unrestrained use of testing, despite any adverse impact on blacks, as necessary for maintaining quality in the workforce. Several legislative models were considered that would have set standards governing employment tests, but none were incorporated in the final version of Title VII. Employers were told by the statute not to "discriminate on the basis of race," but they were not told exactly what kinds of testing procedures might fall under this very broad term. Their uncertainty was scarcely eased by a special section added to the statute, authorizing the use of "any professionally developed ability test" that is not "designed, intended, or used to discriminate because of race."[87]

How does anyone really know whether a specific test is "designed, intended or used to discriminate," unless one has conclusive evidence on the actual psychological intent of the employer or of those who administered the test? What conclusion should be drawn from the absence of such evidence? Was Title VII addressed solely to discriminatory intentions, or did it also reach the disparate impact of innocently chosen practices? The Burger Court was handed this set of questions in several cases during the 1970s, and it drifted into an approach somewhat reminiscent of the strict-scrutiny doctrine of constitutional law.

The major case was Griggs v. Duke Power Co., in which Chief Justice Burger took the expansive view that Title VII was concerned with discriminatory impact as well as documented intentions, basing his interpretation on the "plain" language of the statute. On closer examination, however, Burger's approach focused on proof burdens rather than broad principles. His decision assigned to employers the burden of showing that testing procedures were not used invidiously. In general, he said, "if an employment practice which operates to exclude Negroes cannot be shown to be related to job performance, the practice is prohibited."[88] In the Griggs case, this task was not nearly so formidable as might first appear. All Burger seemed to expect was some respectable quantitative data showing that the test in question could be correlated with objective measures of job performance.[89]

Subsequent Title VII decisions, however, began to build a more rigid doctrinal structure around the burden-of-proof approach taken in the Griggs case, as legal advocates sought to impose on employers the much more onerous burden of proving their lack of discriminatory intent. Burger's opinion set the initial direction, declaring that the Court was willing to shift the burden of proof to defendants, provided the challenger could produce initial evidence that employment practices had a differential impact on groups of employees defined by race.[90] But the Court never imposed a very onerous burden on employers, who, in practical terms, could shift the burden back to employees by providing plausible evidence that the employment practice under review had at least some independent justification, whatever its alleged impact.

Finally, in 1989 the Supreme Court invoked a distinction between two kinds of legal burdens, limiting the employer's burden to the need to produce some exculpatory evidence of valid business objectives. "In this phase, the employer carries the burden of producing evidence of a business justification for his employment practice. The burden of persuasion, however, remains with the . . . plaintiff." In contrast to the impression created by the Griggs opinion and indulged by the Court for almost twenty years, there is no shifting of the key risk of non-persuasion. "The ultimate burden of proving that discrimination against a protected group has been caused by a specific employment practice remains with the plaintiff *at all times.*"[91]

The Presumption of Constitutionality

The importance of assigning the burden of proof in constitutional cases has been well known to judges throughout our history, but it became especially visible after the Civil War with the growth of state and federal economic regulation and the trend toward federal dominance within the nation's legal structure.[92] Examples of judicial management of proof burdens can be found in many cases around the turn of the century, including Lochner v. New York—a decision that assumed symbolic importance, thirty years later, in the unfolding partisan debate over judicial review.[93] The Lochner case provides another perspective on the central role of presumptions in modern constitutional law and clarifies the background to the Court's strict presumption of constitutionality, established soon after the 1937 watershed.

From the standpoint of its progressive critics, the Lochner decision is the evil witch in a long fairy tale, in which the role of intrepid hero belongs to the progressive agenda for socioeconomic reform. It is now perhaps too easy to see the Lochner opinion as a reactionary moment, a curious reminder of the era before enlightened public opinion accepted the role of government in regulating the private market.[94] The case came to a decision in 1905 after the state of New York had sought to regulate conditions in the baking industry, in part by limiting the maximum weekly service of bakery employees to sixty hours. The Lochner opinion struck down the New York law as a violation of the "right of contract between the employer and employees," which was treated as an integral part of "the liberty of the individual protected by the Fourteenth Amendment" due process clause. The decision drew four dissenting votes and occasioned some of Justice Holmes's most famous prose, which has now become the preeminent source for all opponents of judicial activism, both from left and right on the political spectrum.[95]

70

The majority decision is more subtle than its storybook reputation would suggest. Along with the individual right of free contract, it acknowledges the legitimate interest of the states in regulating unsafe or unhealthful labor conditions. Justice Peckham cites several examples of permissible workplace regulations, including laws covering the mining and smelting industries, which the Supreme Court had recently upheld.[96] Peckham's forthright statement of these competing legal principles illustrates a common strategy in twentieth-century Supreme Court decisions, used by conservative and progressive judges alike. Rhetorically this method preempts the criticism that judges are simply imposing their own set of values on the case—the standard refrain of judicial dissenters, of losing parties and their political allies, and of later Supreme Court majorities. If the Court can project alternative ways to conceptualize a legal issue, then it can narrow its task to the classification of specific facts. Thus the Lochner decision does not entirely repudiate the entire regulatory power of government, contrary to legend, but instead renders the more modest judgment that New York's bakery law was not an appropriate occasion for using that power.

Such well-hedged arguments draw support from a subtly planted burden of proof. Peckham's decision classifies the New York statute as an unconstitutional infringement of due process rights, based on a series of negative premises. Note the frequency of negative terms in this key excerpt:

The question whether this act is valid as a labor law, pure and simple, may be dismissed in a few words. There is no reasonable ground for interfering with the liberty of person or the right of free contract, by determining the hours of labor, in the occupation of a baker. There is no contention that bakers as a class are not equal in intelligence and capacity to men in other trades or manual occupations, or that they are not able to assert their rights and care for themselves without the protecting arm of the state. . . . They are in no sense wards of the state.[97]

If the New York statute cannot show itself to be a reasonable device for promoting public safety, even less does it meet Peckham's rigorous test of a public-health measure: "It does not affect any other portion of the public than those who are engaged in that occupation [baking]. Clean and wholesome bread does not depend upon whether the baker works but ten hours per day or only sixty hours a week. The limitation of the hours of labor does not come within the police power on that ground."[98]

In short, this case involves a violation of personal liberty because there is "no reasonable foundation"[99] for treating it as a safety or health law. Although critics now view this decision as the paradigmatic example of the Court's placing ideology above facts, Peckham's rhetoric resists that easy description. He would gladly entertain more facts, he says, but dryly notes an absence of evidence sufficient to prove that state regulation is reasonable in this particular field. The burden placed on factual evidence becomes very high indeed, as Peckham dismisses "the mere fact that the occupation [baking] is not absolutely and perfectly healthy. . . . There must be more than the mere fact of the possible existence of some small amount of unhealthiness to warrant legislative interference with liberty."[100]

Just how fully documented must the legislature's position be in this particular case? Although the Court starts off with two rival legal principles, it selects the liberty principle by default, after noting New York's failure to provide enough facts to justify the alternative principle of public regulation. The amount of factual evidence that would have been required, however, was set impossibly high; not only does the state's evidence fall short, but the Court questions whether any conceivable evidence could be enough: "In our judgment, it is not possible in fact to discover the connection between the number of hours a baker may work in the bakery and the healthful quality of the bread made by the workman. The connection, if any exists, is too shadowy and thin to build any argument for the interference of the legislature."[101]

Until we peer behind the familiar judicial pretense of weighing factual evidence, the Lochner Court's professed standard of judicial review seems unob-

71

jectionable. After all, what could be wrong with requiring the legislature to be reasonable in its actions? We might well question, however, the enormous burden of proof that the conservative majority places on the New York legislature, under conditions where the Court itself believes that no conceivable evidence could establish the reasonableness of regulating health conditions in the baking industry. By default, the Court elevates liberty of contract to an absolute principle, but its rhetoric appears more balanced. It is, indeed, the same rhetoric of neutrality embraced by progressive judges after 1937, when a new majority on the Court was able to shift this staggering burden onto those who would challenge state intervention.

In shifting the burden of proving reasonableness, progressive judges kept the same high standard of proof and the skepticism about the relevance of available facts. The Lochner case presents examples of this progressive style in its two dissenting opinions—one a lengthy commentary by Justice Harlan and the other the famous talismanic prose of Justice Holmes. Harlan recognizes the same competing legal principles as the majority: the "right of the citizen to enter into contracts" and the power of the legislature to regulate health and safety. His classification of the New York statute, however, depends on an explicit shift in the burden of proof:

72

> If the end which the legislature seeks to accomplish be one to which its power extends, and if the means employed to that end, although not the wisest or the best, are yet not plainly and palpably unauthorized by law, then the court cannot interfere. In other words, when the validity of a statute is questioned, the burden of proof, so to speak, is upon those who assert it to be unconstitutional.[102]

Warming to this theme, Justice Harlan offers a catalogue of negative judgments that rivals Justice Peckham's:

> I find it impossible, in view of common experience, to say that there is here no real or substantial relation between the means employed by the state and the end sought to be accomplished by its legislation. Nor can I say that the statute has no appropriate or direct connection with that protection to health which each State owes to her citizens; or that it is not promotive of the health of the employees in question; or that the regulation prescribed by the state is utterly unreasonable and extravagant or wholly arbitrary. Still less can I say that the statute is, beyond question, a plain, palpable invasion of rights secured by the fundamental law. Therefore I submit that this court will transcend its functions if it assumes to annul the statute of New York.[103]

The legal standard of reasonableness and the rhetoric of both opinions are identical. The difference between judicial factions comes down to which party must prove what all the justices acknowledge to be unprovable. Five members of the Court wanted to impose that burden on the state of New York, while four would have shifted it to the opponents of state economic regulation. With hindsight, of course, the underlying differences in political philosophy can be seen beyond the default rhetoric. The progressive dissenters in Lochner, no less than the conservative majority, accepted the same essential technique.

When we come to Justice Holmes's dissent, finally, we encounter something truly new. Holmes uses this occasion to offer a scant page of observations on the general subject of judicial review—a topic on which he is anything but neutral. His opening paragraph declares the real issue in this case to be the "right of a majority to embody their opinions in law." He cites no authority for this right, nor does he acknowledge that it has been subject to serious qualification throughout American constitutional history. He concedes that exceptions may arise when "a rational and fair man necessarily would admit that the statute proposed would infringe fundamental principles as they have been understood by the traditions of our people and our law." But he fails to address the central conclusion of the Lochner majority: that the New York regulation is precisely this sort of infringement. Granted, Peckham reaches this conclusion by a process of indirect reasoning. But one suspects that Holmes would have used the same serpentine strategy had he bothered to apply his own principle about what the "rational and fair man" would do.[104]

Holmes's opinion rose to fame not because of its judicial craftsmanship but because it supplied an apparently neutral argument for shifting the burden of proof in the direction chosen by the progressives. Holmes's argument would base this shift on the presumption of legislative supremacy, offered without apology as an axiom of constitutional neutrality. Lest this axiom appear to abandon the Supreme Court's traditional function within the federal structure, Holmes allows for exceptions, but his formulation raises a standard that few challengers could expect to meet.

Holmes proposes this virtually insuperable barrier to judicial review not as wise social policy, but as a value-neutral position that requires no further justification. He seems to say that judges can avoid taking positions on partisan issues by deferring to the legislative will; if they do not defer, they are necessarily taking partisan positions. The only exception to be found in Holmes's opinion is the extreme case mentioned in the last quotation, which echoes Justice Harlan's position but with no provision for burdens of proof.

73

There is scarcely any doubt why Holmes's philosophy of judicial review delighted the post-1937 generation of judges and progressive legal commentators. In a political context where the legislature seemed to embody progressive values, Holmes's principle effectively transferred the legal finality of the judicial system to the legislative process. And once a new majority of the Supreme Court was able to build this principle into its constitutional practice, it could be routinely invoked, without any reference to the value skepticism and voluntarism that guided Holmes's personal metaphysics.[105]

"This case is decided upon an economic theory which a large part of the country does not entertain," said Holmes. "A constitution is not intended to embody a particular economic theory, whether of paternalism and the organic relation of the citizen to the state or of *laissez faire*." [106] He fails to mention, of course, that he would have decided this case according to a theory of judicial review that (for all he knew) fell equally short of majority acceptance. And by sheer coincidence, that theory, if applied to this case, would have triggered a result favorable to progressive economic and social views.

Holmes's position anticipated the virtually conclusive presumption of constitutionality that the Court built into its jurisprudence after 1937. In 1905, Holmes did not have the votes of four fellow justices—enough to transfer the burden of proof with no further argument—and thus he had to base his position on a presumption that seemed self-evident to him: the reduction of all value questions to political disputes. Any selection of legal principles, on this theory, represents the personal value choice of the justices. A more radical version of Holmes's position would treat his underlying institutional prejudice as just another personal choice, one that might have turned him into a hero of today's CLS movement. As it is, he occupies a more ambiguous position as the patron saint of all those opposed to judicial review and who need a convenient text to lend their opposition the cloak of legal authority. During the Warren period, conservative dissenters kept Holmes's presumption alive, preserving it for all future dissenters attracted by the strategy of default reasoning.

Chapter 3 | Institutionalizing the Challenge to Authority: Justice through Correct Procedure

The Supreme Court's due process decisions extended the logic of landmark criminal-procedure rulings to other branches of state and federal government, thereby creating a powerful model for challenging virtually all bureaucratic and professional authority. This model converts social issues into questions of procedural fairness, with wide-ranging implications dependent on judicial manipulation of presumptions and proof burdens. The due process doctrine institutionalizes a paradoxical kind of authority, whose power to draw inferences evades scrutiny even as it subjects other forms of authority to skeptical critique. However, the same power can just as suddenly be reversed and can thus resume the function of shielding the status quo.

Court Procedure as a Model of Social Justice

In addition to the equal protection decisions, a second Warren Court doctrinal experiment transformed the constitutional principle of due process. As with equal treatment, the notion of fair procedure is deeply associated with traditional values of legality, and its ideals partly define the proper functioning of all branches of government. It is, moreover, an especially powerful norm within the judicial system, where strict observance of procedure has become a self-fulfilling measure of institutional authority.

As courts gradually surrendered their claim to deal in timeless truths—a process spread out over the past century—their legitimacy increasingly depended on expanding the scope of formal procedures. As sociological critics repeatedly exposed the divergence between the formal rhetoric of law and its operating reality, courts developed a thicker procedural shell based on the notion that formal measures are reflexive and self-purifying. The steady expansion of such procedures is now well established within contemporary judicial systems where they encourage strong adversarial combat along the shifting frontiers of the due process doctrine.[1]

Although courts articulated the procedural model of justice initially for their own redemption, more recently they have imposed similar restraints on other bodies. Over the past three decades, a wide range of public and private institutions have adopted new procedural mechanisms, modeled on the judicial process, in an effort to conserve their authority and autonomy. Thus administrative agencies, schools, and other public services have yielded to judicial and popular pressures for grievance procedures, formalized hearings, and other quasi-judicial devices. Likewise, many private institutions, including corporations, nonprofit organizations, and voluntary associations, have accepted at least some court-type procedures, often as a strategy for avoiding formal judicial review in civil lawsuits.

Whatever the ultimate sources of this general trend, its central institutional standards come from an idealized criminal justice system shaped during the 1960s by the U.S. Supreme Court. In projecting this model, the Warren Court found ingenious ways to merge instrumental social reform—now flying the banner of due process—with the reigning philosophy of judicial restraint. By comparison with its equal protection efforts, the Court's due process decisions have proved to be unusually durable. The conservative shift in membership has limited the pace of reform, but it has not dismantled the underlying doctrinal structure.

76

For reasons to be explored in this chapter, the substantive considerations behind the advance of due process are easily masked by the ritualistic nature of procedure, for which the courts have claimed unique expertise and authority. In due process cases, legal issues are typically reduced to the question of whether an organization can prove that its procedures are fair enough to guarantee the absence of institutional bias or discretion. Depending on how high the reviewing court chooses to set the burden of proof, virtually any public or private authority can be forced to modify its actions once it falls under federal court jurisdiction.

The vigorous spread of due process challenges thus transforms the basic idiom of social policy discussion. In place of economic or political competition among interest groups vying for scarce social resources, the federal courts provide a forum for groups or individuals to challenge the operating procedures of complex organizations. Those who view themselves as powerless in political bargaining have an opportunity to recast their claims in the language of priceless procedural rights. In many cases, of course, these rights will carry tangible benefits for the alleged victims of procedural unfairness: acquittal in criminal cases, modification of charges in disciplinary hearings, or the extension of benefits in public welfare hearings. But the distributive consequences of due process challenges are mere by-products of a separate calculus, which is allowed to preempt allocations under prevailing economic or political systems.

Before very much could be done with the concept of procedural justice in the 1960s, Warren and his colleagues had to sidestep two important barriers. First, due process was the infamous rubric under which earlier justices had managed to block major social and economic reforms of the progressive era. By expanding this protean term, the Supreme Court's Lochner decision was able to protect broadly defined property rights from state regulation, including those contractual rights that Holmes derisively associated with the social philosophy of laissez-faire. After the Court's conversion to judicial restraint in 1937, it sought to prevent such inter-institutional conflicts by distinguishing between *substantive* and *procedural* uses of due process. The former were illegitimate, said proponents of restraint, because they involved the courts in the substantive business of other governmental branches.[2]

This distinction left the courts perfectly free to monitor procedural abuses within their own system, as the Warren Court discovered during the 1960s. The self-correcting power of appellate court review, for example, lay completely beyond the progressive critique of judicial activism, which focused on relations between the judiciary and other branches of government. Procedural due process—an awkward pleonasm—thus began its doctrinal career as a means for keeping the courts under house arrest. Under Warren, however, it emerged as an impregnable fortress, supplying an aggressive policy of territorial annexation. Under the excuse of keeping its own house in proper order, the Warren Court was thus able to extend judicial review into other systems that fell within the expanding jurisdictional claims of the judicial process.

The first major task of the Warren Court was to assert jurisdiction over the procedural norms used by all state courts, in addition to its authority over the lower federal courts. Some of the most controversial criminal justice cases of the 1960s did not actually enlarge the definition of procedural due process but merely extended the prevailing federal model to state judicial systems. Although highly controversial from a political standpoint, this shift was doctrinally quite simple. It depended largely on giving parallel readings to the Constitution's two due process clauses: the Fifth Amendment, which applies solely to the federal government, and the Fourteenth Amendment, which is addressed to the states. In conjunction with the Court's tendency to interpret procedural safeguards found throughout the Bill of Rights as emanations from the federal due process clause, the Fourteenth Amendment became the central conduit for passing everything through to the states.[3]

Thus the famous decision in Gideon v. Wainwright, which required state courts to provide legal counsel to indigent defendants in felony cases, was a direct parallel to the prevailing constitutional rule for federal courts based on the Sixth

Amendment right to a fair trial.[4] The same is true for the controversial decision in Mapp v. Ohio, which required state courts to exclude from criminal trials any prosecution evidence gathered in violation of the Fourth Amendment; this case merely extended a rule first imposed on federal courts almost fifty years earlier.[5]

The campaign to transfer federal procedural standards to the states by means of the Fifth and Fourteenth amendments was ultimately successful, at least in doctrinal terms. Since Warren's retirement in 1969, a more conservative judiciary has been unwilling or unable to retreat from it in any substantial way. Once established, the parallel treatment of state and federal court systems meant that any further innovations under the rubric of procedural due process could be directed against judicial actions in either system. As due process was further extended to impose procedural restrictions on legislative and administrative policies, the Supreme Court's reach thus became exceedingly broad.

Procedural due process is perhaps the most subtle tool of judicial activism, because it purports to recognize a clear distinction between procedural means and the substantive ends of public policy. And yet, the decision to require more or less in the way of procedural safeguards can have enormous substantive impact on policy implementation. In the criminal justice system, for example, procedural rules restricting use of tainted evidence in criminal trials were intended by appeals courts to control the behavior of prosecuting officials and police. Similarly, in special judicial structures established for children and family issues—adoption, custody, delinquency, neglect, and related matters—even minor changes in procedural rules can have dramatic influence on the pattern of outcomes. On the whole, whenever courts require other branches of government to hold hearings on controversial policies, they tap directly into the political dynamics of regulation and policy implementation.

No one really denies the instrumental impact of judicial procedures, but courts are careful to express their procedural goals as an exclusive concern with institutional fairness. In other words, courts try to avoid the powerful strictures against judicial activism by emphasizing their traditional authority to curb their own internal tendencies toward error or bias. In an ideal judicial system, such basic procedures as the adversary process, the structured relation of judge and jury, and the hierarchy of appeals can all be functionally understood as promoting impartial judicial decision-making. These traditional outlines of procedural justice have long been part of Anglo-American jurisprudence, coming down to us through a combination of doctrines, rituals, and judicial discretion.[6]

There is a fundamental irony in this resurgence of judicial activism under the doctrinal rubric of procedural reform. Early in this century, critics influenced by sociological jurisprudence argued for vigorous reform within judicial structures. The legal realist school postulated profound new sources of systematic bias in the social and psychological makeup of both judge and jury. Based on this analysis, progressive legal critics sought to transfer some of the most sensitive judicial decisions to other institutions—either to special courts or to other branches of government—for more specialized expertise, less hermetic attitudes toward factual evidence, or (at the very least) more democratic oversight.[7] Thus the Supreme Court, following its 1937 conversion to the principle of judicial restraint, began to contract drastically its constitutional jurisdiction, particularly over the socioeconomic policies of the modern state. For these justices—as for many legal commentators who accepted the legal realist critique—public authority was thought to be more fully represented in the legislative process, where a broader inquiry into relevant facts could be pursued and interest groups were free to bargain over the ultimate definition of social principles.

In the last thirty years, however, in a movement associated with Earl Warren's tenure as Chief Justice, federal courts have vigorously reasserted their power to purify themselves and thus to protect their autonomy from invasion by other forms of public or personal authority. Paradoxically, the self-correcting structure of judicial institutions has now been elevated into a model for other institutions whose procedural flaws and tendencies toward unacknowledged bias have been forcefully accentuated by recent critics. Indeed, as public confidence in expert inquiry and interest-group bargaining has declined, the procedural approach to legitimation—borrowed from images of an ideally functioning judicial process—has rushed to fill the vacuum.

The U.S. Supreme Court actively cultivated this wider role for procedural justice, starting in the 1960s, as it expanded its jurisdiction to reach new forms of public and private action. The larger causes of this trend are difficult to distinguish from the effects, but it seems plain that this phase of Supreme Court activism is the most prominent part of a broader movement to redefine institutional authority on purely procedural grounds.

Due Process and the Burden of Proof

The procedural due process model provides an institutional regimen—a kind of procedural algorithm—from which justice is presumed to follow. Strictly speaking, the means define the end; the model operates with no independent criteria of justice apart from prescribed procedures. The criminal law is well accustomed to following this logic, as reflected in the principle of *legal guilt*.

According to this doctrine, a person is not to be held guilty of crime merely on a showing that in all probability, based upon reliable evidence, he did factually what he is said to have done. Instead, he is to be held guilty if and only if these factual determinations are made in procedurally regular fashion and by authorities acting within competences duly allocated to them.[8]

Packer describes this concept as one "modest-seeming but potentially far-reaching" element in the principle of due process. It gives a distinctive meaning to the traditional presumption of innocence, which has a strong historic association with Anglo-American criminal law procedure.

By forcing the state to prove its case against the accused in an adjudicative context, the presumption of innocence serves to force into play all the qualifying and disabling doctrines that limit the use of the criminal sanction against the individual, thereby enhancing his opportunity to secure a favorable outcome. In this sense, the presumption of innocence may be seen to operate as a kind of self-fulfilling prophecy. By opening up a procedural situation that permits the successful assertion of defenses having nothing to do with factual guilt, it vindicates the proposition that the factually guilty may nonetheless be legally innocent and should therefore be given a chance to qualify for that kind of treatment.[9]

Packer characterized the entire due process model of criminal procedure as "very much like an obstacle course. Each of its successive stages is designed to present formidable impediments to carrying the accused any further along in the process."[10] In the ordinary criminal trial, these obstacles include standard features of the adversary system and the division of tasks between judge and jury. But certain other procedural safeguards, now commonly taken for granted, were added to the traditional trial process only in the 1960s. Some of these devices were viewed by the Warren Court as so basic, in fact, that they entered into the minimal constitutional definition of procedural fairness for other types of judicial proceedings in addition to criminal trials. In a 1967 decision, for example, the Supreme Court imposed the following procedural safeguards on all state juvenile court hearings: (1) formal notice of charges, (2) legal representation, appointed by the court if necessary, (3) the opportunity to confront and cross-examine witnesses, (4) the privilege against self-incrimination, (5) a full transcript of trial proceedings, and (6) access to appellate review.[11]

These and other applications of the due process model were a significant institutional innovation, whatever their practical effects on criminal trials, police behavior, or the treatment of juveniles.[12] Although it is now customary to view the Warren Court as the primary source of such changes, at least some state legislatures and judicial systems were already moving along parallel lines during the 1960s. The sudden desire to place powerful new obstacles in the path of law-enforcement authorities may seem unusual, especially when the courts themselves appeared to take the lead. Moreover, as the public and press quickly discovered, the concrete effects of new procedural requirements could be highly controversial; inevitably, some suspects were found legally innocent, even though common sense would conclude they had committed serious crimes. The concept of legal guilt thus seemed to deny everyday experience in addition to complicating the respective tasks of police, court personnel, social workers, and others forced to negotiate the more demanding obstacle course.

In retrospect, judicial reforms of the Warren period seem to reflect the growing public distrust of professional and institutional authority—now a common diagnosis of shifting public attitudes during the 1960s.[13] In the field of criminal justice and juvenile court hearings, although the courts were nominally addressing their own shortcomings, they were in fact trying to modify the behavior of law enforcement officials, social workers, and other professional groups responsible for implementing public policy. The targets of due process came to include state agencies responsible for investigating the conditions of children in families. Previously decisions by these agencies on matters of custody, adoption, and abuse and neglect had been subject to only cursory court review. The courts also began to scrutinize the states' traditional administrative role in providing involuntary mental health services, including emergency commitment, guardianship appointments, and institutionalized treatment for the mentally ill and mentally disabled.[14]

Throughout the 1960s and 1970s, organized groups of litigants encouraged the federal courts to impose increasingly rigorous procedural review on individual encounters with the police, social service agencies, and the entire public welfare bureaucracy. In each of these cases, the implicit analogy with the treatment of defendants in criminal trials served several purposes. It allowed the courts to confine their action to a purely formal level—the stipulation of procedures—for which their traditional powers and expertise have been widely assumed. It reinforced the libertarian stereotype of government services as inherently coercive, with the individual as a likely victim of whatever bias or error was allowed to creep into the system. And it presupposed a particular definition of institutional fair play, memorialized in Blackstone's maxim that "it is better that ten guilty persons escape, than that one innocent suffer."[15]

Ironically, the central targets of distrust singled out under the due process model included some of the major goals of progressive reform from the preceding half century: the rehabilitative objectives of criminal corrections, the

81

therapeutic efforts of juvenile courts and public mental health agencies, and, in general, the increase in state public welfare services.[16] By 1968, Packer had detected this "mood of skepticism," and attributed it to "doubts about the ends for which power is being exercised," along with a corresponding "pressure to limit the discretion with which that power is exercised." Quoting another commentator, Packer sensed "a peculiar receptivity toward claims of injustice which arise within the traditional structure of the system itself," adding portentously that such skepticism "may be fairly said to be widespread among the most influential and articulate contemporary leaders of informed opinion."[17]

In his discussion of the juvenile court cases, Donald Horowitz takes a similar view that the growing influence of procedural justice reflected "the skepticism of established institutions that was so widely prevalent in the mid-1960s." As far as the Supreme Court was concerned, Horowitz adds, this was merely "skepticism, not hostility. . . . The emphasis is on good intentions gone awry."[18] As was also true with the equal protection cases, the Court's deeds in the area of due process fell short of the utopian expectations of many litigants. The underlying rhetoric in cases like Gault suggested that procedural reform could substantially alter the strategic balance between the state and the individual, but in fact the Warren Court moved somewhat cautiously in extending due process into new institutional settings. For litigators, however, applications of the due process model were potentially as broad as the exercise of institutionalized power in all its forms—both public and private.

Indeed, some civil libertarians staked out a much more radical agenda than even the Warren Court was prepared to endorse. For them, the due process model issued a blanket challenge to public authority and invited the courts to impose so many restrictions that states would eventually cease their coercive activities altogether.[19] During the Warren years, the Court avoided the larger question whether one can ever have too much procedure; it treated the due process principle more like a vector than a precise quantitative tool. So long as the Court was preoccupied with upgrading the obstacle course, libertarians could always hope that state agencies might close down coercive institutions, put an end to therapeutic social intervention, and eliminate constraints on the distribution of public entitlements.[20]

Eventually the Burger Court issued warnings that due process challenges faced inevitable limits, however vague, and that the Court would henceforth seek to balance the competing interests of society and the individual. Paradoxically, this image strengthens the adversarial premise of the libertarian position, and it seems to draw the courts into precisely the sort of policy-making role that was heavily condemned in the Lochner line of cases. As the Court has tried to perform these arcane calculations over the past decade, its decisions fail to suppress the substantive issues that are never far from the surface of the due process model. The justices must now involve themselves in such complex measurements as weighing the liberty interests of children against the interests of their parents and the state in seeking institutionalized treatment.[21] Such imponderable problems could be successfully hidden behind the veil of judicial formalism only so long as the courts treated procedural reform as an unalloyed, costless source of fundamental fairness.

The due process model represents the most highly developed technique for resolving public questions by means of strategic presumptions and the burden of proof. The conditions for its sudden blossoming in the 1960s help explain its pervasive role in contemporary public discourse, even after the courts have apparently chosen to slow the pace of doctrinal advance. Liberated from its judicial setting, the due process principle imposes a burden of proof on any type of authority—bureaucratic, professional, or cognitive. This burden can be met only when the authority in question has satisfied critics that it has eliminated all important sources of error, bias, indeterminacy, and uncertainty connected with any of its actions. As the critic's role blends imperceptibly into that of the neutral judge, that burden can easily be raised to levels that become impossible to meet.

The critical power of this rhetorical strategy was amply illustrated during the 1960s when the appellate judges of the Warren Court institutionalized the working assumptions of the skeptical critic, chiefly in their criminal-justice decisions. Their skepticism was patterned on the legal realist critique of tightly organized rule systems, which emphasized the inescapable presence of discretionary power that transcended formal rules. The same type of skepticism can be extended to most other areas of public life, where the governing rule structures are much less formal than in the criminal justice system. Indeed, it can be argued that rules of all kinds—formal and informal—generate the conditions for discretionary deviations, even though the rules are often designed to limit discretion found in earlier practices.[22]

The most intriguing aspect of the due process model is the elusive nature of appellate judicial authority, whose very task is to question the authority of subordinate judges, as well as the behavior of other public servants who fall within the jurisdiction of legal hearings. At a time when professional authority of every sort has been subjected to public skepticism, the appellate judge seems to be a unique exception. This is not to say that the Supreme Court has been spared all criticism; indeed, it has received its full share—not excluding the Warren Court's decisions on criminal justice. But such criticism typically distinguishes between the legitimate function of the appellate judge and some alleged deviation from that function. Only the most uncompromising skeptics deny that the Supreme Court is capable of speaking impartially and thus with the immunity from higher review that is implicit in the notion of a highest court of appeal.[23]

The powerful attraction of this ideal comes from our desire to believe that final answers to public questions can still be found, if only in principle. (Preferably, they are the same answers that we happen to favor in the course of debate.) The ideal of legal finality makes it possible to distinguish between ordinary disputes, where disagreements may persist indefinitely, and the special case, where one of the disputants speaks with the authority of a court of highest appeal. Strategies of modern discourse have learned that the power to declare finality has overwhelming attractions, especially in debates where both sides appear skeptical that objective inquiry can resolve major differences. To the extent public discourse has fallen under that skeptical spirit, the temptation is overwhelming to seek out strategic ground from which we can impose crushing proof burdens on our opponents.

The Procedural Challenge to Bureaucratic Authority

By the time Warren left the Court in 1969, the due process clause was moving toward the brink of wider application beyond the judicial branch. As with the equal protection decisions, reform-minded litigators eagerly generalized on the logic of court decisions dating from the 1960s. The concern for procedural fairness that had driven the Warren Court to constitutionalize criminal hearings and other state judicial procedures was thus extended to other branches of state and federal government. If the juvenile courts had to offer procedural safeguards, why shouldn't public school officials observe similar rules in student disciplinary actions? And when it came to arbitrary or biased decision-making, the entire public welfare bureaucracy appeared vulnerable to the same skeptical attack previously aimed at the therapeutic services of social workers.

The 1970 decision in Goldberg v. Kelly[24] seemed to fulfill these expectations, as the Supreme Court imposed new procedural requirements on state agencies seeking to reduce benefits for public welfare recipients. But like Shapiro v. Thompson in the field of equal protection, the Goldberg case was a short-lived victory for liberal reform. Soon enough, the Burger Court found ways to slow the momentum of due process doctrine, substituting more flexible rules that would spare public and private decision-makers the most demanding obstacles found in the due process model of criminal justice. But the trend toward more elaborate procedural standards has continued, even without the Supreme Court's active encouragement; and outside the courts, the procedural challenge to authority continues unabated.[25]

Within the criminal justice system the due process doctrine builds on the traditional presumption of innocence, in effect requiring the prosecution to overcome the skeptical presumption that its own actions and judgments may be biased or otherwise tainted. By imposing procedural requirements on public welfare agencies or public schools,[26] the courts have created an analogous presumption, and only those administrative actions that can survive the obstacle course placed in their path are considered fair by constitutional standards. The burden of proof thus shifts from the individual challenger to the public or private decision-maker, and defining sufficient procedures becomes the central strategic focus of further litigation. Once a certain level of procedure is frozen in judicial doctrine, skeptical critics are relieved of any need to supply fresh reasons for their skepticism; the legal system tacitly endorses their critique and sets the terms on which it can be overcome.

The New York program scrutinized in Goldberg v. Kelly was already operating within a procedural framework that allowed welfare claimants to challenge administrative decisions. Under federal, state, and local regulations, New York City was required to give a week's notice before terminating public assistance payments, as well as an opportunity for appeal, before benefits could actually be suspended. If unsuccessful at the appeal stage, a claimant could still challenge the termination—after the fact—in a separate hearing before a state administrative judge, where the claimant had the right to appear personally, offer oral evidence, confront and cross-examine witnesses, and receive a transcript of the hearing.[27]

The question, therefore, was not whether the local welfare department had to run an obstacle course on the way to canceling welfare payments, but precisely how difficult that course ought to be. "The constitutional issue to be decided," said Justice Brennan, ". . . is the narrow one of whether the Due Process Clause requires that the recipient be afforded an evidentiary hearing *before* the termination of benefits."[28] How much due process to require depends largely on the presumptions the Court majority brings to the situation under review. Using the convenient balancing metaphor, which allows justices to shift burdens of proof under the guise of weighing evidence, Brennan lets the decision depend on "whether the recipient's interest in avoiding . . . loss outweighs the governmental interest in summary adjudication." In this instance, the lower federal court had already assigned relative weights to the opposing interests, basing its actions on "one overpowering fact": the assumed economic need of all welfare recipients. "Against the justified desire to protect public funds must be weighed the individual's overpowering need in this unique situation not to be wrongfully deprived of assistance."[29]

The balancing metaphor uses a traditional symbol of legal neutrality, but

85

lends itself more, in this case, to the complementary image of putting one's thumb on the scales. The welfare recipient's "overpowering need" is, in practice, treated like the criminal defendant's innocence; it is a hypothesis or presumption, which admits of no independent measure apart from the outcome of a legal proceeding. Like the presumption of innocence, according to Packer's description quoted earlier, it is a kind of "self-fulfilling prophecy."[30] In the lower court's terms, "To cut off a welfare recipient in the face of . . . [hypothesized] 'brutal need' without a prior hearing of some sort is unconscionable, unless overwhelming considerations justify it."[31]

This style of reasoning is reminiscent of the Warren Court's resort to strict scrutiny in the equal protection cases, which, as Gunther noted, was invariably "'strict' in theory and fatal in fact."[32] Protecting the taxpayers' money, not surprisingly, did not rise to the level of an "overwhelming consideration." "While the problem of additional expense must be kept in mind, it does not justify denying a hearing meeting the ordinary standards of due process." Of course, this statement begs the question of which standards are to be considered ordinary when welfare agencies set out to terminate benefits. For a court sympathetic to claimants, the strength of the initial presumption determines the rigors of the obstacle course that the agency must run. Moreover, in Brennan's view, the "credibility and veracity" of the agency come under natural suspicion in a termination dispute.[33] Thus the agency's interpretation of the recipient's actual level of need must pass through the self-correcting procedures of judicial hearings.

The argument endorsed by the Supreme Court in Goldberg v. Kelly does not finally tell us how much procedure is required, only that more was needed in this instance. Specifically, the welfare department had to start providing formal hearings prior to ending payments. What about further procedural protections, including furnishing the claimant an attorney (at state expense) to take full advantage of these new trial opportunities? Brennan was not prepared to go that far, saying only that "the recipient must be allowed to retain an attorney if he so desires."[34] Under the logic of due process, however, requiring the state to offer free legal counsel was the obvious next move in an incremental litigation strategy. The presumption of brutal need could just as easily be used to argue that if recipients are unable to afford an attorney, they will be denied the essential benefits of formal hearings, complete with cross-examination of witnesses. In general, the presumptions adopted by the Supreme Court in due process cases set the direction of change—toward an increase in procedures—without defining an optimal level.[35]

Like strict scrutiny, the due process metaphor of weighing competing interests supplies a judicial lever for shifting the presumption of constitutionality, while maintaining the fiction that the Court is merely trying to look more closely at the evidence. In the Goldberg case, along with similar opinions from the early years of the Burger Court, the majority challenged the welfare department to find overwhelming considerations for denying the additional procedural reforms requested by the plaintiffs. If saving public funds was not a good enough reason, it becomes difficult to say what kind of evidence the Court might have found sufficient. The Court's tacit presumption thus favored continually upgrading the procedural obstacle course, whose intended purpose was to eliminate the assumed biases and errors of bureaucratic administration. This strategy drove public welfare agencies to insist that they were completely innocent of bias. But their vigorous defense created a larger problem: if they are really so pure, they should have nothing to fear from a bracing regimen of procedural formality. If a little due process is good, then more would seem to be even better.[36]

As in the equal protection cases, this major shift in the burden of proof must be understood as a reaction against the equally stiff burdens applied earlier under the presumption of constitutionality. Critics of Goldberg and related cases couched their arguments in the traditional language of judicial neutrality, but constitutional due process had scarcely been neutral in the thirty years after progressive judges gained control of the Supreme Court. According to Jerry Mashaw, "The history of administrative law from the thirties to the sixties is the history of the judicial development of technical defenses that prevented private plaintiffs from reaching the merits of their claims against government officials."[37] For defendants, the most powerful legal support was the conceptual distinction between *adjudicative* facts and *legislative* facts, with the latter enjoying heavy protection under the presumption of constitutionality.[38]

Using this distinction, earlier courts had drawn a sharp line between administrative bureaucracies and their own system of lower courts. As Justice Frankfurter noted soon after his appointment to the Court helped consolidate the new progressive majority, differences in the origin and function of administrative agencies "preclude wholesale transplantation of the rules of procedure, trial, and review which have evolved from the history and experience of courts."[39] By the 1960s, however, both Congress and the federal judiciary had begun to challenge this administrative immunity from judicial review, leading up to the decision in Goldberg v. Kelly.

> As the brave new agencies of the New Deal became creaky bureaucracies, the body politic and the courts began to lose faith in the administrative state. The civil rights movement and the war on poverty, joined later by the environmental, consumer, and women's rights movements, disclosed that minorities, the poor, and indeed "people" in general, were being left out of the processes

of governance. As the body politic embraced participatory governance, the technical barriers to judicial review came tumbling down.[40]

More passionate reasons for the change in public attitudes can be found in the contemporary writings of litigators, who kept pressure on the courts to expand judicial review: "We should respond to the claims of service professionals as if they were cops. . . . Both serve important social ends, but both are dangerous. Both will violate rights in the course of their jobs if they think it is important enough, *and therefore that is a decision that cannot be left to them.* . . . Service professionals are not the guardians of their clients' liberty."[41] Continuing the same theme that encouraged the Warren Court to impose stricter judicial review on the therapeutic authority of the social service profession, Glasser extended his critique to the entire welfare bureaucracy: "Not until the . . . 1960s did anyone begin to look with skepticism upon these good works. . . . Vast discretionary power thus came to be vested in an army of civil servants . . . , organized into huge service bureaucracies, which began quietly and silently to trespass upon the private lives and rights of millions of citizens."[42] Glasser concluded by announcing the following principle—a skilled advocate's attempt to formulate a new legal presumption by shifting the burden of proof: "Every program designed to help the dependent ought to be evaluated, not on the basis of the good it might do, but rather on the basis of the harm it might do. Those programs ought to be adopted that seem to be the least likely to make things worse."[43]

Although this sort of rhetoric became muted as the 1970s advanced, it was broadcast loud and clear during the late 1960s and doubtless reflects the atmosphere in which the Supreme Court, in Goldberg v. Kelley, undertook to balance the competing interests of welfare agencies and their clients. For several years the Burger Court used a more ad hoc process to weigh adversarial interests, but with inconclusive results—much the same way that the Court vacillated on strict scrutiny. By 1976, however, the Burger Court was ready to announce a more elaborate balancing formula, which was clearly meant to signal a slowing of the "give 'em more process"[44] trend. With a determined show of good craftsmanship, Justice Powell discovered a new coherence in the Court's preceding six years of experimentation with judicial review of administrative action:

> Our prior decisions indicate that identification of the specific dictates of due process generally requires consideration of three distinct factors: first, the private interest that will be affected by the official action; second, the risk of an erroneous deprivation of such interest through the procedures used, and the probable value, if any, of additional or substitute procedural safeguards; and finally, the government's interest, including the function involved and the

fiscal and administrative burdens that the additional or substitute procedural requirement would entail.[45]

Powell's revealing formulation, which imports adversarial strategies into the discursive logic of judicial reasoning, adds an ironic commentary on the use of jurisprudential analogies in practical reasoning. Rather than applying preestablished warrants to unambiguous data, the courts now find themselves reflecting openly on the dialectical options in procedural due process claims. Falling back on the empiricist and utilitarian idioms of our legal culture, the Court envisions a weighing of factlike data that can somehow reduce adverse interests to comparable terms. But considering the Court's self-imposed limits on substantive review—its studied ignorance of how these interests ought to be assessed apart from legislative guidance—it must pass the data through preselected value-filters or presumptions chosen freely in each case. In place of presumptions adopted after the New Deal (favoring the autonomy of administrative agencies) or advanced by the Goldberg case and civil libertarians (favoring the adverse interests of claimants), Powell's formula allowed the Court to shift the burden of proof virtually at will.[46]

Skeptical Views of Bureaucratic Action

Even though the Supreme Court chose not to follow the doctrinal trajectory mapped out by partisans of Goldberg v. Kelly, the federal courts were nonetheless strongly marked by that decision. In his 1975 assessment, Judge Henry J. Friendly wrote of a post-Goldberg "due process explosion," in which "the Court has carried the hearing requirement from one new area of government action to another." The impact on lower courts was especially profound, Friendly noted,[47] an observation confirmed by Mashaw, who found that the volume of procedural due process complaints more than tripled in the decade following the Goldberg opinion.[48]

Whether or not Goldberg was the actual cause of this expansion, it became the main doctrinal reference for legal advocates. It seems more likely that Goldberg and other due process rulings were symptoms of a larger political and cultural challenge to public and private authority, as David Rothman has suggested.[49] The major contribution of judicial activism was its institutionalized dialectic, notably its capacity and willingness to shift burdens of proof from individual challengers to powerful bureaucracies. Although the courts stopped short of granting everything that civil libertarians were asking for in the 1960s, they provided a unique, ostensibly neutral forum for a broad assault on existing institutions. And although the courts eventually lost their own peculiar immunity from skeptical attack, the techniques of due process adjudication have remained central in the rhetoric of contemporary social critique. Proceduralized fairness—based on the ideals of the due process model—has become an independent social principle outside the formal legal system, contributing to an increasingly adversarial climate in the life of modern institutions.[50]

The precise impact of due process decisions on actual administrative behavior has been difficult to measure. Justice Black's dissent in Goldberg predicted certain negative consequences for welfare recipients, on balance, as a result of reflexive bureaucratic caution.

> The inevitable result of such a constitutionally imposed burden will be that the government will not put a claimant on the rolls initially until it has made an exhaustive investigation to determine his eligibility. While this Court will perhaps have insured that no needy person will be taken off the rolls without a full "due process" proceeding, it will also have insured that many will never get on the rolls, or at least that they will remain destitute during the lengthy proceedings followed to determine initial eligibility.[51]

According to Mashaw, the available evidence substantiates Black's specific concerns. But, he adds, "the problems with due process review are more general. . . . In *Goldberg* the Court also seems to have misunderstood what caused decisional errors and vastly overestimated the capacity of welfare bureaucracies to run a hearing system. The risks of judicial intervention may thus include both new dysfunctional consequences for the supposed winners and the ultimate irrelevance of the judicial remedies provided. Impertinence and irrelevance may combine as well as alternate."[52] The same objection, Mashaw adds, can be raised against the Burger Court's elaborate balancing mechanism announced in the Mathews case, which assumed that Courts could accurately predict the impact of procedural remedies on bureaucratic behavior.

Despite its technocratic rhetoric, the Mathews opinion was no less formalistic than Goldberg, resting on a simple reversal of the burden of proof. The underlying legal issues were similar to those in Goldberg, in that a claimant to public entitlements was asserting the right to an individualized hearing prior to termination of benefits; the only difference was that the Mathews case involved Social Security Disability Insurance (SSDI) rather than welfare assistance. The Burger Court performed the ritual motions of weighing and balancing the competing interests, but it undertook no serious empirical scrutiny and relied instead on the formal power of presumptions. Like any good advocate, Powell was able to find a strategically useful difference between the two cases: Goldberg was about public welfare, whereas Mathews was about public insurance. This conceptual distinction enabled him to waive the whole reason for burden-shifting used in Goldberg: the presumption that welfare recipients had some "overpowering need." By contrast, said Powell, "Eligibility for disability benefits . . . is not based upon financial need. Indeed, it is wholly unrelated to the worker's income or support from many other sources." In view of these potential supports, Powell concluded, "there is less reason here than in Goldberg to depart from the ordinary principle . . . that something less than an evidentiary hearing is sufficient prior to adverse administrative action."[53]

Mashaw's extensive study of SSDI claims tries to document how the formal approach taken by Goldberg, Mathews, and similar cases is "impertinent and irrelevant" to the efficient functioning of public programs. He interprets Goldberg as a misplaced attempt to impose a regimen of individualized decision-making on large-scale bureaucracies, running counter to both the classic model of bureaucratic rationality and more recent post-bureaucratic theories of organizations.[54] At the same time, he adds, the tendency of individualized decision-making to produce unsystematic results need not suggest that modern bureaucracies should be left to their own devices—the inference drawn by the Burger Court in Mathews. Indeed, Mashaw finds much to admire in constitutional due process as a model for self-standing "dignitary rights," and he looks for ways to promote those rights more vigorously within the internal structure of administrative agencies.[55]

For most large-scale social programs, including SSDI, the indeterminate nature of eligibility rules cannot be remedied by requiring more individualized decisions. Inevitable uncertainties may frustrate bureaucratic rationality, but they also complicate any effort to reshape the bureaucracy through litigation. In SSDI, perhaps the major source of instability is the ambiguity surrounding the very definition of *disability* in the basic legislation, a widely noted problem in policy debates occurring in other countries as well.[56] Partly medical, but also partly economic and sociological, disability as a principle of entitlement cannot be operationalized without slighting one or more of these elements.

Individualized decision-making does nothing to relieve this dilemma. As Mashaw notes, "There is no external referent, that is, a clear case of disability, with which particular claimants can be compared. Indeed, it may not even be possible to know very much after the fact about the tendency of the system to differentiate appropriately between the able and the disabled."[57] Uncertainty in the very conception of disability does not have to paralyze the entire program; it does, however, guarantee that disputes will arise in marginal cases, where the resolution will always seem arbitrary to determined challengers who control the

91

burden of proof. The problem is largely practical rather than cultural or meta-physical, but it is nonetheless important in a mass program whose results often retrospectively measured by bureaucratic or rational legal standards.

Although SSDI legislation already provides an internal adjudicatory structure for disputed claims, it fares no better than the more elaborate procedures of the due process model. Mashaw sees an inevitable tension between promoting the "intuitive rationality" of individualized justice and strengthening the "systematic rationality" of public programs through stricter rules or tighter administration: "It should be clear that any attempt to systematize decisionmaking through regulation necessarily involves both the construction of general categories and the specification of the effect of finding that a case fits into one or more of those categories. If that regulatory effort is effective, the individual decider will not be able to 'do justice,' all things considered." [58] The demand of cases like Goldberg, which would expand the right to individualized hearings for issues of eligibility, "simply misses the point of the welfare state. . . . The problem has become one of mass, not individual justice. Legal security for the class of welfare claimants lies, not in hearings, but in good management. Unless due process, therefore, comes to terms with administration, becomes systems- rather than case-oriented, it will be irrelevant." [59]

92

From an adversarial perspective, however, Mashaw himself can be accused of missing the strategic point of constitutional due process. He wants to fold procedural safeguards into organizational structures simply by calling on agencies to observe certain dignitary rights, consisting mainly of the formal right to personalized attention and participation in the process of decision. But all procedures can rapidly become systems oriented, whether they consist of individualized hearings or flipping a coin. Indeed, bureaucracies are generally eager to exploit gaps in substantive rules by adopting procedural mechanisms—a classic device found in all large organizations to reduce the appearance of ambiguity in operational decisions.[60] The outcomes of such procedures may, in theory, be open to challenge by disappointed parties, but the strategic advantage belongs to whichever party controls the burden of proof.

Constitutional due process becomes a truly powerful tool only when it forces bureaucracies to carry the burden of justifying disputed decisions according to substantive criteria. Otherwise, all agency procedures (however modest) carry a presumptive force that leaves the challenger with the formidable task of proving that the outcome was a truly substantive error. From a purely functional perspective, formal procedures can either insulate organizations from later challenge or expose their decisions to relentless skeptical attack. The Goldberg opinion was a threat to public welfare agencies not only because it diverted resources from direct services into procedural tasks, but because it also had the potential to broaden welfare eligibility. Depending on the presumptions adopted by judges, the requirement of pretermination hearings gave welfare advocates an opportunity to place bureaucrats on the defensive and thus to push eligibility to the upper limits of the inevitable statutory leeways. Without that strategic mission, Mashaw's dignitary rights would possibly become empty formalities.[61]

The Supreme Court's peculiar role in the allocation of proof burdens masks its own ambiguous authority as an institutional forum for launching attacks on other institutions. Constitutional due process principles seem to offer the archimedean point that is missing from ordinary academic and political debate: the conclusive authority to declare winners and losers without having to base one's selections on any substantive foundation.

Once the Warren Court expanded federal jurisdiction to reach far into the public sphere—and even into some forms of private action—it provided (however briefly) the ideal forum for skeptical arguments against institutional authority. Public school officials, welfare bureaucrats, social service workers, psychiatrists, and everyone else targeted by due process suits was required to justify his or her actions under standards that transcend the capacities of complex organizations and professional practitioners. By a contorted analogy with the conventions of criminal trials, the defendants in due process cases, in effect, were presumed guilty until proven innocent. The challengers, meanwhile, were under no obligation to prove anything, although their advocates had to work hard enough to translate overarching substantive issues into the legal idiom of due process.

This anti-institutional use of the judicial system reenacts on a much larger stage the Warren Court's original attack on the courts themselves, in which constitutional law became the standard for correcting widespread abuses attributed to lower courts. Even in the domain of criminal justice, however, appellate courts have failed to bring actual judicial practice into conformity with constitutional ideals. As the Supreme Court defined more onerous standards of fair procedure for criminal trials, it was unable to halt the parallel growth of plea bargaining and other informal alternatives to judicial hearings. Lower courts and prosecutorial officials now preside over a vast system of informal justice, which deviates from the rising standards of constitutional due process at least as much as mass bureaucracies have strayed from their Weberian ideal.

By the time of Warren's departure from the Court in 1969, it still seemed possible to some critics that this "lower court problem" could be cleared up by further constitutional rulings.[62] But other commentators, such as Abraham Blumberg, noted the separation of judicial reality into two fundamentally differ-

93

ent orders: one "couched in constitutional-ideological terms of due process and rule of law" and the other "the administrative, ministerial, rational-bureaucratic one we have actually institutionalized." It was this latter system, according to Blumberg, that ultimately prevailed. "While we continue to express our preference and reverence for the constitutional ideology, it is the perfunctory and efficacious system of justice that we implement." [63] This style of criticism exposed an ironic weakness in the judicial process: its inability to put its own scandalous house in order despite the doctrinal activism of appellate courts. Rather than disturbing the due process ideal, however, most critics chose to deepen their lament over the conditions of everyday practice, as their empirical assessments documented the increasingly sharp divergence with doctrinal principles. [64] Criticisms of lower criminal courts as failed bureaucracies dominated legal commentary throughout the 1970s. [65]

As the Supreme Court began to dilute the procedural due process doctrine with technocratic formulas and ad hoc presumptions, the constitutional ideal of procedural due process evolved into a moral critique, a transcendental extension of the judicial style immortalized in Goldberg v. Kelly. [66] Three characteristics of this critique derive from the special rhetoric of the Warren Court's activist period. First, it has preserved the burden-shifting techniques and anti-institutional presumptions developed by legal advocates in the late 1960s, generating an ideal jurisprudence as if it commanded a permanent majority on a transcendental Supreme Court. Second, it has condemned adverse Burger Court decisions as unprincipled deviations from an ideal set of fairness principles. On this view, the Burger Court became just another example of incompetent or illegitimate authority, unable to justify its decisions under the stiff burden of proof assigned by this shadow majority. Third, the same critique of authority could be applied to any institution within the moral jurisdiction of this peculiar court. Long after students of formal organizations have absorbed the message that bureaucracies rarely, if ever, conform to the Weberian formal-rational model, the moral advocates of due process continue to use that model as the moral basis for a universal critique of prevailing authority.

Due Process Rhetoric in Family Law: Shifting Cultural Presumptions

A perfectly rational bureaucracy thus became the critical standard against which the due process model measures institutional performance, including the operation of lower courts. The special emphasis on hearings during the heyday of Goldberg v. Kelly was meant to give federal courts the opportunity to scrutinize agency behavior, where the burden of proof was on the agency to demonstrate that its decisions were consistent with substantive criteria of entitlement, as well as with internal procedural criteria. Since few organizations of any complexity could satisfy such exacting scrutiny, case by case, the due process style became a self-fulfilling method for demonstrating that modern institutions never really know what they are doing.

But even if organizations in the modern welfare state could somehow meet these exacting standards, due process arguments can also be used for the more radical mission of challenging organizational goals. Bureaucracies are expected to implement a set of goals originating outside the administrative structure, derived not only from legislation but also from broader cultural norms. In some circumstances, federal courts have the power to test those goals directly against constitutional standards drawn from either the equal protection or due process clause (and often from both). This is potentially the most radical use of judicial review, as well as the logical extension of due process rulings limited to strictly procedural issues. When Goldberg v. Kelly was decided, welfare advocates had no practical need to choose among three distinct litigation objectives: increasing the scope of client participation in agency procedures, forcing the welfare bureaucracy to obey the substantive mandates of legislative policies, and forcing the state to expand the scope of entitlements. By concentrating on the first of these aims, litigators expected that the cumulative impact of further victories would eventually reach all three levels.

Changes in Court membership slowed the due process drive against bureaucratic authority, keeping it focused on the first level of procedural design. However, in the field of family law due process arguments have already reached the level of public goals and their underlying cultural assumptions. Administered largely by lower courts in the various states, family law governs the fundamental relations of parents and children and defines occasions when the state plays a quasi-parental role through guardianship proceedings, foster care, civil commitment of the mentally ill, and emergency protective services for abused children and other dependent people. All of these areas have experienced intense litigation as an outgrowth of the Warren Court's due process jurisprudence, proceeding in tandem with shifting social attitudes toward family responsibilities, mental health, and personal autonomy.

The relations between children and parents raise special problems for judicial regulation. The law has to balance potentially conflicting obligations, and due process claims advanced by one party may oppose the due process claims of another. After divorce proceedings, for example, courts must often decide which of the natural parents will be granted primary custody of children. In contested adoption proceedings, there may be multiple claims from potential guardians, including natural parents, more remote relations, and foster parents. And in child abuse cases, courts must determine when the state's responsibilities to the child supersede the custodial rights of parents. In none of these cases can the courts take much comfort in the anti-institutional rhetoric of due process. Rarely can such conflicts be reduced to the model of the solitary individual versus the powerful bureaucracy, except in the distinct adversarial arguments of separate parties.

During the 1970s Joseph Goldstein, Anna Freud, and Albert J. Solnit, re-examined the juridical relations of parents and children from a perspective deeply influenced by the due process model.[67] Although these proposals obviously lack the status of law, they have nonetheless had a significant impact on legislation and judicial practice.[68] From our perspective, they illustrate the subtle interplay between substantive goals and shifting proof burdens, which were largely hidden in the Supreme Court's major due process decisions. Goldstein and his colleagues are especially forthcoming in discussing presumptions and burdens, drawing attention to the strategic foundations of substantive values served by the law. His consistent skepticism about institutional authority and the evils of discretion echo liberal constitutional trends of the time, and he is refreshingly open about drawing legal consequences from presumed areas of uncertainty, both cultural and professional. He is equally candid in selecting one particular theory out of the morass of professional ignorance and elevating it to a legal presumption: a problematic psychoanalytic theory about what constitutes good custodial care for children.[69]

Like due process jurisprudence in general, Goldstein's views raised a challenge to prevailing legal presumptions that seemed ripe for fresh examination. His main target was a traditional principle known by the phrase "best interests of the child," which had become a common judicial reference point in child custody decisions over several decades. In the eyes of due process advocates, this empty generality gave enormous discretion to lower court judges in cases where courts were required to select an appropriate custodial parent.[70] Most important, Goldstein alleged, this standard had been widely used to rationalize judicial intrusion into family life at the behest of social workers, psychiatrists, and other therapeutic professionals. Legal critics began to question the best-interests standard as both indeterminate and dangerous: indeterminate because it provided no operational definition of best interests, and dangerous because it opened the door to state intervention in family relations at the expense of family rights of privacy.[71]

What exactly are the child's best interests? Goldstein's answer had an attractive simplicity, and it seemed to offer judges and advocates a practical standard for measuring the case-specific advice given by social workers and psychiatrists. Adverting to psychoanalytic theory, Goldstein reduced the abstraction of best interests to a temporal criterion based on "continuity of care," an inertial concept that says children are best off staying with those adult(s) with whom they have already formed a psychological bond. Nearly everything else about what is good for children should be left to the inscrutable judgment of parental opinion, he argued, except this overarching standard of long-term bonding with an adult "parent."[72]

For most children, of course, this criterion converts the bond with natural parents into something intrinsically valuable, no matter how defective or deviant the quality of that relationship might seem to an outsider (especially to an investigating social worker). The implications of the basic theory were that individualized clinical judgments by therapeutic experts could be largely dispensed with; any judge able to count could wield the Goldstein criterion to challenge the interventionist tendencies of professionals. The popularity of Goldstein's theory among legal advocates doubtless comes from this strategic function: it was a powerful answer—often a conclusive answer—to the presumed authority of experts.

This tilt toward nonintervention was not presented as a mere cultural choice favoring natural parents; indeed, the Goldstein theory gave comparable support to long-term foster parents seeking to block further changes in child custody.[73] With no apparent irony, Goldstein (the skeptical critic of clinical expertise) defended his presumption as scientific, although lacking in experimental evidence. But no matter how vulnerable it might have seemed as a scientific principle, as a legal presumption it provided a criterion for measuring the clinical judgments made by human services professionals. Goldstein eventually acknowledged that his principle was derived from libertarian political premises.

Goldstein's approach thus supplied a missing ingredient in the Supreme Court's due process jurisprudence: an affirmative reason, in the form of an ostensible scientific theory, for shifting the burden of proof. As in constitutional argument, Goldstein reversed the presumption that had favored professional or bureaucratic expertise, and he required social service personnel and administrative officials to satisfy the court that their reasons for intervention were good enough. Going beyond mere procedural metaphors, Goldstein handed the courts a substantive principle for making this dramatic shift. Up to this point courts had pointedly resisted basing dialectical reversals on principles other than pure procedural fairness. Indeed, under the constraints of post-realist judicial review, the Supreme Court was not allowed to elevate substantive theories of its own choosing above those contained in legislation. Behind its formal rhetoric, the

Court's ultimate authority for manipulating burdens of proof rested on its pure declaratory power to implement constitutional values.

Several other insights into judicial strategies emerge from Goldstein's second volume, which responded to growing public sentiment for more intervention to protect children from physical and sexual abuse. During the 1970s, many states strengthened criminal penalties against child abuse: they required hospitals, police, and social service workers to report observed instances of abuse, and they increased funding for educational and voluntary service programs.[74] But some legislatures were reluctant to increase the authority of social service officials to investigate abuse and remove children from their homes, for fear of compromising due process values.

In this context, Goldstein constructed an ideal set of legal rules for balancing the opposed interests of child protection and parental privacy. His second book contained no new scientific premises, beyond the continuity-of-care standard. Instead, it rather proudly rested its recommendations on arguments from social ignorance. Unlike Supreme Court justices, who always spoke with unappealable authority, Goldstein was forced to articulate the *ad ignorantium* premises that lie behind due process challenges.

In the second volume, Goldstein declared his "preference for minimum state intervention," which he treated as a more fundamental premise than his psychoanalytic theory of best interests. "So long as a child is a member of a functioning family, his paramount interest lies in the preservation of his family."[75] This formulation, however, begs the question of how one knows when families are truly functioning. Similarly, the concept of minimum state intervention does not define any contextual boundaries; the minimum could well be zero, unless there is also some countervailing measure of the state's affirmative responsibilities.

Both statements were modes of expressing Goldstein's overwhelming skepticism of individualized professional clinical judgments. To be sure, he noted, some families mistreat their children, but "the state may make a bad situation worse; indeed, it may turn a tolerable or even a good situation into a bad one." Therefore, the law should "ask in every case whether removal from an unsatisfactory home is the beneficial measure it purports to be." But how can the courts answer such questions on a case-by-case basis when they have already conceded that professional opinion is unreliable? The only solution, said Goldstein, was for courts to emphasize procedural safeguards embodied in statutes, designed to "prevent judges, lawyers, social workers, and others from imposing their personal, even if professional, preferences upon unwilling parents."[76]

To put the conclusion into more familiar due process language, Goldstein defined parental privacy and state intervention as two competing interests that had to be balanced. That balance was achieved by setting up a procedural obstacle course, which therapeutic authorities had to negotiate successfully before they could interfere with the privacy of the family. Having established which party was obligated to run the course, Goldstein also ensured the rigors of the race by using presumptions, starting with the assumed inability of public services to provide convincing evidence for their actions.

As it turned out, Goldstein's obstacle course was far more onerous than most legislatures were willing to require.[77] But why was the centerpiece of this policy to restrain professional intervention rather than to solve the initial problem of dysfunctional families? The state can make mistakes, but so can families, and neither fact alone is enough to dictate the construction of procedural presumptions. Like the due process model, Goldstein's proposal fell back on presumptions built into the language of criminal trials: "At no stage," he wrote, "should intrusion on any family be authorized unless probable and sufficient cause for the coercive action has been established in accord with limits prospectively and precisely defined by the legislature."[78]

Goldstein was perfectly clear that his ideal obstacle course rested on several key inferences from ignorance, including social, cultural, legal and professional ignorance. On the question of whether medical treatment should be provided to children over the objections of their parents, for example, Goldstein emphasized that medical opinion is often "conflicting," and "societal consensus" is often lacking for deciding precisely when the risks of medical treatment are worth taking. Under these circumstances, no one can

99

> be presumed to be in a better position than the child's parents to decide what course to pursue if the medical experts disagree about treatment. The same is true if there is no general agreement in society that the outcome of a proven treatment is clearly preferable to the outcome of no treatment. Put somewhat more starkly, how can parents in such situations be judged to give the wrong answer when there is no way of knowing the right answer? . . . The burden must always be on the state to establish what is wrong and not on parents to establish that what may be right for them is necessarily right for others.[79]

This last phrase glosses over the critical issue of what may be right for the child, which was, supposedly, the guiding principle behind both books. In the absence of sufficient medical or social information (and we are not told exactly how high the standard of proof should be set in these cases), there is also no reason to presume that the parents know what is right or that they are better equipped than child-welfare specialists to weigh the probabilities of alternative outcomes. Nonetheless, Goldstein advances his presumption in the clearest possible language, basing it on his acknowledged preference for minimizing therapeutic intervention in family life. In his view, uncertainty should always be resolved against the advice of experts, whose proposals are often thinly disguised "personal preferences," "coercively" imposed on parents.[80]

Although acknowledging that this basic position may strike some people as controversial, Goldstein defended his argument with an even bolder presumption against the use of state power in general. Any substantial doubt about social intervention, he argued, should always be resolved against the authority of the state and therapeutic experts.[81] Here we can see the essential logic behind due process reasoning, freed of all legal formalism. Goldstein's endorsement of nonintervention, as he cheerfully conceded, is purely a matter of his personal preference. By the end of his analysis, however, he has elevated that preference into a presumption, placing the burden of proof on his opponents to demonstrate the superiority of any alternative social principle. Had he been writing for a majority of the Supreme Court, of course, he would never have grounded this presumption on a personal preference.

The Goldstein volume illuminates the paradoxical notion that judicial institutions are immune from the general critique of authority—one of the most striking premises of the due process movement. On the question of state intervention to prevent child sexual abuse, Goldstein expressed his usual doubts that therapeutic experts can accurately identify those occasions when intervention is preferable to a continuation of family privacy. Instead he would entrust these decisions to the criminal law, by requiring the state to convict a parent of criminal sexual abuse charges before allowing the termination of custodial rights.

100

> Sexual relations between parent and child tend to remain well-guarded family secrets. When suspicion is aroused, the harm done by inquiry may be more than that caused by not intruding. The harm already inflicted upon the child—and it may be difficult to learn its extent—is aggravated by violations of family integrity, particularly by the investigation that is triggered. . . . For these reasons, justification for separating the child and offending parent seems best left to the criminal law—to its high standard of evidentiary proof and its goal of reinforcing society's moral position. . . . Thus, the authority to assume the risks of intervention, including the termination of parental rights, arises only after the parent-child relationship has been severed by the criminal process.[82]

Although unwilling to trust the judgment of experts, Goldstein seemed unusually trusting of the criminal trial process with its vast auxiliary realm of plea bargaining and its unmanageable bureaucratic imperfections. No doubt this attraction came from the fact that criminal conviction is the steepest hurdle one can place in the path of therapeutic experts and thus would ensure the least intrusive standard that society could be expected to endorse, given its concern about child abuse. As a strategic matter, in other words, Goldstein endorsed the procedure that would authorize the fewest number of interventions. Perhaps the judicial process had no greater access to truth than the judgments of experts; but at least it came equipped with presumptions already in place that tend to minimize the occasions for intervention.[83]

Conclusion: Ironies of Institutionalized Skepticism

Judicial challenges to administrative action may be ineffective, cumbersome ways of influencing organizations, but their underlying appeal was always something more than the lure of incremental reform. The surge of due process cases, beginning in the late 1960s and continuing into the present, should rather be seen as one phase of a more fundamental cultural conflict between liberal values and the mass bureaucracies of modern society. They are thus a continuation, in a popular guise, of the "crisis of legitimacy" in organizations, long noted by sociologists and social critics.[84] The source of this crisis, seen from a legal perspective, is the failure of modern organizations to live up to an ideal procedural model related to the Weberian theory of bureaucracy. The burden of proof under a strict standard of rational behavior is simply too great, leaving modern authorities vulnerable to legal challenge.

101

Even without constitutional changes introduced by the Warren Court's due process jurisprudence, courts see themselves as uniquely situated to identify instances where public or private bodies depart from strict legality. Their expertise was implicitly acknowledged by Congress in the Administrative Procedures Act of 1946 and in countless statutory clauses imposing procedural formalities on administrative agencies. As the Warren Court swept aside earlier presumptions that had kept these provisions from being fully utilized, the courts became the inevitable forum for public discontent with contemporary administrative policies and practices. The presumption of constitutionality, raised to its highest level by progressive legal advocates during the New Deal, may have limited or delayed the judicial investigation of bureaucratic lapses; but the burden-shifting strategies favored by the Warren Court guaranteed that barriers to judicial review fell rapidly once they began to falter.

Organization theory does not provide any single model for summarizing the dilemmas of mass justice in public administration. Most contemporary approaches are united in trying to supplement the Weberian model, settling for theories of *bounded rationality* and highlighting the psychological or structural mechanisms that cannot be captured by formal rules.[85] Although much of this literature follows the standard sociological format of the exposé—the discovery that things are not as they seem and that organizations typically abandon their formal goals for the sake of survival or growth—social scientists have not adopted that uncompromising suspicion of discretion implied by the constitutional due process model. Indeed, much of the sociological literature finds unexpected virtues in the informal, adaptive, organic, evolving characteristics of organizations in much the same sense that the field of practical reasoning finds healthy relief from the desiccated forms of abstract logic.[86]

A less accommodating attitude stands behind the due process trend in legal thinking, which originated in a kind of self-purification ritual designed to protect the judicial system from the legal realist critique of judicial discretion. Within the special organizational context of the criminal law, it seems plausible (although perhaps impossible to test empirically) that the negative effects of bias can be reduced by an adversary process, appellate review, judicial independence, and a strong presumption of the defendant's innocence. Even if these devices seldom have any measurable effect, they doubtless enhance public perceptions of judicial fairness.[87] There is considerable irony, however, in the tacit presumption that the due process model is a natural remedy for discretion elsewhere in public life. As Joel Handler has noted: "From the perspective of legal rights advocates, the single most important problem presented by all public agencies . . . can be summed up in the word *discretion*. Discretion is the opposite of fixed, clearly defined, and precisely stated eligibility rules and conditions. Discretion gives officials choices."[88] In other words, having taken a dose of their own medicine, lawyers have been eager to recommend the cure to others, even at the trouble of projecting their own self-admitted illness onto other groups across the whole of society.

102

Chapter 4 | Antinomies of Interpretation: Critical Perspectives on Burden-Shifting

The central inference behind the argument-from-ignorance can be viewed with the same ambivalence that critics have shown toward possible limits of rationality. Thus the rejection of limits (and hence of ignorance) identified with neo-Aristotelian critics shares the same inferential logic as the radical skepticism of post-structuralist critics; both positions use the argument-from-ignorance as leverage for reaching opposite ends of a single antinomy. Seeking to avoid this antinomy, proponents of pragmatic or practical reason translate the problem of rational limits into procedural terms, emphasizing the concepts of performance and dialogue. However, their efforts encounter the fresh dichotomy of finality and legitimacy; and, unlike judicial systems, they are forced to choose between procedural closure and indefinitely postponed consensus.

Jurisprudential Perspectives on Bounded Rationality

As the judicial strategies examined in preceding chapters flourished, various crises of public authority were sweeping through political debate, scientific inquiry, and cultural analysis. Courts have remained unique in their capacity to withstand such crises, as they are somehow able to protect their own elusive authority while helping to consolidate the skeptical critique of other public bodies. Their skill in transmuting substance into procedure becomes a peculiar source of strength, greatly envied by more vulnerable institutions. Hence the contemporary extension of judicial idioms and ideals well beyond the jurisdiction of actual courts. And with that extension comes an increasingly adversarial spirit to accompany the procedural rituals of modern life.

Judicial procedures institutionalize forms of argument that remain largely hidden in other arenas. In particular, judicial virtuosity in handling presumptions and proof burdens offer important clues to a tacit dimension of broader public discourse, in which central presumptions are virtually exempt from direct scrutiny. To pursue the jurisprudential analogy still further: judicial techniques for managing the fundamental premises of public discourse can shed new light on comparable movements in current policy debate, academic discussion, and even ordinary language. The jurisprudential analogy can help diagnose some of the pathologies of modern argument, even if, in the final analysis, judicial procedures fail to provide effective remedies.

Over time, courts grow uneasy with their dialectical authority to shift proof burdens, which imposes severe strain on the formal idiom of judicial argument. Judicial resolutions motivated by limited strategic interests may prove difficult to sustain. Thus the Warren Court, by modifying the presumption of constitutionality, met with limited success in turning judicial review into a tool for progressive social change. The Warren majority never found the doctrinal structures for preventing conservative successors from applying similar strategies to opposing social goals. Today, the struggle over proof burdens has become a routine skirmish in the daily conduct of adversarial combat, gradually undermining the aura of neutrality that has supported judicial authority in American society.

Meanwhile burden-shifting strategies have been spreading rapidly into new arenas of professional and academic discourse. The result is the philosophical extension of adversarial combat: polemical debates, in which each party asserts the dialectical privileges of judge and jury. In addition, judicial forms play an expanding role in practical fields dominated by technological and ethical uncertainties, including environmental policy and medical ethics. At first, judicial procedures seem to offer public opinion a method for reaching closure on intractable issues, without sacrificing the perceived legitimacy of results. But eventually the adversarial spirit reasserts itself in battles among rival experts, who have learned to sharpen their forensic skills.

104

It makes no sense to label this drift toward a more judicialized culture as inherently liberal or conservative, since nearly any point of view stands to gain short-term advantages by controlling the strategic boundaries of discourse. Where it is no longer possible to win on substance, a procedural victory may suffice; but the significance of victory depends on who ultimately controls the procedural playing field. Over the long run, the respective adversarial strength of competing groups will determine whether that field becomes a tougher obstacle course for public institutions or an increasingly uphill struggle for individuals locked in battle with entrenched bureaucracies. Perhaps the inevitable result is some unhappy combination of both competing futures, in both the practical sphere and its philosophical extensions.

Within their own jurisprudential domain judicial bodies face major paradoxes in resolving public disputes under conditions of cultural and political uncertainty. These paradoxes are the contemporary expressions of the broad philosophical problem of defining boundaries or limits to human reason. Kant's restatement of this classic problem at the end of the eighteenth century narrowed its focus to the boundaries of empirical reason, the kind of knowledge associated with the growth of scientific investigation. Over the past two hundred years, unprecedented advances in pure and applied science have kept the problem of boundaries under continual review. The relation between scientific knowledge and possible alternative modes of understanding is now an issue that penetrates deep into our culture, down to everyday matters. In an important sense, today's judicial institutions have inherited the problem for which Kant sought a philosophical solution, and they tend to approach it in similar terms.

Kant formulated his ingenious solution to the problem of rational boundaries as a jurisprudential exercise, conducted by a tribunal of uncertain composition.[1] Although Kant's "tribunal of pure reason" basically supported the growing claims of empirical science, its own authority seemed to presuppose the existence of yet another sphere, one in which the whole question of boundaries might be reopened from a higher or "transcendental" point of view. This transcendental realm—by default, the source of boundaries for empirical reason—plays a fateful part in the jurisprudential paradoxes of our own time. Depending on how one sees it, the transcendental sphere can become a dumping ground for would-be knowledge that fails the test of rationality, which empirical reason alone is authorized to administer. But the transcendental sphere can also become the haven for any self-appointed court of appeal eager to review judgments reached under the prevailing regime.

This intriguing Kantian compromise, which will receive extended analysis in chapter 7, offers potential comforts for highly diverse interests. It protects the prevailing wisdom by branding its competitors as illusory modes of knowledge. But it also points to another kind of authority beyond the reach of prevailing wisdom: an inaccessible authority, and yet the source of legitimacy for whatever we can truly know. Apart from possible theological analogues, the closest secular embodiment of Kant's transcendental authority is the judge in an idealized judicial process, the final voice at the top of a jurisdictional hierarchy.

At the close of the twentieth century, renewed interest in this transcendental standpoint stems from open ambivalence toward the fruits of scientific reason in modern life. A common theme for expressing this ambivalence—whose roots extend back to Kant and well before him—is the idea that modern scientific knowledge, whatever its achievements, demands the sacrifice of intrinsically valuable human traditions. Max Weber, one of the first social analysts who made this sense of loss the subject of scientific investigation, summed it up eloquently in his 1918 essay "Science as a Vocation": "The fate of our times is characterized by rationalization and intellectualization and, above all, by the 'disenchantment of the world.' Precisely the ultimate and most sublime values have retreated from public life either into the transcendental realm of mystic life or into the brother-liness of direct and personal human relations."[2] As for the conduct of scientific activity, Weber believed that the problem of limits could be avoided only by keeping rational inquiry within the controlled conditions of the laboratory or the classroom, where the relation of means and ends can be investigated without re-gard for what the final ends ought to be. As Weber acknowledged, however, even the scientist who exploits technical reason under controlled conditions will often face practical difficulties, as does, for example,

> the technician, who in numerous instances has to make decisions according to the principle of the lesser evil or of the relatively best. Only to him one thing, the main thing, is usually given, namely, the end. But as soon as truly "ultimate" problems are at stake for us this is not the case. With this, at long last, we come to the final service that science as such can render to the aim of clarity, and at the same time we come to the limits of science.[3]

The painful discovery of boundaries to instrumental reason has generated periodic crises of scientific authority. Ironically, the spectacular growth of sci-entific and technical knowledge has ensured an expanding frontier of ignorance, paralleling the limits of science. The implications of such limits are somewhat different for academic, political, and popular discussion, but in each area the symptoms are identical: distrust of expert authority, suspicion of prevailing rules and procedures, and skepticism that even minor problems—not just the ultimate ones—can be objectively settled. In recent years, our weary acceptance of social ignorance and institutional bias has strengthened an academic revival of Kantian ethics, with its special sensitivity to intrinsic values of individual autonomy. Not-withstanding their strong ambitions, however, these efforts have remained at such high levels of abstraction that they offer little concrete guidance in the everyday political world. At the most practical level, the great unsolved problem remains our paradoxical need to exercise public control in areas alleged to lie beyond the authority of experts.

According to contemporary versions of this theme, Western culture seems to have suffered a serious loss of common understanding in matters that touch human life very deeply, including political programs, ethical relations, and reli-gious belief. During the twentieth century, periodic revivals of Kantian ideas have provided only short-lived relief for our malaise and may well have deep-ened the sense of crisis with each cycle. Ever since the important neo-Kantian movement at the end of the nineteenth century, transcendental distinctions have accompanied the penetration of scientific principles into law and public policy, academic disciplines, and even ordinary discourse.

Herbert Simon's concept of "bounded rationality" has become a popular term for capturing the neo-Kantian dualism that separates instrumental reason from its transcendental framework.[4] In contrast to Weber's distinction between science and politics as discontinuous vocations—between the laboratory and the "streets" as metaphorical arenas where separate issues must be dealt with— Simon's concept describes a more pervasive boundary. For Simon, even in the laboratory, human reason remains an elusive ideal; it is always hemmed in by an array of unspecified and contingent conditions, supplementing mankind's imperfect grasp of the natural world, the limits of human ingenuity, and the inherent constraints of organized social behavior. But practical problems do somehow get solved, notwithstanding the imperfect conditions under which individuals invariably act, and Simon's work has suggested practical ways to conceptualize whatever lies beyond the operational boundaries of rationality.

One such force is the modern "organization," an entity that Simon and his co-author James March treat functionally as the primary "absorber" of contextual uncertainty in the rational calculations of human beings.[5] Although the term is meant to apply literally to complex social organizations, various commentators have noted its wider significance as a model of contemporary authority, a largely faceless power that shapes the epistemological environment of individuals. In contrast to some other views of organizational authority, bounded rationality "is not bottom-up, emphasizing the power of the subordinate to grant authority to the superior," as Charles Perrow puts it.

> Instead, the superior has the power or tools to structure the subordinate's environment and perceptions in such a way that he or she sees the proper things and in the proper light. The superior actually appears to give few orders . . . but rather sets priorities ("we had better take care of this first"; "this is getting out of hand and creating problems, so let's give it more attention until the problems are cleared up") and alters the flow of inputs and stimuli. . . . An organization develops a set of concepts influenced by the technical vocabulary and classification schemes; this permits easy communication. Anything that does not fit into these concepts is not easily communicated. For the organization, "the particular categories and schemes of classification it employs are reified and become, for members of the organization, attributes of the world rather than mere conventions."[6]

Perrow concludes by noting that, according to Simon and March, "we learn that it is the premises of decisions that are important, rather than the decision-making capabilities of individuals—once it is established that they are not superhuman."[7]

Simon and March's organization thus performs tasks comparable to those addressed by judicial review. By construing the general clauses of the American Constitution, courts set the parameters of public debate—much as organizations supply the boundaries of rationality in modern institutional life, except that courts are expected to articulate objective reasons for these parameters. As Nonet and Selznick have argued, however, this unique ambition for the legal system itself presupposes a political and cultural environment that is, at best, a fragile accomplishment.[8] More likely, in a period of increasing skepticism about the common goals of a political community, the legal system tends to break down into one or both of the pathologies explored by Nonet and Selznick: "legalism," the pursuit of procedural order for its own sake, or "repressive law," which attempts to harness legal authority to the special interests of some limited portion of that community.

The Revolt against Ignorance: Taking Control of Rational Boundaries

At critical moments during this century, commentators on public affairs have offered spirited rebuttals to the whole notion of social ignorance. In many cases their response has included a heavy lament for earlier cultural periods when problems now viewed as irresolvable were allegedly within the grasp of human judgment. The call for a return to such a golden age invariably suggests that modern dilemmas are the result of some avoidable malaise, rather than of strict cognitive boundaries. With the right sort of resolve, we might recover our sense of values or virtue or at least the basic cultural literacy that seems merely to have been mislaid.[9]

Ironically, such arguments shrewdly employ burden-shifting strategies of their own, following the same logic that allowed the Supreme Court to find substantive content in the indefinite principles of constitutional law. The implicit premise can be detected, for instance, in Walter Lippmann's eloquent plea for a higher law of public order. "If there is no higher law," Lippmann said, "then there is no ground on which anyone can challenge the power of the strong to exploit the weak. . . . The denial that men may be arbitrary in human transactions *is* the higher law."[10] In other words, so long as the case for ignorance can possibly be resisted, it should be presumed false: no one can disprove our incapacity as a political community to discover normative principles for handling important social problems. In some popular academic versions of this argument, conspiracy theories have been used to explain how an entire culture might forfeit its deepest access to social truths and thus betray our rightful claims to normative self-mastery.[11]

Despite their apparent optimism, such arguments (when placed in an affirmative mode) invariably retain a clear sense of transcendental limits, while emphasizing the subtlety and fragility of any useful cultural intuitions.[12] Even when the higher law cannot be ruled out on grounds of objective evidence, it is usually found in the attenuated form of a Kantian imperative or regulative ideal.[13] Purcell has thoroughly explored this peculiar combination of intellectual bravado and strategic hedging in arguments from the 1930s, including the famous defense of democratic principles offered by Robert Maynard Hutchins.

> The rational, ethical basis of those principles, [Hutchins] argued, consisted of five logically related ideas in which men "must believe" if they were to justify democracy: that man acted not from instinct alone but through the power of reason; that non-empirical truth existed; that an objective ethical standard existed; that the proper end of man was the fulfillment of his moral and intellectual powers; and that the preceding truths could all be known explicitly through the process of right reason.[14]

Hutchins put forward this series of beliefs as an alternative to the relativism and nihilism in what Purcell calls scientific naturalism, which appeared to place the content of political principles beyond our intellectual reach. But if moral truth were really so accessible, as Hutchins insisted, why did other academics, professionals, and public figures express such paralyzing doubt about it? Like any skilled lawyer, Hutchins challenged the prevailing presumption of moral ignorance by trying to reverse it, using the common belief in democracy as a point of leverage. But, as Purcell asks: "Why, then, was his system better than the others? The only answer he gave was essentially pragmatic—that his ideas necessarily led to democracy. Why, indeed, was democracy itself desirable? That was the question Hutchins had attempted to answer, but instead he used the apparent ethical goodness of democracy as a justification for his philosophical assumptions. It was a circular argument that never resolved the central difficulty.[15]"

109

Hutchins's philosophical manifesto, although constructed on a hypothetical foundation, sought to deny the hypothetical nature of moral truth. Under this bold strategy, arguments-from-ignorance must be rejected; they are cowardly efforts to draw conclusions from defective premises, rather than affirmative truths based on rational insight. To be sure, assigning the burden of proof may become a practical necessity in certain legal disputes when the social order demands some procedure for deciding everyday questions, for which adequate evidence is simply not available. But proof burdens have no legitimate role on the level of theoretical, cultural, or moral inquiry. In many textbooks, accordingly, the *argumentum ad ignorantiam* is classified as a logical fallacy: an offense against rational principles, comparable to embracing a contradiction.[16]

Paralleling these discussions, modern treatments of rhetoric reveal a turbulent debate over possible ethical constraints on rational persuasion. The connotations of "mere rhetoric" reflect the opposing view: that all arguments are simply tools of persuasion to be used for good or for ill by those who can master them. Argument strategies that require shifting burdens of proof may not conform to strict principles of deductive logic, but the same can be said for almost any concrete instance of persuasion, at least in public discourse. Thus it may be asking too much to demand that persuasion always be anchored in some demonstration of an underlying truth or moral virtue, providing a sure criterion to help the unwary distinguish between "good" and "bad" rhetoric.

A spirited rejoinder to this position arose from the same abhorrence of relativism and nihilism that prompted the philosophical pronouncements of Robert Hutchins. With their cascading references to the works of Plato and Aristotle, this neo-Aristotelian school included Hutchins's close associate, Mortimer Adler, and remained an especially strong influence at the University of Chicago well after both men had resigned.[17] The theory of good rhetoric maintains that all genuine public argument carries certain presuppositions, including a metaphysical commitment to the existence of affirmative, accessible, moral truths—like those truths invoked by Hutchins in the argument cited above.[18] Richard Weaver (another University of Chicago figure) developed this notion in popular texts published around 1950, which followed Hutchins and Adler in seeking to elevate public discussion beyond "mere scientific demonstration" to the level of "speculative wisdom."[19]

Although philosophically this movement paid homage to Plato, Aristotle, and Aquinas, its basic elements came from the modern neo-Kantian distinction between empirical and ethical truth. Kant himself had prescribed strict limits on rational inquiry separate from empirical investigations, but his philosophy could not rule out the intriguing possibility that some future cognitive discipline might roam freely across the uncharted plane of pure reason. Drawing on Adler's early work, Richard Weaver concluded that dialectic must be that discipline, taking his formulations of this term from both Plato and Aristotle. When practiced properly, dialectic was a purely intellectual, intuitive examination of conceptual meanings modeled on Platonic forms—"the true nature of intelligible things" and "axiological systems which have ontic status."[20] In addition to these purely intellectual insights, according to Adler and Weaver, humans also have the capacity to recognize concrete applications of dialectical forms as part of their daily practice. Although no one can actually demonstrate these situational, rhetorical applications, their possibility cannot be disproved. And besides, their elusive authority can be classically anchored in the Aristotelian verb *phronein*, whose un-

110

translatable nuances testify to the shameful loss of our cultural heritage in the modern era.[21]

For Weaver, all rhetorical applications of dialectical insights presuppose the metaphorical use of language as a "bridge between the phenomenal and the noumenal world." According to one of his current defenders, "If the metaphoric account of meaning-making is correct . . . , we can say that a term becomes meaningful to the extent that we can place it in the formula 'A' is like 'B' with respect to 'C' in which 'A' is the matter under consideration, 'B' is a paradigm case advanced as clarification, and 'C' is what I call the 'criterial absolute.' "[22] The reason given for this formulation of the criterial absolute, however, seems oddly contingent. The metaphoric account of meaning is correct if we are to have any secure path from the everyday world into the noumenal realm of absolutes. ("It is absurd to speak of . . . meaning in . . . the contingent sphere of human knowledge without the assumption of an existent beyond this—a realm, Weaver asserted, where values have ontic status."[23]) Moreover, according to Weaver, everyday terms have meaning only to the extent the criterial absolute can be utilized. ("Appeals [to truth] are incoherent and certainly non-compulsive without a criterial absolute."[24]) As with Hutchins's circular defense of similar philosophical claims, Weaver's strong denials of moral indeterminacy rest on a strategic foundation. No one can disprove the efficacy of dialectical principles, and operating without them thus becomes absurd.

Weaver's arguments illustrate how proponents of good rhetoric projected a transcendental value realm as a self-justifying strategy for rescuing public discourse from relativism and nihilism. But the strategy did not in fact prove widely successful, and the neo-Aristotelian school soon found itself mired in partisan battles among competing approaches to rhetoric, in addition to playing an adversarial role on major issues of public policy.[25] It was not enough for just this small group of thinkers to reverse the presumption of ignorance so long as others were free to accept it, thereby making it self-fulfilling.

As later generations of transcendental theorists have sought to revive certain arguments of the neo-Aristotelians, they frequently invoke the prestige and authority of the judicial process, both literally and analogically. Today they include surviving veterans of landmark Warren Court battles, concerned to find solid philosophical grounding for the constitutional methods of that era. As one of the most prolific members of this group, Owen Fiss has argued that federal judges are uniquely equipped to identify the "true" or "proper meaning" of American public values.[26] "The task of the judge is to give meaning to constitutional values, and he does that by working with the constitutional text, history, and social ideals. He searches for what is true, right, or just. He does not become a participant in interest group politics."[27] Although the true meanings alluded to by Fiss seem to cluster near the liberal end of the Supreme Court spectrum, his philosophical presumption is that of the rhetorical conservative as characterized by Weaver:

> The true conservative is one who sees the universe as a paradigm of essences, of which the phenomenology of the world is a sort of continuing approximation. Or, to put this in another way, he sees it as a set of definitions which are struggling to get themselves defined in the real world. . . . This type of conservative is sometimes found fighting quite briskly for change; but if there is one thing by which he is distinguished, it is a trust in the methods of law. For him law is the embodiment of abstract justice; it is not "what the courts will decide tomorrow," or a calculation of the forces at work in society.[28]

Years after the Supreme Court ceased to function as the oracle of progressive public values, the authority of impersonal law has inherited that transcendental status which the neo-Aristotelians attributed to philosophical dialectic. In a recent, elegant formulation, Joseph Vining offers a judicialized vision of Weaver's noumenal realm as the only possible guarantor of public order.

> If that which produces law and statements of law is a mindless system, how can we see it as something else without deluding ourselves . . . ? This is a bit like asking whether we must live in delusion and listen to voices that are not there in order to save ourselves from a state of such utter solitude and silence that we might be driven to hearing voices and seeing visions that are not there. The question seems a mad one. How could we do such a thing? Does not the question answer itself?[29]

Not entirely secure in this rather sinuous answer, Vining acknowledges elsewhere that "the question is always with us." Lawyers continually ask themselves whether their presupposition of an impersonal legal authority is a reasonable one.

> Are they foolish to engage in this kind of activity? Is it a front, a cover? Is it beside the point, superfluous or superstructural? . . . The shape of the answer that will emerge should be evident. It is an answer of the not-if kind. Not foolish, not superfluous, if law is to have authority. Not if law is to hold us, evoke our willing acceptance rather than our resistance. Not if law is to be a source to be looked to in discovering what we ought to do. Perhaps we do not or ought not to want that; but if we do not, then we cannot complain about disintegration, disappearance of authority, or respect, and of self-respect, or loss of meaning in the modern state.[30]

Vesting such extraordinary authority in judges raises unusual dilemmas for legal commentators who must conjure with the legacy of legal realism, with judicial restraint, and with the mocking dissent of Justice Holmes in the Lochner case. Fiss is not ready to abandon the accomplishments of the Warren era as just another example of judicial usurpation, but their justification requires a heroic view not only of judicial capacities, but of the whole nature of public values. Like Robert Hutchins and Allen Bloom, Fiss deplores a distinctively modern failure of nerve:

> We have lost our confidence in the existence of the values that underlie the litigation of the 1960s, or, for that matter, in the existence of any public values. All is preference. That seems to be the crucial issue, not the issue of relative institutional competence. Only once we reassert our belief in the existence of public values, that values such as equality, liberty, due process, no cruel and unusual punishment, security in the person, or free speech can have a true and important meaning, that must be articulated and implemented— yes, discovered—will the role of the courts in our political system become meaningful, or for that matter even intelligible.[31]

This lament for a lost sense of moral certainty has a more parochial context than the earlier neo-Aristotelian movement. Instead of idealizing the process of practical judgment in classical Athens, Fiss appears to be nostalgic for the litigating climate of a mere two or three decades ago—for that moment, in short, when the burden-shifting strategies of progressive litigators had captured the unique power of the federal judiciary to impose finality on contested social issues. By contrast, as long as a majority of the Supreme Court went along with these strategies, progressive reformers remained faithful to their pragmatic roots; the truth behind new readings of constitutional principles was still functionally related to the practical results of landmark court decisions.

After 1970, however, as the Supreme Court interrupted the radical logic of burden-shifting, a pragmatic theory of truth had to be replaced by a transcendental theory; only then, in Fiss's terms, "will the role of the courts in our political system become meaningful." In retrospect, therefore, the Warren Court had to be discovering truth in some timeless sense, not merely shifting the burden of proof on intrinsically undecidable issues. And if cynical remnants of the Warren era now doubt that such truths are accessible, they risk encouraging the further erosion of normative insight—that insidious loss which threatens to separate us forever from Fiss's golden age.

Transcendental theories of legal and moral truth cannot avoid the risk, however, that opposing interest groups will fight over the exclusive right to define its contents. During the past decade, opponents of progressive tendencies in constitutional law have also found comfort in postulating a realm of timeless truth,

113

to which others have been too timid to gain access. The keys to that particular kingdom are allegedly found in the doctrine of *original intent*—the notion that constitutional values remain frozen in time and that the specific values enunciated by the Founding Fathers remain obligatory in current constitutional interpretation. The strategic purposes of this doctrine were somewhat clumsily revealed by the zeal with which the Reagan administration's Justice Department campaigned for its acceptance.[32] Ironically, these highly partisan efforts mocked the transcendental perspective by advocating the appointment of only those judges who embraced the faith of original intent. Meese's vision would seem to meet all the conditions laid down by Owen Fiss for a meaningful judicial role, except for the partisan reversal of Fiss's radical agenda.

By rejecting the view that legal and moral issues are hidden behind a veil of ignorance, critics like Hutchins, Adler, and Fiss have attempted to escape the relativism and nihilism that threaten the very possibility of public moral debate. Their strategy undercuts that goal, however, by treating meaningful discourse as a transcendental postulate whose authenticity is presupposed and defended by its reliance on the argument-from-ignorance. Once we concede the possibility that social conflicts have absolute answers, this unfulfilled ideal operates like a vacuum to attract conflicting speculations on its precise contents. In law, the predictable result is an adversarial struggle to control the Supreme Court's unique doctrinal powers. And in the broader field of moral theory, comparable battles are carried out on a transcendental plane, where partisans have staked out dogmatic positions, based on a presumption of ethical foundations.

114

Transcendental Skepticism: The Anti-Foundationalist Presumption

By the 1980s, survivors of the Warren period had divided the legal academy into two hostile camps. One group drifted toward some version of the transcendental faith in judicially defined constitutional values as developed by Fiss and Dworkin, among others. But another group decided to put this faith on trial; they reversed its unexamined presumptions and struck a deliberate pose of disillusionment with the idea of judicial institutions as neutral authorities. These proponents of critical legal studies have concluded that all constitutional controversies boil down to political struggles[33] and thus that the debate over judicial review "is essentially incoherent and unresolvable."[34]

Proponents of CLS have experimented with a broad style of skepticism borrowed from European post-structuralism, although strong pragmatic reflexes seem to hold them back from the farthest implications of this esoteric movement.[35] Post-structuralism performs a complete reversal on the neo-Aristotelian presumption that the boundaries or foundations of public discourse are open to rational examination. It develops with monological determination the presumption that such boundaries are never fully accessible and that efforts to formulate them invariably end in self-contradiction.

As numerous commentators have pointed out, the very constancy of the post-structuralist critique raises paradoxical questions about its own foundations.[36] Although it lacks an institutional dialectic, post-structuralism shares with recent constitutional trends the urgent need to find a presuppositionless authority, an intellectual standpoint from which it can safely cast doubt on all pretensions to rationality. Like the Warren Court, CLS advocates have learned the value of burden-shifting strategies in formalizing skepticism, while still protecting themselves from charges of self-contradiction.

Critical legal studies scholarship illustrates some of the jurisprudential strategies lurking behind the elusive arguments of post-structuralism. A central theme in both movements is an uncompromising denial that conventional texts may be taken at face value. According to this view, public discourse always contains a hidden subtext that undermines the literal message, however skillfully the author or speaker may try to disguise it.

For many readers (including those sympathetic to the results of post-structuralist analysis), this theory raises painful questions about its underpinnings. To what extent does the post-structuralism strategy undermine its implicit claims for coherence and authority? Such questions have forced the movement's leading figures to adopt notoriously cryptic narrative styles. But CLS literature remains refreshingly direct in confessing its foundations in a utopian commitment to social reform. Paul Brest, for example, has pondered the critical options facing the descendants of Warren Court jurisprudence. In his view, the solution is "simply to acknowledge that most of our writings are not political theory but advocacy scholarship—amicus briefs ultimately designed to persuade the Court to adopt our various notions of the public good." Does this mean that a radical social vision lacks intellectual authority beyond the partisan strategy of a legal brief? No one can answer this question, says Brest, but one should never give up hope:

> Finally, the truly courageous—or the most foolhardy—among us might go the next step and, grasping what we understand of our situation, work toward a genuine reconstitution of society—perhaps one in which the concept of freedom includes citizen participation in the community's public discourse and responsibility to shape its values and structures. Those who explore this

115

route may discover that in escaping one set of contradictions they have just found themselves in another. But we will not know, until despair or hope impel us to explore alternatives to the world we currently inhabit.[37]

The key notion that alternatives to the status quo should be granted at least the presumption of normative force is a recurring theme in CLS scholarship. This is a strategic reversal of the presumption often denounced as *privileging*, which denotes the conceptual primacy extended by the dominant culture to established ideas and values: liberalism, the rule of law, value subjectivity, social atomism, and other familiar targets of neo-Marxian political theory.[38] Dominant points of view, by endorsing in advance each of these terms in preference to their respective contraries, obviate the need for upholders of the status quo to prove a series of answers to indeterminable issues: "The privileged term is presumptively entitled as a normative matter to govern disputes; it is simply assumed, as a descriptive matter, to govern the bulk of situations; and most subtly, but perhaps most significantly, departures from the purportedly dominant norm . . . are treated as *exceptional*, in need of special justification, a bit chaotic."[39] Kelman's presumptions play the same sociological and psychological role as organizations in the theory of bounded rationality: they inhabit abstract ideals and reify them, thereby imposing unconscious limits on what ordinary human beings tend to observe as a matter of standard experience. Thus the presumption of individual autonomy tends to support the customary belief that social behavior is mostly voluntary rather than coerced. Similarly, the presumption of rationality predisposes us to interpret official behavior as rule-following rather than discretionary.[40]

In exposing these presumptions, Kelman warns us that any general form of interpretation invariably distorts a more complex reality. Abstract ideals can never describe the whole of social life, and the critic's job is to resist cognitive conformity, to play up the exceptions, and thus to challenge the privileged rule. It is, according to Kelman, "one of the foremost . . . political accomplishments of CLS . . . to arm left liberals against more politically conservative ones . . . by resuscitating the unprivileged positions, by noting the degree to which they remain pervasive in the face of complex efforts to repress their presence."[41] Much of Kelman's book, accordingly, is devoted to showing that the generalizations of conventional liberal theory (not to mention libertarian versions) are never entirely adequate to social events.

But precisely what conclusions follow from this epistemological gap between the general and the concrete, which any prudent observer or theorist must be forced to admit? The CLS strategy, as explained by Kelman, exploits a familiar judicial practice: it places the generalization on trial where it can be judged guilty

116

unless it manages somehow to illuminate the infinite details of concrete social life. "Critique" becomes an intellectualized civil rights battle, in which the oppressed particulars protest their domination by powerful generalizations. Operating like a conceptual Supreme Court, CLS analysis shifts the burden of proof, which no longer shields the presumptions of the dominant discourse. A long string of witnesses are called to testify to specific occasions when liberal values have broken down, thereby exposing the hypocrisy of allegedly free markets, democratic political systems, and meritocratic universities. Once the evidence is in, judgment follows swiftly: the dominant discourse always fails to defend its privileged position.

The attractions of this technique are identical for a post-realist Supreme Court and the post-structuralist critic. It permits anyone who challenges prevailing authority to build a winning case on negative terms. It alters boundaries of rationality without requiring a definitive map; it undermines conceptual foundations without rearranging them in any specific fashion. As Terry Eagleton has said, "It allows you to drive a coach and horses through everybody else's beliefs without saddling you with the inconvenience of having to adopt any yourself." [42]

Opponents of CLS sometimes accuse their adversaries of nihilism, in recognition of this predominantly negative form of reasoning. But CLS members are no more nihilists than were liberal judges and advocates during the days of the Warren Court; they obviously possess an affirmative vision but are restrained by the strategy of their critique from articulating it. [43] Ironically, it is precisely those unstated values of Warren-era liberalism that are now being subjected to radical critique by the next generation of legal commentators. Once these values are taken out of the shadows of appellate argument and brought within the boundaries of reflection, they become easy targets for skeptical attack.

The major casualties of that critique are the specific efforts by Fiss, Dworkin, and others to find conceptual foundations for liberal values. It was, after all, Fiss who defined the alternatives as either judicial authority or social chaos, using indirect arguments of his own to make the uneasy case for shifting judicial activism onto some transcendental level. In placing the dominant discourse on trial, CLS must first construe that discourse in the categorical form into which Fiss and his colleagues have obligingly put it.

Critical legal studies members remain advocates in the same sense that can be applied to Fiss, Tribe, and other participants in the golden age of progressive litigation. They have adapted a negative form of judicial argument for their own heretical purposes, but they remain essentially strategic partisans of an alternative vision. Their rhetoric requires them to be sparing in depicting that vision, but the general outlines are hardly mysterious. Implicitly, they extend privileged

117

status to a set of social practices that were widely idealized during the 1960s: some variation on the themes of small-community life, democratic participation, and face-to-face conversation. Gerald Frug has given us an especially rhapsodic version of this utopia, echoing the remarks already quoted from Paul Brest: "The alternative to 'foundations' is not 'chaos' but the joint reconstruction of social life, the . . . quest of participatory democracy. Acting together, we could begin to dismantle the structure of bureaucratic organizations—not all at once, but piece by piece. In their place we could substitute forms of human relationship that better reflect our aspirations for human development and equality."[44]

Both Kelman and Frug seem to suggest that these countercultural values spring directly from an underlying social reality, one which we could all recognize if our vision were not obscured by the veil of dominant discourse.[45] Their reflexive realism maintains the foundational confidence of a legal generation that has never challenged the regnant pragmatism in American intellectual culture. Placed on trial, the nostrums of group process and democratic participation would reveal as many gaps as the liberal principles that have failed to carry their burden of proof in CLS courtrooms.[46]

There is a more penetrating critique of rational boundaries and philosophical foundations in recent writings of European post-structuralism, which has gained wide acceptance in American circles of literary and social criticism. Many of these works practice the burden-shifting strategies of constitutional jurisprudence, even as they draw attention to patterns of discourse in other writers.[47] The post-structuralist strategy of *deconstruction* has become a well-known critical tool, which posits a dichotomy between truth and rhetoric in public discourse. In many respects, the analysis of constitutional argument presented in chapters 2 and 3 follows the same lines as deconstructionist treatments of literary texts; in both cases the analysis reveals a suppressed level of argument, or subtext, which controls the surface discourse. The demonstration that much of recent constitutional law rests on tacit manipulation of burdens of proof is consistent with the basic premise of deconstruction: all arguments contain both more and less than first meets the eye.

For adjudication, there are historical reasons why judges feel compelled to suppress substantive values in constitutional adjudication, based on legal and political events going back to the beginnings of this century. At the same time, the judicial process has the authority to make final decisions, notwithstanding conditions of doubt or uncertainty. This power to reach categorical conclusions, without revealing their presumptive foundations, gave the courts rhetorical privileges unknown to other institutions. Amid growing public skepticism toward political authority and professional expertise, the adversarial parties to constitutional disputes were able to perfect an indirect style of argument: preserving the rhetoric of evidence and rational decision, while manipulating the onus of decision.

According to the late Paul DeMan (a subtle master of deconstruction techniques), we can expect to encounter rhetoric in any text whenever "it is impossible to decide by grammatical or other linguistic devices which of . . . two meanings (that can be entirely incompatible) prevails. Rhetoric radically suspends logic and opens up vertiginous possibilities of referential aberration." [48] In complete opposition to Richard Weaver's neo-Aristotelian theory of good rhetoric, deconstruction presumes that all texts harbor rhetorical levels that remain hidden from both author and reader. For Weaver, public argument presupposed that rational individuals were somehow capable of discerning "the true nature of intelligible things" and "axiological systems which have ontic status." [49] Metaphor was the bridge that carried us from the "phenomenal" world of language into the "noumenal" realm—that postulated domain of "criterial absolutes." De Man's work mercilessly attacks this approach, concluding instead that metaphor invariably leads in multiple directions and thus ensures the radicial uncertainty of written texts.

Other post-structuralist critics have raised similar objections to a variety of philosophical positions adopted by preceding generations of European scholars. The works of Derrida, Lacan, and Foucault, among others, challenge an alleged tendency in contemporary philosophy to postulate conceptual foundations for modern thinking. Ironically, the philosophical targets of post-structuralist critique are often thinkers who, in turn, took a critical stand toward past philosophical traditions. Husserl's phenomenology, for example, which has become a recurrent point of reference for post-structuralists, emerged from a tireless search for presuppositionless reflection. But while it proposed a more complex philosophical method than American neo-Aristotelianism, Husserlian phenomenology was likewise the response to a relativistic crisis, which Husserl attributed to the methodical dominance of empirical science. [50] Along with Heidegger and other contemporaries, Husserl reacted strongly against the destabilizing cultural consequences of instrumental reason; but he never denied the elusive, transcendental status of possible countervailing foundations. These qualifications are frequently lost in the polemical discourse of post-structuralism.

The charge of conceptual nihilism has perhaps more substance when applied to the post-structuralists than to their American legal cousins, considering the broader scope of their rhetorical critique. In the field of literary criticism, for example, where fierce polemics mark the debate between deconstructionists and descendants of American New Criticism, post-structuralist methods have been used to challenge the fragile postulates that permitted New Critics to balance the subjectivity of interpretation with the alleged objectivity of aesthetic meaning.[51] Without suggesting any close analogy between Warren-Court activism and New Criticism, it is still possible to compare the sense of vulnerability that haunts academic survivors of once-dominant strategies as their presuppositions come under rigid scrutiny by many of their brightest students. As Art Berman has suggested in his penetrating study of this confrontation,

> French post-structuralism is imported to dissolve the bond that reconciles opposites for the New Critics, to replace it with an indeterminacy in literature that is then extended to cover all language (a disciplinary imperialism).
>
> The post-structuralist challenge to New Criticism has been extended to other disciplines that presuppose a similar "balance" between two incompatible perspectives—disciplines that had hoped to accommodate scientific procedures within traditional cultural life. The same uncompromising indeterminacy has been postulated by those deconstructionists who analyze social and cultural systems as "texts." And within legal scholarship, deconstructive readings of legal texts have become a prominent style of academic discourse, even if not yet the dominant one.[52]

Shifting the burden of proof remains a delicate operation, calling for careful craftsmanship in its judicial setting and for artful narrative in its broader uses. The strategy seems most effective when it is focused somewhat narrowly on the specific presumptions of a reigning but fragile orthodoxy in a critical climate open to greater diversity of thought. The risk, however, is that the technique will become the vehicle for new orthodoxies and new interest groups, whether defined in political, legal, or academic terms. Even Paul De Man's patient, case-by-case analysis of textual indeterminacy threatens to become a dogma about the inescapable nature of language.

Similarly, Jacques Derrida's flamboyant readings of philosophical texts appear to emanate from certain unexamined presuppositions, which are nonetheless predictable for being herded under the paradoxical rubric of *différance*. As Peter Dews has argued: "The characterization of this principle as non-self-identical makes no substantial alteration to its status, since absolute difference—which is what Derrida's term '*différance*' indicates—is ultimately indistinguishable from absolute identity; *différance* is no less inwardly unified, though historically deployed, than Heidegger's *Sein* or Hegel's *Geist*."[53] In exposing philosophical presuppositions that preserve the traditional "metaphysics of presence," Derrida cannot avoid raising questions about his own critical standpoint. As Dews further notes,

Derrida's deconstruction does not seek to *challenge* or *transform* the relationship between subjectivity, truth and presence (for example), but rather seeks to lay bare its structure. Although this manoeuvre then generates for Derrida the difficulty of explaining the point from which he himself is speaking, perhaps even more importantly it represents—in a paradoxical sense—an attempt to *preserve* the security and priority of philosophical discourse. Derrida's conception of deconstruction as an eternal vigilance, as an incessant attempt to escape the illusion of presence, seems to support this interpretation. Deconstruction cannot learn from its objects, but occupies a position of superior insight . . . : in this way the successor to philosophy continues to evade the exposure of thought to the contingency of interpretation.[54]

No doubt Derrida would strenuously resist the drift of this analysis, for clearly he intends to write without a priori principles and empty absolutes and to tolerate no exceptions to the relentless attack on conceptual foundations. However, the same defense could be made for most post-Kantian continental philosophers, including Hegel, Nietzsche, Husserl, and Heidegger. It is simple enough for whoever comes last in this line to stand in opposition to "the tradition" and to point out respects in which prior thinkers have been forced into tacit metaphysical commitments. But it is also reasonable to expect that the same exercise will be repeated in the near future by some ascendant critic, who will dwell especially long on the ironic failures of the most recent predecessor.[55] In an intellectual climate receptive to such frequent reversals, the odds favor the continued proliferation of interpretive schools, not to mention charismatic intellectualizing and plain, small-minded backbiting—matters that are perhaps better left to the sociologist than to philosophers or self-styled critics.

Wherever possible, it is useful to analyze critical movements in concrete terms as attempts to reverse specific presumptions held (explicitly or implicitly) by some proximate source. The members of CLS have essentially been challenging the presumption of judicial neutrality implicit in the Warren Court's experiment in judicial activism. To be sure, their critique has often expanded to reach the customary targets of neo-Marxist and post-structuralist critics. But CLS commentators are least compelling when they move too far beyond their own national and professional horizons.

It bears repeating that the presumptions placed on trial by CLS operate below the surface of judicial argument in Warren-era progressivism. The rhetoric of that vanished era exploited the strategies of burden-shifting precisely to avoid formulating substantive presumptions. Moreover, the fact that progressive liberalism—however briefly—actually spoke through the Supreme Court lent a special purity to its presumptions: these were not the values of any mere interest

121

group, so it seemed, but those of impersonal law. It was not until the sun had begun to set on progressive litigation that survivors formulated the transcendental postulates—the philosophical visions of Fiss, Dworkin, and Meese—that provide the easiest targets for deconstruction. The issue of foundations is ultimately joined on this level of absolutes: either truth or chaos says one side; either critique or lies, says the other.

The case of post-structuralism is admittedly more complex. Whereas some critics have dismissed the entire movement as a surreptitious absolutism or nihilism, the most generous commentary sees it as a limited response to preceding trends in French structuralism and European phenomenology. Although these movements were, in turn, inspired by efforts to reject still earlier presumptions that had allegedly hardened into dogma, the post-structuralists (each one in a distinctive way, of course) produce evidence to show how their mentors succumbed to the lures of metaphysics. Derrida finds such metaphysical commitments in any implicit claim to capture truth, no matter how carefully that claim had been hedged by structuralists and phenomenologists. As Dews observes: "For Derrida, there can be no other truth than truth as defined by metaphysics—an assumption which drives him into a posture of incessant harrying of an unbeatable enemy. Whatever the inconsistencies and self-contradictions of philosophical discourse may reveal, they cannot be read as signs of 'untruth,' even though they are, in some sense, signs of illusion." [56] Both structuralism and phenomenology, in their respective heydays, had pointedly disowned subjective relativism in favor of an allegedly more objective approach to human knowledge, even if that standpoint had to be consciously constructed. Derrida preserves the same set of alternatives but exposes the constructivist strategy of his predecessors as a simple deception. Either constructivism or chaos, said his predecessors. Either deconstruction or illusion, was his response.

Taken together, the neo-Aristotelian and post-structuralist positions form a classic antinomy: the antinomy of bounded rationality. [57] They share the nineteenth-century neo-Kantian model of human reason as bounded by a set of indeterminate presuppositions. But they differ in characterizing that boundary as something that falls entirely within, or entirely without, the territory accessible to reason. They would agree, nonetheless, that the boundary question cannot be categorically resolved either way; and thus they are each left to articulate the familiar argument-from-ignorance.

The neo-Aristotelian insists that no one can prove that the major presuppositions of thought are beyond all possibility of comprehension, and in the absence of such proof, we might as well hope for the best. To do so offers at least a pragmatic barrier to relativism and nihilism. The post-structuralist, meanwhile, pleads the opposite case. No one can prove that the foundations of reason can ever be grasped, even in principle, and thus we might as well face up to our limitations. To do so requires vigilance and self-discipline, but at least it protects us from illusory universal principles dictated by the dominant interests in contemporary culture.

In the judicial process, whenever two adversaries take such sharply opposed positions on the meaning of an underdetermined legal principle, the judge plays the dialectical function of assigning the burden of proof. For an interpretive antinomy, however, no court has obvious jurisdiction—not even Kant's tribunal of pure reason, which was not prepared to rule on questions that transcended all empirical evidence.[58] Each claimant, in sum, must serve as both advocate and judge in a fragmented dialectic that may become the dominant style in current academic debate.

Pragmatic Reason and the Boundaries of Legitimacy

In recent decades, many critics have sought to avoid the antinomy of rational boundaries by emphasizing the dynamic, interactive qualities of reason, consciously replacing the more traditional static, logical view.[59] If human reasoning is to have a foundation at all, according to this approach, it cannot be located in the abstract essences of the neo-Aristotelians; instead it must emerge through practical activity, interactions with the cultural environment, and interpersonal dialogue. In chapter 1 I examined two influential products of this movement: Toulmin's theory of knowledge as warranted belief and Perelman's theory of rhetoric as public persuasion. Both theories made a case for their respective dynamic elements as irreducible, intrinsic features of human reason and not merely as arbitrary or edifying descriptions. And both relied heavily on jurisprudential analogies as models for the dynamic structure of reason and not merely as suggestive metaphors for a purely logical system.

Neither Toulmin nor Perelman, however, took his analogies seriously enough. By failing to explore the dialectical structure of adjudication, they overlooked important problems endemic to the judicial model. In the next two sections I shall examine these problems through yet another antinomy: that between *finality* and *legitimacy*. Finality yields the presumption that human activity can (at some ideal level) be referred to a coherent body of rules, from which specific actions may derive determinate meaning and value. Its emphasis on closure within a unified, axiological structure achieves the same purpose as jurisdictional coherence within a legal system. What counts as legitimate is thus the product of structure and procedure, and "ought" emerges out of "is."[60] An opposing presumption challenges this lodging of legitimacy within any particular procedural regime. It rescues the prospect for normative critique of existing institutions, but it leaves the whole issue of legitimacy hostage to adversarial interpretations. "Ought" remains separated from "is" and appears in multiple, conflicting guises.

Modern analytic thought has long been aware that human discourse is riddled with unarticulated presumptions. Indeed, among the most celebrated quests of twentieth-century British philosophy has been the detection of tacit metaphysical premises in quite innocuous statements, going back to Russell's celebrated analysis of "The king of France is bald."[61] During the 1950s, encouraged by fresh perspectives circulating among the students of Ludwig Wittgenstein, some philosophers relegated the whole search for metaphysical foundations to the heap of meaningless pursuits. In its place they promoted a relentless behaviorism, launching a calculatedly mundane inquiry into linguistic exchanges where interlocutors seemed to be uttering appropriate responses. Appropriateness was measured against the implicit conventions of ordinary speech, taken as the distillation of everyday behavior. Such tacit rule systems were the only foundations one needed to explore, and to do so required little more than cultivated reflection on everyday discourse and not the ponderous nomenclature of academic philosophers.[62]

124

Toulmin's pragmatic description of the everday uses of argument illustrates this new pattern. Toulmin wanted to replace traditional theories of knowledge with dynamic, operational criteria of validity.[63] But his study was also one of the first to reveal the troublesome pluralism that plagues all such efforts to approach rationality through codes of behavior: is there only one code, or are there many? If more than one, then each separate code would measure the same action by different jurisdictional standards; what was appropriate for political debate might not be appropriate for professional discussion among nuclear scientists. Toulmin seemed ready to acknowledge such diverse "fields" of specialized discourse as natural features of pragmatic reason. But the regulative ideal of a single, all-encompassing standard ("ordinary language") remained paramount for most of his colleagues, perhaps reflecting what some critics have characterized as the sheltered intellectual climate in which "ordinary language philosophy" flourished.[64]

As long as public arguments could all be placed within discernible codes or fields, Toulmin's jurisprudential analogy was a graceful image for pragmatic language philosophy. The very definition of a field made short work of possible dilemmas in rational discourse. It presupposed that all the important dialectical problems had been resolved: questions about the nature, relevance, admissibility and weight of evidence; problems in matching general rules with specific factual findings; procedures for eliminating good-faith differences about the interpretation of general rules; a default mechanism for resolving underdetermined cases; and a uniform code for conflicts of law among multiple jurisdictions.[65]

Curiously, these assumptions tend to convert arguments into something analogous to final, uncontested judicial decisions. A better analogy would compare them to legal briefs submitted to appellate courts, where the merits of rival claims must be extracted from conflicting interpretations of important procedural questions. At least some arguments—including many ordinary political and academic controversies—unfold in the same way a modern criminal trial addresses the issue of legal guilt. The parties bring opposing interests to the debate that are extrinsic to the formal rules, lending an adversarial edge to the entire process. Very little in the way of evidence is accepted as given, and the central facts emerge only after strategic conflict has shaped the classification of testimony and other raw data. Beyond matters of evidence, conflicts relevant to appellate review play an even more central role. For it is here that the parties present opposing views on how much process is due or what the full roster of appropriate legal rules should be in order to conform with broad constitutional principles. Finally, for specific applications of these broadest principles, we can expect to find polarized doctrines for assigning burdens of proof.

In the end, of course, the highest court willing to hear an appeal must render final judgment; and only then is the entire controversy frozen into a Toulmin-like tableau vivant of warrants and data. To call this artifice the argument is to ignore the vital activity beneath the surface of the final decision.[66] It mistakes the result for the process—an ironic twist, considering that this is the very complaint lodged by partisans of practical reasoning against formal logic.

Most important, Toulmin's limited use of the jurisprudential analogy misses the reflexive aspect of interactive argument. A great deal of judicial energy is spent in determining how the underlying substantive conflict will be resolved—a process in which the adversaries are encouraged to participate. These arguments about arguments necessarily pass beyond the parameters of a single field; they characterize the restless boundary disputes that accompany any truly dynamic area of argument, whether judicial, academic, or political. By assuming that all standards of validity are internal to established fields, Toulmin's analysis casts metaphysical suspicion on the validity of dialectical debate, which is concerned with the definition and future direction of prevailing disciplinary standards.[67]

This is precisely the sort of suspicion that has haunted American judicial review throughout the twentieth century, ever since pragmatists and legal realists finished denouncing the pretensions of legal formalism. To the extent that judges were found to be doing something more than applying preestablished rules to known facts, they were held to be legislating rather than judging. For progressive legal critics, this revelation became a self-evident argument for minimizing the role of judges in broad constitutional interpretation (the policy of judicial restraint) and for referring all the indeterminate questions of public policy to the political arena.

By contrast, Toulmin has no institutional alternative to his argument fields and their circumscribed, discontinuous authority. Within each field, that authority must be considered self-validating or declarative, with no significant role for dialectical disputes about constitutive rules or their application. This set of conditions approaches the tunnel vision of Kuhn's normal science conducted under a paradigm, which tolerates only a limited range of internal disputes—puzzles rather than anomalies.[68] Toulmin's only conceptual alternative to this balkanized approach to rationality is to accept definitions of validity that transcend single argument fields; but that would open the door to the dreaded metaphysics.

For Toulmin, the jurisprudential model of self-executing rules presumes conceptual stability and finality for all potential disputes about validity—at least within distinct fields. It is the same picture one finds in legal textbooks that organize the specialized fields of legal practice into "black letter" summaries.[69] It is also the impression that courts deliberately cultivate in their official rhetoric.

126

Judges interpret their own dialectical duties through a dedicated body of procedural rules, notwithstanding the decades of realist attacks on this formalist pretense.[70] Accordingly, it might appear that all such troublesome reflexive issues could be transferred to some postulated metalevel of rule-following behavior.[71] As was noted in earlier chapters, even for the most dramatic shifts in judicial strategy, it is always possible for a skillful majority to frame its decision within the boundaries of stable rules and deductive logic. There is, for example, a growing body of doctrine on burdens of proof in many areas of civil procedure, which contains relevant warrants for judges who want to readjust the traditional division of burdens between plaintiffs and defendants. But, the procedural doctrines applied by trial judges and appellate courts have an especially volatile dialectical career. Over time, they appear stable and self-executing, but only as long as judges resist any challenge to them or when they are so heavily protected by presumptions that challenges are futile.

Even the most strongly worded presumption, however, can suddenly reveal its complex dialectical structure. The examination of two historic shifts in the presumption of constitutionality—during the mid-1930s and again in the Warren era—showed that even heavily entrenched procedural doctrines can be dramatically altered, given sufficiently powerful dialectical support. In each period, of

course, critics immediately complained that judges were placing private preferences above objective law. But this is a ritual argument heard from all losing
parties in major constitutional struggles. If the dialectical shift is strong enough,
the usurpers will control all the symbols of impersonal law, both at the moment
of change and, increasingly, as change continues. They will eventually reinterpret judicial history, reaching back to prescient dissenting opinions from prior
decades to embellish the wisdom of current orthodoxy.[72]

Courts of law must struggle daily, with all their craftsmanlike skill, to maintain the fragile structure of rules that philosophers like Toulmin take for granted
in the definition of argument fields. In essence, this façade of rational closure, determinate rules, and finality of decisions offers pragmatic reason the secure foundations demanded by the neo-Aristotelians and the transcendental defenders
of the Warren Court. Even though pragmatists scoff at static limits placed on
logical or empirical knowledge, they must eventually entertain similar limits for
rational action. Any resulting crises in pragmatic authority will quickly reignite
antinomies like those analyzed earlier in this chapter.[73]

The American realists tried to obviate this challenge by shifting their allegiance to the legislative branch of government, which became the new procedural
source of finality. In the first decades of this century, the progressive views of
most realists made it easy for them to presume that the current political system
had replaced the courts as the embodiment of rational action. Politics had to be
rational in some ultimate sense, because the alternatives were either to return to
the legal formalism of the judiciary or to the social anarchy of economic markets.[74]
Over time, however, the steady erosion of this progressive presumption opened
the way for a neo-conservative shift in American public policy. Gaining strength
during the 1960s, this movement shrewdly transposed the progressive postulates
of political rationality and market failure, occasioning a dramatic change in the
basic premises of academic theorizing and political debate.

Such revolutions in unarticulated presumptions underscore the cost of ne-
glecting the dialectical elements behind established fields of argument. At least
three different frameworks for conceptualizing the problems of public policy can
be identified, depending on whether one is prepared to assign final rational authority to courts, legislatures, or markets. Each approach tries to monopolize the
field; and its academic partisans, by controlling the burden of proof, can proceed
quickly to bury the pretensions of dissenting arguments. Rationality and validity
thus achieve an outward stability, and public problems are reduced to technical
puzzles within the competence of the favored set of institutions—courts, legislatures, or markets. But this stable condition lasts only as long as the underlying

presumptions resist hostile scrutiny. When the burden of proof eventually shifts, the finality of argument fields remains intact, but a dramatically different form of legitimacy is thereby conserved.

Argument as Process: Transcendental Dialectics

The central question raised by the jurisprudential analogy asks how practical decisions or arguments gain legitimacy. Are judgments in public discourse deemed correct because they follow the prevailing criteria, or can these operating criteria be judged critically by their ability to generate correct judgments? The second option takes us back to the antinomy of bounded rationality; it begs the issue of whether we have access to criteria of correctness that are independent of active judgments.[75] By contrast, the first option—legitimation by reference to an exemplary method—seems to avoid such metaphysical hazards. It resolves the whole question of legitimacy by making it the pragmatic function of prescribed procedures.[76]

Almost immediately, however, there emerges a new dilemma, based on whether one adopts an internal or external perspective on procedural norms. From a point of view internal to any single method, legitimacy changes from an insoluble puzzle to a trivial certitude; judgments are self-executing. There is simply no other source of validity or truth, and anyone who challenges a fully vetted judgment is flirting with civil disobedience—also known as shifting to a different field or deciding to play a different language game. On the other hand, postulating an external perspective on procedural standards suggests that we can somehow remove ourselves from the procedural confines of any particular field. It leaves us suspended among multiple jurisdictions without criteria for selecting any one of them as the final authority. The tension between these perspectives creates a new antinomy, one in which the alleged weakness of either position becomes the dominant argument for accepting its opposite.[77]

Recent attempts to mediate this antinomy have posited a series of self-transcending procedures, which allow for mediation across discontinuous frameworks consisting of either personal, cultural, or field-based systems. The dominant image found in these theories is one of genuine dialogue, distinguished from its allegedly false imitations by various stipulations of integrity and sincerity. The pragmatic turn behind standard versions of this approach takes equal exception to dogmatism and relativism, the Scylla and Charybdis between which the heroic practical reasoner must navigate. However, the actual mechanism for this procedural self-steering is subject to much dispute. Candidates range from the ineffable human competence displayed in everyday linguistic exchange, to various ethical maxims stressing the utility of cooperative strategies, to transcendental conditions for the whole concept of legitimate discourse. I shall briefly compare all three to the dialectical mechanism of adjudication, whose unique blend of legitimacy and finality remains the central attraction in the jurisprudential analogy.

For each of these mechanisms, the legitimating dynamics of method or procedure puts a momentary end to the antinomy of external and internal perspectives. But legitimacy is gained at the price of finality, for each separate procedure lacks the dialectical equivalent of a court of highest appeal over all the others. Habermas acknowledges that final authority eludes the decision procedures embedded in public argument; and yet it remains a necessary postulate, in his view, if there is to be any hope of criticizing the positions taken by either false or multiple supreme courts.[78]

The pragmatic perspective on discourse fields presupposes a distinction between arguments as products and as processes.[79] The latter concept captures the irreducibly dynamic element that distinguishes an entirely new idiom—one that elevates argumentation over argument, speech acts over statements, discourse over speech, pragmatics over semantics, dialogue over utterance, practical reasoning over formal deduction, and rhetoric over logic. Nevertheless, the enduring prestige of formalism in academic linguistics and language philosophy has continually undercut the distinction between product and process, between result and event. A process without any product seems entirely too mysterious for most analytical theorists.

Thus the history of recent pragmatic approaches to argument reveals a two-stage pattern: the pragmatic iconoclast undertakes a new campaign to escape the dead formalism of the past, while the conservative formalist rushes forward to impute conditions that would convert pure activity back into discrete, rule-governed events. Such retrospective treatments are often called "rational reconstructions," and they are instantly recognizable by their florid but arcane notations.[80]

For a long time, these reconstructions were heavily influenced by Noam Chomsky's model of generative grammar.[81] Chomsky postulated an ordered series of discrete, rulelike patterns through which ordinary language statements could be displayed as outcomes of a unified, comprehensive process. The relentless formalism of generative models offers subtle rational support to the flexible, creative dimensions of language. Prior to any formal reconstruction, expressions in a particular language are already known by native speakers to be syntactically correct, based on their self-validating exercise of competent judgment. Rational reconstruction is not the source of their correctness, but rather the functional

129

equivalent of an objective, interpersonal test; the validity of competently spoken sentences can thus be explained by showing how they could have been derived by specified procedures. To the extent that underlying procedures can also be generalized across natural languages, dialects, and cultural schemes, they seem to provide a unifying syntactic framework for all language.[82] Moreover, from a technological point of view, they suggest one possible route by which artificially constructed discourse could be machine-generated, thereby joining the wider conversation of mankind.

The Chomskian model lost much of its appeal in the early 1970s, however, as linguists increasingly followed the lead of certain language philosophers in exploring the nonuniversal, situational aspects of speech. In place of a mechanism conceived as a single regime of generative rules, philosophers found a set of conventional practices, open-textured principles, and ethical maxims to validate the many nonsyntactic aspects of everyday speech. Like the warrants in Toulmin's fields of inquiry, these practices tend to blur the distinction between description and prescription. John Searle, for example, summarized general types of "felicity conditions," under which speakers can successfully project the many practical uses of language in everyday speech. And Paul Grice postulated his principle of "cooperation," along with other "maxims," as implicit conventions for explaining the apparent success with which ordinary speakers convey their intended meanings to an audience.[83]

As with Toulmin's self-executing warrants, however, these reconstructive principles of valid discourse have been removed from any dialectical context. Quite evidently, these are not yet the kinds of speech events in which persuasion takes place, in which communicative norms are negotiated, or in which the boundaries of conventional inference are critically examined. Indeed, there is virtually no sociological data to indicate how frequently these conventions are in fact observed and no recognized authority whose function it is to resolve uncertainties, anomalies, and novelties in the daily application of such maxims.[84]

After some three decades in which followers of the Oxford school have been sketching in these somewhat hazy principles, they have yet to tell us much about concrete argumentation, in which discourse often loses its self-certifying qualities. Most of these analyses concentrate on teasing out potential ambiguities of single utterances. Perhaps the closest approach to interpersonal discourse can be found in Grice's work on conversational implicature, which traces the assumptions under which an ideal hearer might successfully reconstruct a particular meaning intended by the speaker.[85]

This modest yield takes us little farther than Toulmin's doctrine of good reasons, in that it freezes a supposedly interactive field within a preexisting frame of self-executing rules. Grice even adds to Toulmin's nondialectical epistemology a matching theory of personal psychology, according to which rational behavior in argument is defined as conformity with putative preestablished norms. Such a theory writes its own inference-ticket, Grice explains, since:

> [I]t should be possible to derive strong motivations on the part of the creatures subject to the theory against the abandonment of the central concepts of the theory (and so of the theory itself), motivations which the creatures would (or should) regard as justified. Indeed, only from within the framework of such a theory, I think, can matters of evaluation, and so, of the evaluation of modes of explanation, be raised at all. If I conjecture aright, then, the entrenched system contains the materials needed to justify its own entrenchment; whereas no rival system contains a basis for the justification of anything at all.[86]

Among linguists who have carefully analyzed the dialectical challenges of public discourse, the theory of speech acts has recently been broadened to reach more interactive communication. Several Dutch linguists, for example, have criticized speech-act theory for failing to apply its terms to argumentation.[87] In place of the passive listener attempting to reconstruct the idiosyncratic meaning of a speaker, van Eemeren and Grootendorst envision an active respondent equipped with an opposing point of view:

> Language users performing speech acts do not, in principle, do so with the sole intention of making the persons to whom they address themselves understand what speech act they are performing: rather, by means of those speech acts they hope to elicit from their listeners a particular response (verbal or otherwise). This means that their language must serve not only a *communicative* but also an *interactional* purpose.[88]

The process of argumentation continues until one of the parties persuades the other to change his or her mind, using the kinds of arguments that would appeal to a postulated rational judge. It is important for this exchange that the outcome could, in principle, go either way, depending on the force of the "better" argument: "Argumentation is a speech act consisting of a constellation of statements designed to justify or refute an expressed opinion and calculated in a regimented discussion to convince a rational judge of a particular standpoint in respect of the acceptability or unacceptability of that expressed opinion."[89]

Accordingly, the Amsterdam School has elaborated certain dialectical elements of speech events—by which they mean, following Wenzel, "a structure of discourse marked by critical intention." In order to achieve "the critical testing of expressed opinions," argumentation must be "regimented" under a set of appropriate procedural rules.[90] To be sure, everyday argumentation may occur outside these rules—and probably does in most practical situations—but it can earn the description of *rational* or *proper* argumentation only by faithful adherence to a set of ideal standards.[91] Van Eemeren and Grootendorst thus propose a "dialectical code of conduct for rational discussants," consisting of seventeen detailed prescriptions. The essence of this code is summed up by the authors in the form of certain assumptions about the participants:

> We assume the discussants to be ordinary language users in ordinary circumstances, acting of their own volition and seriously, saying what they mean and regarding themselves as committed to what they say, understanding what is said and basing their judgement on it, permitted to adopt any point of view that they may wish to adopt, and to advance any information that they may consider relevant, saying nothing that they do not consider relevant, permitted to attack any statement that they consider worth criticizing, and prepared to defend any statement of their own that may be criticized by other discussants.

Above all, the code of conduct assumes discussants "who wish to resolve a dispute about an expressed opinion by means of a [rational] argumentative discussion." [92]

132   Of special interest is the rule formulated in this quasi-judicial code for apportioning the burden of proof. Van Eemeren and Grootendorst dismiss most of the important issues surrounding the burden of proof, since their performance-based model leaves no role for ambiguity, uncertainty, or indeterminacy in practical argumentation. They assume that issues will be resolved on the basis of rational examination of evidence and thus that the burden of proof does little more than assign responsibility to one of the parties for producing relevant evidence. "The question of who bears the burden of proof presents no problem in principle, since . . . *both* language users have an obligation to defend their own points of view, so that *each* bears the burden of proof for his own point of view. The question is therefore not on whom 'the' burden of proof rests, but which language user is the first to begin defining his point of view." [93]

Like countless legal commentators who reduce the dialectical functions of courts to a self-executing system of procedural rules, van Eemeren and Grootendorst concentrate exclusively on the burden of going forward, assuming that the enlightened conversation about to occur will resolve all issues to the rational satisfaction of both parties. In the absence of such results, argumentation (unlike judicial proceedings) can be suspended without resolution. It might, for example, degenerate into some different interactive process that appears rational and proper but in fact is not. In the end, the Amsterdam School is able to ignore the risk of non-persuasion. Following the normative strategy of speech-act theory, it defines performance as successful performance. It thus seeks to capture the legitimacy of practical discourse in a set of ideal rules, but in exchange it must abandon all hope of using those rules to ascertain finality in concrete disputes. In the end, Oxford-style analysis is a feeble tool for making the dialectical transition from process to procedure. Its performance-based norms leave judgments in discourse open to perpetual revision, punctuated only by ephemeral flashes of intuitive assessments among diverse participants.[94]

The procedural model of argumentation guided by self-fulfilling ethical ideals thus falls short of the mechanism represented by adjudication, which simultaneously bestows legitimacy (through fidelity to rules) and finality (through recognition of a judicial hierarchy) on disputes that reach its jurisdiction. Nevertheless, the Amsterdam theorists have at least postulated the dialectical nature of interpersonal discourse, unlike either Toulmin or Grice. They have also indirectly shown why, in many cases, arguments are not terminated rationally under customary, field-dependent warrants or by means of general maxims of conversational cooperation. Rational argumentation requires the further set of conditions embodied in the complex ethical code recommended by van Eemeren and Grootendorst—or, at least, something much like it.[95] In their treatment, speech-act theory takes a large step toward redefining its felicity conditions in transcendental terms, anticipating the direction laid out by Habermas in his theory of the ideal speech situation.

Before pursuing this transcendental path, it is important to note the rich sociological literature devoted to empirical elements of public discourse viewed as a performance or process. Sociolinguistic investigators have shown that most verbal interactions serve implicit goals other than (or, at least, in addition to) rational deliberation and the striving toward rational cooperation. Brown and Levinson, for example, have interpreted discourse behavior as an elaborate process of negotiating personal status—what sociologists call "saving face." Although their study treats this remarkably subtle process as an adjunct to linguistic communication, it establishes the diversity of communication goals, in terms of which public discourse may be interpreted as reasonable.[96]

Their work only scratches the surface of sociological approaches to purposeful negotiation over the norms of everyday living. Going beyond linguistic activity, Erving Goffman's well-known studies postulate the alternative goals of personality-definition and impression-management as central tasks of personal interaction. And ethnomethodology, notably in the work of Harold Garfinkle, expands the list of purposes still further, to include the perpetuation of discrete, group-defined enterprises, each serving its own parochial interests.[97]

Taken together, these ramifying approaches to rule-governed interaction undermine any assumption that procedural validity can resist the relativizing antinomies of logical validity. To be sure, along with Toulmin, one can simply presume that argument procedures sort themselves into a few complementary validity domains. But that presumption faces a strong challenge from the rising volume of empirical research on everyday norm-governed behavior. Toulmin's presumption—like that of the Oxford School—ultimately rests on strategic grounds; without it, the whole notion of procedural validity fails in its stabilizing mission.[98]

Growing interest in the dialectics of contemporary argument is shared by many specialists in speech communication, encompassing the study of debate, public speaking, and other common uses of rhetoric. Over the past decade, this diverse group of scholars has energetically pursued the contextual study of argument in conjunction with theories of rhetoric. Following the distinction noted by Wenzel, they endorse the threefold division of argumentation into separate levels concerned with products, processes, and procedures. They associate these multiple approaches to argument, respectively, with logic, rhetoric, and dialectic. According to Wenzel, the study of public discourse has recently been advancing along this continuum, to the point where it is now possible to focus on the dialectical aspects of argument or the procedures by which arguments are commonly vetted to meet public expectations of either legitimacy or finality.[99]

Of the numerous approaches to public discourse surveyed in this chapter, the work of Jürgen Habermas is doubtless the most comprehensive and ambitious. Habermas has conscientiously attended to the major interpretive trends of his generation, steering a middle course between the widening extremes of prevailing antinomies. Although he has responded perhaps too generously to the linguistic rationalism of both generative grammar and speech act theory, Habermas remains critically concerned with the social and cultural conditions surrounding practical reasoning.[100]

The tortuous path of Habermas's prose leads finally into the airy reaches of transcendental philosophy, returning to the neo-Kantian environment in which today's interpretive antinomies first took their distinctive shape. Habermas approaches this destination with caution; rather than escaping the antinomies of practical reason in one question-begging leap, he postulates ideal standards that remain stubbornly embedded in everyday discourse. And yet, unlike the generative metaphors, ethical maxims, and argument codes mentioned earlier, Habermas frames his model of genuine discourse in avowedly transcendental terms. This vertiginous move allows a qualified separation of evaluative standards from contextualized reasoning, thereby opening a space for critical reflection based on either perspective. Habermas uses the ideal standards to stir radical doubts about prevailing conventions of reasoning, but he also insists that ideal standards can be realized only in culturally specific arguments.[101]

In developing this subtle balance of perspectives, Habermas assigns a pivotal role to dialectic in public discourse, as though to mediate in the struggle between "rational" logic and "pragmatic" rhetoric. Along with Wenzel, he defines dialectic as the procedures of public argumention, in contrast to both products and processes.

> A communicatively achieved agreement must be based in the end on reasons. And the rationality of those who participate in this communicative practice is determined by whether, if necessary, they could, under suitable circumstances, provide reasons for their expressions. Thus the rationality proper to the communicative practice of everyday life points to the practice of argumentation as a *court of appeal* that makes it possible to continue communicative action with other means when disagreements can no longer be repaired with everyday routines and yet are not to be settled by the direct or strategic use of force.[102]

Habermas is prepared to go much farther than Toulmin, for example, in facing the consequences of disagreement over how argumentation should be handled in specific situations—and in treating these meta-arguments as critical events in socially organized reasoning. By locating his court of appeal in transcendental territory, Habermas leaves open the possibility that people can be systematically mistaken about their apparent success in resolving such disagreements. Indeed, as Habermas has argued, hidden power relationships may subvert practical reasoning when the strategic aims of particular actors distort the rigorously symmetrical conditions of the "ideal speech situation."[103] Finality and legitimacy can be assumed to coincide only in this transcendental, or counterfactual, space.

As Habermas is acutely aware, his transcendental move cannot eliminate the many paradoxes of practical reasoning as a part of human culture. The actual social practices by which public argumentation is commonly ended may not correspond to the ideal conditions that alone can ensure their legitimacy. In hypothetical terms, finality and legitimacy can come together only if the wider public shares a common vision—a set of premises that can resolve disagreements, with clarity and completeness, in the opinion of all participants. This is indeed a heroic vision; in contemporary culture, final decisions will remain vulnerable to critical attack, and any moral claims to either authority or legitimacy may prove undecidable. Even tacit discord over basic presumptions will lead to strategic competition, which may become public and adversarial if rival groups insulate their bedrock presumptions from public scrutiny.

> Cultural values do not count as universal; they are, as the name indicates, located within the horizon of the lifeworld of a specific group or culture. And values can be made plausible only in the context of a particular form of life. Thus the critique of value standards presupposes a shared preunderstanding among participants in the argument, a preunderstanding that is not at their disposal but constitutes and at the same time circumscribes the domain of the thematized validity claims.[104]

The notorious opacity of Habermas's work may stem from his stubborn refusal to collapse the competing claims of finality and legitimacy. This makes him an ambiguous ally of most of the interpretive schools examined in this chapter, notwithstanding their widely divergent presumptions. In keeping with the openness and tolerance represented in his model of the ideal speech situation, Habermas seems determined to repel the tendency of argument communities to close themselves off from dialogue. In his most recent work, he postulates the broadest possible "preunderstanding" for placing contemporary critics on common ground, despite their bitter struggles against each other.[105] Thus, in place of the antinomies documented in this chapter, Habermas tries to see beyond adversarial conflict to the transcendental vanishing point in which all differences are reconciled. It is a noble vision that incurs singular risks, not the least of which is an eclecticism that can mislead his followers into believing that the day of world harmony—while not here yet—is moving closer.[106]

Avoiding the hazards of presupposing foundations, Habermas's strategy is to reserve transcendental ground as a place to park the standards of legitimacy in public discourse. Once consigned to this utopian space, his model of ideal discourse has been stripped of all dialectical elements. Habermas can describe it only through indirect discourse: it is the place where strategic concerns have ceased to function, where intuitions carry stronger convictions than inferences, and where rationality is reduced to a pure product, innocent of procedure. This aspect of Habermas's complex theory shows the lasting influence of the Marburg neo-Kantians, nurtured by the eschatological strain in Frankfurt neo-Marxism. His vision of pure communicative action can take its rightful place alongside other utopias in both traditions, but it gets us no closer to understanding the varied forms of practical reasoning that continue to develop in our increasingly litigious, procedure-conscious world.[107]

In a public arena filled with suppressed strategic reasoning, Habermas's ideal model offers an irresistible temptation to anyone prepared to use the power of decisional finality as a substitute for legitimacy. When a community seems to

136

attach complete faith to any set of norms, whoever controls their specific application will view that process as a self-executing system of rules based on universal consensus. This is true not only in most philosophical and academic debate, but also in practical reasoning based on the authority of either scientific method or particular ethical standards.[108]

The reasons for this capture of legitimacy by procedural authority appear most clearly in the context of judicial proceedings, as discussed in earlier chapters. In particular, the sudden reversals in Supreme Court doctrine in recent decades illustrate the extraordinary capacity of practical reasoning to structure almost any set of decisions as the logical consequences of preexisting principles. The dialectic behind such procedures remains hidden behind unarticulated presumptions. In most cases, those presumptions can be detected only in moments of dramatic change, signaled by shifts in burdens of proof. Meanwhile, the custodians of final authority within any existing normative system may easily assume that the transcendental kingdom is already at hand, simply because no one bothers to challenge the unanalyzed presumptions that stand behind it.

Let us imagine, for instance, that an ideal speech community openly endorses the principles of equality and fairness that Habermas properly demands. As with comparable principles discovered in the American Constitution during the Warren Court era, the opportunities for strategic debate continue as specialized decision-makers struggle to apply these lofty principles to the ambiguities and uncertainties of everyday life.[109] Taken without Habermas's important diagnosis of contemporary cultural trends, his ideal model may suggest the practical reality of self-executing principles, mimicking the rhetoric of judicial review. But so long as his postulated "preunderstanding" of public life fails to extend all the way down to the details of modern culture, consensus on general principles will inevitably give way to strategic action in procedural execution.

A healthy counterweight to the transcendental side of Habermas can be found in the writings of argumentation theorist Charles Willard, which lead down a more terrestrial path. Willard's approach postpones the examination of ideal standards and concentrates directly on the procedures that enforce finality within contemporary argument communities. Reversing the emphasis in Habermas, he tries to view "rationality as a rhetorical phenomenon," premised on the inscrutable presuppositions that characterize any field.

> It is pointless to debate whether a field should seek impersonal and universal guarantors of knowledge. . . . My claim is that knowledge is in fact balkanized and that critical epistemics ought to consider carefully the problems this divisiveness raises. Put crudely, it is our present epistemic situation that we seek to know the truth in contexts ruled by authority and consensus. The study of

authority, consensus, and legitimation . . . is the twentieth century's principal epistemic project. It is our present epistemic situation that we do not know (for sure) whether there is a difference between genuine and conventional claims; we have no agreed-upon principles for drawing such contrasts.[110]

The linguistic pragmatism of recent years obscures the central rhetorical dilemmas of modern argument. At best, it uses transcendental logic to reassure us on the possibility of meaningful interpersonal communication, based on the same anti-bureaucratic utopian vision that was identified as the leading presumption of the CLS movement. But such models have little to say about contemporary reasoning, which is not just interpersonal but institutional in nature. Modern publics are searching for ways to address problems that impede a collective approach to the social environment and to common values. In the next two chapters, I shall explore the difficulties of building public consensus in the areas of technology and ethics. The dramatic extension of judicial analogies and procedures into environmental policy and medical decision-making points to the missing dialectical ingredients in modern debate. As Willard reminds us, it is still too early to congratulate ourselves for public accomplishments that have not yet been brought down from transcendental heights.

138

Even if we think we shall end up applauding the continued tension of contentiousness of the public sphere, even if we think argument principles will survive scrutiny, it would be a mistake to start out by taking them for granted. The public sphere is a disaster area, not an accomplished epistemic community; its history is filled with incrementalism and the traces of past compromises. We have "muddled through" rather than triumphed. We count ourselves lucky to get through a year without megadeath. We congratulate ourselves on pious holidays that the planet has not yet been destroyed. Whatever else the public sphere may be, it is full of objects to be handled with rubber gloves. We wipe our feet before leaving.[111]

Part II | Philosophical Presumptions

It is one of the strange facts of philosophy . . . that issues
that at one moment seem crucial, and about which
the hottest debate rages, suddenly, by a shift of light,
seem not only devoid of point,
but even without a plain sense:
we not only do not care about their
answers, but we have ceased to know what the
relevant questions mean.

—J. N. FINDLAY

Chapter 5 | The Erosion of Scientific Authority

The strategic underpinnings of scientific authority are revealed most clearly in the relation between science and public regulatory policy. Judicial proceedings have sharpened the question whether scientific hypotheses should be presumed innocent or guilty in the absence of definitive proof. And philosophers of science have raised the same issue in the broader context of scientific inquiry. Increasingly, the antinomy of finality and legitimacy has influenced the political and academic response to scientific reason. Unless the objectivity of science is carried to the vanishing point of transcendental consensus, or secured by a postulated criterion of reality, it seems to need quasi-judicial institutional structures for bringing closure to issues of public significance.

Authority and Community in Science and Technology

As the peculiar authority of judicial review grows in both public and rhetorical prestige, its success overlaps a corresponding decline in the privileged status of scientific reason. Unlike earlier crises in scientific authority (extending back more than three hundred years), this modern legalistic challenge is resolutely secular in nature and presents itself as a superior critical force. It thus reverses the standard presumption in prior conflicts between science and established religion, or between science and traditional morality. In the eyes of some critics, scientific reason has itself come to represent the pale wisdom of tradition, for which more progressive alternatives need to be found. The leading candidates, however, must still be described through indirect means, as they emerge slowly from some transcendental space posited beyond the scope of naturalistic inquiry.[1]

From the standpoint of scientific reason, which maintains an ambiguous claim to privileged status within the modern disciplines of social science, these meta-scientific critiques can be analyzed as secular religions along the lines pioneered by Durkheim.[2] Their contemporary expressions include the judicial fundamentalism of Owen Fiss and Edwin Meese, and also the rapidly ascending authority of ethical criticism in many academic as well as applied fields.[3] Moreover, such challenges draw support from both extremes of the antinomy of bounded rationality—not only from the neo-Aristotelian revolt against scientific naturalism but also from the post-structuralist rejection of foundationalist discourse. Even the process-oriented methods of practical reasoning add weight to this challenge, as dialectical elements of modern discourse lend themselves to transcendental speculation.[4]

Scientific authority is closely identified with objectivity—with the primacy of facts and other brute realities over mere ideas or subjective interpretations. Paradoxically, from at least the time of Descartes, human access to these objective standards has been forced to stand on circumstantial evidence that falls short of pure objectivity. Indeed, the appeal of scientific authority lies in its presumed indifference to human perspectives and desires.[5] By the beginning of this century, accompanying the spectacular rise of modern technology, this type of authority had become the central postulate for academic disciplines in the natural and social sciences, dominating rival claims from religious, political, and cultural traditions.[6] Freud's indignant dismissal of personal religious belief captures the resolve of scientific standards to preempt all competition. Despite the broad indulgence with which he greeted the darkest fantasies of the human psyche, Freud recognized scientific procedures as the highest tribunal for adjudicating claims to truth.

142

Justifications for scientific authority, nonetheless, have proved elusive; even simple explanations of how the tribunal of science functions (or ought to function) leave philosophers and scientists more or less dissatisfied.[7] Although this failure remains a nagging source of embarrassment, it has not prevented the continuing jurisdictional expansion of scientific standards. Important questions arise, however, in boundary conflicts between scientific norms and their political, cultural, and transcendental rivals; indeed, in the past several decades, such conflicts have yielded a predictable sense of crisis.[8] Whereas it was once believed that scientific procedures might ultimately guide the political and cultural spheres toward greater enlightenment, it is now more fashionable to investigate the political and cultural frameworks surrounding scientific expertise. All of a sudden, scientific reasoning seems to have sprouted its own set of dialectical procedures, to which judicial metaphors and institutional structures can be applied. These changes mark the erosion of traditional boundaries that once separated the competing jurisdictions of scientific investigation, technological applications, and the conduct of public policy.

Scientific authority in the twentieth century rests on a set of assumptions that have fallen chiefly to philosophers for interpretation. In reversing the idealist presumptions of various nineteenth-century movements, modern philosophical realism generally follows the "critical" direction taken by Kant.[9] According to this view, scientific theories do not directly correspond to an independent reality; at best they can be correlated with predigested forms of human experience. Verification in scientific procedure gets no farther than the structured knowledge of particular scientific communities, but it is nonetheless assumed to refer to a reality that transcends human experience. According to one early twentieth-century exponent of this Kantian postulate, "The very nature of knowledge . . . unconditionally presupposes that the reality known exists independently of the knowledge of it. . . . It is simply impossible to think that any reality depends on our knowledge of it."[10]

The activity of science thus calls for highly refined procedures that reflect a functional image of reality, much as the judicial process assumes a rigorously functional approach to justice. Taking into account both the natural and social sciences, this inventory of procedures includes the mathematization of data, operational definitions, hypothetical-deductive methods of theory construction, controlled conditions of experimentation, canons of interpretation for experimental results, and conventional standards of reliability.[11] Although lacking the institutional hierarchy of legal systems, scientific procedures are identified with distinct communities of investigators, through which judgments of scientific validity are rendered.[12]

143

Just how well this network serves the dialectical goal of finality, in practical terms, is open to dispute. In response to the familiar claim by philosophers of science that experimental inquiry is infinitely reviewable, I shall explore later in this chapter the critical role of presumptions in the scientific approach to finality. Whether all theories are deemed guilty until proven innocent seems to depend on the skill of prevailing scientific communities in manipulating burdens and standards of proof.

The procedural framework of scientific inquiry, including personal and social contexts, has long been a standard theme in American pragmatism.[13] The close connection between scientific procedures and legal dialectic was often emphasized by Dewey, who was fond of applying scientific procedural analogies to law—an intriguing reversal of Toulmin's basic strategy. Joining the attack on the legal realists' favorite target, "mechanical jurisprudence," Dewey criticized the "failure to recognize that general legal rules and principles are working hypotheses, needing to be constantly tested by the way in which they work out in application to concrete situations." Such failure, Dewey notes, leads to the legalistic fixation on rules rather than applications, and it "explains the otherwise paradoxical fact that the slogans of the liberalism of one period often become the bulwarks of reaction in a subsequent era."[14] The crucial decision whether to stick with prior legal interpretations rather than substituting new ones is always a situational judgment, according to Dewey, rendered by the custodians of judicial procedure in every new case. This analogy draws attention to the dialectical context of rules that was largely ignored by the jurisprudential rhetorics examined in chapter 4, all the way from Toulmin to speech-act theories of argumentation.

It is worth pursuing Dewey's scientific analogy still further, as he applies it to the practice of formal reasoning within legal systems. His highly contextual model of inquiry brings to center stage precisely what gets shifted to the background in recent theories of action based on postulated generative-rule systems.

> As a matter of fact, men do not begin thinking with premises. They begin with some complicated and confused case, apparently admitting of alternative modes of treatment and solution. Premises only gradually emerge from analysis of the total situation. The problem is not to draw a conclusion from given premises; that can best be done by a piece of inanimate machinery by fingering a keyboard. The problem is to find statements of general principle and of particular fact that are worthy to serve as premises.

Applying this conception to legal decisions, Dewey reverses the customary legal pretense that preexisting rules dominate conclusions.

144

> We generally begin with some vague anticipation of a conclusion (or at least of alternative conclusions), and then we look around for principles and data which will substantiate it or which will enable us to choose intelligently between rival conclusions. No lawyer ever thought out the case of a client in terms of the syllogism. He begins with a conclusion which he intends to reach, favorable to his client, of course, and then analyzes the facts of the situation to find material out of which to construct a favorable statement of facts, to *form* a minor premise. At the same time he goes over recorded cases to find rules of law employed in cases which can be presented as similar, rules which will substantiate a certain way of looking at and interpreting the facts. . . . In strict logic, the conclusion does not follow from premises; conclusions and premises are two ways of stating the same thing.[15]

Dewey's scientific metaphors for jurisprudence were simply a footnote to his larger theory of experimental logic.[16] For him, the dialectical structure of law followed from the social and institutional demands of scientific method, which grounded the selection and testing of hypotheses in all types of inquiry. Instead of locating scientific authority in transcendental levels of objectivity, as philosophical realisms continually recommend, Dewey looked to the existing community of scientific investigators, operating under the guidance of political institutions.[17] This made Dewey more than just a persistent champion of the coherence approach to truth, which seeks to avoid the paradoxes of realist-inspired correspondence theories. In addition, Dewey analyzed the social, political, and dialectical procedures by which coherence is created, identified, and maintained in everyday communities. This degree of contingency would seriously overload most recent linguistic and semantic approaches to coherence, whose model is dominated by the spontaneous, nondiscursive process of competent performance in language use.[18]

Dewey was also keenly aware that the conditions for successful inquiry, by his definition, were dependent on the political and cultural strengths of specific communities. Neither legitimacy nor finality in social decisions could be guaranteed by procedure alone but were available (if at all) only in the retrospective judgment of future communities.[19] Hence the fundamental irony, noted by critics of pragmatism, that the intelligent society never actually knows anything but is always about to have known everything. Inferences of any consequence were invariably based on some degree of ignorance, under the expectation that society would always find some practical way to deliberate over its basic presumptions and would eventually come to deal explicitly with burdens and standards of proof.

As Dewey became an increasingly astute observer of political processes, he lost his initial faith that democratic institutions were strong enough to perform these difficult epistemological tasks. Indeed, his ruminations on "the public and its problems"[20] acknowledged that the social achievement of both finality and legitimacy was slipping beyond the grasp of the public sphere. As my theory in this book has suggested, this perceived loss of communal self-confidence has hastened the skeptical turn in public discourse. The contemporary distance from Dewey's approach can be measured precisely by the return of judicial review as a public rhetorical style, popular not only in the judicial process itself but in the post-structuralist mode of cultural criticism.

Technical Authority and the Uses of Presumption

In human endeavors requiring the cooperation of modern technology, the construction of guiding premises presents a significant challenge to both social and scientific procedures. Indeed, in most cases this process goes virtually unnoticed, and the premises of action are established largely by default. This happens in part because the respective communities that administer social and scientific procedures rarely overlap; and, in fact, either one may become fragmented in ways that stall the progress of inquiry. Nonetheless, to the extent scientific authority can be made to speak in a clear voice, it is often invoked in public debate as a source of fundamental premises for social action.

In the absence of social or cultural norms with broad popular support, such appeals to underlying facts based on scientific theories have enormous strategic value in shifting the risk of non-persuasion. The very concept of the burden of proof obscures this strategic function in the central metaphor of empirical science: when individual points of view come into conflict, we simply let "the evidence" decide between them. As Charles Willard has noted, "Science is the public sphere's evidentiary standard. The public sphere is utterly dependent upon the argument-from-authority, and science is its paradigm case."[21]

In recent years, however, rival sources have emerged within public discourse to challenge the putative authority of science, especially in the complex political debate over environmental policy. In the past, such rivals have been easily dismissed as reactionary in contrast to the objective (if confidently forward-looking) posture of empirical science.[22] But more recently, critiques of scientific expertise have emerged that purport to rest on higher, transcendental authority. Social commentators in earlier decades raised similar claims, including the higher law invoked by Lippmann and Hutchins in the 1940s. The fact that such arguments by-passed the use of scientific evidence was vital to their appeal; their superior jurisdiction over neutral science was based on a peculiar, self-validating moral authority.[23]

146

Today these transcendental critiques are no longer so peculiar. A novel idiom of public argument has emerged, entirely different from the appeal to evidence, in order to challenge the objectivist rhetoric of empirical proof. The rhetorical deadlock between science and ethics is our reward for decades of tacit adherence to the fateful neo-Kantian dichotomy between facts and values. It scarcely needs saying that this conflict becomes self-perpetuating, in that its resolution cannot be effected by either facts or values in isolation from the other. Perhaps the only serious chance for rhetorical compromise rests with the institutional authority of the legal process, with its unique aspirations to satisfy social demands for both finality and legitimacy.[24] But legal systems are susceptible to abrupt pendulum shifts in basic presumptions and thus become fragile guardians for protecting any particular moral vision.

In most settings, however, there remain powerful attractions to arguing one's position on the strength of facts, especially when the opposing view can thereby be relegated to a noncognitive realm of subjective intuition. Students of public decision-making have documented such strategies, often in settings involving high-technology decisions. In a recent survey of American science policy, for example, David Dickson finds a resurgence in the 1980s "of an almost religious belief—dormant for much of the 1970s—in the powers of science based technology." According to Dickson, this development parallels a steady sharpening of rhetorical conflicts between two perspectives on public regulation of technology: "the *democratic*, embracing values that supporters describe as humane and socially just, and critics deride as emotional and irrational; and the *technocratic*, defended by the same critics as scientific and rational, criticized by others as unfeeling and anti-democratic."[25]

Even within a purely technical domain, however, facts play a complex strategic role in organizational decision-making. In a study of events surrounding the ill-fated Challenger space mission in 1986, Richard Ice argues that factual controversies are often heavily structured by tacit presumptions, which become the default assumptions embedded in organizational dynamics.[26] Instead of actively constructing the major premise of their deliberations—the ideal behind Dewey's model of scientific inquiry—the scientist-administrators at NASA imposed a presumption structure in evaluating the now-famous O-rings, whose malfunction was later blamed for causing the accident. According to Ice, in the days before the Challenger launch, NASA officials were operating with a guiding philosophy that controlled the deployment and evaluation of facts concerning the safety of the Challenger craft: "Management at NASA presumed flight readiness and that those questioning that readiness shouldered the burden of proof." This interpretation is supported by testimony before the Presidential Commission that investigated the accident: "Since the earliest days of the manned space flight program that I've [Crippen] been associated with and Mr. Armstrong has been associated with, our basic philosophy is: Prove to me we're ready to fly. And somehow it seems in this particular instance we have switched to: Prove to me we are not able to fly."[27]

When engineers from Morton Thiokol (manufacturers of the O-rings) questioned the possible effect of record-low temperatures only one day before the Challenger launch, they came up against an opposing organizational presumption. They were told by NASA that their initial recommendation was "appalling" to space officials and ordered to reexamine their data.

> Thus when the members of the Thiokol group were sent into caucus, they felt they needed to come back to the main teleconference with "conclusive" data which demonstrated that they should not certify flight readiness.
>
> Indeed the members at Thiokol believed that they had to prove that the flight was not ready. As Robert Lund put it: ". . . we [the engineers at Thiokol] were trying to find some way to prove to them it wouldn't work and we were unable to do that. We couldn't prove absolutely that the motor wouldn't work."

According to still another Thiokol engineer: "This was a meeting where the determination was to launch, and it was up to us to prove beyond a shadow of a doubt that it was not safe to do so. This is a total reverse of what the position usually is in a preflight conversation or a flight readiness review. It is usually exactly opposite that." [28] In short, the burden of proof was assigned to those who questioned the decision to launch, under circumstances where scientific proof was less than conclusive.

The need to conjure with burdens of proof grows out of the peculiar kind of uncertainty that accompanies all scientific investigation. This uncertainty is not simply due to lack of relevant information, but also to the gap between particular evidence (in any quantity) and the universality of scientific laws. The same gulf separates evidence and theories, whether one adopts the inductive model of scientific method or the hypothetical-deductive model. [29] In the everyday practice of scientific inquiry, investigators must reach tacit agreement about the problematic status of hypotheses, which can be treated as either guilty or innocent pending the termination of inquiry. But since the whole notion of termination is left to the dialectical framework of scientific procedure, the underlying presumption of guilt or innocence can be indefinitely conserved or abruptly reversed. Thus there is no escape from the dilemmas of legitimacy and finality that were described in earlier chapters. Appeals to scientific authority in public policy debates are invariably wrapped in complex argument strategies, from which no bedrock notion of facts can extract them. [30]

The presumption of guilt or innocence for scientific hypotheses can be variously approached under competing techniques of empirical inquiry. In environmental policy disputes, such variations may account for conflicting reactions from scientists about prominent risks to public health and safety. In recent years, traditional laboratory science has come into conflict with epidemiological research methods, which have generated a rich fund of hypotheses connecting injuries and health risks to hazardous substances, cultural patterns, and personal behavior. Although both methods rightly claim to be scientific, they supply quite different premises for public regulation of environmental risk, based on fundamentally different approaches to causation.

Laboratory science treats the risk of human injury as an extrapolation from smaller causal hypotheses that have survived laboratory analysis. In the case of cigarette smoking and lung cancer, for example, the link has been postulated largely on the basis of chemical analysis and animal studies involving massive exposures. But specific hypotheses from such studies are always subject to revision, and the critical leap of extrapolating to human beings in a nonlaboratory environment is itself intrinsically untestable. If public policy for regulating public risk is supposed to wait until scientific evidence supplies a solid basis for intervention, it may have to wait for decades. Indeed, no hypothesis is ever strong enough to preclude later falsification; and in this sense a presumption of guilt clings to all hypotheses until scientific inquiry is closed off.

By contrast, the risk of human injury counts as a basic datum for epidemiology, starting from broad statistical correlations between environmental events and suspected agents. Since it is not based on inductive logic, epidemiological research never even tries to show that any particular event (for example, a single diagnosis of lung cancer) was actually caused by a particular agent (cigarette smoking, asbestos, radiation). Its statistical method starts with broad categories and then moves slowly, by the controlled manipulation of aggregate variables, toward more concrete conclusions. Along the way, any significant correlations of harmful events and environmental agents may serve as premises for public intervention. If residents near the site of a major toxic waste dumping site fall victim to an unusual number of serious diseases (beyond the standard base rates for a control population), that relationship starts to speak for itself. The logic of epidemiology—reinforced by public opinion—will change this initial presumption of causation only when more discriminating correlations have been established. Until that time, the initial correlation (like the criminal defendant) enjoys a presumption of innocence.[31]

149

In public debate over environmental regulation, contrary presumptions are frequently established for dealing with potential health risks, based on contrasting appeals to scientific evidence. This dichotomy is strikingly similar to the broader rhetorical choice of presumptions in public debate, which G. Thomas Goodnight has characterized as "liberal" and "conservative" ways of allocating burdens of proof.[32] Goodnight defines *presumption* as: "that advantage which resides with one side in a dispute which, absent the dispute, would be successful. The side which is not attributed presumption need not even argue, absent a prima facie case presented by the opposition. The question, why one side is favored and the other not, is central; in its answer can be found the epistemological and axiological assumptions of any theory of argument." Goodnight views social negotiation over presumptions as a symptom of public attitudes toward the risk of being wrong.

> Presumption is that tension between the premature denial of new knowledge, falsely retaining old knowledge, on the one hand, and the premature acceptance of new knowledge falsely denying old knowledge on the other. Although this tension is implicit in every argument, the reasons why some risks are taken and not others may not be fully understood or even rendered expressible. Over the long term, however, which risks are accepted as routine and

which in so far as possible are avoided discloses the structure of presumption for an individual, method, and community.[33]

In the heat of controversy over public regulation, the *structure of presumption* is subject to volatile changes. Whenever legislative standards succeed in defining some presumption within a limited field of regulation, opponents can either meet the formidable burden of proof assigned to them or attack the official standard as unscientific.

The second option has been the overwhelming strategy of interest groups opposed to the Delaney clause of the national Food, Drug, and Cosmetic Act, which blocks federal approval of food additives that carry any risk of public injury.[34] David O'Brien has reviewed the great saccharin controversy of the late 1970s, which placed the Delaney clause at the center of adversarial debate. Notwithstanding the likely political commitments of many scientists and commentators on the topic of cancer-causing agents, O'Brien shows how this controversy also involved rival models of scientific procedure. "Depending on whether some or all of [the] assumptions identified with the no-safe-threshold model of carcinogenesis are accepted, risk assessments will take either a conservative or a liberal bias toward regulation of alleged health-safety or environmental risks."[35]

Legislative hearings and court proceedings are common forums for disputes over scientific presumptions. In a detailed study of Congressional oversight hearings on the problem of hazardous waste, Jane Kronick and her colleagues have analyzed the strategic implications of conflicting appeals to scientific authority. After describing the inherent "tension between knowledge and action," Kronick concludes that "the consensus requirements for dealing 'scientifically' with the problem of hazardous waste in America is either presently simply impossible or impractical."[36] In testimony by corporate officials whose companies were implicated in various environmental disasters, she finds "a common pattern of defense," which consists of "an appeal to ignorance and presumes that the burden of proof of damage rests with the presumed injured parties, or, perhaps, with government agencies."

> The first line of defense is that no one can prove that there has been any damage. If evidence of damage is compelling, then there is no sufficient proof that the company is the source of the damaging toxic substance. If somehow there is strong evidence that the company is the source of the contaminants, then the officials urge that they were in conformity with government regulations, that there may have been carelessness by some of their personnel or inadequate supervision or inadequate record keeping.

Kronick also compares the strengths and weaknesses of epidemiological and laboratory-science approaches to documenting public health risks. Epidemiology plays "only a very limited projective role" and is more a source for future research hypotheses than a set of conclusions. Laboratory-science techniques, based on case-by-case controlled experiments, are inordinately costly and time-consuming. "Insofar as many health problems have a lengthy latency period, one might only know several generations after the exposure, assuming one can keep track of several generations, whether there has, indeed, been any harm effected." If critics require "that officials 'know' in some strong 'scientific' sense before they act, then action and policy are paralyzed and the call to science amounts to the impossibility of public policy and public action."[37] This conclusion aptly describes public debate during the 1980s over broad environmental problems like acid rain, ozone depletion, and the greenhouse effect.

In judicial proceedings, the structure of presumption hovers close to the surface, in part because the failure to change the status quo usually has immediate consequences for parties to a lawsuit. In complex litigation surrounding environmental accidents, it is not unusual for courts at different levels of the judicial hierarchy to shift presumptions; and adversarial argumentation ensures that lucid alternatives are never far from reach. For cases involving scientific assessments, the judicial rhetoric of evidence and burdens of proof offers the court virtually unlimited flexibility.

The full range of available presumptions can be found in the judicial record of a case involving the Reserve Mining Company of Minnesota, as summarized by O'Brien.[38] Reserve Mining came under investigation in the 1960s for its practice of extracting iron from taconite, thereby sending large quantities of potentially hazardous residues into Lake Superior. In 1969 a variety of environmental interests brought suit to enforce stricter controls on the disposal of taconite waste ("tailings"). By the time the Reserve Mining case entered the federal courts in the mid-1970s, extensive evidence had been collected by both sides, leading to a trial that "lasted 139 days, with testimony from over 100 witnesses and scientific experts, and more than 1,600 exhibits entered into evidence. The trial transcript eventually exceeded 18,000 pages."[39]

Ruling against Reserve Mining, the trial court judge endorsed the reasoning of his court-appointed expert, who inferred a duty to intervene from the very uncertainty of the hazards.

As a physician, I take the view that I cannot consider, with equanimity, the fact that a known human carcinogen is in the environment. If I knew more about that human carcinogen, if I knew what a safe level was in the water,

151

then I could draw some firm conclusions and advise you in precise terms. That information is not available to me and I submit, sir, it's not available to anyone else. But the presence of a known human carcinogen, sir, is in my view cause for concern, and if there are means for removing the human carcinogen from the environment, that should be done.[40]

Initially, the Court of Appeals blocked the lower court's decision pending review, based on a response to scientific uncertainty that was, in O'Brien's words, "basically the opposite of [lower-court Judge] Lord."[41]

We do not think that a bare risk of the unknown can amount to proof in this case. Plaintiffs have failed to prove that a demonstrable health hazard exists. This failure, we hasten to add, is not reflective of any weakness which it is within their power to cure, but rather, given the current state of medical and scientific knowledge, plaintiffs' case is based only on medical hypothesis and is simply beyond proof. We believe that Judge Lord carried his analysis one step beyond the evidence. Since testimony clearly established that an assessment of the risk was made impossible by the absence of medical knowledge, Judge Lord apparently took the position that all uncertainties should be resolved in favor of health safety.[42]

Upon full review, however, the Court of Appeals accepted the initial ruling; and although Judge Lord himself was later removed from the case, the lower court was able to negotiate an agreement ending the discharge of taconite tailings into Lake Superior.[43]

Paradigm Shifts and the Dialectic of Scientific Theories

Alongside the fragmentation of scientific authority in public policy debates, philosophers of science over the past several decades have raised skeptical doubts about the nature and evolution of scientific theories. As a result, science as a tribunal for determining truth or certainty has lost much of its presumed authority to speak with finality and legitimacy.[44] This challenge to science has opened the door still wider to various metascientific rivals, as well as to greater judicial oversight of scientific opinion in the conduct of public policy.

The philosophical assault on scientific finality was led by Karl Popper, who argued that no amount of material evidence could definitively establish the universal laws demanded by modern scientific theory.[45] The tribunal for matching basic facts and theories had to remain in continuous session, and thus science could be understood only as a process rather than the product of inquiry. Going beyond Popper's procedural analysis, Thomas Kuhn's historical treatment of the physical sciences popularized the concept of *paradigm* as the mutative cloak of scientific legitimacy.[46] Along with other studies emphasizing the social and cultural frameworks of scientific communities, Kuhn's work seemed to qualify the validity of all scientific pronouncements: outside the narrow professional circles of "normal science," according to Kuhn, scientific truth became a problem rather than a premise.[47] Kuhn's paradigms can be interpreted as yet another manifestation of dialectical presumptions lurking behind the inescapably social procedures of public discourse. Moreover, his scientific revolutions can be seen as historical examples of institutionalized shifts in the burden of proof, similar in their effect to the major pendulum swings known to occur in other tribunals.

In light of Kuhn's theories, Popper's revisions of the classic scientific model now seem relatively moderate. Nonetheless, they were influential among philosophers of science for shifting the measure of scientific authority away from approximations to independent truth and toward the ideal of correct procedure.[48] Beyond this shift to proceduralism, Popper's theory of science took a highly polemical approach to the relation between experimental evidence and scientific theories. By declaring the goal of science to be falsification of theories rather than verification, he directly reversed the standard presumption of scientific method, established by Francis Bacon.[49] At issue was the conclusion scientists were entitled to draw from a type of ignorance that Popper described as endemic to science. Because of the epistemological gap between timeless, universal theories and timebound, particular evidence, Popper argued that their correlation would always be imperfect—no matter how coherent or plentiful the evidence might be. Theories could thus never be proved innocent, in Popper's view, although they might be found guilty under properly controlled conditions.

The process of scientific inquiry, according to Popper, was a system of hurdles deliberately placed in the path of hypotheses. Failure could be inferred whenever any hurdles got knocked down; but the obstacle course was infinite in scope and thus could offer no respite for the heroic scientist. Moreover, Popper viewed the distinctive virtue of scientific practice as launching vulnerable hypotheses down the track, even as the entire course was being lengthened and upgraded in difficulty.[50]

From an historical view, the parallels are striking with the basic strategy of due process jurisprudence under the stewardship of the Warren Court. Both models reflect the postulates of proceduralized reason that has grown skeptical of its traditional task: discovering truth in the objective correspondence of theory and reality. In addition, both models tacitly presume that the dominant purpose of inquiry is to defeat certain claims of innocence (claims raised by scientific hypotheses in one realm and by bureaucratic actions in the other).[51]

153

Finally, both models are compelled to find practical limits to the idealism of their respective missions. Beyond the isolation of pure theory, modern technology needs scientific hypotheses that are good enough for everyday use; just as modern societies depend on collective action that goes beyond checking its own transgressions. In practice, most of what passes as scientific theory never confronts the rigors of testing against the facts, any more than the courts are able to review all the actions of public agencies. Popper increasingly faces up to this condition in his later writings through his problematic notion that theories can be "corroborated," even if not verified.[52]

Popper's approach to scientific method is thus both selective and normative, and not merely descriptive. Wise scientific practice presumably calls for some of the passive virtues extolled by judicial moderates during the Warren Court era and requires a kind of situation-sense about when to apply the skeptical review implied by Popper's doctrine that true scientific progress occurs with falsification rather than verification. Universal application of this skeptical standard would result in the sort of relativistic chaos that Popper eventually came to oppose even more than the positivist dogmas of verifiability. To apply Popper's norm selectively, however, suggests a strategic context in which scientists must continually determine whether to exercise strict scrutiny of experimental results or to presume the maintenance of the status quo. As Kuhn would suggest, a demurrer to prevailing scientific conclusions is usually not part of a conscious strategy, but rather a sign that the scientific community no longer shares common standards.

When Popper's falsifiability doctrine shifts the burden of proof onto upholders of prevailing opinion, it supports a strategy that can represent itself as costless: skepticism thus retreats behind the cover of neutral science. By contrast, the civil rights lawsuit acknowledges its zero-sum consequences through the adversary structure, which pins the cost of due process violations on particular agencies or individuals. Popper can identify no comparable representative of the scientific status quo, except to suggest darkly its potential conspiracy with repressive social power. Popper's attack on the "enemies" of the "open society" matches the suspicion of the civil liberties litigator in exposing official misconduct.[53] Indeed, one suspects that the passion with which Popper and his followers defended his model of science (an ironic sentiment, considering its self-critical posture) came largely from a desire to counter the disintegration of nonscientific culture by reasserting traditional liberal ideals of tolerance and openness.[54]

Popper originally developed his approach at a time when realist theories of science were running out of strategies for reconciling the increasingly baroque constructions of twentieth-century science with common-sense views of brute reality. His position shared numerous assumptions with the Viennese positivists,

154

even though his distinctive contribution was to reverse their heroic presumption that scientific theory held up some kind of mathematical mirror to an independent, material reality. For Popper, that reality became as remote and inaccessible as the Kantian world of things-in-themselves. Human experience, by contrast, was a network of artful constructions that reached their highest level in scientific theories, including the models created by Viennese positivism.[55] This explains why Popper would later find himself labeled a positivist by critics who otherwise shared his assimilation of truth and procedure but who chose to explore procedures altogether different from scientific method.[56]

As with other philosophers who substitute investigatory procedures for direct correlations between theory and reality, Popper was attracted to judicial analogies. His focus, however, was restricted to the determination of basic facts as opposed to the dialectical implementation of rules. In passages reminiscent of legal-realist statements on "fact skepticism," Popper declared that "every test of a theory, whether resulting in its corroboration, or falsification, must stop at some basic statement or other which we *decide to accept.*"[57] The Viennese positivists had postulated such basic statements ("protocol sentences") as reports on direct human contact with an assumed independent, physical reality.[58] Popper rejected both the empirical-realist and the linguistic-transcendentalist interpretation of basic statements and considered them instead the products of psychological judgments reached by scientific investigators. They are analogous, he said, to the determinations of fact reached by juries in criminal trials, which he referred to as "verdicts."[59]

> By its decision, the jury accepts, by agreement, a statement about a factual occurrence—a basic statement, as it were. The significance of this decision lies in the fact that from it, together with the universal statements of the system (of [rules of] criminal law) certain consequences can be deduced. . . . The verdict is reached in accordance with a procedure which is governed by rules. These rules are based on certain fundamental principles which are chiefly, if not solely, designed to result in the discovery of objective truth. They sometimes leave room not only for subjective convictions but even for subjective bias.[60]

Although Popper's iconoclasm was focused on this eminently disputable point found in his Viennese predecessors, he seemed to ignore any larger application of the judicial analogy in relation to legal rules.

> In contrast to the verdict of the jury, the judgment of the judge is "reasoned"; it needs, and contains, a justification. The judge tries to justify it by, or deduce it logically from, other statements: the statements of the legal system,

155

combined with the verdict that plays the role of initial conditions. This is why the judgment may be challenged on logical grounds. The jury's decision, on the other hand, can only be challenged by questioning whether it has been reached in accordance with the accepted rules of procedure; i.e. formally, but not as to its content.[61]

Popper uses his judicial analogy to explain the inescapable relativity of basic statements—those elusive tangents between scientific authority and a supposed independent reality. Although more daring forms of relativism were already poised to invade the philosophy of science, Popper fortified his challenge to the troubled realism of the Viennese positivists with graphic metaphors suggesting the cosmic impermanence of scientific foundations.

> The empirical basis of objective science has thus nothing "absolute" about it. Science does not rest upon rock-bottom. The bold structure of its theories rises, as it were, above a swamp. It is like a building erected on piles. The piles are driven down from above into the swamp, but not down to any natural or "given" base; and when we cease our attempts to drive our piles into a deeper layer, it is not because we have reached firm ground. We simply stop when we are satisfied that they are firm enough to carry the structure, at least for the time being.[62]

156

If Popper's role was to bring fact-skepticism to the tribunal of science, Kuhn added the equivalent of rule-skepticism.[63] Like Viennese positivism as a whole, Popper's theory of scientific method accepted the self-executing model of deductive reasoning as a sufficient means for ordering multiple levels of scientific axioms and theorems; the problem was in contriving some factual basis on which to rest the entire deductive edifice. Popper encountered a different type of problem, however, in approaching the methodological norms (or conventions) that guide the logical development of theories and regulate all contact between hypotheses and judgments of fact.[64] Kuhn can be understood as extending Popper's procedurally based skepticism to include the deployment of methodological norms in addition to the vetting of basic facts.

Kuhn's paradigms have been widely discussed, and their protean meanings have been exhaustively catalogued and debated.[65] Rather than torturing Kuhn's definitions any further, let us compare his concept to the procedural dialectic of public discourse, which is institutionalized most concretely in the process of judicial interpretation. Seen in this light, the paradigm encloses the nonformalized context in which rules of any depth are interpreted and applied to concrete situations. Paradigms are the diverse presumptions that stand in the background and unify a field of practice but are ordinarily invisible to the practitioners who employ them. They define discrete jurisdictions within which rules may be interpreted as self-executing, much like Stephen Toulmin's fields of argument. They ultimately determine what counts as proof (including what the jury may reasonably discover to be true in particular situations), but they also assign the risk of non-persuasion on matters that are understood to lie beyond the scope or competence of judge and jury.

The very plasticity of Kuhn's term seems congenial to the judicial model: a paradigm covers everything from an exemplary experiment to tacit personal knowledge, and on further to metaphysical presuppositions.[66] In the same way that judges can be variously understood as following a landmark precedent, introducing personal bias into a case, or drawing on unstated normative assumptions, the paradigm covers a potentially wide range of scientific judgments oriented to either concrete or abstract presumptions.

Judges retroactively reconstitute the rules of their trade in ways that offer a rational path through the decisions they reach. Rule-skepticism does not ignore this rhetorical convention in law; but it reverses the traditional priority between outcomes and rules, treating the selection of rules as symptoms of unarticulated presumptions. Kuhn discovers a similar relationship between the rules formulated in normal scientific inquiry and the tacit assumptions that supersede them.

Scientists work from models acquired through education and through subsequent exposure to the literature often without quite knowing or needing to know what characteristics have given these models the status of community paradigms. And because they do so, they need no full set of rules. The coherence displayed by the research tradition in which they participate may not imply even the existence of an underlying body of rules and assumptions that additional historical or philosophical investigation might uncover. That scientists do not usually ask or debate what makes a particular problem or solution legitimate tempts us to suppose that, at least intuitively, they know the answer. But it may only indicate that neither the question nor the answer is felt to be relevant to their research. Paradigms may be prior to, more binding, and more complete than any set of rules for research that could be unequivocally abstracted from them.[67]

Kuhn compares the process of articulating a paradigm within a scientific community with the elaboration of legal rules by an active judiciary. "A paradigm is rarely an object for [mere] replication. Instead, like an accepted judicial decision in the common law, it is an object for further articulation and specification under new or more stringent conditions."[68] The analogy with adjudication helps clarify the dialectical features of science that contribute both to its steady evolution during normal periods and to the sudden revolutions to which Kuhn draws special attention. Novelty and change quickly outstrip the formal structure of a closed deductive system, but they are the normal expectation for any active legal process. As long as new cases can be easily assigned to the loose categories provided by existing precedents, the entire process remains one of conservation. The precedents invariably harbor potential uses that were not anticipated at their creation, and they must continually be shaded and embellished to remain part of a coherent, dynamic body of law. Judicial craftsmanship is expected to perform these tasks while drawing as little attention as possible to the gaps, open textures, discretionary judgments, and split decisions that haunt the operational legal systems of heterogeneous societies.[69]

Kuhn's chronicle of theoretical science emphasized the periodic breakdowns in this evolutionary model. For reasons that fall completely outside his explanatory categories, Kuhn noted, scientific communities may suddenly find themselves in a state of crisis, in which the extension of a prevailing paradigm no longer seems automatic to its interpreters. The new cases cease to fit the existing precedents; mundane problems that were previously settled quietly by skilled technique suddenly become anomalies that fragment the community. The comfortable open texture that allowed continuous expansion becomes a yawning gulf that divides polarized factions. The legal system actually lives somewhat closer to this edge than the scientific community, since the adversary structure of adjudication encourages the parties to articulate opposing views on all aspects of the normative status quo.[70]

Kuhn's paradigms—although they can be mistaken for static concepts—have a dynamic life similar to the activity of adjudication. They bring the same unifying force to scientific communities that we have identified more broadly as the dialectical framework of public discourse. They are not to be confused with the rules, whether declared or tacit, according to which the community may account for its own activity. In a passage cited earlier, Kuhn concluded that "Paradigms may be prior to, more binding, and more complete than any set of rules for research that could be unequivocally abstracted from them."[71] In contrast to the rule-centered models of generative grammar and interactionist sociology, Kuhn believes that scientific activities cannot be fully explained in terms of constitutive rules. "One is at liberty to suppose that somewhere along the way the scientist has intuitively abstracted rules of the game for himself, but there is little reason to believe it."[72]

Indeed, Kuhn continues, the articulation of rules may be a signal that the paradigm has lost its earlier hold on the community: "Normal science can proceed without rules only so long as the relevant scientific community accepts without question the particular problem-solutions already achieved. Rules should therefore become important and the characteristic unconcern about them should vanish whenever paradigms or models are felt to be insecure." Kuhn insists that historical analysis bears out this tendency. Outside the range of normal science, one finds

> frequent and deep debates over legitimate methods, problems, and standards of solution, though these serve rather to define schools rather than to produce agreement. . . . Debates like these . . . recur regularly just before and during scientific revolutions, the periods when paradigms are first under attack and then subject to change. . . . When scientists disagree about whether the fundamental problems of their field have been solved, the search for rules gains a function that it does not ordinarily possess.[73]

Whereas Kuhn's main interest lies in documenting these patterns in the history of scientific theory, my purpose here is to understand the contemporary erosion of scientific authority in the wider field of public policy. Extending Kuhn's theory about the relation of paradigms and rules, one can speculate that judicialization of scientific argument reflects the fragmentation of authority presupposed by public appeals to scientific proof. The paradoxes are comparable to those attending scientific revolutions under Kuhn's model, when rival parties put forward conflicting models of reality in the absence of definitive tests that might select one model over the other.

It is perhaps more precise to say that definitive tests exist but that they are internal to the warring paradigms; what ensues is a jurisdictional battle for the privilege of imposing finality on otherwise intractable issues. From the internal standpoint, of course, each paradigm will experience the struggle as a battle between truth and error, not as a conflict to determine who will have the final authority to declare truth. As with the highest court in a jurisdiction, declarations by the prevailing paradigm establish a revised orthodoxy—complete with a redrafted set of rules that define the recent struggle as the suppression of civil rebellion against the immutable ideal of truth, rather than flat-out revolution. Courts project formal doctrines to consolidate the shift in proof burdens as part of the mopping-up process that accompanies legal revolutions.

The link to the shifting of proof burdens comes with Kuhn's notion that old paradigms are never abandoned until new ones are already firmly in place. The failure of a paradigm is not the result of a mismatch with neutral evidence from reality (as the victor will later insist), but rather it indicates a shift in standards by which proof is defined. Until some clear priority is established, the disputants speak at cross-purposes.

> Neither side will grant all the non-empirical assumptions that the other needs in order to make its case. Like Proust and Berthollet arguing about the composition of chemical compounds, they are bound partly to talk through each

other. Though each may hope to convert the other to his way of seeing his science and its problems, neither may hope to prove his case. The competition between paradigms is not the sort of battle that can be resolved by proofs.[74]

The invention of new proof standards by the victorious paradigm is concealed in the very process of change. Only the dissenting community of scientists will insist that a new paradigm lacks hard evidence. But the loser inherits the heavy burden of producing convincing evidence to challenge judgments endorsed by the new majority, under circumstances where the newly ascendant paradigm would exclude most conflicting evidence as irrelevant. The empiricist rhetoric of proof conceals this shift in standards that accompanies all dialectical revolutions, but the underlying change rises closest to the surface in landmark judicial opinions. There the underlying events are at least possible to discern, owing to the unique responsibility of judges to reconstruct their judgments in the idiom of deductive logic and empirical proof. Often it is the disgruntled dissenters (the prior majority) who call sharp attention to the change and to the hasty arguments assembled by an opportunistic majority.

Kuhn describes the analogous circumstances in scientific revolutions.

> Ordinarily, it is only much later, after the new paradigm has been developed, accepted, and exploited that apparently decisive arguments—the Foucault pendulum to demonstrate the rotation of the earth or the Fizeau experiment to show that light moves faster in air than in water—are developed. Producing them is part of normal science, and their role is not in paradigm debate but in postrevolutionary texts.
>
> Before those texts are written, while the debate goes on, the situation is very different. Usually the opponents of a new paradigm can legitimately claim that even in the area of crisis it is little superior to its traditional rival. . . . The older paradigm can presumably be articulated to meet these challenges as it has met others before. . . . In addition, the defenders of traditional theory and procedure can almost always point to problems that its new rival has not solved but that for their view are no problems at all.

Kuhn's conclusion could serve equally well as a commentary on the judicial trends examined in chapters 2 and 3: "In short, if a new candidate for a paradigm had to be judged from the start by hard-headed people who examined only relative problem-solving ability, the sciences would experience very few major revolutions. Add the counterarguments generated by . . . the incommensurability of paradigms, and the sciences might experience no revolutions at all."[75]

In light of these conclusions, Kuhn experienced a peculiar difficulty in documenting the historical reality of paradigm shifts. With no congenial sociological, political, or rhetorical categories of explanation ready to hand, Kuhn invented a series of colorful metaphors that doubtless enhanced the skeptical appeal of his overall theory. "The transfer of allegiance from paradigm to paradigm is a conversion experience that cannot be forced." Paradigms, he said, represent a practical solution to scientific crises, which are terminated

> not by deliberation and interpretation, but by a relatively sudden and unstructured event like the gestalt switch. Scientists then often speak of the "scales falling from the eyes" or the "lightning flash" that "inundates" a previously obscure puzzle, enabling its components to be seen in a new way that for the first time permits its solution. On other occasions the relevant illumination comes in sleep. No ordinary sense of the term "interpretation" fits these flashes of intuition through which a new paradigm is born.[76]

Rather than borrowing Kuhn's language of religious conversion, gestalt psychology, lightning flashes, or somnambulism, the study of proof burdens offers a conceptual fulcrum for supporting the sudden shifts that afflict not just scientific theory but also academic inquiry and public policy debate. Shifts in the burden of proof may seem less dramatic than gestalt switches, but their conceptual nature makes it possible to combine specific principles or dogmas into a polarity that unites two adversaries. The overall relationship between these parties can thus be interpreted as one of specific negation rather than the blanket opposition projected by either party. In most cases, a residual continuity still unites the two parties through common presumptions that remain in place despite the shift of particular burdens.

161

The Judicialization of Scientific Conflict: The Science Court

Quite apart from trends in the philosophy of science, the practice of science came under closer public scrutiny during the 1970s as the United States began implementing a series of national policies for regulating the human and natural environment. Scientists found themselves entangled in public controversies over such issues as food additives, ozone depletion, toxic waste, nuclear power, and acid rain, and eventually scientific authority began to mimic the fragmented discourse of political conflict. No serious interest group could afford to enter the political arena without assistance from a scientific staff, preferably one well stocked with prize winners and department heads from leading research universities. These bespectacled, lab-coated, technically fluent scientific experts conserved the outward images of scientific authority, but their conflicting messages sounded more like the legal briefs of skilled advocates.[77]

As public policy decisions began to lean more heavily on scientific premises, the boundaries of scientific authority became evident to a larger circle than professional philosophers. In political debate, an appeal to facts was meant to lend legitimacy to policy positions otherwise identified with special interests. But for reasons explored by the philosophy of science, the thin connection between factual evidence and hypotheses in laboratory research can never quite stretch to cover the wider gap between evidence and political decisions. Without the protective assumptions of normal-science paradigms, inference is little more than a bold surmise, and it cannot be expected to transfer the legitimacy of scientific procedure into public policy.

By locating the burden of proof in the Popperian manner, both scientific and lay partisans have learned how to cast significant doubt on affirmative uses of scientific evidence without risking any hypotheses of their own. Faced with unwelcome policy conclusions, critics can play the part of objective arbiters by documenting the inevitable failure of opposing experts to verify their hypotheses. As with legal criticism under the due process model, the safest role for scientists in public discourse is to play the hard-nosed skeptic. This strategy forces the opponent to bear the burden of proving scientific facts, preferably under an unattainable standard of proof. The same considerations apply to evidence drawn from the social sciences, which are even more likely than natural sciences to draw methodological crossfire from competing research programs.

162

The surest way to protect the legitimacy of scientific inferences from preemptive critique is to sacrifice the equally central dialectical goal of finality. Constructive advocates of scientific approaches to environmental policy are often successful in deflecting the nihilistic implications of Popperian skepticism, in much the same way that philosophers of science have softened the rigors of the falsifiability principle. They must, however, hold the tribunal of science in continuous session if they wish to prevent this metaphorical court from reaching final conclusions on the innocence or guilt of policy-related hypotheses. Alternatively, the potentially universal scope of scientific authority can be divided into discrete jurisdictions, where competing scientific communities are free to reach conflicting verdicts based on competing presumptions for defining facts and articulating rules. This outcome is perhaps no different from what happens to group debate in academic and political discourse, but it removes any strategic value that might be gained from an appeal to objectivity.[78]

Scientific knowledge now enters into public discourse through a series of dialectical conventions, which have evolved separately within the political arena, various knowledge communities, and the broader cultural sphere.[79] In the political setting, formal judicial institutions have now assumed the major responsibility for regulating applications of scientific findings to policy goals. This control can be shaped by legislative standards (and especially by rules for allocating the burden of proof), although the standards themselves remain subject to judicial review. In addition, courts hearing environmental lawsuits have to make count-less decisions on the admissibility and weight of scientific evidence, often with far-reaching consequences for future disputes. Increasingly, courts must adapt their institutional epistemology, built on the empiricism of Bacon, Bentham, and J. S. Mill, to the more complex hypotheses of modern epidemiological research.

Before the judicial system assumed this burden, an intermediate form of judicialization was widely discussed during the 1970s. Over many years, repre-sentatives of major scientific associations pondered the intriguing notion of a special *science court*, sometimes referred to as a Supreme Court of Science or a Technical Court of Inquiry. The science court initiative never stirred much en-thusiasm among a wide circle of scientists or policy-makers. However, through the efforts of a few indefatigable and well-placed sponsors, the concept was kept alive until the 1980s, and it was briefly considered as a concrete mechanism for resolving a bitter public dispute over power lines in Minnesota.[80] Even though the judicialization of scientific authority has since followed a very different route, the original aims of the proposed science court offer useful insights into the dia-lectical structure of science. To champions of the proposal, at least, this idealized judicial body supplied the missing ingredients for extending scientific knowledge more successfully to public purposes.

Contemporary views on the scientific grounding of public policy must be understood in their historical context. The federal government has a long record of reliance on scientific experts for policies concerned with environmental con-trol, national defense, and general commerce.[81] The scientific ideal and its poten-tial applications to public problems was critical to the rise of social science disciplines in the United States and was also closely tied to the political agenda of progressivism.[82] At the apex of this harmonious vision stood the pragma-tist theory that democracy and expertise were complementary functions, with Dewey's "public" serving as the normative community within which scientific research found both inspiration and salience.[83]

But if science gained its political foothold by supporting the liberal critique of traditional (nonexperimental) authority in religion and morality, that same skep-ticism later turned against the authority of expertise. In the aftermath of World War II, the presumption of harmony between public values and scientific leader-ship seemed to lose popular support: it became a troubled postulate instead of a self-evident premise.[84] Controversies over peaceful and military uses of nuclear power (in addition to other instruments of national defense) anticipated some of the polemics that would soon widen the gap between science and politics, stranding scientists on opposite sides of political questions. The environmental movement of the 1960s greatly accelerated these divisions. As a national environmental agenda took shape during the ensuing decade, scientific inference moved onto the battlefield of public discourse.

In 1976 a special task force drawn from President Ford's Science Advisory Group expressed cautious support for the science court proposal. According to the task force, success would depend on the new court's ability to separate "scientific fact" from "value-laden issues" that had begun to paralyze regulatory agencies. "Should fluorocarbons be banned because of their impact on the ozone layer? Is Red Dye #40 safer than Red Dye #2?" These were the kinds of questions the task force thought needed a new procedural response.[85] In evaluating this proposal, however, we must look beyond the dichotomies of fact/value and science/politics, which were quickly attacked by critics as simplistic.[86] The science court was never meant to dictate policy decisions but to halt the fragmentation of scientific authority.

As Arthur Kantrowitz, the author of the main proposal, had pointed out in 1967, science was increasingly called on to render final opinions on factual matters before the standard procedures of science were prepared to issue a verdict. "The federal government has had to make decisions on questions which have an important scientific component—that is, which involve areas of science so new that no unanimity has been achieved in the scientific community and so important that the decisions inevitably have important political and perhaps moral implications. I refer to these as mixed decisions." The nature of contemporary political decisions put intolerable strains on the natural dialectical processes of science, according to Kantrowitz. Paradoxically, these burdens could only increase with future advances in technology.

164

> We now face a variety of mixed decisions—in connection, for example, with control of our physical environment, with the relationship of weapons technology to disarmament, and so on. The enormous gains that can be foreseen from the application of modern technology to medical problems will present us with a variety of great mixed decisions. . . . These decisions must be made before unanimity exists in the scientific community. The problem of communicating with a divided scientific community is and will remain one of the most difficult aspects of making mixed decisions.[87]

Leaving aside for a moment the question whether a unified scientific authority would be good or bad for public policy, we need to draw from this discussion some sense of the conditions under which science might be made whole. Kantrowitz seemed most concerned about the inability of scientists to draw balanced inferences from their immediate work: those scientists "who have gone deeply into the subjects under discussion" will have "preconceived ideas about what the outcome should be," as opposed to scientists who are "unprejudiced" and "relatively uninformed" on the same subjects.[88] Although he made no references to Thomas Kuhn, Kantrowitz evidently believed that partisanship was essential to good science; but his greater concern was to ensure dispassionate scientific judgment in the face of public pressure to reach finality. "Scientists are traditionally advocates, and judicial functions in small-scale science have never had an importance comparable to that of advocacy."[89]

Kantrowitz identified partisanship with individual creativity and entrepreneurship, in contrast to Kuhn's view of partisan communities unified by unstated presuppositions. Like the "private-enterprise, laissez-faire system in which I firmly believe," Kantrowitz also believed in a market-place of scientific wisdom. But the invisible hand moves slowly, and time constraints dictate that some other group has to make the mixed decisions demanded by politics. Moreover, the increasing scale and expense of modern experiments impose serious restrictions on the number of ideas that can be fully tested. These conditions suggest the need for an institutionalized judicial function within science, carried out by "a group of distinguished people who will devote themselves to scientific judgment."[90]

In 1976, quite a number of distinguished people attended a special colloquium designed to move Kantrowitz's idea from entrepreneurship toward brute reality.[91] No one commented on the irony of using the colloquium format for promoting agreement on the structure of a quasi-judicial body, which was defined as the institutional format sine qua non for generating scientific unity on controversial issues. In a further irony, the stated purpose of the meeting was to establish an experiment for determining the value of a science court, although no rigorous model of experimental procedure was used to guide the discussion. Perhaps it is inevitable, in a contest among rival principles of authority (science, law, economics, politics), that the central metaphors of each system have to bear the main strategic burdens.

What should an institutionalized supreme court of science look like? Everyone agreed that the judges should be objective, but how were suitable candidates to be selected? Kantrowitz received a mixed response to his preference for scientific nonspecialists. The least controversial alternative was to select randomly from a vast list of respected specialists and nonspecialists.[92] How would issues be presented to the judges? Some kind of adversary procedure seemed essential (after all, there had to be a controversy worthy of adjudication), but was its purpose to let participants find the truth or win the argument? The lawyers taking part in this discussion grabbed hold of the second horn of this dilemma, whereas most of the scientists clung tenaciously to the first.[93] Nearly all participants agreed that some kind of cross-examination was essential to the process, but without the dramatic presentations or heavy legal procedures found in conventional courtrooms (and, of course, on television).[94]

The full *Proceedings* offer a fascinating glimpse of popular assumptions about both science and law, few of which have changed in the intervening years. (Judging from the transcript, none were altered radically after three days of civilized colloquy.) What emerges most clearly is the frustration of professional scientists with the apparent disintegration of authority derived from scientific ideals. This is especially true for scientists in the regulatory process, who were deeply involved in decision-making on drugs, food, environmental health standards, and consumer-product safety. Indeed, their frustration provoked strong outbursts against the whole policy process, and politics was blamed for disturbing the dialectical boundaries of scientific procedure. For these participants, a science court was the postulated mechanism for purifying such boundaries, a dignified alternative to the professional shame of endless wrangling.

As Kantrowitz was keenly aware, however, science must confront its own boundaries in meeting the demands of public policy. The central limitation reflects a conflict of two dialectical goals within science; the demand for closure compromises the entire procedural legitimacy of science. Among participants in the colloquium, this dilemma was squarely identified by H. Guyford Stever: "There has been a call for knowledge with more certainty and action with less risk. . . . Whereas it is the nature of science usually to raise more questions than it answers and of technology to introduce new risk with every benefit it bestows."[95] Science ordinarily relies on tacit presumptions (such as Kuhn's paradigms) to minimize dialectical conflict, although even science has its revolutions. But in the regulatory state, scientific authority can be severely tested in even the most ordinary decisions. Only legal authority can still presume to unite legitimacy and finality, and therein lies its great attraction for scientists seeking professional repose in regulatory proceedings.

This book has explored the rhetorical conditions under which legal institutions live up to their bold presumptions. Courts can bring finality to public discourse, but often with the sacrifice of perceived legitimacy. Skillful judicial assignments of proof burdens can eke out this appearance, but it cannot disguise the sudden pendulum swings that accompany important shifts in the burden of proof. Both science and ethical authority stand ready to exploit this weakness in the legal process. A unified authority for science—institutionally capable of delivering opinions on public issues—could scarcely expect to escape the identical critique. Thus opponents of the science court argued that it would inevitably undermine its own authority. As one colloquium participant observed, "The extent to which the court is successful is the extent to which it is dangerous."[96] By reaching closure on issues that remain scientifically indeterminate, a science court could preempt future scientific inquiry:

> If institutionalized as part of the policy-making process, the science court proceeding might lend a false validity to its findings and, by the authority of its institutionalization, might mask or suppress ongoing scientific disputes. The end product would be a truncation of scientific inquiry in favor of false certainty in policy-making. In areas involving environmental policy . . . the possibility of inhibiting scientific inquiry would indeed be a hazardous prospect.[97]

Postulating a Higher Reality

By failing to institutionalize their proposals, advocates of judicialized science lost an opportunity to create new public procedures for imposing finality in factual disputes. Indeed, by drawing attention to dialectical elements that are normally suppressed in science, they may have hastened the diffusion of scientific authority across multiple procedures. Many disputes will still find their way to expert fact-finding panels, just as ordinary litigation can sometimes shift to voluntary mediation. But the structure and management of fact-finding procedures remain part of the strategic battleground, as parties seek to empower their own experts, to impose their own time horizons, and to preserve any provisional victories by manipulating presumptions and proof burdens.

167

Under pressure to respond definitively to public problems, the community of inquirers envisioned by Peirce and the early pragmatists tends to break into jurisdictional fragments. If the demand for public consensus can somehow be postponed, it may be possible to preserve a semblance of scientific unity within entrenched research programs, stretching into the indefinite future. Nonetheless, with the rise of environmental issues on the public agenda, the same dispersion of authority that has long haunted social science research has now spread farther into the natural sciences.

Trying to defer scientific conclusions has become a standard adversarial maneuver, similar to postponement strategies commonly used by attorneys. But with no Supreme Court to unify the juridical framework, the partisans of scientific deferral face unusually high costs of indecision, including the perpetual risk that influential courts of public opinion may turn against them. Thus a definitive ruling remains a strong attraction for all parties joined in scientific polemics; short-term beneficiaries try to lock in their gains, while their opponents hope to reverse the presumptions that allocate burdens of indecision. Scientific authority can serve neither group very well when its power is diffused through the inconclusive procedures used by multiple communities of inquirers.

A much stronger claim for scientific authority can be based on a subtle theory of transcendence. This approach protects scientific truth from fragmentation by projecting it onto a level of reality somewhere beyond the realm of human activity. Borrowing from Kantian philosophical strategies, the assertive realist draws a critical inference from the very lack of finality in the leading forms of human inquiry. The sudden leap to a reality beyond method starts from the central presumption that human indecision, although inescapable, cannot rule out the existence of some natural standard for adjudicating important human questions. Indeed, the space available for such standards grows in direct proportion to human ignorance, measured by systematic limits to inquiry. The breakdown of procedurally defined truth into warring jurisdictions strengthens the realist's argument for removing truth to a different sphere.

According to Roy Bhaskar, who has presented an eloquent case for this transcendental shift, the defense of scientific authority requires a strategic reversal of standard arguments in philosophy of science. Rather than justifying scientific procedure by establishing an independent reality to which scientific conclusions happen to conform, Bhaskar "assumes at the outset the intelligibility of science . . . and asks explicitly what the world must be like for those activities to be possible." [98]

Bhaskar projects a naturalistic standard whose juridical function is to win acquittal for the "generally recognized activities" of professional scientists. [99] That victory is placed in jeopardy, argues Bhaskar, if reality is identified too closely with sense experience or with concrete objects situated somewhere beyond human consciousness. This leaves him with a "profusion of terms . . . to specify the newly identified realm . . . of the real or its cognates—powers, tendencies, structures, generative mechanisms, transfactuality, normic statements." [100]

According to Bhaskar's presumption, scientific activity can redeem its ambitious claims only if these dynamic entities are invited to populate a transcendental space reserved for juridical authority. There may still be competing visions of precisely which structures, tendencies, and mechanisms carry the legitimacy of scientific truth, but human inquiry can at least proceed on the conviction that truth is attainable in principle. As political scientist Ian Shapiro has argued, "Science holds out the hope that we can get beyond the welter of conflicting opinions and ideological claims to the truth of a matter, that we can come to hold a set of beliefs about an entity, event, or action that is most reasonable under the circumstances. . . . Although this is often difficult in practice, there is no reason to rule it out in principle." [101]

Chapter 6 | The Rise of Ethical Authority

The decline in scientific authority contrasts with the recent ascendance of ethical authority. In some respects, the turn to rights-based arguments in political and academic debate extends popular judicial models into transcendental jurisdictions. Unlike the U.S. Supreme Court, these postulated courts can immunize themselves from sudden reversals caused by changing judicial coalitions; but the price for stable majorities seems to be the proliferation of rival tribunals, each vying for exclusive jurisdiction. Although appeals to such "higher" courts may be an inevitable response to the politicizing of actual courts, the resulting fragmentation of ethical authority can paralyze political institutions and academic disciplines. Despite certain strategic advantages for players in both systems, the long-term effects of postulating new ethical jurisdictions include sudden pendulum swings in dominant presumptions.

The Transcendental Turn

"Saints should always be judged guilty until they are proved innocent," wrote George Orwell, introducing his "Reflections on Gandhi."[1] By reversing the standard presumption of innocence, Orwell wanted to distinguish secular norms, which apply to everyday mortals, from the more exclusive codes of self-appointed exceptions. And by urging a skeptical response, Orwell was essentially echoing Freud's advice on religious belief, based on similar premises.

Orwell wanted to reserve our evidentiary standards and moral presumptions for those occasions when actions can be measured by human proportions. Visitors from another realm should always be evaluated under the everyday norms of an imperfect world: "Gandhi's teachings cannot be squared with the belief that Man is the measure of all things, and that our job is to make life worth living on this earth, which is the only earth we have. They make sense only on the assumption that God exists and that the world of solid objects is an illusion to be escaped from." In Orwell's view, Gandhi's opposition to eating animal products (among other impractical convictions) underlined the fundamental divergence between humanistic and religious attitudes. Unlike the rest of us, for Gandhi "there must . . . be some limit to what we will do in order to remain alive, and the limit is well on this side of chicken broth."[2]

These reflections, including the gentle witticism, now have a somewhat dated quality. Forty years later an entirely different set of presumptions has won popular and academic acceptance. The perspective has shifted, such that standards of justice are increasingly found in the higher world, to which we must demand some form of access. This cosmology suggests a point of view quite opposed to Orwell's: ordinary judgments involving ethics and values can now earn true acquittal (if at all) only in some transcendental court. Unlike the ephemeral rulings of earthly judges, this tribunal deals in categorical truths. Its jurisdiction is defined as transcendental because it cannot be overruled by the highest authorities of everyday legal and social systems, those ambiguous guardians of Orwell's humanism.

This breathtaking shift in presumptions has dramatically changed the climate for discussion of ethical issues since Orwell's day. Especially in the last twenty years, public desire for categorical ethical standards has reached a new intensity. Philosophers have taught us to take them seriously, and the professions of law, business, and medicine have felt compelled to adopt higher principles of professional responsibility. Ethicists have become professionals in their own transcendental discipline, and prudent politicians run the other way rather than face the new tribunals of institutionalized ethics.[3]

170   A distinctive vocabulary marks this shift in orientation, centered on the language of rights. A more openly skeptical generation, closer in spirit to Orwell's humanism, had viewed rights somewhat dubiously as the byproducts of social conditions. Rights were fluid and situational, but also vulnerable to manipulation by powerful groups overrepresented in social deliberations. The problem was to distinguish valid complaints about the fairness of social procedures from the inevitable lament of sore losers.

But what happens if rights were understood strictly as detached, self-sufficient principles, rather than the fragile outcomes of imperfect procedures? The exponent of such rights could pursue a powerful brand of social critique, similar to the strict scrutiny of the U.S. Supreme Court under Chief Justice Warren. Under the new due process doctrines of the Warren era, courts became an independent forum for challenging any established authority that could be brought under expanding federal jurisdiction. This shift in authority released the dormant power of judicial review, which allows the federal judiciary to preempt actions taken by other governmental bodies. In effect, courts can impose higher-order constraints on the pluralist mechanisms used to balance social interests. The vocabulary and strategies of constitutional rights litigation thus became the model for a distinctive ethical authority.

The transition from Orwell's stubbornly secular vision to contemporary transcendental ethics[4] can be broken down into two stages, the first of which was the constitutional phase explored in chapter 3. I shall approach the second phase through the works of contemporary social philosophers. Ronald Dworkin's essays from the late 1960s and 1970s, which admonished readers to "take rights seriously," transferred the Warren Court's rhetorical techniques to a distinctive ethical realm that became a progressive haven as the federal judiciary grew more conservative. When John Rawls's treatise on justice was published in the early 1970s, it supplied a coherent political philosophy modeled on progressive constitutional doctrines, even as those doctrines were being revised by new members of the Supreme Court. Soon thereafter, Robert Nozick (among others) demonstrated how transcendental ethical authority, which Rawls and Dworkin assumed would underwrite further progressive reform, could just as logically support an extreme brand of libertarianism.[5]

Ethicizing the Law: The Shift to Transcendental Authority

Dworkin and Nozick cunningly built their respective theories on the inability of opponents to prove that certain rights do not exist (using formidable standards of proof). Both were somewhat mysterious about the process of postulating affirmative conclusions, but their main accomplishment was to pursue the logical implications of popular liberal presumptions. Rawls created a sensation by turning the argument-from-ignorance into one of his main themes. In essence, he suppressed his own authorship of the postulated "theory of justice" and attributed it to the whole of humanity, reduced to a legion of inference-makers hidden behind a "veil of ignorance."

171

Dworkin's initial essays in the transcendental[6] vein appeared as the Warren Court fell under heavy attack for innovative decisions on political equality, criminal justice, and personal privacy. Dworkin acknowledged the "continuing embarrassment" of the Court's liberal defenders, who had been hard pressed since the 1954 ruling in Brown v. Board of Education to show that their decisions were not just instrumentally prudent, but also legally and morally correct.[7] In contrast to the ambiguous defense by Alexander Bickel, which carved out a narrow role for judge-led, enlightened prudence, Dworkin took the more ambitious position that court decisions should be measured ultimately by categorical standards of legal correctness.

Although he was not prepared to demonstrate the correctness of specific constitutional decisions, Dworkin shifted the burden to the Court's critics to prove that its controversial opinions were not correct. Taking rights seriously signaled this strategic shift in perspective. Given our apparent inability to prove that certain fundamental rights cannot be categorically defined and applied to legal cases, we have "no reason" to restrain judges who were conscientiously trying to define and apply them. Ironically, there are also some good reasons (meaning prudential arguments) for urging courts to play this elusive nonprudential role.

> Some readers may object that, if no procedure exists, even in principle, for demonstrating what legal rights the parties have in hard cases, it follows that they have none. That objection presupposes a controversial thesis of general philosophy, which is that no proposition can be true unless it can, at least in principle, be demonstrated to be true. There is no reason to accept that thesis as part of a general theory of truth, and good reason to reject its specific application to propositions about legal rights.[8]

This rhetorical tour de force opens up entirely new avenues of legal and moral inquiry, as well as some characteristic puzzles. In contrast to the dominant presumptions of legal realism, Dworkin used the argument-from-ignorance to presume that legal rights are essentially categorical and that judges are properly concerned with discovering them. Still further presumptions seemed to suggest that judges were the best (if not the only) interpreters of the transcendental realm of legal rights. As can be expected with any wholesale reversal of long-established presumptions, Dworkin's strategy seemed to turn everything on its head. Indefensible arguments under the old regime became impregnable fortresses, and arguments previously deemed self-evident could be summarily dismissed as absurd. The effect was much like the doctrinal revolution initiated by the Court itself.[9]

To consolidate such revolutions, partisans of newly dominant presumptions must invent new concepts, disguised as mere elaborations of older doctrines and fortified by common sense. Dworkin's accomplishment was the philosophical analogue to this shift in legal practice. If judges were appropriately concerned with interpreting categorical rights, there had to be some vocabulary for talking about these previously banished notions. Dworkin also needed to replace the whole legal-realist theory of how judges think. This older view had put creative judges squarely in a dilemma between mechanical jurisprudence and unrestrained discretion. Instead of following commentators like Bickel in searching for a route between the Scylla and Charybdis that haunted realist presumptions, Dworkin set out on an entirely different mission.

It was, all the same, an odyssey of heroic proportions. Dworkin decided to cease apologizing for the Supreme Court's furtive references to fundamental rights in constitutional cases. To be sure, in practice the Court seemed to treat these rights instrumentally, using them as conceptual leverage for shifting the presumption of constitutionality. But, said Dworkin, that fact should not stop us from interpreting rights in a more categorical sense. Legal and moral arguments may often be expressed in terms of "policies" (instrumental premises), but they can also be based on fundamental "principles" (noninstrumental—or categorical—premises). More precisely, no one can prove that such principles are not engaged by the characteristic reasoning of conscientious judges. In the absence of conclusive proof to the contrary, Dworkin presumed that "the Constitution fuses legal and moral issues, by making the validity of a law depend on the answer to complex moral problems." [10]

Having thus laid claim to a whole new region of transcendental space, Dworkin offered his remaining analysis as a massive hypothetical case: if fundamental principles provide the moral substance of judicial reasoning, then they also require a distinctive method of analysis and properly qualified personnel. In Dworkin's theory, these functions are to be performed in a manner strikingly similar to the Warren Court's technique of strict scrutiny. And they are eventually entrusted to a transcendental authority with all the characteristics of a high appellate judge. [11]

Dworkin's defense of the Warren Court was typically ambitious and uncompromising, and it went far beyond the modest descriptions of judicial craft authored by the justices themselves. Whereas liberal members of the Court often seemed muddled in reconciling the novelty of their decisions with post-realist ideals of craftsmanship, Dworkin painted a heroic portrait of the entire judicial enterprise. No system of rules could be assumed to apply itself; and thus judges should become actively involved in interpreting even the most explicit statute, not to mention the normative subtleties of constitutional law. The realist attack on judicial activism is misguided, Dworkin concluded, because it tries to prove too much. If true, it would make the task of judging not just difficult, but impossible. "Unless at least some principles are acknowledged to be binding upon judges, requiring them as a set to reach particular decisions, then no rules, or very few rules, can be said to be binding upon them either." [12]

Dworkin's shift in perspective had dramatic implications. If judges (by definition) really do use principles rather than mere pragmatic policies as their starting premises, it follows that their reasoning process must be qualitatively different from that of political actors. But the principles supporting fundamental rights are not necessarily rulelike commandments; they might instead be seen as a swirling complex of intellectual notions. And if so much is presumed true, then judicial energy and integrity become vital in defining legal rights. Judges have no choice but to weigh or balance an array of shapeless principles emanating from the shadows of the Constitution and from the whole political and cultural tra-

173

dition. In determining the scope of a broad principle like equal protection, for example, the courts must ponder "an amalgam of practice and other principles in which the implications of legislation and judicial history figure along with appeals to community practices and understandings." [13] "We argue for a particular principle by grappling with a whole set of shifting, developing, and interacting standards (themselves principles rather than rules) about institutional responsibility, statutory interpretation, the persuasive force of various sorts of precedent, the relation of all these to contemporary moral practices, and hosts of other such standards." [14] No formal hierarchy of concepts can impose mechanical order on this process. Principles cannot expect deductive support from a body of absolute premises and must therefore rely on an active judiciary to identify overlapping lines of mutual support.

> We should argue for [our principles of legislation, precedent, democracy, or federalism] not only in terms of practice, but in terms of each other and in terms of the implications of trends of judicial and legislative decisions, even though this last would involve appealing to those same doctrines of interpretation we justified through the principles we are now trying to support. At this level of abstraction, in other words, principles rather hang together than link together. [15]

174

This remarkable theory of adjudication can be broken down into three major presumptions, all resting on arguments-from-ignorance.

> 1. We can presume there are correct answers to questions about legal rights, even though we may not know (or be able to prove) what they are.
> 2. We can presume there is a complex procedure appropriate for discovering rights in controversial situations, even though that procedure cannot itself be formulated as a series of rules.
> 3. We can presume that judges are uniquely placed to perform this procedure, even though no one else is in a position to measure their success against independent criteria.

Dworkin's elaborate and subtle theory is a philosophical vindication of the practice labeled "strict scrutiny" by liberal advocates in the late 1960s. [16] It offers a strategic rejoinder to the critique of judicial activism, carefully constructed to withstand any argument that might prove it wrong. For Dworkin, fundamental norms, procedures, and personnel all belong to a transcendental order over which no critic can claim proper jurisdiction. To take this self-fulfilling argument seriously means to grant it a presumption of innocence, understanding full well that no one will ever be in a position to impeach it. And if it is not taken seriously, Dworkin warns, our whole legal and moral order could be jeopardized.

What does this baroque structure of untouchable presumptions tell us about our controversial Supreme Court? In the early days of the Warren era, it might briefly have been possible to blur the jurisdictional lines between the federal judiciary and the kind of tribunal postulated by Dworkin. By opening up a previously uncharted region of legal and moral norms, Dworkin provided a plausible rationale for the jurisprudential innovations of the Warren period, which seemed cramped and suspicious by the conventions of post-realist legal criticism. In particular, Dworkin predicted in the late 1960s that equal protection doctrines were destined to reach the most fundamental level of moral reasoning. He also assumed that the courts had found the proper idiom for articulating fundamental rights: as restrictions on government interference in decisions appropriately left to individuals.[17]

Before 1970 it was not yet apparent that similar judicial creativity might be used to slow or even stifle progressive reform. The conservative opposition to Warren Court activism was still being channeled through the impotent rhetoric of judicial restraint. It arguably took more than five years for Justice Rehnquist's opinions to demonstrate what was implicit in Dworkin's theories: that uninhibited transcendental judging was destined to produce a wide range of results wandering all across the political spectrum.[18] Until that moment eventually came, judicial strategists of the Warren era (and their supporters within the litigation community) had the transcendental field entirely to themselves. In the spirit of Dworkin's bold challenge, who among the Court's conservative critics could prove that these judicial innovations were not in touch with fundamental values? It was an ennobling line of defense, which seemed to rescue the larger cause from self-doubts by wavering commentators like Alexander Bickel. These strategic concerns were doubtless among the "good reasons" alluded to by Dworkin for starting to take fundamental constitutional rights seriously.

Dworkin never directly asserted that the Supreme Court was the temporal voice of transcendental rights. To defend such a conclusion, he would have had to presume some independent access to a definitive roster of fundamental rights, against which he (and others) could then measure the Court's performance. Furthermore, his early essays had suggested that isolated reasoners might follow their own judgelike paths and come out at different points than the courts. This argument, to be sure, appeared at the height of domestic protest against the Vietnam War, and it explored the possibilities for civil disobedience based on considered judgments of individual conscience.[19] But Dworkin also emphasized that

175

the law is frequently "uncertain" and that even appellate courts sometimes over-rule themselves.[20] Still using the rhetorical strategy of negative proof, Dworkin concluded that: "A citizen's allegiance is to the law, not to any particular person's view of what the law is, and he does *not* behave unfairly so long as he proceeds on his own considered and reasonable view of what the law requires . . . . When the law is uncertain, in the sense that a plausible case can be made on both sides, then a citizen who follows his own judgment is *not* behaving *un*fairly." [21]

Locating fundamental norms in transcendental space helps us make sense of judicial activism (it helps us take it seriously), but it makes equal sense of activism directed to either liberal or conservative ends. Ironically, it also spon-sors an unceasing critique of current court decisions, since it is impossible for courts to prove that their opinions offer a definitive account of rights. Dworkin's argument-from-ignorance, which starts from the premise that no one can prove enough to block the transcendental turn, thus leads to divergent implications that Dworkin himself left unexplored. If "we cannot assume . . . that the Constitution is always what the Supreme Court says it is," nor can we assume that consti-tutional rights have been properly stated by any other putative authority.[22] Nor, paradoxically, can we assume that such authorities do not speak for the Consti-tution or for some other source of transcendental norms. From Dworkin's initial starting point, almost any conclusion is possible because none can be definitively disproved.

To bring order into this potential fragmentation of normative authority, Dworkin introduced the figure of a transcendental appellate court judge. Dworkin's deeper intuitions had already confirmed that "lawyers or political philosophers" were best situated to perform the conceptual tasks central to tran-scendental exploration.[23] His 1975 essay on "Hard Cases" turned that assignment over to a fictional but philosophical judge named Hercules, "a lawyer of super-human skill, learning, patience, and acumen." Hercules "must suppose that it is understood in his community, though perhaps not explicitly recognized, that judicial decisions must be taken to be justified by arguments of principle rather than arguments of policy." [24] And, presumably, Dworkin's readers must suppose that Hercules must be taken to resolve hard cases at a level of performance sufficient to produce correct results.

Most striking of all about this Herculean task, it differs radically from the application of antecedent rules to specific fact situations. Even though the rights Dworkin wants us to take seriously are assumed to be categorically binding rather than pragmatically selected (the difference between principles and policies, re-spectively), the process of discovering them and applying them to concrete situa-tions was nonetheless a highly speculative task. Like Toulmin, Dworkin believes that criteria of validity already exist; but for Dworkin they cannot simply be drawn from a compendium of rulelike warrants. Like Hart he believes that a secondary order of norms is essential for the proper application of primary rules; but for Dworkin that secondary order must be actively constructed by the judiciary. Like our own notion of dialectic, Dworkin's theory of principles emphasizes process and procedure over product. Making practical use of transcendental rights rests on a procedure in which the proper personnel are as vital as the rule-defined process.

Hercules performs the requisite task of making complex principles operational in specific situations. He surveys judicial precedents and discerns their "gravitational force" within an applied field.[25] He interprets legislative rules against the background of legislative intent (no simple notion in itself), and he measures the results against a well-developed political philosophy that weighs legislation alongside other elements of legality. Hercules further extends that political philosophy to give it historical and moral dimensions. He must fully assimilate the dominant moral views of his time, while taking into account the degree of diversity tolerated by the wider culture.[26]

However daunting this list of cognitive challenges, Hercules's true power comes from his strategic position at the summit of transcendental authority. With no higher level of appeal available, even in principle, the dialectical finality of Hercules's position is far more important than his mythical intellectual capacities. If Hercules's ability to perform these unreviewable tasks is ever doubted, there are no relevant criteria by which to rate his performance. Hercules's pledge to "take into account" the entire checklist of legally relevant factors may be reassuring, but there can be no further evidence that the process itself was properly performed—and thus no independent evidence that Hercules has found the right answer.

Transcendental presumptions, by their very nature, inhabit a postulated realm of categorical values, unaffected by the pragmatic needs or purposes of calculating humans. We are not meant to stare directly at the beauties of this higher world; it is enough to postulate its existence for whatever stability it may bring to our otherwise baseless ethical experience. At the same time, some procedure for eliminating potentially competing interpretations of transcendental standards is desperately needed, and all the weight of categorical truth gets transferred to that procedure.

What can be said about the accuracy of Hercules's judgments? Dworkin's blunt reply is the inescapable consequence of transcendental reasoning: "Though we, as social critics, know that mistakes will be made, we do not know when because we are not Hercules either." But can any conclusion whatsoever be drawn from the sheer possibility that Hercules might get it wrong? Dworkin responds by placing the burden of proof on critics of judicial supremacy to find any better interpreter of transcendental mysteries. Hercules wins his place at the top of the jurisdictional pyramid not by talent or success, but by default. Moreover, some of this authority seems to rub off on terrestrial judges.

> Hercules' technique encourages a [real] judge to make his own judgments about institutional rights. The argument from judicial fallibility might be thought to suggest two alternatives. The first argues that since judges are fallible they should make no effort at all to determine the institutional rights of the parties before them. . . . But that is perverse; it argues that because judges will often, by misadventure, produce unjust decisions they should make no effort to produce just ones.

But is this argument any more perverse than the default solution that emerges from Dworkin's argument-from-ignorance? The sharp dichotomy between "no effort to produce justice" and unreviewable Herculean efforts is an artifact of Dworkin's transcendental logic. The Orwellian humanist would urge us to seek out less ambitious standards of justice. But where else, Dworkin asks, can we turn: "The second alternative argues that since judges are fallible they should submit questions of institutional right . . . to someone else. But to whom? There is *no reason* to credit any other particular group with better facilities of moral argument."[27] Unless we are prepared to prove to Dworkin's satisfaction that someone else is better able to perform these Herculean tasks, we are admonished to leave them with the self-appointed Hercules's of the judicial system. In 1975, when these arguments were being aired, the Burger Court was ready to make substantial breaks with progressive doctrines of the Warren period. Was this not the Court Dworkin wanted us to follow?

Ethical Authority: Foundations in Transcendental Procedures

Looking across current philosophical literature, there is nothing unique about Dworkin's free use of arguments-from-ignorance in mapping out a territory of categorical rights. The transcendental status of ethical authority compels its interpreters to practice indirect methods of argumentation, which surround their topic with an irrebuttable presumption of innocence. Without that presumption, normative judgments would face unbeatable odds under the skeptical standards of modern scientific authority, by which ethical statements have often been dismissed as sheer nonsense or as mislabeled emotional energy. The neo-Kantian movement of the last century discovered how to preserve both kinds of authority by confining each to its separate, nonoverlapping territory. We are relearning that strategy one hundred years later, stimulated in part by jurisprudential analogies.

Advocates who practice before transcendental tribunals seem fully as contentious as their counterparts in temporal jurisdictions. In some cases, of course, the practitioners are the same, with Dworkin as perhaps the leading example. His assertion of a dichotomy between principles and policies captured the central philosophical presumption behind the Warren Court's historic shift in the burden of proof for certain constitutional challenges to legislation. His selection of principles as privileged criteria placed a transcendental framework around the Court's fragile doctrinal experiments with strict scrutiny and due process, and it gave defenders of judicial activism the moral high ground in their continuing battle over the proper scope of judicial review. From another standpoint, however, Dworkin's work added little more than timely judicial metaphors to an existing stock of Anglo-American moral philosophy, based largely on Kant's critique of utilitarian concepts and methods.[28]

Within this broader academic context, transcendental theoreticians do battle not only with cosmic rivals, but also with each other. Confined to a jurisdiction with no written statutes or published caselaw, these advocates are especially accomplished in adducing presumptions to warrant specific conclusions, even though their "clients" remain at the level of abstract theory. Their techniques include skillful use of arguments-from-ignorance, in which the favored result is posited as the default or prima facie conclusion. The strategies are identical to those commonly found in legal briefs filed in constitutional litigation.

Consider the following example in David O. Brink's recent defense of moral realism (a theory that attributes a special kind of existence to moral rights and principles, rather than viewing them as mere constructs or postulates). "Realism is the natural metaphysical position," Brink writes. "Moral realism should be our metaethical starting point, and we should give it up only if it does involve unacceptable metaphysical and epistemological commitments. . . . We have reason[s] to accept moral realism that can be overturned only if there are powerful objections." Brink commends his case to the court with the following challenge:

> If my argument has been correct, general considerations about the nature of inquiry . . . are most easily explained on the assumption that moral inquiry is directed at discovering moral facts that obtain independently of our moral beliefs and at arriving at evidence-independent true moral beliefs. I take this conclusion to establish a presumptive case in favor of moral realism and to shift the burden of proof to the moral antirealist. That is, the burden of proof is on the antirealist to explain why the apparent realist presuppositions of commonsense morality are mistaken.[29]

179

The merits of Brink's case will have to be determined by an appropriate tribunal. For our purposes, we need to pursue the philosophical presumptions that accompany this style of argument throughout the transcendental realm, regardless of who (or what) the notional client may be. This path leads to John Rawls's works, which pay extraordinary attention to methods of justifying moral reasoning. His monumental treatise, *A Theory of Justice,* popularized two imaginative supports for moral arguments, both of which incorporate burden-shifting strategies: a decisionist theory of normative procedure in his doctrine of the original position and an inductive theory of moral evidence in the doctrine of reflective equilibrium.[30] Although both theories continue to receive extensive professional commentary, their subtle use of arguments-from-ignorance has yet to be fully explored.[31]

Rawls's striking theory of the original position commanded immediate attention when *A Theory of Justice* appeared in 1971. This elliptical phrase refers to Rawls's variant of social-contract theory: it supports his postulated theory of justice by invoking the authority of ideal decision-makers, whose original position lies somewhere in transcendental space. Rawls turned to this chorus of Kantian selves (rather than, for example, to Dworkin's transcendental judge) because he wanted to find normative authority for an entire social system. Decision-makers in their original position do not decide concrete cases; they select "basic social structures," including procedural principles to operationalize the notion of justice in complex social settings. What they choose, according to Rawls, is a set of principles compatible with "justice as fairness," the leading theme in Rawls's earlier writings.[32] In accordance with Rawls's constructivist and pragmatic philosophical presumptions, fairness is to be defined by procedures rather than outcomes: justice is thus presumed to be a matter of selecting fair institutional structures and has no pretensions as a timeless absolute.[33] Assigning that selection to ideal decision-makers is entirely consistent with this procedural emphasis.

Among other strategic purposes, Rawls's original position device sought to allay potential fragmentation of ethical authority as it entered the basic social structures of Rawls's postulated "well-ordered society."[34] As in Dworkin's work, a unified ethical jurisdiction becomes increasingly difficult to maintain as one approaches the concrete conditions in a nonideal world. A theory of justice on the scale projected by Rawls must encompass the normative relations of a diverse social community, including the procedural mechanisms through which ethical authority reaches specific situations. Rawls tried to insure a higher unity for this potentially disparate field by moving his decision-makers back in time to prehistory and by allowing them to select only from general principles. They do, nonetheless, enjoy full psychological and moral development, even though their original position removes them from life's vicissitudes.

Only by constructing this transcendental device could Rawls find a point of view from which to conserve the notion of a self-standing ethical authority, independent of the conditioned desires and secular interests that haunted the utilitarian categories of Orwell's style of humanism. Structural principles for the just society were validated in being chosen by individuals placed behind a carefully constructed "veil of ignorance."[35] Rawls wanted to ask precisely these individuals to make the critical inferences about preferred social structures; their lack of information about the specific consequences of their action, or about the conventions of a specific culture, guaranteed that their selection could not be based on mere temporal calculations. The original position theory was thus a transcendental application of the argument-from-ignorance. It gave an absolute preference to inferences made in a postulated temporal vacuum, where transcendental norms were presumed to be the default criteria.

Like the choices of his hypothetical decision-makers, Rawls's arguments depend on default reasoning, which comes to the surface only when the proper rhetorical questions are asked. If the shape of basic social structures were not a transcendental choice but a mere temporal fact, how could such structures ever be considered part of a moral order? And if Kantian selves did not make this transcendental choice, who else could be in a position to do so? After assuming that there were no affirmative answers to these questions, Rawls posited his celebrated hypothetical constructions. His overarching presumption was that justice needed a transcendental warrant. In the absence of any other validating procedure, the original position device earned that job by the logic of default.[36]

Richard Dien Winfield has noticed the same pattern of reasoning in Rawls, but he approaches it from a somewhat different direction. According to Winfield, Rawls's constructions are default inferences from a set of premises long identified with the political tradition of liberalism. These premises include a recognition of ethical authority but deny that it can be cognitively apprehended as a set of timeless goals. For liberalism this dilemma supports the inference that ethical authority must therefore be practical or pragmatic—something expressed through human activity, rather than a collection of static norms.

> Rawls' recourse to prudential calculation is predicated upon the basic move that gives liberal theory its point of departure. . . . This consists in the repudiation of the appeal to privileged givens defining teleological ethics, an appeal represented by the latter's cardinal assumption that justice can only be ascertained by first conceiving a highest good from which all valid norms derive.[37]

181

Other philosophers, in fact, have been willing to postulate the existence of a highest norm, from which ethical reality could be suspended in a deductive relation.[38] As Winfield properly notes, however, Rawls belongs to a different tradition, which looks for transcendental authority within the process of human decision-making.

> Congruent with any move from privileged givens to a privileged determiner, Rawls' turn to pure procedural justice has meaning only if ethics can no longer prescribe what ends conduct should realize. Rawls himself admits as much, acknowledging that pure procedural justice, which aims at furnishing a procedure that is just regardless of what its results may be, is employable provided no independent criteria are available to mandate the valid outcome of a fair course of action.[39]

So far I have said nothing about the products of the original position decision: the operating principles of "justice as fairness," which have been the focus of enormous commentary over the past twenty years.[40] Much of this reaction—positive and negative—accepts the basic strategy of transcendental reasoning and concentrates on Rawls's elaborative techniques and conclusions. Some critics wonder if Rawls's original position device extended far enough into transcendental regions to tap the full source of ethical authority. Others have questioned whether it yields the proper principles for ordering human institutions on a truly just basis.[41] The results of such inquiries are as varied as the normative presumptions with which commentators approach the highly malleable conceptual tools Rawls placed in their hands.

Dworkin provides a convenient illustration of how other advocates for transcendental authority have exploited Rawls's suggestive techniques. From the outset he presumes that Rawls's general method has touched on something highly profound and that its true meaning therefore lies beyond the reach of skeptical critics who raise doubts about the separation of transcendental norms and temporal facts. Some critics, for example, argue that any contractual agreement (especially a fictional one) makes an unlikely source for valid, prospective principles of justice. Dworkin concedes the point but draws an unexpected inference: "We must *therefore* treat the argument from the original position as . . . a device for calling attention to some independent argument for the fairness of [Rawls's] principles—an argument that does not rest on the false premise that a hypothetical contract has some pale binding force. What other argument is available?"[42] Some thirty pages later, Dworkin concludes that Rawls was really trying to defend the same ideals that Dworkin himself had previously endorsed: a bedrock principle of "equal respect," resembling Dworkin's Kantian reading of the equal protection clause of the U.S. Constitution, and institutional procedures, in which the hypothetical Hercules could eventually play a pivotal role. Having shown that his own transcendental principles were at least compatible with the Rawlsian apparatus, Dworkin then issued the inevitable challenge to potential critics to prove that such principles do not rest on transcendental authority. Here is his summation and peroration: "These arguments [of Rawls] may, of course, be wrong. I have certainly said nothing in their defense here. But the critics of liberalism now have the responsibility to show that they are wrong. They cannot say that Rawls's basic assumptions and attitudes are too far from their own to allow a confrontation." [43]

Ethical Authority: The Search for Temporal Foundations

Beyond these bold rhetorical inventions, Rawls takes yet another approach to transcendental authority: the theory of reflective equilibrium. This formidable term designates a method of grounding ethical authority that resembles both empirical verification in science and legal justification in common law judging. As a method of validation, reflective equilibrium has potentially broad applications within moral theory, beyond specific uses in *A Theory of Justice*. Its distinctive procedure supplements the arguments-from-ignorance that are characteristic of contemporary moral philosophy, and it says a great deal about the philosophical presumptions of transcendental reasoning.

In later essays, Rawls has sought tirelessly to defend the baroque conceptual design of his celebrated treatise with its interlocking definitions and mutually confirming postulates. [44] It is all part of the complex task of invoking an authority whose relevance for "us" (for "you and me," [45] says Rawls) consists entirely of postulated or constructed theories. His theory of justice is the sort of doctrine that

> interprets the notion of objectivity in terms of a suitably constructed social point of view that is authoritative with respect to all individual and associational points of view. This rendering of objectivity implies that, rather than think of the principles of justice as true, it is better to say they are the principles most reasonable *for us, given* our conception of persons as free and equal, and fully cooperating members of a democratic society. [46]

Transcendental authority is posited by "us," but it is constructed in such a way that it takes the form of a self-justifying system of objective principles. "Apart from the procedure of constructing these principles, there are no reasons of justice." These constructions may have emerged from the pen of John Rawls, but validation can come only from their acceptance by "you and me," as we choose whether to find objective authority in the kinds of principles Rawls has nominated. "Thus, the essential agreement in judgments of justice arises not from the recognition of a prior and independent moral order, but from everyone's affirmation of the same authoritative social perspective."[47]

Rawls has provided no less than three perspectives from which to view his elaborate enterprise: two are constructed perspectives standing within the transcendental theory, and only the third belongs to "you and me" as dialectical judges of the finished construction. In Rawls's words, the three points of view include "that of the parties in the original position, that of citizens in a well-ordered society, and finally, that of ourselves—you and me who are examining justice as fairness as a basis for a conception of justice that may yield a suitable understanding of freedom and equality."[48]

The first two perspectives are modeled on the "companion moral ideals" of Kantian personhood and the well-ordered society. Their postulated authority is used strategically within Rawls's system to lend impressive order and plausibility to a wide-ranging set of theorems. "These distinctions are incorporated into justice as fairness through the description of the parties as agents of construction and the account of how they are to deliberate. Charged with the task of agreeing to a workable conception of justice . . . , the parties can find no better way in which to carry out this task." However, for us their efforts are premised on a contingency, since we are privy to Rawls's functional strategy. "Thus the reason why a constructivist view uses the schematic or practical distinctions we have just noted is that such distinctions are necessary *if* a workable conception of justice is to be achieved."[49]

Nearly all of Rawls's work (and the overwhelming proportion of professional commentary thereon) concentrates on articulating the two internal perspectives as a coherent system. As such, these writings describe a self-contained world where the skeptical doubts of Orwellian humanism can be entirely forgotten and where analysts eager to enter that realm can engage in artfully framed controversies. Nothing prevents a reader from embracing such constructions in the benign spirit that pervades this vast literature; and Rawls has given his audience all the conceptual tools they need to conduct civilized (if sometimes contentious) debates over transcendental topography.[50]

The argument-from-ignorance provides the license for entering this territory, based on the fundamental presumption that no one has the authority to revoke it. Rawls's consistent refusal to assign any metaphysical status to his normative realm, other than that of a construct, remains an important part of his accomplishment. With no independent perspective from which to map the transcendental landscape, Rawls's readers are ultimately free to arrange it according to their own needs and desires.

> The idea of approximating to moral truth has no place in a constructivist doctrine: the parties in the original position do not recognize any principles of justice as true or correct and so as antecedently given; their aim is simply to select the conception most rational for them, given their circumstances. This conception is not regarded as a workable approximation to the moral facts: there are no such moral facts to which the principles adopted could approximate.[51]

Rawls's tantalizing allusions to a third perspective ("you and me") lift the veil of abstraction from the strategic considerations embedded in arguments-from-ignorance. Why should readers construct this moral reflections in the way Rawls has advised or in any of the countless alternate patterns that have emerged from a torrent of transcendental speculation over the past two decades? Without benefit of a presumption of innocence, constructivist moral philosophy cannot certify its own acquittal in the temporal courts of the third perspective. And Rawls admits as much: "It may turn out that, for us, there exists no reasonable and workable conception of justice at all. That would mean that the practical task of political philosophy is doomed to failure."[52]

Here Rawls addresses the reader directly, who can apparently choose not to adopt the pessimism borne by skeptical presumptions that would impede transcendental reasoning. It could always turn out (at least, no one can disprove the possibility) that readers will find themselves endorsing the constructions of ideal moral theory.[53] And if we did, according to Rawls, their method of confirmation should follow the procedures of reflective equilibrium.

> The third point of view—that of you and me—is that from which justice as fairness, and indeed any other doctrine, is to be assessed. Here the test is that of general and wide reflective equilibrium, that is, how well the view as a whole meshes with and articulates our more firm considered convictions, at all levels of generality, after due examination, once all adjustments and revisions that seem compelling have been made. A doctrine that meets this criterion is the doctrine that, so far as we can now ascertain, is the most reasonable for us.[54]

Reflective equilibrium promises to bring (at long last) the transcendental realm into direct contact with everyday experience. It is a technique by which each person can match his or her specific moral intuitions against general moral propositions and, by a process of trial and error, modify both sides of the equation until they find a state of harmony. Despite Rawls's strikingly modest claims, as reflected in the above quotation, this is the only method he suggests for validating normative principles that does not postulate a transcendental presumption of innocence. And as L. Jonathan Cohen has argued, it may also be the major validation technique used by the whole analytic movement in philosophy since the 1950s—and not just in moral philosophy.[55] The close connection between reflective equilibrium and burden-of-proof strategies thus merits close attention.

The immediate analogy for reflective equilibrium comes from the procedure of hypothesis-testing in science, with its mutual adjustment of generalizations and particularized evidence.[56] Paradoxically, these naturalistic metaphors trade on the prestige of scientific authority, which is presumed to be absolute in the temporal realm, where "you and I" lead our ordinary lives. Following the model of empirical induction, reflective equilibrium treats each person's intuitions about specific moral questions as ultimate data, against which a succession of postulated moral principles can be tested, rejected, revised, and (finally) accepted. Moreover, in Baconian fashion, the process of testing is deemed to sharpen and direct a person's intuitive reflection, so that both data and hypothesis undergo mutual adjustment in a long-term (and perhaps endless) process.

As Cohen points out, however, the jurisprudential analogy is even closer than scientific method to reflective equilibrium in moral inquiry, where the basic data are not subject to the controlled observations of natural science.

> In experimental reasoning the data for inductive inference are the observed experimental results, whether these observations occur before, or after, anyone thinks up a hypothesis that they check. . . . What corresponds to this where inductive reasoning is not concerned with problems about causes and matters of fact? In jurisprudence reported judicial decisions constitute the corresponding data, though it is not always easy to extract the precise principle in accordance with which the decision should be taken to have been made.

Cohen's sympathetic account suggests that validating moral principles by means of reflective equilibrium is procedurally comparable to reaching judicial decisions based on past precedents. This view recalls the main strategy of Toulmin's jurisprudential analogy, which looked to legal procedures to help bridge a perceived gap between common methods of proof and the notion of logical validity. Law represents an attractive model, since it is generally presumed that judicial procedures unite finality and legitimacy without departing the temporal sphere.

As with Toulmin's analogy, however, Cohen's comparison may eventually point toward certain tensions in reflective equilibrium, if the judicial process turns out to be more complex than he assumes. And like Toulmin, Cohen fails to acknowledge the essential role of dialectical procedures in adjudication.[57] To be sure, he concedes that "it is not always easy" for courts to "extract the precise principle" from earlier cases; but the dialectical demands are more profound than this challenge to mere craftsmanship. There can be as many interpretations of past precedents as there are adversarial interests waiting to exploit them. Under the pressure to reach decisions in contested cases, courts can resolve such indeterminacies only with the strategic use of presumptions, both explicit and implicit.

The limits of Rawls's moral methodology can be seen by applying a dialectical analysis of judicial procedures to its postulated analogue in practical reason. The major points were discussed in earlier chapters around the dilemma of rational boundaries and the antinomy of legitimacy and finality. The same conflicts were also reflected in purely scientific disputes, some of which spilled over into the political arena whenever public policy demanded closure on technical controversies. In the sphere of moral deliberation, the resolution of facts and rules is reduced to the behavioral experiences of singular individuals. Moral jurisdictions become even narrower than Toulmin's fields of inquiry; judgments about social values must be validated separately by "you and me."

Current moral philosophy has largely avoided the potential conflict of jurisdictions by turning to linguistic analogies. Both the scientific and the jurisprudential analogies may illuminate some features of reflective equilibrium, but linguistic analogies supply the public dimension to this fragmented procedure. Although Rawls traces his method back to Aristotle, its most obvious direct source is the linguistic turn in analytic philosophy, especially the ordinary language school associated with Oxford in the 1950s and with Wittgenstein's *Philosophical Investigations*. [58] As this movement lost some of its initial luster in the 1970s, it was quickly reinforced by the Chomskian model of linguistic competence. For Chomsky, the intuitions of the native speaker provided an empirical-behavioral grounding for the postulated deep structures of language grammar. Defenders of reflective equilibrium have exploited both of these linguistic movements in order to justify procedures for validating transcendental authority.

For many years, the overwhelming characteristic of the ordinary-language school was its willingness to find normative authority—first and foremost—in common linguistic expressions. Its current proponents vehemently disavow any rigid reduction of philosophical and ethical problems to questions of the proper use of language; but they seem ready to assign more or less conclusive presumptions to epistemological and ethical norms embedded in linguistic idioms. Language use thus becomes prima facie evidence for nonlinguistic conclusions, and the burden of proof then shifts to opponents to disprove the commonsense wisdom of speech. This strategic shift first arose in a philosophical climate of profound distrust toward all nonlinguistic evidence on philosophical issues. The resulting argument patterns are closely analogous to court opinions tempered by judicial restraint, as embodied in the progressive presumption that existing legislation is constitutional unless shown to be unreasonable under practically impossible standards of proof.[59]

Cohen's highly sympathetic "analysis of analytical philosophy" suggests that this linguistic presumption was just a passing phase of the movement's youthful exuberance. He argues that reflective equilibrium has been the true "underlying presupposition" all along, and that it emerged from behind its linguistic cover as early as the 1950s.[60] The linguistic emphasis was merely the first stage in a larger pragmatic strategy designed to treat traditional philosophical problems as behavioral deviations from social-contextual norms. The process of "semantic ascent" was an initial test to see which problems could be summarily dismissed as linguistic confusions.[61] "But even where semantic ascent is the appropriate strategy to use," says Cohen, "it may not suffice to ground a resolution of the issue. . . . The crucial, underlying problems are rarely, if ever, just semantic."[62]

If we follow Cohen's interpretation, all the question-begging "talk about talk"—based on the presumption that what we say establishes the baseline norm for analysis—is just a lingering idiom for something more fundamental: the basic intuitions held by separate individuals as the ultimate data against which all generalizations (philosophical, moral, scientific, academic) need to be tested.[63] This is the same reflective procedure cited by Rawls as the overarching test for his theory of justice; and for other moral philosophers as well, it purports to be a foundational level of proof—for "you and me"—for grounding the transcendental claims of ethical authority.

Philosophers often turn to the Chomskian model of generative grammar for an intuitive illustration of this intuitionist mode of induction. Rawls does so in *A Theory of Justice* following his initial statement of the equilibrium method:

> A useful comparison here is with the problem of describing the sense of grammaticalness that we have for the sentences of our native language. In this case the aim is to characterize the ability to recognize well-formed sentences by formulating clearly expressed principles which make the same discriminations as the native speaker. This is a difficult undertaking which, although still unfinished, is known to require theoretical constructions that far outrun the ad hoc precepts of our explicit grammatical knowledge. A similar situation presumably holds in moral philosophy.[64]

Both kinds of linguistic analogy—ordinary usage and grammatical deep-structures—reflect the aspirations of moral philosophy to achieve the universal coherence of a common language and the systematic rigor of rule-governed syntactic structures. Once postulated, these analogies can be treated as presumptive possibilities for moral reflection in a social context, which is all that Rawls claims for them.[65] It would be futile to try to disprove the mere possibility of reaching greater social consensus on normative issues using the method now practiced by moral philosophers. If we cannot bring it off, perhaps some future Herculean society can; at least we cannot rule it out.

But a postulated procedure—the successful, social pursuit of reflective equilibrium—is still not the bedrock evidence that can ground transcendental authority in the current temporal environment. For such analysis to become anything more than a hypothetical mode of analysis, there must be a tribunal prepared to make authoritative judgments. Cohen proposes that such a tribunal can be recognized within each individual's innate capacity for analyzing non-immediate intuitions. It is a bold suggestion, rich with paradox and based finally on arguments-from-ignorance. Unless one is prepared to treat individual intuitions as the ultimate test of moral (and philosophical) validity, one is condemned to keep all transcendental reflections on a hypothetical level. Cohen's defense follows the familiar pattern of shifting the burden of proof: "Those readers who find themselves unwilling to accept [this] account of intuition and its function in analytic philosophy need to ask themselves what alternative source of philosophical premises they would propose. Or would they wish to confine analytical philosophy to the hypothetical mode of procedure?"[66]

All of the ironies of transcendental authority are present in this rush to construe individual intuitions as messengers from the constructive world of transcendental ethics, bringing ethical authority into the temporal realm in which all of us are forced to conduct our lives. According to this argument, moral intuitions must issue from some higher region, or else we are all stuck in a world of meaningless description, pure self-assertion, and irresolvable social conflict—the kinds of horrors that traditional philosophers since the days of Plato have sought to avoid. Paradoxically, each one of us needs to make one simple question-begging inference, and the entire universe then becomes a place where common-sense judgments can find a firm foundation: "Even when a[n intuitive] premise accords with the official tenets of some non-philosophical doctrine, it must be assumed to have an independent standing and authority. Only thus can it provide, *without circularity*, a deductive or inductive basis for passing judgement on that doctrine. Only thus can analytical philosophy carry out a radical critique in which *nothing* is taken for granted."[67] The transcendental authority that "must be assumed" cannot rest on anything so contingent as social agreement. Personal intuitions supply the initial premise, but a tacit structure of presumptions immediately raises that premise to the status of a normative principle. This infer-

189

ence follows the general pattern discussed throughout this book, in which the desired result has been presumed as the default solution to an otherwise irresolvable, unanswerable problem. Ironically, here the default position has been defined as something independent, authoritative, noncircular, and not taken for granted. The argument-from-ignorance on which it is based remains invisible, so long as personal intuitions constitute the highest tribunal in the jurisdiction of analytical philosophy.[68]

The Dispersion of Ethical Authority

Once they gain some foothold in the intuitions of separate individuals, transcendental norms stand on foundations more secure than the hypothetical constructions of analytical philosophers. It is, nonetheless, a narrow point of contact between two distinct realms; for intuitive norms, the contingency of their validation stands in stark contrast to the broad authority they presumably carry. This identical gap was reflected in Rawls's distinction between the temporal perspective belonging to "you and me" and his special constructed viewpoint that remains within the transcendental system, occupied by his mythical persons in their original position.

190   Contemporary moral theory, to the extent it uses transcendental constructions, rests on a paradox: its theorems are a rich set of categorical, unconstrained normative standards, but their underlying justification is the shifting, evolving accomplishment of multiple tribunals. I shall examine these tribunals in this section, using the same analysis applied to other court-type procedures in previous chapters. As in the discussion of practical reasoning in chapter 4, I will focus primarily on the antinomy of legitimacy and finality in the career of ethical authority.

The dilemmas affecting ethical authority are not the fault of current moral philosophers but are based rather on antinomies intrinsic to the transcendental enterprise. In its desire to find normative standards that are free from situational compromise, transcendental ethics is pulled in two opposing directions. On the one hand, categorical norms are presumed to enter everyday experience through the self-justifying medium of intuition. On the other hand, the separate, enclosed worlds of individual experience potentially subdivide ethical authority, distributing it across as many jurisdictions as there are persons with lively intuitions. We are thus stranded within a monadic ethical universe, in which all self-reflecting souls can gaze directly upon categorical norms, but only from a discrete range of singular perspectives.

This fragmented metaphysics is the source of both enormous energy and endless contention within contemporary ethical theory and practice. As with the Warren Court's historic change in the presumption of constitutionality, the philosophical shift to a presumption of innocence for transcendental ethical speculation helped launch an era of intense discovery. New value schemes began to appear in profusion, and even those that now seem highly traditional are methodologically quite radical. Above all, they turn the tables on previously dominant assumptions of scientific authority, which can now be criticized as mere positivism.

Some of the initial products of this movement—notably those contributed by Dworkin and Rawls—were decidedly progressive in their substantive values, and thus they appealed especially to the anxious partisans of 1960s judicial activism. It was simply a matter of time, however, until the sheer variety of ethical systems began to branch off in all ideological directions. Just as a more conservative Supreme Court learned how to harness the creative flexibility of judicial review to different public goals, so has the range of ethical visions been expanded. Moral philosophers now report widely varying fundamental intuitions on practical topics like abortion and medical decision-making, on political conduct, and on ordinary business practices—including such detailed matters as airline frequent-flyer programs.[69]

Unlike the formal judicial system, however, these competing tribunals of ethical judgment are not ordered in any single hierarchy. New orthodoxies appear on the scene with great regularity, but the old ones remain; tribunals proliferate, even though each one assumes the authority to speak for the entire moral domain. Value discussions in public life thus come to reflect not only the positive aspirations of transcendental ethics, but also its inherent adversarial tendencies.

Robert Nozick's *Anarchy, State, and Utopia* burst on the academic scene just as commentators were still absorbing the unfamiliar philosophical methods and progressive messages of Dworkin and Rawls. With an equally fertile imagination and a livelier writing style, Nozick postulated a very simple default principle for social theory: individual rights and prerogatives are unlimited, unless and until adequate justification for interference by state or public power can be found. According to Nozick, the burden of proof should always lie with proponents of public intervention, notwithstanding the historical presence of state power for numerous practical (if not ideal) purposes.

At the very outset of his argument, Nozick declares that "the fundamental question of political philosophy, one that precedes questions about how the state should be organized, is whether there should be any state at all. Why not have anarchy?"[70] Any skilled appellate lawyer can see immediately the strategic power of this approach. It defines a preferred solution as the residual or default

191

position, which emerges unchallenged after its rivals have been subjected to merciless critical scrutiny. Nozick also makes sure that the standard of proof will be set very high and that it will specifically not allow for utilitarian evidence or any evidence that requires comparing the interests of one person with those of another.[71]

This uncompromising position follows from the structure of Nozick's central presumption that personal rights impose absolute prohibitions or constraints on the authority of others to invade a residual sphere of personal autonomy. From a rhetorical point of view, this position can become the founding presumption for a complete social system, reflecting the bedrock intuitions of Nozick-the-philosopher: "The moral side constraints upon what we may do, I claim, reflect the fact of our separate existences. They reflect the fact that no moral balancing act can take place among us; there is no moral outweighing of one of our lives by others so as to lead to a greater overall social good. There is no justified sacrifice of some of us for others."[72] As with other foundations cast in the form of presumptions, the theory of rights as exclusionary constraints is also the conclusion of an implicit argument-from-ignorance—carefully constructed by Nozick-the-strategist but scarcely alluded to in an otherwise free-wheeling text.[73] Perhaps Nozick's foundational argument is left unstated because its basic presumption is so familiar within the liberal political tradition: the lack of relevant criteria on which to ground intervention in the life of another human being.[74]

In a subsection entitled, "What Are Constraints Based Upon?" Nozick briefly entertains an opposing line of thought, as he searches in vain for any positive evidence that individuals are entitled to absolute autonomy: for "an intervening variable M . . . which has a perspicuous and convincing connection to moral constraints on behavior toward someone with M."[75] However, even at the abstract level of "that elusive and difficult notion: the meaning of life," Nozick cannot explain how the bare capacity for directing one's own life can "bridge an 'is-ought' gap," even though this sort of capacity has "the right 'feel'."[76] In the final analysis, Nozick asks, why couldn't life just be meaningless? He concludes this revealing section with assurances that he plans "to grapple with these and related issues on another occasion," but not in this book.[77]

I shall not take time to explore the calculatedly extreme libertarian theorems Nozick derived from his starting premises, which now seem less *outré* to the general reader of moral philosophy than they did fifteen years ago. But it may be useful to pause briefly over his equally striking speculation on the comparative rights of persons and animals—a topic that has likewise grown familiar and can now boast its own specialized journals and robust intramural dissension.

Nozick understood that the same negative premises on which he built his defense of personal rights could apply just as well to other living creatures. The inability to justify interference with persons, using utilitarian arguments, seems equally manifest when it comes to animals, and perhaps also with inanimate nature. We generally assume that the interests of humans outweigh those of animals, says Nozick, but how can we ever really be sure? If at least some animals are deemed to have worthwhile interests in their own right, precisely "how much do they count, and how can this be determined?" True, says Nozick, there may be no affirmative evidence that animals have dignitary rights—or rights not to have their liberties tampered with. But the same affirmative evidence is lacking for human liberties too; surely, we would never conclude from this fact alone that humans have no rights! If the lack of evidence generates one result for humans, why not the same result for animals?[78] Nozick's text is full of such sharply punctuated questions; and whereas he seems to discard the whole topic as a bit of playful rhetoric, he nonetheless takes time to share his personal intuitions on behalf of vegetarianism.[79]

Animal rights are no casual concern for many moral philosophers. The term *speciesism* has been coined by those who take animal rights seriously and who demand evidence from their opponents that such rights do not exist. Among this group is Mary Midgley, who has pondered the moral implications of speciesism: "What points does the word *speciesism* exist to make? Its most obvious use is to deny the . . . supposition that the species boundary not only makes a difference, but makes the gigantic difference of setting the limits of morality, of deciding whether a given creature can matter to us at all. Here speciesism corresponds to the most extreme form of racism, which takes the same line."[80] The parallels with antidiscrimination logic are important for Midgley. "Is there any clear principle," she asks, "which would prohibit absolute dismissal of entire classes of people, and still allow it for animals?"[81] The argument is precisely the same one that Warren-era litigators used on behalf of new suspect classifications. As Midgley points out, many of the criteria considered good reasons for treating animals as subhuman have, at one time or another, been applied invidiously to certain classes of human beings. But modern societies now reject those criteria in their human application, and they have yet to produce adequate proof to justify their use with animals. The convenience of human beings is not, of course, the kind of evidence that is allowed to count in this tribunal.[82]

Protected from skeptical critique by our inability to prove them wrong in a court of higher appeal, the varied presumptions of ethical discourse have been left to flourish over the past two decades. The climate has been so favorable, in fact, that it is difficult to imagine how any species of argument could fail the test of sheer survival—provided it stays close to the transcendental definition of rights. In this chapter I have examined the notion of rights as legal entitlements, defined and delivered by virtuoso judges; rights as the procedural byproducts of social machinery, chosen by persons in their transcendental state of nature; rights as absolute prohibitions on collective action, in the absence of consent (the type of consent found chiefly in the marketplace); and rights that constrain human relations with animals (and perhaps also inanimate nature), more or less parallel to constraints on invasions of human autonomy.[83] The literature in this field has been growing exponentially, and it gives every indication of expanding further along its centrifugal course.

One cannot dismiss the possibility that reflective equilibrium will eventually start to exert the kind of unifying force that its theoretical partisans sometimes imagine—not only within the experience of single souls, but across groups as well. But nor can one presume that consensus is the natural tendency of the reflective method. As one proponent has expressed it, reflective equilibrium "aspires to be of universal significance, or at least of significance to anyone who broadly agrees in the particular judgments of the theorist which supply the theory's data base. How far the theorist may expect to secure such agreement, and in particular whether agreement may be expected across cultural barriers, is a controversial question."[84] Cohen finds nothing worrisome about this dispersion of cognitive or ethical authority occasioned by the desire to approach normative problems through nonscientific modes of reasoning. Indeed, he sees the lack of closure in philosophical debate as one of its great strengths. "The objective progress of philosophy has to be judged . . . by appraisal of its merit as a dialogue between people who do not necessarily all share the same premises and principles." Popper gave a similar endorsement to the never-ending struggle he associated with the authority of science.[85]

Whatever the quality of dialogue set in motion by the transcendental turn in moral philosophy, there are few signs it is leading any closer to social consensus. As Cohen notes:

> The actual dialogue of analytical philosophers disappoints all expectations of finality and finds no shortage of new problems, new arguments, and new solutions. . . . The method . . . has now apparently lent itself . . . to the exposition of a vast variety of conflicting philosophical doctrines, without any of the emerging consensus that distinguishes the progress of science and was originally expected from logico-linguistic philosophy. . . . Above all the expectation of an eventual consensus seems radically flawed.[86]

As Cohen further emphasizes, this prognosis implies no lack of dedication or skill on the part of current philosophers. On the contrary, the dialogue in ques-

194

tion cannot avoid "appealing, at certain crucial points, to the far from unanimous tribunals of intuition, common sense, or general acceptance . . . , while science respects instead the normally united tribunal of experience." In the end, "philosophical dialogue has a natural tendency to generate opposing theories."[87]

If ethical dialogue cannot ensure social agreement, what then can it accomplish? Perhaps its main contribution has been to encourage a fresh look at the problems of legitimacy that plague most ongoing social enterprises. The ethical critic's removal to a transcendental perspective remains vital to this mission, if everyday events cannot otherwise reveal their ethical dimensions to the casual observer. In contrast to situational lay judgments, ethical authority presumes that the highest standard of legitimacy must be universalistic. Human beings must either have access to this higher authority, or else they are condemned to the morally fragmented level of particular interests.

In a society that often seems to have misplaced its ability to resolve value questions through civilized discussion, new ethical systems respond to a self-diagnosed social malaise. Transcendental authority fills the vacuum left by the retreat of customary values, which scientific expertise can no longer plausibly replace. Like the courts in everyday public life, constructed ethical schemes can be invested with residual normative authority, especially if the only alternative is assumed to be further decline into cultural ignorance. As Cohen bravely suggests, "By its systematic exploration of reasons and reasoning, analytical philosophy helps to consolidate the intellectual infrastructure that is needed for systems of social organization within which disputes are reflected in argument and counter-argument." Its task is to "clarify, evaluate, improve, or redesign the various rational frameworks within which people can determine the optimal solutions of their personal, social, cultural, technical, or scientific problems."[88]

195

The positive constructions produced across multiple ethical jurisdictions seem to share a common rhetorical foundation in negative critique. Thus moral philosophers have an ambiguous stake in the very diagnosis of ignorance, whose effects they seek to mitigate. Rather than simply responding to cultural ignorance, they must first postulate a deeper, transcendental, dimension to the contemporary malaise. It is because other normative procedures cannot possibly provide appropriate remedies that one must entertain the constructions of analytical philosophy.

Perhaps there is nothing remarkable about this strategic foundation, even for a system that aspires to universal authority. After all, the major intellectual target of recent moral philosophy—utilitarianism—based most of its own improbable postulates on the alleged incurable failures of its predecessors, including natural-law theories, religious authority, and traditional superstition. The technocratic idiom embedded in utilitarian theories helped to ensure their parallel rise along-side scientific authority throughout the nineteenth century, and (with periodic setbacks) into our own century as well. If the time has come to search for some new idioms, there may be nothing stronger for their foundation than the weak-ness of prior concepts. As with most intellectual shifts discussed throughout this book, this one seems to depend on magnifying the deficiencies of its rivals. It relies on implicit antinomies to support a transcendental distinction between policies and principles, between everyday self-interest and choices exercised in the original position, and between pluralistic interests and individual autonomy.

As in constitutional due process litigation, the critique of any preceding dominant discourse can sometimes strike a neutral (and perhaps even heroic) posture. It is on this basis, for example, that Cohen gives transcendental ethics (and analytic philosophy generally) such high marks as a form of dialogue.

> By virtue of its preoccupation with rationality [analytical philosophy] pro-motes awareness that the intellectual merit of a person's opinion does not hinge on his membership of a particular party, priesthood, or hermetic tra-dition. And, with its interest in picking out ultimate issues for discussion, it tends to undermine any support for the view that certain accepted principles, prerogatives, or presumptions are intrinsically immune to rational criticism and appraisal. No tenets are sacrosanct for it.[89]

196

Neutral due process litigation depended heavily on a judicial framework in which to operate, with its central dialectical procedures fully institutionalized. Similarly, the critique originating with transcendental tribunals rests on a frame-work of philosophical presumptions, which support the norms and intuitions that come under transcendental scrutiny but are not themselves subjected to critique. From a dialectical perspective, there is special irony in the claim of analytical philosophy to occupy itself "with a search for hitherto unnoticed presuppositions or implications," with "normative problems about reasons and reasoning," with critical concern for "permissive inferential rules," and with "the nature of philo-sophical inquiry itself." [90] To aspire to all these goals, and yet to remain silent on the strategic or dialectical foundations of its own practice could indicate that transcendental method has reached its farthest limits.

Further indications of limits appear whenever ethical interpreters announce that the time has come to stop talking. In line with the old Wittgensteinian ap-prehension about reaching "the limits of our language," the leading exponents of ethical authority have a sure sense of precisely when transcendental courts need to take a strategic recess. An especially blunt example comes from Ronald Dworkin, in response to an encounter with post-structuralist skepticism about the notion of objective interpretation.

I have no interest in trying to compose a general defense of the objectivity of my interpretive or legal or moral opinions. In fact, I think that the whole issue of objectivity, which so dominates contemporary theory in these areas, is a kind of fake. We should stick to our knitting. We should account to ourselves for our own convictions as best we can, standing ready to abandon those that do not survive reflective inspection. We should make such arguments to others, who do not share our opinions, as we can make in good faith and break off arguing when no further argument is appropriate. I do not mean that this is all we can do because we are creatures with limited access to true reality or with necessarily parochial viewpoints. I mean that we can give no sense to the idea that there is anything else we could do in deciding whether our judgments are "really" true.[91]

Putting Ethics into Practice: Judicializing the Professions

Despite the historic shift to broad principles in moral philosophy, much recent ethical debate has been focused on intensely practical questions. Probably the most widely discussed issues have arisen in medical settings, where the new field of bioethics has become a powerful influence on professional reflection and daily practice. Ethical conundrums, conflicts, and dilemmas have increasingly punctuated the routines of all the professions, including business and politics. Even legal and judicial practice have now lost their anomalous immunity, which protected them during the era when courts encouraged broad scrutiny of professional decision-makers in other public settings.[92]

As the transcendental movement in ethics becomes a stronger institutional force in practical affairs, its intimate connections with jurisprudential logic take on increasing importance. Ethical analysis will doubtless continue to displace constitutional law as the highest tribunal for reviewing all other forms of public authority, especially those elements of professional and academic practice that rest on scientific expertise. At the same time, as ethical principles take on a broader practical jurisdiction, their interpreters will be forced either to adopt some of the institutionalized procedures of the judicial system or to invent their own court-type structures.

The major influence of recent ethical perspectives within medical practice has been to challenge dominant professional and legal presumptions that were based on scientific method as an ultimate authority.[93] In operational terms, transcendental ethics seeks to disrupt the delicate compromise reached between scientific expertise and the normative strategy of utilitarian calculation. By positing a completely new ethical jurisdiction, in which utilitarian measurements are deemed to be poor evidence, ethicists have engineered a major shift in presump-

197

tions, accompanied by a shift in standards of normative proof. Measured against the categorical norms of transcendental ethics, all particularized and quantified values come up short. None of the counting, weighing, balancing, and comparing—activities that are commonly informed by professional expertise—can move a society closer to universal ethical principles. Prior to the transcendental turn, by contrast, utilitarian data were the only kinds of normative evidence admissible in tribunals dominated by the presumptions of positivistic science.

In displacing utilitarian or interest-based evidence in practical decision-making, transcendental ethics initially creates an immense normative vacuum, which its own professional exponents then hasten to fill with new presumptions serving a wide range of ideologies. Whatever their ultimate objectives, ethicists commonly start from general concepts of personal autonomy as basic operating principles. Their guiding procedure is to impose proof burdens (of varying degrees) on anyone seeking to contradict such postulated autonomous judgments. This general strategy derives from the transcendental monadology that makes each person the final court of appeal on his or her own moral goals—a metaphysical presumption implicit in the Rawlsian doctrines of the original position and reflective equilibrium and explicit in Nozick's libertarian theory of rights as preemptive constraints on public intervention.

198

Many bioethicists, in short, construct a normative presumption in favor of choices that are deemed to flow from the privileged authority of individual autonomy. They then assign varying proof burdens to medical professionals, public officials, social workers, relatives, friends, and other supporting players who are most likely to question the choices people commonly make in pursuit of their own, unreviewable vision of the good. Within this strategic framework, of course, there remain a great many variables that require further collective definition. For example, what are the socially recognizable criteria of a genuine personal choice? Who can make such choices, on which occasions, and concerning what kinds of events? What do we say when personal choices have an impact on third parties?

Depending on how such questions are answered, the practical results of bioethical analysis can vary enormously, even without disturbing the ethical primacy of individual autonomy. The bioethics literature is filled with borderline cases for every conceivable parameter, against which individual ethicists must continually test their intuitions. As it happens, many of these situations are also favorite topics for the popular media: the moribund patient who refuses further life-saving treatment; the eccentric homeless person who prefers the bitter cold of the streets to warm, paternalistic public shelters; the Jehovah's Witness parents who refuse to authorize an emergency blood transfusion for their injured child. Although popular attention may create the impression that bioethicists are professionally equipped to give authoritative solutions to these difficult problems, most ethical specialists disclaim any expertise beyond logical skill in clarifying conceptual boundaries.[94] However, precisely these boundary-maintenance tasks can have powerful strategic implications, as they support the dialectical implementation of transcendental constructions.

Bioethics ends up paying a considerable price for its commitment to transcendental norms. The diffuse nature of bioethical postulates (especially the principles of personal autonomy) ensures an endless succession of borderline cases, which must somehow be adjudicated according to practical dialectical procedures. Throughout this chapter, I have noted the inherent dilemmas of entrusting categorical standards to temporal institutions. If ethics wants to preserve its overriding concern for universal legitimacy, it requires a collective tribunal that runs like Dworkin's Herculean courtroom or like Rawls's assembly of Kantian souls in their original position.

To achieve determinate results with any hope of temporal finality, however, ethical authority must cooperate with supplementary jurisdictions, both in the philosophical realm of reflective equilibrium and in the practical realm of institutionalized, dialectical procedures. Either of these arenas may contaminate categorical ethical judgments with strategic elements, which are endemic to particularized perspectives and organizational structures. The resulting compromises can thus become the source of deep torments for bioethicists. As perennial critics of everyday ethical decisions by established bureaucracies, their arguments echo the rhetoric of losing parties in constitutional litigation, with indignant complaints about the biased judgments, the dim grasp of reality, and the poor craftsmanship of ethical tribunals that come out the wrong way.

In many respects, the field of bioethics is still a loose constellation of intellectual forces, united mainly by their strategic opposition to the dominant authority of professional opinion. Important efforts are now under way, however, to place the field on a more systematic footing and to repress boundary issues that plague the level of theory. One such project, unusually ambitious in scope, comes from bioethicist H. Tristram Engelhardt. Engelhardt has addressed a wide field of ethical indeterminacies with a series of presumptions, which he offers as philosophical "foundations."[95] Among its other virtues, his work shows how arguments-from-ignorance might eventually be used to channel the flow of strategic action within institutionalized ethical tribunals.

No doubt many other such treatises will appear in coming years, as bioethics moves down that same ramifying course of dialogue that Cohen has charted for analytical philosophy. But Engelhardt's work sets an imposing architectural standard; his framework of presumptions surrounding the concept of personal autonomy is so exhaustive that it seems likely to influence the style of many future constructions. Moreover, Engelhardt sees his work as continuing the philosophical enterprise spurred by Dworkin, Rawls, and Nozick—perhaps even improving on their theories. He clearly acknowledges the philosophical presumptions on which all of these ethical systems have been based, and he accurately traces their source to the transcendental method used by Kant and his successors.

Engelhardt's default framework for transcendental ethics shows its strategic origins in his philosophical rejection of alternative normative approaches, especially those methods that try to calculate collective goals by mixing discrete, particularized quantities of welfare. Engelhardt uses familiar analytical techniques to postulate a categorical ethical standard, presumed to correspond to "what we really mean" when "we" talk about morality—the same argument found in Dworkin, Rawls, Nozick, and other recent philosophers.[96] Having posited this standard, Engelhardt takes extraordinary trouble to deny that any substantive moral content whatsoever can be derived from it. To be sure, he acknowledges that some ethicists have used the transcendental turn to breathe new life into traditional values, harking back to prescientific cultures. Others have exploited the freedom of transcendental speculation to dignify the visions of new moral prophets. But all such moral systems, Engelhardt believes, are conditioned by the personalized intuitions of their beholders. The ethical monadology implicit in recent moral philosophy takes an especially rich form in Engelhardt's treatise: one can know that an ethical realm exists, he says, but no one is in a position to prove that any particular moral perspective can cover a wider, collective jurisdiction.

Engelhardt uses a subtle philosophical strategy to carry his bioethical presumptions to a degree of voluntarism comparable to Nozick's libertarianism. For Engelhardt, ethical authority is universal in meaning but highly particularistic in its temporal guise: each person has the potential to identify categorical normative standards, but only as they apply to his or her own personal development. As in Leibniz's metaphysical system, any vision of ethics *sub specie aeternitatis* can appear only in the mind of God; for us, the ethical world is divided into as many absolute jurisdictions as there are rational individuals. Each person's ethical judgment (his or her autonomy) is therefore inviolable: we have no truly collective moral life, but only such coalitions and associations (based on prudence) as sovereign individuals elect to create. Violations of personal autonomy constitute coercion and cannot be vindicated in any normative jurisdiction larger than the particular viewpoint of the coercer.

None of this elaborate ethical and social framework can itself be proved except as a series of default judgments, based on strategic reasoning that would require potential opponents, at every crucial step, to prove that Engelhardt's theorems cannot be valid. Engelhardt concedes that his argument yields a very slim basis for any public conception of the moral life, but he accepts this voluntaristic universe as a natural inference from the failure to establish any alternative moral structure.

> The hope of establishing through secular arguments the moral probity of any particular concrete moral viewpoint appears unfounded. The monotheistic presumption has in short collapsed. . . . If the expected means for establishing the correctness of a particular moral viewpoint fails, then without some new approach one will not be able (1) to establish *a* particular moral viewpoint as *the* proper moral viewpoint, and therefore (2) one will not be able to establish public policy bodies or individuals as having the moral authority to impose any particular moral points of view by force.[97]

Having thus excluded the possibility of discovering an operational collective morality through reason, tradition, or political action, Engelhardt falls back on his default notion of consent as a working principle for social cooperation: "If the authority of good arguments and common inspiration fails, the final possibility remains of deriving authority from the consent of those who fashion a community. There is still a generally understandable meaning to acting with moral authority—that is, with the consent of all those involved. . . . The only remaining source for authority will be common agreement."[98]

201

In theory, a relatively homogeneous society could discover a significant overlap of personal moral perceptions; and even in our own pluralistic, secular culture, numerous communities of common moral interest are known to exist. But Engelhardt declares that the only acceptable evidence for such moral consensus is the voluntary assent of individuals. By contrast, communities maintained through the privileged insights of professional or priestly authorities are presumptively coercive, as are all procedural devices (such as democratic politics) that merely assume the voluntary consent of participants: "Within a secular, pluralist society, not only will one not be able to identify who has embraced the *true*, concrete view of the good life, but agreement to moral claims by simple pluralities of the individuals involved in a controversy, or by majorities of two-thirds or three-fourths, also will not provide authority, unless *all* can be presumed to have agreed in advance to such procedures."[99] Many commentators, of course, would challenge Engelhardt's readiness to presume the voluntary nature of economic markets, in contrast to his skepticism about political systems.[100]

Engelhardt's libertarian social philosophy may be usefully compared to that of Nozick, who likewise imposes an overwhelming burden of proof on all coercive or political forms of social interaction, and who also postulates a residual category of voluntary interactions as requiring no special justification. Nozick's view of rights as preemptive constraints on public action (unless excused by an individual's voluntary consent) corresponds to Engelhardt's position that society's obligation to exercise forbearance requires no affirmative justification. The only social duty that emerges from this scheme is the negative obligation to leave each other alone, unless and until an invitation is properly delivered that initiates voluntary interaction. Nonintervention in the lives of sovereign individuals thus becomes a neutral principle.[101] But all this is just another way of stating that no other form of social practice has met (or can meet) the extraordinarily demanding ethical standards that Engelhardt shares with Nozick: "Apart from any arguments in principle on behalf of this view of toleration . . . , one might ask under what circumstances there could ever be a peaceable union of the peoples of the earth, save through acquiescing in the policy that persons may do with themselves and consenting others whatever they wish, despite what others might think and feel in the matter." [102]

For all the intellectual elegance and consistency of Engelhardt's approach, it leaves the concerned bioethicist with an immense collection of unresolved issues. As Engelhardt would doubtless concur, general principles of autonomy, nonintervention, and consent cannot be applied to concrete situations without some expenditure of dialectical energy. One must, as a practical social matter, be able to determine when a particular mentally impaired patient is no longer able to exercise the postulated power of autonomy; when the state's failure to intervene in a certain family's way of life places neglected or abused children in peril; and when a person's consent to certain health risks is based on ignorance or fear, rather than autonomous judgment.[103] In addition to the general principles of bioethics, one must also consider how concrete problems are classified and brought under those principles.

In the formal legal system, these interpretive tasks are handled (often quietly) by the institutionalized dialectic of judicial proceedings. This is in fact where the most difficult bioethical questions are ultimately delivered, although the courts can resolve only a relatively small number of cases. In the complex environment of medical settings, however, less formal mechanisms fulfill these dialectical functions, starting with professional judgments by individual practitioners, which are increasingly supplemented by the countervailing authority of medical review committees and ethical tribunals of varying formality.[104] Both types of dialectical power rely heavily on presumptions—both explicit and implicit—which define the residual or default conclusions on biomedical questions under conditions fraught with both scientific and cultural uncertainty. With its deeply skeptical challenge to the presumptions residing in professional expertise, the bioethics

202

movement has thus fostered competing dialectical forces, even though it cannot offer a fully institutionalized alternative.

No matter how much energy and ingenuity are expended on quasi-judicial structures, all dialectical procedures ultimately fall short of transcendental ethical standards. Even the judicial system is subject to residual challenge on ordinary legal questions, although most such challenges are muted by the social custom of investing courts with final authority to resolve disputed issues. In other words, society's collective need to find closure or finality in everyday legal disputes is generally strong enough to deflect unanswerable challenges to the legitimacy of those decisions. As Supreme Court Justice Robert Jackson wryly noted, the Court owes a large part of its normative authority to its unique institutional status as the final temporal authority on legal questions. In bioethical settings the need for determinate and orderly judgments is likewise very strong, but here the pursuit of finality works at cross purposes with transcendental standards of legitimacy.

The field of bioethics, as represented in works like Engelhardt's treatise, has codified a fundamental shift in presumptions that resembles the Warren Court's historic return to active judicial review. The same general (perhaps even neutral) principles of equal treatment and fair procedure stand behind both movements. So does the strategy of summoning the dominant authorities—in both cases, professionally trained experts and government officials—before a tribunal where their actions can be given close scrutiny under skeptical standards of review. In the case of bioethics, however, this shift has not been engineered by the courts, and thus it cannot fall back on a default procedure—like the federal judiciary—with some traditional claim to unite the dichotomous interests of legitimacy and finality.

Bioethics is the offshoot of a broad cultural challenge to scientific authority, which has been forced to presume the existence of a worthy rival. Because the power of this new authority depends on its postulated removal from contextual or situational judgments, its supporting structures are inherently problematic. Ethical standards can always find expression in working dialectical procedures, but only by risking their own dispersion across multiple and conflicting jurisdictions, including existing court structures, ad hoc institutional procedures, the constructive systems of moral philosophers, and the nonreviewable judgments of individuals in reflective equilibrium.

Paradoxically, the transcendental turn studied in this chapter can be rescued from this fate of dismemberment by situating it historically, culturally, and strategically in late-twentieth century skepticism about the exclusive authority of scientific and professional expertise. As the latest in a recurring cycle of such conflicts, the recent explosion of interest in both moral theory and professional ethics may be seen as an academic and a popular rebellion against a set of social presumptions that have accompanied the unprecedented influence of science and technology. Perhaps it is the same cultural message—albeit in scrupulously secular form—as the rejection of socioeconomic modernization in societies where traditional, prescientific values remain very strong.

This interpretation of contemporary ethics as a higher (but still somehow secular) authority places the central emphasis on a negative argument: the rejection of a cultural realm in which scientific authority stands as our highest court of appeal. It may be tempting to view this whole argument as a somewhat scrofulous strategy for smuggling ethics in through the back door by the indirect route of default reasoning. But such a dismissive critique runs the risk of ignoring the negative argument as a significant expression in its own right. Even if the resulting default position becomes a matter of some controversy, the current strength of cultural ambivalence about scientific authority should not be lost in the analysis.

Taken in the abstract, negative arguments retain something of a bad odor: a truly honest argument would seem to come right out and state its affirmative message. Even Orwell might listen politely, although his final verdict was already sealed in advance. In the case of transcendental ethics, however, the consistent failure to produce flesh-and-blood alternatives to scientific authority should not be dismissed as cowardice. Rather, it reveals a complex rhetorical posture, whose philosophical presumptions extend at least as far back as Kant.

204

Chapter 7   Transcendental Foundations

The conflict between scientific and ethical authority ripened in the historical context of neo-Kantian philosophy at the end of the nineteenth century. Although the central figures in this important movement have been curiously neglected in twentieth-century debate, their rhetorical practices have remained highly influential, especially for the growth and critical aspirations of social science. Their distinctive presumption was to create separate jurisdictions for science and values, certified by a transcendental tribunal with its own problematic claim to authority. The original convenor of this tribunal was Kant himself, whose philosophical method firmly anchored the rhetorical conditions for modern polemical debate. The fragmentation of neo-Kantianism into disputes between (and among) foundationalists and contextualists reveals the inescapable tensions of transcendental argument, anticipating adversarial trends in public discourse.

Modern Discourse and the Conflict of Authorities

Contemporary debates reflect the growing skills of proponents in waging polemical battles based on sweeping philosophical presumptions. These practices have important antecedents in intellectual movements from the past two centuries, centered on the recurring struggle between competing sources of rational authority. This struggle is often understood to define a distinctly modern temperament shaped by religious and scientific events marking the transition from the Middle Ages.[1] The enduring challenge for the modern spirit has been to find a procedure for adjudicating such fundamental conflicts. This strongly pragmatic desire points toward an elusive, overarching type of authority: a unifying force that serves as an impartial court of final appeal, operating with both finality and legitimacy.

The notion of a powerful tribunal for human reason emerged fully with Kant's efforts, at the end of the eighteenth century, to qualify the status of scientific authority and to find a workable procedure for resolving conflicts between science and its various challengers.[2] Kant's enigmatic shift to a transcendental mode of reflection provides the central model for contemporary argument patterns, starting with the strategic use of self-diagnosed ignorance. Despite the otherworldly sound of the term *transcendental,* Kant's philosophical method invokes a distinctively humanistic perspective, one designed to strike a delicate balance between contingent evidence and timeless principles.[3] Implied in this presumption is the power of human reason to mediate conflicts between the expanding empirical sciences and various residual sources of authority, including ethical, religious, and aesthetic realms that supplement the appearance of objects in space and time.[4]

Kant explicitly called for a philosophical "tribunal" to resolve the otherwise interminable tensions within human reason, even though his reliance on legal imagery raised new ambiguities for the whole problem of authority.[5] Many subsequent thinkers have drawn profound inspiration from this self-justifying humanism (along with Kant's taste for jurisprudential metaphors) as a strategic response to changing physical and social environments. At several historic junctures, indeed, critics have found themselves turning "back to Kant" to rebuild their philosophical foundations and to clarify their sense of practical direction.[6]

In many respects, the contemporary battle of scientific and ethical authority can be understood as one more variation on a cultural theme formed in a Kantian mode. The conflicts discussed in chapters 5 and 6 have an especially close kinship with debates from the end of the nineteenth century and may profitably be seen in that context.[7] Both then and now, public controversy centers on the status of scientific method, following on periods of revolutionary achievement in science and technology. With each historical return to this type of conflict, the intellectual forces challenging science seem farther removed from their original base in custom or traditional belief. For Kant, as for the first great wave of neo-Kantians, organized religion was still a potent alternative to ascendant scientific authority. For us, however, the challenge is to supplement a rapacious science with whatever alternatives we can plausibly find—but not necessarily those rooted in past belief systems. Kant's transcendental perspective provides most of the tools we need for confronting this contemporary problem. His concepts and procedures place limits on science without embracing traditional belief as the sole residual authority. Kant's philosophy thus encourages the growth of new orientations, but it may also become the unwitting source of recurring disillusion and pessimism.[8]

Intimations of our contemporary challenge can be found in the writings of the Scottish philosopher Edward Caird, who helped introduce Kant to the English-speaking world a century ago. In his influential 1889 commentary, Caird suggested the Kantian term "criticism" for the task of mediating conflicts of authority—the task Kant had earlier assigned to his philosophical tribunal. For Caird, criticism had two major phases, the first of which was illustrated by the growth of science as the skeptical opponent of traditional belief:

Criticism is always the result of the fact that the intelligence has found its way blocked by some difficulty, which has awakened a suspicion against the universal applicability of the categories or methods which it had been using. In this sense criticism was at the very birth of science, and it has mediated every transition to a new point of view, by which science has widened the scope of its investigations and brought the concrete fact of the world in its diversity and unity more definitely within the reach of the intelligence.[9]

Eventually, Caird noted, a shift in critical tasks becomes necessary with the tendency of modern science to extend its own methods beyond their skeptical, situational context, a tendency to develop new principles of "universal applicability." According to Caird, the habit of successfully deploying empirical methods has led quite naturally to the assumption that these same methods should be applied to all problems.

It is in the attempt to universalise the principles of such science that the metaphysical difficulty makes its appearance. These principles have a sphere in which they are continually verifying themselves by making new conquests, and therefore, the intelligence is only following a natural impulse when it tries to use them as guides in other spheres. So long as we are dealing with the material world, we find no reason to doubt their applicability; why should we hesitate to apply them to the solution of questions as to the spiritual world,— questions as to the nature of the soul, the mode of its presence in the world, and the way in which it acts and is acted upon by other beings and things?[10]

The resulting confrontation of scientific method with residual forms of authority gives rise, according to Caird, to an "antinomy between the principles of physical science and that unscientific consciousness of spiritual reality which is expressed in religion and morality."[11]

The intensity of the conflict which thus arises finds its measure only in the importance of the interests arranged on either side. On the one side, the intolerance, with which the scientific man regards any refusal to admit the universality of his method, really springs from one of the deepest intellectual instincts of man, which will not let him treat anything as truth that is not universally valid. . . . On the other hand, those who resist the extension of these principles to the new region, though often unable to oppose to them any distinct principle of their own, are supported by a consciousness of the facts of their own spiritual life, and by a perception that these facts, which to them are the most certain of all, must be treated as illusory if the claims of science be admitted.[12]

207

Unlike Kant, Caird never tied the process of criticism to jurisprudential concepts, metaphorical or otherwise. His imagined critic played the role of questioner and qualifier, searching for inevitable limits to the most powerful ideas of the moment and not halting to declare winners or losers. Most major debates in philosophy, Caird assumed, display the same stubborn structure, in which "opposite but complementary aspects or elements of a truth are taken for absolutely contradictory views of that truth." These controversies "attempt to settle by a simple 'yes' or 'no' questions which cannot be thus simply answered. Hence each answer involves an absurdity and is open to an irresistible attack from the other side, and that disputant will be victorious who can secure the attack and force his opponents to act on the defensive." [13]

The special role of criticism is to "get beyond the sphere in which a controversy is carried on, and to throw new light upon it from a point of view which is above that of either of the disputants, though it is also a point of view which both the disputants tacitly acknowledge." [14] Unless they face up to this distinctive task, philosophers (and other disputants) remain metaphorical adversaries, separated by rival arguments delivered as absolute, dogmatic positions. Significantly, Caird also locates the skeptic within this same adversarial forum, the partisan who categorically condemns other positions as dogmatic and mutually defeating.

208

> A dogmatism is an attempt to explain the whole universe by a principle which applies only to a fragment or phase of it, while the opposite dogmatism denies that that principle has any validity whatever, and puts an opposite principle in its place. Finally, the resulting scepticism is simply the unlimited rejection of both the opposite dogmas. But if this is so, it becomes obvious that all the combatants are fighting within a closed arena where no conclusive victory can be gained. The only way to put an end to the dispute is to break through the narrow conditions under which it has been carried on. And it is just this which Criticism seeks to do. [15]

In 1889, Caird saw "the special intellectual task of the present age" as the need to apply procedures of criticism to "the fixed opposition between the material and the spiritual world." [16] More than a century later, that task remains largely unfulfilled; indeed, the stultifying effects of fixed oppositions seem to have increased. Rather than bringing conflicts to a peaceful result, contemporary tribunals appear to sharpen existing divisions, even as jurisprudential authority descends from its transcendental abode and shapes the everyday world according to the demands of litigation.

Kantian Origins of the Argument-from-Ignorance

Kant's critical tribunal sought to accommodate both science and ethics by partitioning human experience into fundamentally distinct levels of reflection. His overarching strategy of assuming discontinuous kinds of experience, or "perspectives,"[17] is a major source of the narrative obscurity found throughout Kant's writings—but surely also the secret of their perennial appeal. By investing opposing perspectives with presumptive authority, philosophers were able to draw radically distinct messages out of Kant's works from the moment they appeared. With their extraordinary flexibility, Kant's multiple perspectives provide a durable framework for intellectual debate in an adversarial mode that was by no means limited to academic philosophy. Over the past two centuries, virtually every major school of Western thought has found strategic comfort in this Kantian scheme with its elusive juridical powers.

The Kantian strategy of partitioning human reason into multiple camps is especially useful for challenging a point of view that has acquired the dominance of an inertial force. Kant's approach creates an impregnable base for subversive operations, from which the critic may safely attack a more powerful adversary. Kant wanted to impose a truce on the debilitating cultural battles of his own day, and this has often been taken as his legacy. But more frequently the Kantian framework has stimulated dramatic shifts in the intellectual balance of power, as rival camps seek to redraw the boundaries separating their philosophical redoubts.

Depending on how it is applied, Kant's juridical authority can offer strategic advantages to a variety of claimants. It may strengthen an ascendant or dominant perspective (the Newtonian physics of Kant's day, for example) against attack by either traditionalists or skeptical philosophers. It may also revive declining or less powerful perspectives, just as Kant sought to inject new life into ethics and religion. Both kinds of support are provided by Kant's distinctive transcendental boundaries, which prevent adversaries on both sides from mounting a direct attack on their opponents. From the standpoint of the parties, these jurisdictional lines define a strategically postulated zone of ignorance—a presumption of conceptual discontinuity, such that neither side can absorb the other. The parties' future relations are governed by this reciprocal inability to produce evidence that both sides will accept as definitive. Negative arguments thus come to play an indispensable role in Kantian debate.

The plasticity of Kant's approach is reflected in the shifting emphases across his own major works, especially his efforts to balance the competing authority of science and ethics.[18] A powerful brief for the dominant authority of scientific method has often been taken from the *Critique of Pure Reason,* especially by nineteenth-century schools of realism and naturalism.[19] The First *Critique* encouraged these movements with its highly restrictive definition of knowledge, reflecting an empiricist emphasis on spatial-temporal data in human experience. Styles of Kantian scholarship periodically return to this reading, which elevates rule-governed, spatial-temporal experience into an epistemological standard immune to skeptical attack.[20]

At the same time, an equally strong brief can be written for the separate claims of ethics and religious belief, based on Kant's ethical writings and a crucial negative inference drawn from the First *Critique.* By making knowledge so restrictive, Kant ensured its inability to preempt those creative reflections, for which spatial-temporal data are said to play no significant role.[21] Included among these privileged insights—in addition to ethics and religion—are Kant's philosophical doctrines: the transcendental judgments delivered by his famous tribunal.

As Kant pointed out in the preface to the second edition, the very question of whether there may be other kinds of knowledge beyond the rule-governed, spatial-temporal field cannot itself be answered by means of spatial-temporal evidence. This negative premise opened up all the space Kant needed to postulate a separate realm for "faith," for a distinctive "practical reason" immune to skeptical arguments derived from empirical science.

210

> On a cursory view of the present work it may seem that its results are merely *negative,* warning us that we must never venture with speculative reason beyond the limits of experience. Such is in fact its primary use. But such teaching at once acquires a *positive* value . . . since it thereby removes an obstacle which stands in the way of the employment of practical reason, nay threatens to destroy it. . . .
>
> Though [practical] reason . . . requires no assistance from speculative reason, it must yet be assured against its opposition, that reason may not be brought into conflict with itself. To deny that the service which the Critique renders is *positive* in character, would thus be like saying that the police are of no positive benefit, inasmuch as their main business is merely to prevent the violence of which citizens stand in mutual fear, in order that each may pursue his vocation in peace and security.[22]

Although it is plain that Kant recognized the strategic implications of his own philosophical doctrines,[23] he was not content to rest his views simply on pragmatic effects. Kant also demanded a special juridical authority to separate the overlapping claims of science and ethics. This "tribunal of pure reason" implies yet a third perspective, going beyond both the empirical and the practical but

nonetheless vividly imagined by Kant as the final court of appeal for all jurisdictional questions. In his preface to the first edition, Kant invoked this tribunal
with his famous challenge: "a call to reason to undertake anew the most difficult
of all its tasks, namely, that of self-knowledge, and to institute a tribunal which
will assure to reason its lawful claims, and dismiss all groundless pretensions,
not by despotic decrees, but in accordance with its own eternal and unalterable
laws. This tribunal is no other than the *critique of pure reason.*"[24]

Although Kant relied freely on jurisprudential metaphors, he never explained
very clearly the nature of juridical authority, whose higher-order efficacy became one of his own unexamined presumptions.[25] The tribunal of pure reason
"insists upon laws"[26]—not simply personal opinion or strategic compromise—
for grounding its jurisdictional rulings. Justifications for the tribunal's decisions
"have to state the right or the legal claim," and Kant gives them the technical
jurisprudential label of "deductions."[27] He defends this aspiration for his unique
transcendental perspective by extending the jurisprudential analogy to encompass the *quaestio quid juris* of Roman law, the question of right as opposed to
mere determinations of fact.[28] Kant needed an unassailable authority to certify
transcendental boundaries within human reason, and yet he offered little more
than colorful imagery to describe this unique regulative function.

At least two sections of the First *Critique* shed important light on Kant's jurisprudential presumptions. The formal discussion of method in part 2 explicates
juridical authority with lucid (but paradoxical) indirection: by showing what it is
not. Second, the notoriously difficult "transcendental deduction" of the "pure
categories of the understanding" tries to capture juridical authority in a vanishing moment of self-certification. Both of these discussions can help clarify the
strategic implications of Kant's historic effort to settle the competing claims of
science and ethics.

Part 2 of the First *Critique* contains the most accessible of Kant's scattered remarks on his own philosophical assumptions. Paradoxically, these passages yield
no important examples of those assertoric, "apodeictic," or ostensive arguments
that Kant sometimes said were essential for backing the pronouncements of
juridical critique.[29] Instead, Kant provides an intriguing series of indirect, "apogogic" arguments, which preview the basic pattern of arguments-from-ignorance
developed over the next two centuries.[30] By showing how philosophical authority
should not be defended, Kant rests his case for the elusive affirmative qualities
of philosophical (or transcendental) proof.

Although Kant's arguments in these sections risk self-defeat, his basic
strategy shows a rare simplicity, descriptive clarity, and rhetorical sensitivity. For
contemporary readers, moreover, it contains important clues for understanding

211

public debate under modern conditions, in an era that still embraces the ideal of authority modeled on judicial finality but disagrees about who can properly speak for that authority. Kant thus prepares us well for the many trials awaiting public discourse under the presumed jurisdiction of a single highest court, as conflicting parties vie to control that court's unappealable pronouncements.[31]

Kant gives a telling description of rhetorical conflict between intellectual combatants in what he calls the "polemical employment of pure reason."[32] Advocates in such confrontations defend their views "dogmatically," finding comfort in their opponent's inability to disprove their respective positions: "Here the contention is not that [one's] own assertions may not, perhaps, be false, but only that no one can assert the opposite with apodeictic certainty, or even, indeed, with a greater degree of likelihood. We do not here hold our possessions upon sufferance; for although our title to them may not be satisfactory, it is yet quite certain that no one can ever be in a position to prove the illegality of the title."[33] This familiar battle of indirect arguments, in which each side rests its claim on the inability of the other to offer conclusive counter-evidence, can lead only to endless dispute, according to Kant. Whenever an opponent relies on such indirect grounds, "it is an easy matter to refute him. The dogmatist cannot, however, profit by this advantage. His own judgments are, as a rule, no less dependent upon subjective influences; and he can himself in turn be similarly cornered by his opponent."[34]

Kant illustrates this futile style of debate in one of the central topics of his own philosophy: the status of "practical" authority in morality and religion. For this analysis, Kant borrowed the substantive results of his philosophical critique: that science and ethics have no commerce with each other but belong rather to two fundamentally different orders of reflection. (In part 1, Kant had surveyed this debate from the viewpoint of a transcendental judge, whose unique perspective was there simply presumed.) Here Kant shifts his attention to the principal adversaries: the overzealous champion of experience, who reduces everything to the standards of scientific method, and the ardent believer, who uses alleged spiritual insights to challenge scientific experience. "Both parties beat the air, and wrestle with their own shadows, since they go beyond the limits of nature, where there is nothing that they can seize and hold with their dogmatic grasp. Fight as they may, the shadows which they cleave asunder grow together again forthwith, like the heroes in Valhalla, to disport themselves anew in the bloodless contests."[35] Such polemical arguments have a leveling effect, according to Kant, since neither side can offer conclusive evidence on behalf of its own dogma. "This equality of fortune [in the ventures] of human reason does not . . . favour either of the two parties, and it is consequently the fitting battle-ground for their never-ending feuds."[36]

212

This symmetrical relationship can suddenly shift, Kant notes, owing to an important strategic advantage devolving on proponents of ethical authority. According to the compromise that allowed Kant to "make room for faith," ethical authority has been elevated to a higher jurisdiction where empirical proof no longer decides. The advocate for ethical authority has a peculiar rhetorical stake in positing transcendental ignorance[37] at the margins of scientific knowledge. So long as hypotheses about morality and religion avoid making empirical claims on their own behalf, they enjoy a kind of negative presumption within their own special sphere, sanctioned by the transcendental court of pure reason.

Such presumptions have no value whatsoever in the empirical tribunals of scientific method, but they become irrebuttable within the projected domain of practical reason. An easy victory in the court of spatial-temporal experience will be summarily reversed in a different jurisdiction, entered by way of a rhetorical tour de force.

> In the practical sphere, reason has rights of possession that it does not have to prove, and for which, in fact, it could not produce any proof. Thus the opponent is expected to prove his case. But since the latter knows just as little of the object under question, in trying to prove its non-existence, as does the former in maintaining its reality, it is evident that the former, who is asserting something as a practically necessary supposition, is at an advantage. For he is at liberty to employ, as it were in self-defence, on behalf of his own good cause, the very same weapons that his opponent employs against that cause.[38]

Within this specially defined practical sphere, Kant grants the advocate of ethical authority broad creative power to invoke hypotheses. However shadowy their origins, these postulates enjoy intriguing rhetorical privileges in their battles with empiricist critics.

> Hypotheses are not available for the purposes of basing propositions upon them, [but] they are entirely permissible for the purposes of defending propositions; that is to say, they may not be employed in any dogmatic, but only in polemical fashion. By the defence of propositions I do not mean the addition of fresh grounds for their assertion, but merely the nullifying of the sophistical arguments by which our opponent professes to invalidate this assertion.[39]

Kant's whole notion of polemics can now be seen in a different light. By endorsing the polemical use of hypotheses as a defensive maneuver, Kant acknowledged the strategic functions of an otherwise sterile form of argumention. In a juridically defined sphere where uniform standards of evidence no longer govern the outcome of arguments, self-defense takes the place of truth.[40] The field for indirect argument expands as the authority of science faces stricter transcendental scrutiny—and as its pretensions to universal authority are countered by the assertions of practical reason. The argument-from-ignorance thus becomes the natural ally of any advocate who challenges a position based entirely on empirical standards. Under these conditions, the balance of power between contenders may shift back and forth, and the rhetorical battle falls to whoever can command the transcendental high ground.

Kant's description of the polemical uses of reason, with its careful attention to strategic interaction, serves an important negative function within the First *Critique*. Kant describes polemical argument as the antithesis of the kind of reasoning by which philosophical authority must be established. But he cannot provide, in affirmative terms, any proof structure for this higher pattern of reasoning. He gives it the unique force of juristic deduction and insists that it must be direct, apodeictic, and ostensive, rather than indirect, apogogic, and defensive. But his chapters on method say nothing about the structure of a transcendental deduction, except that it is posited as something greater than logical deduction and evidence-based induction. Accordingly, the unique authority of Kant's philosophical tribunal rests on the same rhetorical shift—the same negative foundations—as the hypotheses of practical reason. Although rich with paradox, this was the only method Kant found for escaping the conceivably greater paradoxes of two alternate strategies: an infinite regress of authorities or an appeal to personal intuition.

214

To be sure, Kant had already offered a single controversial example of transcendental deduction earlier in the First *Critique*, when he sought to demonstrate the role of "categories" ("pure concepts of the understanding") in everyday experience of rule-governed spatial-temporal events. This was not a proof of philosophical authority as such, nor even a bare description of philosophical proof procedure. It was, rather, a concrete illustration of how such a procedure might work for one particular case, taken from the heart of his own epistemological theories. This case is widely conceded to be the most obscure passage in all Kant's works, if not in all of modern philosophy.

There can be little doubt that the fog surrounding this notorious deduction is deepened by its strategic importance for Kant's entire philosophical project. If philosophical reason cannot supply the proof for its own authority, then Kant's epistemological teachings are reduced to dogmatism, unable to live up to their critical aspirations. Kant's tribunal might still issue its famous rulings, but it could not vindicate its command over a universal jurisdiction, its claim to be the court of last appeal on matters of human reason. Its ability to speak on behalf of "our" reason—which Kant assumed was common to all human beings—would become deeply relativized: the limits of our world would suddenly vary according to the particular tribunal under whose limited jurisdiction we happened to fall.

Unless the process of transcendental deduction can somehow prevent this prolif-eration of tribunals competing for final authority, Kant's teachings are destined to sharpen the polemical tendencies of public discourse.

Even without this dispersion of philosophical authority, moreover, Kantian philosophy greatly expands the strategic importance of presumptive limits to knowledge. By positing transcendental ignorance as a boundary zone front-ing onto a higher jurisdiction, advocates compete to map the presumptions under which this elevated tribunal shall be assumed to operate. Arguments-from-ignorance become the standard rhetorical tool for advocates of competing transcendental postulates. The polemical battle between science and ethics, as described by Kant, thus becomes the general model for an adversarial mode of discourse, centered on irresolvable disputes over the proper location of transcen-dental boundaries. For Kant, the distinction between experience and practical reason became a polemical antinomy, in which scientific proof can always be challenged at the margin as limiting the scope of human freedom. Here is the prototype of the neo-Kantian dichotomy of facts and values, as well as the leading twentieth-century dualism of thought and being.

Perhaps Kant understood all too well the rhetorical implications of his whole enterprise and thus looked to the elusive process of transcendental deduction to curb the polemical tendencies within his philosophical project. Despite his own subtle command of indirect-argument strategies, with their novel presumption of transcendental ignorance, Kant insisted that all apogogic proofs were ulti-mately self-destructive unless founded on a transcendental deduction.[41] In order to halt the "endless disputes of a merely dogmatic reason,"[42] Kant thought, he must certify the authority of that uniquely powerful tribunal belonging to pure reason: "Everyone must defend his position directly, by a legitimate proof that carries with it a transcendental deduction of the grounds upon which it is itself made to rest. Only when this has been done, are we in a position to decide how far its claims allow of rational justification."[43]

Kant pleads his case for a foundational deduction by invoking Hobbes's argu-ment for political authority.

215

In the absence of this critique reason is, as it were, in the state of nature, and can establish and secure its assertions and claims only through war. The critique, on the other hand, arriving at all its decisions in the light of fun-damental principles of its own institution, the authority of which no one can question, secures to us the peace of a legal order, in which our disputes have to be conducted solely by the recognized methods of legal action. In the former state, the disputes are ended by a victory to which both sides lay claim, and which is generally followed by a merely temporary armistice, arranged by some mediating authority; in the latter, by a judicial sentence which, as it strikes at the very root of the conflicts, effectively secures an eternal peace.[44]

With so much apparently riding on transcendental deduction, generations of readers have puzzled over Kant's elliptical efforts, in a few tortuous illustrations, to suggest its general method.[45] After two centuries of commentary, the experts cannot agree on the very criteria for measuring Kant's performance in this most fully developed example (the deduction of the categories), let alone the standards for assessing his method as a whole.[46] This interpretive state of nature obviously runs counter to Kant's objective. To fulfill his philosophical ambitions, transcendental deduction would have to justify its own legal title through a process of self-certification. Such a proof would necessarily exceed the boundaries of induction, deduction, and even transcendental deduction, for which it supplies the very foundations.[47]

Despite Kant's unqualified claims for this climactic argument, he manages to hedge his position rather carefully, moving along the strategic path that also leads to the realm of practical reason. Whatever else one might say about it, the success of Kant's transcendental deduction is a rhetorical necessity; without it, the central epistemological doctrines of the First *Critique* would be reduced to mere polemics.[48] Notwithstanding his uncompromising methodological ideals, Kant surrounds this heralded deduction with presumptions and negative inferences, combined into an early model of default reasoning. As Palmquist describes this important Kantian strategy:

> It is the reasoned decision to treat as true a presupposition which cannot be defended objectively, but which is suggested by the objectively known facts to be the best (or perhaps, the only) choice available which will enhance the unity of the system to which it belongs. When Kant adopts rational faith in the thing in itself, it generates a systematic movement of thought through the whole spectrum of human knowledge, which comes full circle to rest where it began, with faith in the unknown, considered now as the tool of practical reason.[49]

Despite Kant's repeated insistence that the transcendental tribunal should directly certify its own authority, his rhetoric follows the defensive strategies associated with polemical reasoning. The vaunted authority of his philosophical tribunal rests, in the end, on something akin to moral conviction in the practical sphere. With its strategic foundations, "moral certainty" carries with it the seeds of jurisdictional disintegration. As Kant says of moral conviction in the religious sphere: "No one, indeed, will be able to boast that he knows that there is a God, and a future life. . . . No, my conviction is not *logical*, but *moral* certainty; and since it rests on subjective grounds . . . I must not even say, '*It is* morally certain that there is a God, etc.,' but '*I am* morally certain, etc.' " [50] As for later philosophical critics who have found Kant's deduction successful in reaching the highest level of apodeixis, their revelations too are conditioned by subjective causes and are therefore confined within the moral jurisdiction of single individuals. [51] In contrast to the Hobbesian authority of transcendental deduction, Kant offers a more pluralistic theory of transcendental persuasion or conviction: "For reason has no dictatorial authority; its verdict is always simply the agreement of free citizens, of whom each one must be permitted to express, without let or hindrance, his objections or even his veto." [52]

Thus Kant leaves little hope that polemical battles will ever cease in philosophy as long as arguments-from-ignorance are present in the transcendental deduction of philosophical authority. Perhaps this is "still enough to satisfy us, so far as our practical standpoint is concerned," but it opens the way to radically divergent professions of faith, issuing from the shifting venues and the multiple sessions from which transcendental courts deliver their unreviewable decisions. Unable to resolve controversies on the basis of evidence, Kant's tribunal opens the door to polemical manipulation of normative postulates. It forces debate into multiple arenas separated by rigid dichotomies, governed by opposing presumptions about the very nature of evidence, and subject to continual shifts in the rhetorical balance of power. [53]

217

The Transcendental Argument-from-Ignorance: A General Model

It is now time to summarize the general course of this powerful style of reasoning, derived from Kant's pioneering efforts. Transcendental arguments-from-ignorance proceed through four connected stages:

1. Projecting postulates for resolving conceptual tensions at a new, higher level of discourse.
2. Conflating alternative positions and treating them as strict adversaries through the use of conceptual dichotomies.
3. Showing the inability of opposition parties to disprove the transcendental postulates, which are placed in the default position.
4. Articulating the coherence of these postulates (taken now as foundational principles) with ordinary forms of knowledge.

In the following analysis, I shall refer to these steps more briefly as (1) projecting transcendental postulates, (2) polarizing the opposition, (3) imposing the burden of proof, and (4) consolidating the postulates. Each stage could also be characterized by analogy with strategic moves in ordinary judicial proceedings: (1) changing the venue, (2) filing a complaint and joining all parties in opposition, (3) shifting the risk of non-persuasion, and (4) drafting the court opinion for a victorious judgment.

The transcendental argument-from-ignorance follows this basic pattern, which outlines the implicit framework supporting its advance. Reconstructing this conceptual context will nearly always prove controversial, as most practitioners of transcendental rhetoric move quickly to suppress their strategic premises immediately after winning the protection of transcendental tribunals. Like courts that bury their dialectical functions in tacit assumptions, procedural ritual, formal doctrine, and deductive logic, the argument-from-ignorance disowns its strategic foundations as unworthy of the very highest authority. The conclusions of transcendental reasoning are typically delivered in broad, confident declarations, using the same deductive idioms, appeals to self-evidence, and lofty common sense found in majority opinions from courts of last resort. Skillful advocates for transcendental conclusions will move swiftly to discredit any reference to their own rhetorical strategies, much as a court majority will brush aside an ad hominem dissent. Once strategic presumptions have been raised to the level of unappealable axioms, those opponents who still remember them as presumptions are reduced to nihilistic outbursts in conflict with simple logic and plain reality.

218

Kant acknowledged some of these strategic elements in his unusual method, especially the maneuver to "limit knowledge in order to make room for faith." Similar concessions can be found among the writings of neo-Kantians, who were united in the larger cause of protecting political, ethical, and aesthetic discourse from the imperious authority of modern science. By reconstructing a conceptual context for these strategic events, my rhetorical observations are not meant to attack the nobility of such ideals as faith, legality, scientific truth, or ethical correctness. My point is that adversarial techniques remain adversarial, no matter how commendable the humanistic objectives of leading advocates. Background rhetorical strategies become especially important, as arguments-from-ignorance leave their partisans vulnerable to sudden and wrenching shifts. Among equally skilled advocates, transcendental reasoning can support multiple, often conflicting aims, including the skeptical rejection of humanistic values.

Projecting transcendental postulates. Transcendental arguments are borne of frustration in addressing otherwise intractable mysteries. These arguments stubbornly refuse to accept ignorance and indeterminacy as excuses for indecision; indeed, paradoxically, they seek to convert the most extreme degrees of ignorance into a source for new solutions. This heroic process begins with an act of creative imagination, in which a conceptually rich solution is first envisioned, then placed into a venue where it can be shielded from its most powerful challengers. Kant signals this stage with his well-known formula of asking "how x is possible," where x is some laudable human accomplishment (synthetic a priori knowledge, ethical decision, aesthetic judgment), which has come under siege by an overbearing conceptual system (materialism, historicism, skepticism). By relocating his philosophical postulates in a transcendental realm, Kant creates a special venue that lies beyond these unanswerable attacks.

Transcendental postulates are meant to be different from scientific hypotheses, intuitive first principles, and customary beliefs. They cannot be disproved by empirical evidence because they were never candidates for empirical verification. Their function is to define the conditions under which empirical evidence enters into human activity. At the same time, these postulates are not to be secured by direct revelation. It would limit their scope to base them on contingencies of time and place, if and when they disclose themselves to particular individuals. Postulates are not real, but rather constructed; and their rhetorical power comes from precisely this difference. Finally, they are not to be confused with traditional beliefs, which are subject to endless cultural diversity and historical evolution.

Kant's philosophical method led him to define transcendental postulates in negative terms—concentrating on what they were not. When it finally came time to describe the transcendental venue in affirmative terms, Kant announced a special proof procedure—the notorious transcendental deduction—that was presumed to lend apodeictic certainty to at least some of his own philosophical postulates. But even this procedure needed support from its transcendental argument-from-ignorance, which allowed Kant to establish the possibility of transcendental arguments.

Considering the strategic importance of this proof for Kant's whole enterprise, it is understandable that his interpreters face a quandary in reconciling its peculiar proof-structure with its strategic underpinnings. To invoke Kant's jurisprudential analogy, the whole problem is rather like questioning the juridical authority of a court of last resort. As with any transcendental argument, the strategic context tends to disappear in the rhetoric of "consolidation" (stage 4). However, once transcendental authority itself becomes fragmented in its social reception, the suppressed context quickly reemerges in a burst of adversarial discourse. Ironically, the academic debate on Kant's transcendental deduction has become a premier example of the polemics that haunt arguments-from-ignorance.[54]

Polarizing the opposition. The next two stages work together to establish the postulates as default principles, from which the triumphant move to consolidation will follow. Transcendental postulates achieve this residual status through aggressive litigation: by gathering all conceivable opposition parties and joining them to the suit. Conceptual dichotomies mark the dividing line between contending parties. The paradigm for this maneuver is Kant's statement (to quote it once again) that he was forced to "limit knowledge to make room for faith." Kant's restrictive definition of knowledge (rule-governed spatial-temporal experience) was narrow enough to leave ample room for religious faith, for the whole realm of practical reason, and for the transcendental tribunal itself. In their own realm, of course, the claims of knowledge were unimpeachable; but they could never cross the zone of transcendental ignorance that kept them from dominating the claims of faith.

As in a standard lawsuit, transcendental reasoning assumes that the number of claimants is limited and that a clear and final decision must eventually be delivered on the major issues in controversy. Potential intervenors must be identified as early as possible and assigned to categories of friend or foe—even if it means substantially reinterpreting their expressed positions. Once again, conceptual dichotomies help serve this rhetorical need for a closed structure, from which a result can eventually emerge by default. The transcendental framework presupposes jurisdictional unity, finality of decision, and a definitive outcome all at once. Within that framework, the strategist must guide the argument the way a good advocate shapes the issues in a judicial proceeding; the client's virtues are painted in the purest shades of white, while all defects in the opposition are exposed down to the level of deepest black.

There were numerous examples of this litigious strategy in earlier chapters: Perelman's new rhetoric versus the dark forces of determinism and relativism; Toulmin's pragmatic theory of argument fields versus rigid deductivism and skepticism; the neo-Aristotelian defense of moral or legal absolutes versus the demons of relativism; the post-structuralist demand for deconstruction versus the façade of foundationalism and dogmatism.

This second stage in transcendental reasoning emphasizes the universal and final quality of judgments reached by the transcendental tribunal. It categorically rejects the position implicit in skeptical arguments (and in many judicial dissents) that contending issues reveal diverse, mutually exclusive aspects or perspectives. As legal fundamentalists in every generation have argued, the very concept of a tribunal for resolving disputes suggests the presence (somewhere) of a hierarchical standard of judgment, from which ultimately there is no further appeal.

Imposing the burden of proof. The third stage in transcendental argumentation concerns the burden of proof. This entire reasoning process hinges, finally, on whether the postulates can be granted an absolute presumption of innocence.

The self-validating power of transcendental rhetoric succeeds only when the opponent carries the full burden of showing that projected postulates are not, in truth, what they presume to be. Of course, the facts available to the opponent in this special venue are always inadequate to the task.

Let us not rush past this ingenious maneuver too quickly. A split-second before the trapdoor opens beneath the opposition, the argument-from-ignorance reaches its point of greatest vulnerability. The transcendental reasoner gestures wildly to divert attention from the pivotal issue of where the burden of ignorance ought to fall. Since the days of Bishop Whately, after all, theorists of ordinary argument have commonly assumed that all novel ideas (including all self-declared postulates) should bear the entire risk of non-persuasion.

Once the burden shifts over to the opposition, the presumption of transcendental ignorance can repel all adversarial attacks based on empirical, intuitionist, or customary evidence. But the ability to blunt an attack is not yet enough for a successful transcendental argument, as Kant's description of polemic vividly reminds us. Before the opposition's failure can be converted into an affirmative victory, something more is necessary. It is always possible, for example, that the controversy can be left hanging or that the issue is ultimately undecidable or nonjusticiable.

Such indeterminate outcomes, however, have already been seriously undermined by the adversarial terms of transcendental debate. Conceptual encounters are staged so that the potential outcomes are limited to the extremes in a preclusive dichotomy. Arrayed against the bright hope of an optimistic postulate, we find the dark horror lurking in the limited alternatives: social chaos, rigid determinism, radical skepticism, bad faith, ideological distortion. Either we have synthetic a priori knowledge, said Kant, or we can have no real assurance of a law-abiding natural world—no science of mechanics applicable to the future, no guarantee that the sun will rise tomorrow.[55] Kant's default argument gathers strength from raising to intolerable levels the destructive potential of its consolidated opposition.

At precisely this juncture—an eyeblink before the default argument takes its fateful shape—transcendental rhetoric pauses to strike a noble pose. Even if the rewards promised by transcendental postulates should elude our grasp, they describe the only honorable path open to us. With everything that humankind holds valuable hanging in the balance, where is the judge who would dare to place the burden of proof on these heroic ideals? For Perelman, the alternative to presuming a new rhetoric was to face the bleak dilemma of rigid dogma and blind self-assertion. To whatever extent we can influence the assignment of proof burdens, should we not give every advantage to the values we hold dear?

These questions may seem unusual in the context of philosophical argument, but they appear quite openly in constitutional litigation. The U.S. Supreme Court in the 1970s developed ad hoc doctrines for apportioning the presumption of constitutionality in certain civil rights cases, based on the Court's comparative assessment of opposing interests. Here is a practice filled with paradox: rather than securing values by consulting preexisting principles, the Court adjusts the principles by consulting predetermined values. Are the correct legal outcomes determined by legal rules, or does the selection of rules depend on a prior selection of desired outcomes? Like the victorious constitutional advocate, transcendental reasoning wants it both ways: it demands control over the vital assignment of proof burdens, while it concedes no limits to the tribunal's objectivity, once the court has reached a favorable judgment.

Consolidating the postulates. The final stage of transcendental argument strikes an entirely new pose, fundamentally different from the creative projection, the adversarial pleadings, and the heroic idealism of the three preceding steps. Dominating the written exposition of transcendental arguments, the fourth stage treats postulated principles as foundational authority for conclusions that are no longer shrouded in ignorance. According to this quick descent to the finish line, synthetic a priori judgments are indeed possible because that is precisely how Kant's epistemological machinery of intuitions and categories must be presumed to work.[56] The transcendental tribunal has issued its final judgment: the outcome is no longer simply our hope or desire, but the conclusion reached by unappealable authority.

Most of Kant's demanding text, in fact, is devoted to explaining how the transcendental machinery really works, and relatively little time is spent recalling why anyone should ever have doubted its reassuring presence. Later transcendental strategists show the same remarkable tendency to treat their initial constructions as firm foundations. Schools of thought grow up around the fine points of articulating these principles, showing elaborate concern with the purely internal fit between principles and conclusions.[57]

It is rare for philosophers to draw attention to the problematic authority behind transcendental principles in the way that John Rawls went behind the principles of his theory of justice. Rawls brings the transcendental tribunal into his theory, using poetic terms to evoke a community of individual decision-makers in a mythical original position. It is their judgment that certifies the principles of justice, according to Rawls, and not his own. Similarly, Ronald Dworkin personifies the tribunal in his mythical judge, whose choice of principles cannot be reopened on appeal to the reader's private judgments.[58] These artful constructions seek to provide exactly what Kant wanted from transcendental deductions:

unappealable reasons for accepting the authority of compelling principles. But they would appear to be no more successful than Kant's attempted proofs, considering the adversarial reactions that are still working their way through the courts of academic opinion.

The final stage in transcendental argumentation reveals its suppressed tensions most clearly in everyday judicial pronouncements, especially in the constitutional jurisprudence of the U.S. Supreme Court. On the surface, these opinions adopt the traditional rhetorical pretense that decisions in constitutional cases are deductions from stable principles of constitutional law.[59] But virtually no one still believes that these principles are self-interpreting; and often they require elaborate reconstruction before they can be placed against the particular facts in a lawsuit. Once the majority has selected its interpretive path, however, the constructed postulates change immediately into axioms; they become the necessary and sufficient source of concrete rights the Court is required to protect.

The most remarkable feature of constitutional cases, however, is the degree to which courts have institutionalized the process of choosing among alternative guiding principles. Appellate courts conduct a large part of this strategic exercise in public: inviting opposing sides to offer competing interpretations of legal principles, suggesting their own alternatives during oral argument, and developing special doctrines for shifting proof burdens. By opening their dialectical responsibilities to public scrutiny, courts weaken the thrust of inevitability that otherwise dominates the activity of adjudication. If they might have chosen premises that support opposing deductions, the courts would seem to face a difficult challenge in protecting the legitimacy and finality of their fragile authority.

These four stages of transcendental reasoning describe a style of argument that stretches far beyond deductive syllogisms and empirical inductions. The transcendental argument-from-ignorance always starts with a preferred conclusion and works backward to its intellectual justification. It is not content, however, to treat these conclusions as contingent facts about the world, pure intellectual revelations, sincere personal convictions, or products of skilled persuasion; it demands their certification by universal law.

The secret behind the strategy is the distinctive juridical procedure through which that law is defined. The reasoner posits a congenial set of presumptions and then dares the opponents to prove that these principles are not valid. Success is ensured when the burden of proof falls on the opposition, in a forum where empirical, traditional, metaphysical, and other kinds of evidence will never be sufficient. When competing transcendental arguments collide, the risk of nonpersuasion may swing wildly from side to side.

223

Neo-Kantian Variations on Transcendental Polemics

Kant's rhetorical legacy was passed down through the writings of neo-Kantian intellectuals, going back to the second half of the nineteenth century.[60] Despite strenuous criticism and then neglect from their twentieth-century successors, it would be difficult to exaggerate the impact on modern thinking of figures like Rudolf Hermann Lotze, Hermann Cohen, and Wilhelm Windelband.[61] Their works exploit fully the strategic implications of Kant's transcendental method, and together they have created the rhetorical arena where public discourse still takes place. Neo-Kantian influences on modern academic disciplines have helped institutionalize these adversarial strategies, which continue to guide major shifts in intellectual fashions.

Despite important variations within this diverse movement, the neo-Kantians shared common philosophical interests. They firmly opposed any claims of natural science to exclusive, final authority over matters of religion and ethics. Like Kant, they defended scientific procedures within a limited sphere of rule-governed, spatial-temporal experience, but they were determined to preserve other spheres for further kinds of inquiry. Their quarrel with science was entirely jurisdictional, and they identified their main adversary as the reductive misuse of scientific procedure by contemporary schools of materialism.[62] Neo-Kantians also rejected the German historical school's determinism and relativism on moral questions, while opposing any return to the alleged mysticism associated with academic remnants of Hegelianism.[63] Even today, the neo-Kantian posture coincides with popular notions of healthy common sense. Crude materialism and the metaphysical excesses of historicism were the Scylla and Charybdis forever haunting these neo-Kantian adventurers. Still another hazard (at least by the end of the century) was Marxist historical materialism, whose very name suggests an odious mixture of both major perils.

A recent historian of neo-Kantianism has summarized the appeal of Kant's philosophical system to the first generation of this complex movement, which included such advocates of ascendant natural science as Hermann Helmholtz and Justus Liebig:

> Kant's dualism was attractive to the defenders of Christian doctrine because it preserved an "unknowable" noumenal domain for the regulative ideas of God, freedom, and immortality transcending physical laws. Men of a scientific disposition could have at the same time both their faith and their science.... Kant's dualism was, to many German thinkers, an appealing compromise in an age of transition from Christian belief to a wholly naturalistic view of the universe.

It was vital to this movement that Kant could be safely invoked without endorsing the romantic critique of empirical science, conservative nostalgia for traditional social values, or unfashionable Hegelian doctrines on the primacy of spirit over nature: "To the extent that Kant had demolished the claims of metaphysics without denying the ultimate truths of religion, he also appealed to the skeptical temper of a generation disenchanted with speculative philosophy and enamored of physical science but not yet ready to jettison its transcendental beliefs altogether."[64]

The special influence of Lotze on later German thinkers, and on generations of visiting British and American students, has been emphasized by Willey and others as important for spreading the Kantian revival into professional philosophy, practical ethics, and politics. Once again, the reasons can be understood in strategic terms: "Perhaps the main reason for his popularity was his reputation as the man 'who could see [. . .] through the difficulties of adjusting the old biblical authority to the new authority of science'; this was exceedingly attractive to a generation of men experiencing difficulties in their Protestant faith."[65]

Despite significant internal differences, the neo-Kantian movement cohered around common rhetorical practices. Most important was the strategy of positing transcendental conceptual boundaries to protect favored principles, which dealt variously with ethical, religious, and aesthetic values and value judgments. Neo-Kantians sheltered these fragile presumptions from powerful rivals by splitting the conceptual universe into separate jurisdictions, assigning their own postulates to a higher juridical level. This procedure allowed them to exploit the strategic advantage Kant had discovered in the polemical claims of practical reason: the power to turn adversarial battle into rhetorical victory via the transcendental argument-from-ignorance.

The neo-Kantians perfected this subtle maneuver by combining rhetorical strategies that Kant had applied separately: the leap to practical reason and the process of transcendental deduction.[66] They invested the argument-from-ignorance with the full authority of Kant's transcendental tribunal and thereby found a way to transform their creative postulates into conceptual foundations for everyday experience. This procedure can be compared to the powerful rhetoric used by courts of last resort, as a majority of judges select and definitively shape the fundamental rules of decision. As with constitutional courts, the crisis of neo-Kantian authority appeared when rival camps sought to monopolize transcendental procedure. At this new level of competition, the adversaries are multiple *Weltanschauungen* battling for presumptive authority to determine legitimacy and finality in public discourse.

In emphasizing the discontinuity of transcendental space, neo-Kantians of all varieties learned to project unbridgeable conceptual dualities: science and ethics, reason and meaning, facts and values, belief and truth, essence and existence, thought and being, logic and history, person and community. Although each of these dualities can be linked with particular controversies now buried in history, they all share certain strategic features. The first term of any dichotomy names something deeply rooted in human experience, which is nonetheless marked by the fatal tendency to overstate its own importance for the whole of experience. The second term points to something beyond immediate inspection, which is nonetheless invested with a higher mission of regulating the ambitions of its adversary.[67]

The imprecise location of the transcendental realm guaranteed its full strategic power.[68] It provided a secure haven for ideas or beliefs threatened by powerful rivals, variously defined in such pejorative terms as reductionist science, metaphysical abstractions, skeptical or relativist doubts, or ruling-class values. At the same time, this privileged domain provided a staging area for corrective missions. Like the constitutional rules framed by the highest court in a unified judicial system, the transcendental postulates held final authority for ordering significant relationships within the everyday world.

Challenged by their own projections, the neo-Kantians became bold (if often eccentric) adventurers. They repeatedly launched heroic expeditions to map out the conceptual realms that were waiting just beyond their immediate horizons. In reviewing their works, we generally find them poised at the start of a perilous journey: staring across that wide sea, whose farther end could only be imagined as conjecture or construction. The inspiration for their paradoxical quest, of course, was Kant's own strategic inference to the realm of practical reason, to which they assigned the authority of a transcendental deduction.

The division of neo-Kantianism itself into adversarial schools reflects inherent tensions within the broader Kantian rhetorical framework. Although Kant's legal metaphors tried to keep these tensions in balance, the neo-Kantians came to emphasize different aspects of legality. One branch, centered at the University of Marburg, concentrated on the jurisdictional unity and finality of transcendental postulates (stages 2 and 3 in the model described earlier in this chapter). The Southwest German (or Baden) School, by contrast, emphasized the careful selection of postulates and their consolidation within common human experience (stages 1 and 4). Both branches used arguments-from-ignorance but seized on different elements to represent the core of transcendental authority. The Marburg School wanted to preserve the legal purity of the tribunal, but it could never convincingly integrate that ideal vision with concrete earthly concerns. The Baden School and its progeny tried to capture transcendental authority in more functional postulates but could not prevent the dissolution of authority into disparate jurisdictions.[69]

This divergence within neo-Kantianism follows the general structure of Kant's famous antinomies, according to which the putative limits of the universe may be interpreted as falling either outside or inside that universe, based on equally convincing and unshakable arguments. An antinomy represents the same endless conflict as Kantian polemics, but it permits both sides in a debate to assert the strategic benefits of arguments-from-ignorance.[70] Such antinomies are to be found in countless intellectual battles over the past century, down to current debates between foundationalism and deconstruction. In the sharpness of adversarial exchange, it is easy to miss the comparable strategic aims of both parties, as they assert their higher authority to define transcendental boundaries.[71]

Through its leading figure, Hermann Cohen, the Marburg School explored the more strictly juridical functions of transcendental reasoning: the quality of legal finality that allows postulates (whatever they might be) to bring closure to major controversies, which might otherwise descend into mere polemics. For Cohen, the most important feature of these postulates was their legal force; he emptied Kant's transcendental realm of its mysterious "things in themselves" and replenished it with juridical notions.[72] Transcendental space thus provides the sustaining atmosphere for all normative judgment. Cohen's vision focuses on jurisprudence as a process, rather than any particular set of rules or standards dealt with by historical legal systems. In strategic terms, Cohen defended the human capacity to issue universal, critical tastes amidst the increasingly diverse values, political agendas, and aesthetic judgments that pervaded the cultural atmosphere of Wilhelmine Germany: "All the human sciences share the presupposition of the mathematical natural sciences that thought is able to give and to secure fixed, determinate and unchanging creations. The identity of Parmenides is the pole-star of all science and all research, of all thinking."[73] In its negative insistence that intellectual standards should not be modeled on pure mechanics, biological imperatives, or blind economic forces, Cohen's postulate was a deeply humanistic commitment, never fully separated from his personal religious convictions.[74]

The very purity of these transcendental capacities made it especially difficult for Cohen to apply them to concrete events found in the world of everyday judgment. He arranged his postulates for the specific purpose of unifying the authority that sets boundaries between science and ethics, but he left no provision for the remaining dialectical elements of legal systems. Cohen's transcendental principles capture the process of legality while ignoring the procedure, in which finality and legitimacy are joined with particular events.[75] His vision of Kant's

227

tribunal left no place for the historical evolution of laws, for situational judgments in classifying novel conditions, and for pragmatic insights in matching general rules with particular situations.[76]

The juridical implications of Cohen's system were developed by his Marburg colleague Rudolf Stammler, who applied a similar approach to concrete legal systems. Stammler's jurisprudential postulate—the "rule of right law"—was derived by familiar strategies of indirect reasoning: its mission (indeed, its whole raison d'être) was to steer the tightest possible course between the opposing hazards of determinism (the closed fate of natural law) and relativism (the shifting standards of positive law). "Our purpose . . . is to find . . . a universally valid formal method, by means of which the necessarily changing material of empirically conditioned rules may be so worked out, judged and determined that it shall have the quality of objective justice."[77] But Stammler could take the Marburg approach no farther than to posit the paradoxical vision of "natural law with variable content," and he, too, was ultimately unsuccessful in persuading later critics that his method could fulfill its regulative goals.[78]

The rhetorical strengths and weaknesses of the Marburg strategy anticipate the course of similar arguments used by later generations. Their finest hour comes at the moment of polarizing the opposition; the primary virtues of Marburg postulates are their steadfast resistance to the twin demons of value indeterminacy (the lack of definitive standards) and value reduction (deriving norms from contingent material conditions or from vague biological or psychological forces). And indeed, when the alternatives are so formulated, who would not demand the most conscientious search for universal legality, answering to our noblest human aspirations? Similar arguments, resting on this same adversarial posture, were discussed in earlier chapters, including the neo-Aristotelian manifestoes of Adler, Hutchins, and Weaver and the analogous legal theories of Fiss and Vining. Ronald Dworkin's theory of rights follows the same rhetorical path blazed by Stammler's legal philosophy.[79] No group of thinkers has ever taken law (or norms) more seriously than the Marburg School.

Marburg strategy shows its strongest side in its passionate rejection of rival positions. It condemns materialism and relativism as unacceptable to the human spirit, even though strangely powerful and seductive. The transcendental turn to universal normative ideals remains the only honorable option left, if mankind can have any hope of avoiding either danger. That turn is all the more worth taking, even if (and, paradoxically, especially if) the pursuit should become a lengthy or infinite task. The very difficulty of the journey becomes the measure of how vigorously one must reject alternative positions. At the outset of this improbable journey, at least one can be confident that postulated ideals will never be disproved by the opposition. These ideals are presumed to rest safely within their own privileged jurisdiction, however remote or inaccessible they might seem to weary or fallible researchers. The skeptic can always question these postulates as bloodless formalism or timid foundationalism, but no such challenge can survive the highest court of conceptual appeal.

Argument strategies similar to Marburg universalism have proved remark-ably persistent despite the easy targets they provide for skeptical response. Such attacks are often merciless; and they, too, are unappealable, since to reject these postulates is to reject the entire jurisdiction of the particular higher authority assigned to protect them.[80] But skeptical counter-arguments cannot mask their vulnerability whenever they try to build positive inferences from negative prem-ises. It would seem that Kant's polemical discourse has never truly ended but continues through these modern surrogates.

It is a disservice to the Marburg strategy to concentrate solely on its polemical employments. It remains a significant stimulus to creative research in numer-ous disciplines (from which, of course, new forms of skeptical attack eventu-ally emerge, after creative arguments bear fruit). Today's philosophers have lost all interest in Hermann Cohen's reconstruction of sensory experience through mathematics,[81] but they probably remember the excitement in academic circles during the 1960s, when Chomsky and others brought Marburg-style postulates to the field of theoretical linguistics.[82] There are, of course, significant differ-ences between these two important academic movements, separated by nearly a century. For one thing, linguistic universalism found tactical support in new computational and notational technologies, which allowed legions of research-ers to join in the creative task of projecting underlying presumptions.[83] These differences worked to infect large numbers of researchers with the bold neo-Kantian spirit of adventure. Abundant practical applications seemed to lie just over the horizon, from machine translation to talking computers; but one could also glimpse a noble humanism in the distant presumption that tied all of us—at a suitably "deep" level—into a single network of communication.

After reviewing some of the cultural tensions that characterized this historical period ("potential mass self-destruction, potential conquest of space, pervasive moral doubts, and awareness of social failures"), Roy Harris has identified three distinct social expectations that prepared the way for linguistic theory. "What was needed," first, was some "reassurance that language provided the means of making a mere agglomeration of individuals into a society in the fullest sense: a fellowship in which all shared a common understanding through participating in a common means of communication."[84] Second, the peculiarities of linguistic bonds set up a new tension between this purpose and the need to reach below

229

the surface of specific languages to deeper universal structures. For we also wanted reassurance "that language was not in the final analysis a barrier which must inevitably divide nation from nation and people from people, but a bond which afforded the basis for a potential brotherhood of man." Third, this more penetrating linguistic quest created still further tensions, as mankind struggled to define a clearer relationship to the natural environment; eventually we also needed reassurance "that *homo sapiens* was not a lonely Caliban-figure, isolated in an otherwise languageless universe, alienated by the mysterious gift of tongues from all other living creatures."[85]

If taken seriously, such strategic considerations clarify the ambitions and weaknesses of the Marburg style of neo-Kantianism. Harris's perspective on linguistic universalism suggests the kinds of tensions that can be expected in other settings, tensions that eventually lead to the fragmentation of transcendental inquiry into competing schools: "The more modern analysis of man's linguistic abilities could provide one of those [three] reassurances, the less it seemed able simultaneously to provide the others. How the concept of a language can fulfill a role consistent with these conflicting demands upon it remains the underlying dilemma of contemporary linguistics."[86]

The Marburg emphasis on juridical aspects of transcendental reasoning was one side of an antinomy that haunted the nineteenth-century Kant revival. It exploited one important theme in Kant's works: the presumption of a higher authority with jurisdiction to check the imperial ambitions of materialism and historicism. Like Kant's practical postulates, however, Marburg universals were elevated to the level of distant imperatives. They issued legal exhortations to fulfill "the law" to its fullest extent but offered no authoritative guidance as to what this law required in concrete instances. This arid legalism did not prevent Cohen from construing his transcendental standards in favor of democratic socialism, a political agenda that received substantial energy from the idealistic humanism implicit in the whole Marburg program.[87] But the gap between normative foundations and political practice was simply too broad to sustain, and Cohen's prescriptions increasingly acquired the status of legal imperatives that were simply unenforceable in their historical context.

The Fragmentation of Transcendental Authority

By the start of World War I, the Marburg program had drawn substantial charges of empty formalism. Fearing that transcendental speculation was leading its proponents into an intellectual desert, the new opposition emphasized a central dilemma within neo-Kantian method: the conflict between transcendental purity and the desire to apply transcendental insights to everyday concerns. During preceding decades, the Baden School of neo-Kantians had already prepared the ground for this critique. Whereas both major branches of the neo-Kantian movement shared similar humanistic concerns,[88] they emphasized divergent aspects of transcendental reasoning. The Baden philosophers, anticipating the conceptual needs of emerging social and cultural sciences, experimented with a more functional approach to transcendental postulates, blurring the distinctions between transcendental rhetoric and the formation and testing of hypotheses in natural science.[89]

Their efforts helped channel transcendental reasoning into the resurgent realist movements of the early twentieth century, which included the constructive realism of Mach and Poincaré, the logical positivism of the Vienna Circle, the phenomenological realism of Husserl, James, and Scheler, the "new ontology" of Hartmann, the vitalism of Bergson and Nietzsche, and the existential realism of Heidegger.[90] Despite obvious and important differences among these movements (which still dominate today's major adversarial battles), they all share the same ambivalent relationship to transcendental reasoning. Using transcendental dichotomies, they posit an elusive higher reality somewhere beyond the merely subjective contents of everyday life. This impersonal, noninstrumental, nonstrategic domain of reality is defined in specific opposition to the personalized, instrumental, and patently strategic concerns that inhabit more familiar social and conceptual experience.

According to the reconstituted tribunal of twentieth-century realism, transcendental reasoning itself must come under the strictest possible scrutiny. This is an important shift from the days of neo-Kantian philosophers, who took great trouble polishing and embellishing their transcendental postulates. To contemporary taste, their tolerance for elaborate hypothetical constructions seems hideously self-indulgent, an extravagant misallocation of mental resources and the likely product of a privileged academic environment.[91] In a complete reversal, modern realist movements seek the first opportunity to cut loose from their transcendental moorings. Using the characteristic dichotomy of thought and being, the heirs of neo-Kantian transcendentalism consign their strategic frameworks to the realm of thought, thereby barring them from that higher reality where the old tribunal still allegedly resides. The rhetorical consequences are registered in twentieth-century polemics among diverse realist schools, in heroic battles with their consolidated "idealist" opponents, and in periodic waves of skepticism, which exploit the ironic distance between realist constructions and their suppressed transcendental foundations.

The Baden School launched the critical transition between neo-Kantian rhetorical styles and the repressed transcendentalism of twentieth-century movements. This branch of neo-Kantianism accelerated the inevitable fragmentation of transcendental authority, preparing the way for a contentious series of competing doctrines, each claiming reality as its juridical foundation. The Baden philosophers never abandoned the universal presumptions implied by the tribunal metaphor, but they shifted critical attention to more diffuse issues of contextual plurality. Their overriding purpose (however paradoxical) was to strengthen transcendental defenses against value relativism, while acknowledging the diversity of values reflected in history and across cultures.[92]

Opposition to empty formalism in transcendental reasoning became a major insurrection, starting within neo-Kantianism, which eventually brought the whole transcendental method into conflict with itself. Such antiformalist critiques have their own deep roots in Kant's epistemological distinction between form and content in sensory experience. Kant introduced this important dichotomy in the *Critique of Pure Reason,* declaring that "synthetic a priori knowledge" was possible only as a constructed unity, an organic bond between perceptual content and conceptual form.[93] These lawlike forms, the "pure categories of the understanding," were Kant's principal rejoinder to the skepticism of Berkeley and Hume. Kant's categories secured the universal significance of scientific knowledge, so that the prediction of tomorrow's sunrise became something more than a contingent induction by observers of past sunrises.[94] Kant posited his categories as transcendental structures embedded in all empirical understanding and dependent on sensory content from some independent source. Perceptions without the categories were "blind," Kant concluded; but pure categories without perceptual content were "empty."[95]

If the Marburg School paid more notice to the first half of this formula, the Baden School (along with most later critics of the whole neo-Kantian movement) emphasized the second part, which it applied to the very relations between transcendental reasoning and its putative contents. On the one hand, the unique authority and finality of transcendental method presuppose a giant leap beyond worldly experience—to a vantage point where definitive boundaries can be properly assessed. On the other hand, the strategic role of transcendental method in public debate draws it back into direct commerce with everyday phenomena. Kant's writings yield two opposing models for construing transcendental method: his projection of an autonomous practical realm and his more restrained model of context-bound formal categories.

There is no point calling on the transcendental tribunal to resolve this kind of divergence, which begs the very nature of that tribunal's own unique functions. After summoning the tribunal to settle more specific conflicts, Kant had little to say about the source of its unique authority or the scope of its exclusive, transcendental jurisdiction. The neo-Kantians inherited all the unsolved problems of transcendental method, a procedure whose own possibility could only be presumed. Was the projection of transcendental principles like a creative expression of practical reason: utterly free (within its autonomous sphere) to legislate in universal terms? Or was it more like the silent operation of formal categories: empty speculation until joined with residual content from the everyday world?

The dualism of form-content held innumerable paradoxes, to the extent it implied that transcendental authority was contingently related to something external to itself.[96] Kant had warned repeatedly against using categorical language to describe the categories; such talk was illusory, and yet the only conceivable alternative was to leave the whole transcendental realm as an unsecured postulate—the tribunal sui generis. Thus the Baden School began its delicate inquiry into the twilight realm of contingent relations surrounding transcendental postulates, focusing on the initial and terminal stages of reasoning: projection and consolidation.

The Baden School hoped to redraw the maps of transcendental territory to make its boundary features more accessible. Windelband and Rickert laid out a conventional philosophical landscape with specially adapted objects and subjects; but in the foreground they placed a new descriptive figure, modeled on the Kantian notion of judgment.[97] In their treatment, judgments straddle elements of form and content. Judgments presuppose values as their content or referent, even if transcendental logic prevents cataloguing these values in abstraction from particular value judgments. Like everything else at this highest level of reflection, values are not real (that is, they are not part of the spatial-temporal order);[98] but they nonetheless have validity, which means they are inseparably tied to formal warrants that supply their structure and unchallengeable authority.[99]

Judgments can thus be posited as the unified expression of values and warrants, all the while surrounding the transcendental realm with new ambiguities. Are these judgments like so many legal pronouncements from a unanimous court, which purport to subsist at a higher level than the process that created them, weaving themselves into a timeless doctrinal fabric? Or are they more like particularized events, conditioned by circumstances that bind them to the sphere of everyday understanding where they can be manipulated for personal ends?[100] Both interpretations were implied by the Baden program, which stimulated a new range of explorations, including joint ventures between philosophy and social science.

The lasting influence of Baden neo-Kantianism comes from this unresolved tension in its treatment of transcendental postulates, which shifted continu-

233

ally between the presumptions of transcendence and immanence.[101] The Baden School reasserted the unique rhetorical privilege of transcendental strategy: winning an argument by default because no one else could ever prove it wrong. In this context, the putative unreality of values provides the license to exercise higher authority. Value judgments are not just ethical prescriptions (as in Kant's practical sphere); they are also the measure of truth in scientific procedure and logical analysis.[102] Indeed, the very act of asserting higher authority—part of the structure of all transcendental reasoning—is itself a value judgment and thus a charter member of its own domain.

At the same time, the Baden School renounced formalism, and it exploited this countervailing Kantian theme to bring transcendental principles closer to human experience. Indeed, as the higher moment within experience, transcendental judgments assumed the role of content, in contrast to the formalism of empty rational procedures.[103] Transcendental values, accordingly, endow life's richest moments; they make possible our true fulfillment in meaning and purpose. Transcendental judgments give us access to intrinsic values, without which our lives are mere empty shells.[104] Precisely because they are unreal, these postulated, unconditioned values supplement the impersonal or mechanical aspects of knowledge—reality in its bleakest form. One can no more say where these values come from than Kant could explain the origins of perceptual content, but they stand revealed through the medium of judgments.[105]

An entirely new model of human experience emerges from these reconfigured Kantian arguments: a composite of empty formal procedures (systematic observation, scientific experiment, deductive logic) and concrete meaning (the unreal value judgments). This startling picture turns Marburg universalism upside down. The lawlike (nomothetic) side of experience takes second place to the creative, particularistic (ideographic) side.[106] Despite the presumed normative preeminence of the ideographic, however, neither side can escape its complement. Without some systematic structure, the ideographic realm is blind (in Kant's terms)—inexplicable, and hence irrational. But purely rational inquiry is empty—abstract, and hence without meaning or purpose.

Through these imaginative forays into transcendental territory, the Baden School tried to tame the unruly paradoxes surrounding Kant's notions of transcendence and immanence. A strikingly similar set of ideas took root in Max Weber's sociology, which gave a naturalistic and historical twist to the Baden School's philosophical postulates. Such parallel journeys in philosophy and social science are no coincidence. In addition to the close friendship between Weber and Rickert,[107] the intrinsic ambiguities of transcendental reasoning made it available for both philosophical and sociological deployment. Baden neo-

Kantianism transformed an esoteric style of philosophy into a potentially power-ful tool of social analysis. Following lines of conceptual tension traceable to Kant, the Baden philosophers shifted repeatedly between the immanent and transcen-dent aspects of transcendental reasoning. And while they were busy constructing transcendental postulates that could explain the possibility of such easy fluctua-tions,[108] social scientists began to investigate the historical and cultural conditions for postulate construction.

The Weberian theory of "rationalization" reaches the spectacular conclu-sion that modern societies suffer from an impoverishment of ideographic mean-ing.[109] The powerful impact of Weber's theory—including the many controver-sies joined by its critics—can be traced to its rich transcendental roots. In effect, Weber treats as historical contingencies the dualistic elements in neo-Kantian methodology, which in turn had been taken from Kant's epistemological model of form and content. Seen now as irreducible historical forces, formal reason and human purpose have diverged, according to Weber, through such historical events as the rise of Protestantism, the development of capitalist economies, and the spread of bureaucratic organizations.

Protestantism, with its doctrines of ascetic denial, favored the hyperdevelop-ment of formal, procedural ways of thinking and living, thus preparing the way for modern scientific method and the growth of capitalist economic organiza-tion.[110] As this autonomous rational force continues its rampant growth, however, it eclipses the value-laden spirit that gave Protestantism its dynamic energy—its emotional intensity and sense of purpose. Under late-capitalist conditions, advances in scientific method, technology, economic rationality, and organiza-tional planning developed their own momentum, leaving human beings (still the confluence of both historical forces) with the sense that life has been drained of value and meaning. At the end of his famous study of capitalism, Weber imag-ines future generations in an "iron cage," leading a pale existence as "specialists without spirit, sensualists without heart." [111]

Whether one ultimately accepts the substance of Weber's theory, it illustrates the volatile tensions within neo-Kantian rhetorical practices. The fragile unity of rationality and meaning, projected as a transcendental postulate by the Baden School, suddenly falls apart when treated as an historical contingency. At this level, a simple shift in the burden of proof can challenge the reigning presump-tion of cultural unity: apologists for the social status quo inherit the impossible task of proving that the present age has found the proper balance between these two independent forces.[112]

In addition to pessimistic historical diagnoses, this shift in presumptions has ignited periodic revolts against scientific practices. Weber himself thought that rational procedures work against life's deeper purpose by hastening the "disenchantment" of the world.[113] Many current movements take up similar notions as the basis for challenging dominant social institutions. Any opponent whose authority can be traced to scientific expertise, instrumental thinking, or long-term planning (that is, almost any example of institutionalized authority) can be charged with obscuring life's fundamental meaning.[114] In earlier chapters some of these adversarial shifts in political and academic discourse were explored, including the recent revival of transcendental ethics.[115] Even though contemporary writers would disavow some or all of the transcendental mode of reasoning, we had little trouble reconstructing their implicit arguments-from-ignorance.

Neo-Kantian rhetoric fostered yet another important movement in social inquiry, the sociology of knowledge. In Karl Mannheim's influential presentation, this approach was devised to play a pragmatic, socially constructive role: the mediation of contentious ideologies that had fragmented the interwar European scene. The conflict of ideologies was no mere clash of personal convictions or class interests, according to Mannheim, but a battle between incommensurable value systems: "total ideologies."[116] By definition, there were no direct intellectual connections among these systems, no effective diplomatic channels, even assuming the good will of interlocutors. Mannheim assigned sociology the default task of looking behind these conceptually closed systems: to discover their source in a social reality posited beyond the ideas themselves, and then to let that reality serve as the tribunal for resolving ideological conflicts.[117]

Mannheim's project was an important extension of the sustained rebellion against neo-Kantian formalism, which soon engulfed even the Baden philosophers. In rhetorical terms, however, Mannheim's approach remains firmly within the strategic sphere of transcendental arguments-from-ignorance. It uses transcendental reasoning to posit a carefully defined reality, specifically designated as higher than mere constructions of the philosopher's imagination. This invidious distinction between levels of reality targets a new adversary: the imperialism of subjective conceptual thought, for which the neo-Kantians were considered the latest and most extreme apologists.[118] Without some access to an external realm of "being," mere thought was like the empty Kantian forms of understanding and was also subject to irreparable fragmentation into separate (ideological) thought-jurisdictions. The Baden School had prepared the way for this critique but had not yet taken the decisive step: shifting the burden of proof and thus forcing the philosopher to show how thought can break out of its presumed isolation to touch the higher reality of "being."[119]

The strategic patterns of transcendental reasoning dominate this remarkable tour de force, as Mannheim was prepared to concede. His new sociological enterprise becomes possible, according to Mannheim, only if "thought" surrenders to a process of "self-transcendence and self-relativization," in which "individual thinkers, and still more the dominant outlook of a given epoch, far from according primacy to thought, conceive of thought as something subordinate to other more comprehensive factors—whether as their emanation, their expression, their concomitant, or, in general, as something conditioned by something else." [120] With no hint of irony, Mannheim advises us that "we may escape" the alleged isolation of self-enclosed thought "by conceiving thought as a mere partial phenomenon belonging to a more comprehensive factor within the totality of the world process." [121] "We have to do here with an act of breaking through the immanence of thought—with an attempt to comprehend thought as a partial phenomenon within the broader field of existence, and to determine it, as it were, starting from existential data. The 'existential thinker,' however, asserts precisely that his ultimate position lies outside the sphere of thought." [122]

The goal, in short, is to find a route by which thought can transcend its presumed isolation—a one-way path, leading back from a more fundamental level of reality, which terminates in the everyday cognitive world. This constructed reality exercises the familiar juridical authority of the Kantian tradition, determining which of the many competing thought systems bears the closest relation to an otherwise unknowable standard. Although this normative reality cannot be observed directly, the sociologist can nevertheless presume its authority.[123] An awkward but necessarily indirect method of approaching this tribunal forces us to bundle up all our thoughts into distinct conceptual frameworks, for which the sociologist of knowledge posits a causally sufficient social and historical context. By presuming that each person's complete ideology ("the totality of [one's] mental world, the whole superstructure") is "a function of . . . social existence," [124] Mannheim hoped to resolve conflicts among socially conditioned points of view.

Mannheim's delicate constructions turned out to be no more secure than the Baden School's heroic efforts to combat the relativism of social perspectives. Instead of a Kantian kingdom of values, Mannheim posits a self-declared naturalistic authority, which is accessible to the "scientific" sociologist. But there has been little enthusiasm for his notion that an academic intelligentsia should be deemed to speak for the normative tribunal of reality.[125] Like both Rawls and Dworkin in recent years, Mannheim was looking for a plausible surrogate for transcendental authority. The strongest argument in favor of Mannheim's solution is built on the scandal and chaos of accepting any alternative. Unless some group has direct access to this elusive set of social norms, Mannheim's notion of total ideologies plays into the hands of his rhetorical adversaries: the proponents of radical conceptual discontinuity.

237

Recent debates over the status of conceptual schemes, competing scientific paradigms, and cultural mentalities raise the same questions that inspired Mannheim's program.[126] In all its forms, the postulate of cultural discontinuity encounters stern criticism. The shrewdest adversaries reject the very idea of such a postulate and seek to replace it with the opposing presumption of conceptual continuity.[127] A simple shift in the burden of proof changes Mannheim's default principle, so that conceptual schemes, paradigms, mentalities, languages, and cultures are all deemed to be continuous—until somebody proves the contrary. From the beginning, both sides in this textbook example of transcendental polemic understand that their opponent will never be able to produce any competent evidence. The core controversy is not about evidence at all but about assigning strategic burdens.

Much of the literature on cultural difference grows out of specific controversies in anthropology, in which the presumption of discontinuity is frequently used to correct the tendency for one culture (usually assumed to be a dominant culture) to measure another by its own contingent standards.[128] Placing a wide gulf between cultures makes room for new and perhaps unorthodox ways of thinking, much the way Kant limited knowledge to make room for faith. Instead of Kant's unified transcendental domain, however, this approach leaves space for an infinite number of separate value jurisdictions.

The critical strategic moment arrives when proof burdens are shifted onto the dominant method or culture, immediately unmasking its pretensions as a universal standard. In social science, the presumption of cultural discontinuity lifts that burden from the party raising new or alien value claims, on whom the burden had been placed (by default) since the days of Bishop Whately. This sudden change forces prevailing normative criteria onto the defensive, subjecting them to the same kind of strict scrutiny the courts have imposed on bureaucratic action under recent constitutional law. To be successful, this strategy of reversal does not have to prove any affirmative normative claims of its own; its only obligation is to be provocative. Used in standard scholarly polemics, it has accounted for iconoclastic works on topics ranging from African witchcraft to medieval Icelandic sagas.[129]

The flexible strategies of Baden neo-Kantianism are equally adapted to philosophy and to the social sciences, differing only in their respective emphases on the normative authority of postulates and the immanent presence of postulates in everyday life. For social scientists, the investigation of normative structures erases the line between neo-Kantian value theory and standard scientific procedure. Interpretive social science turns the participant-observer into a Baden-style philosopher, whose interpretive hypotheses assume the strategic role of neo-Kantian postulates. Just as empirical evidence was unavailable to challenge the Baden School's kingdom of values, the immanent norms hypothesized by the interpretive social scientist cannot be falsified by direct observation.

Until recently, most American social scientists would have approved this activity only as preliminaries to broader research programs: as exercises in theory-building and "thick" description.[130] But it is now clear that many interpretive practitioners would place higher value on these constructions than on the explanatory procedures of science.[131] Their distinctive method, in its very difference from scientific procedure, may even hope to restore the higher meaning lost in the disenchantment of the world, building on Weber's historical diagnosis. The strategic goals of interpretive social science thus converge with the humanistic purposes of Windelband and Rickert. Instead of the Baden School's focus on value judgments, social scientists now look for normative ends in the a priori patterns of everyday living: in rule systems, role structures, language games, action frameworks, and classification schemes.

By treating these formal patterns as a social and cultural residue—beyond the reach of empirical authority (if not entirely beyond empirical observation)—social science postulates unconditioned categories of meaning. Like the projected values of Baden neo-Kantianism, these structures cannot be tested against some absolute standard of evidence; rather they define the multiple jurisdictions of meaning, within which the whole notion of evidence becomes possible. Like Kant's categories of the understanding, these normative patterns are assigned the role of default structures, the postulated authority for all evidence-based arguments.[132]

Chapter 8 | Dialectical Alternatives

The Kantian treatment of dichotomies contrasts with an important philosophical alternative adapted from Hegel's dialectical logic. Transcendental and dialectical reasoning differ over the absolute character of what Kant called "antinomies," which Hegel viewed as provisional dualities that can be systematically rejoined within a fluid conceptual structure. A better understanding of Hegel's approach to dichotomies can potentially lessen adversarial tensions in modern discourse. Admittedly, the strategic power of polarized argumentation will always deliver short-term benefits to successful advocates, thereby strengthening popular reliance on transcendental reasoning. Over the longer term, however, dialectical reasoning offers everyone a less divisive accommodation with arguments-from-ignorance by limiting their authority to restricted domains within a broader conceptual horizon.

Presumptions, Paradoxes, and Conceptual Blind Spots

On the whole, twentieth-century philosophical movements have abandoned neo-Kantian reflection on transcendental reasoning, although they continue to employ its central strategies. We stumble across these strategic underpinnings mainly in the form of riddles and paradoxes. Certain thinkers have been conspicuously eager to bring these riddles to our attention, while denying us the authority to pursue them in the neo-Kantian spirit of adventure. This is the case, for example, with Wittgenstein's well-crafted paradoxes, which conclude his *Tractatus Logico-Philosophicus* on a note of unfathomable mystery:

> My propositions serve as elucidations in the following way: anyone who understands me eventually recognizes them as nonsensical, when he has used them—as steps—to climb up beyond them. (He must, so to speak, throw away the ladder after he has climbed up it.)
>
> He must transcend these propositions, and then he will see the world aright.[1]

Some readers prefer to overlook these cryptic suggestions, which skim the surface of modern dilemmas in transcendental reasoning. Yet it is impossible to ignore such a pivotal allusion to transcendental method: the entire text, according to its author, provides the supporting structure for a particular vision of the world; but these strategic foundations vanish just as the end is in sight. Some aspect of this vision—indeed, its keystone—is posited to lie beyond reasoning, beyond method, and beyond transcendental reflection, even though these very procedures provide our only access to it.

Wittgenstein's teasing allusions to a "mystical"[2] realm point indirectly toward Rickert's *Zwischenreich*, lying somewhere beyond the bedrock facts that Wittgenstein posited as referents for well-formed linguistic expressions. This powerful null-point of the *Tractatus* is the modern guise of Kant's tribunal, summoned now to certify Wittgenstein's early theories about language and the world. Without that certification, these baroque constructions are mere private speculations; and yet the whole juridical process of certification cannot itself be explained through the linguistic theories it protects. For all its heightened mystery, the tribunal remained essential to the movement inspired by Wittgenstein's vision. Its presence was registered in the normative injunction to remain silent about everything beyond the linguistic theory, including its juridical underpinnings.[3] As J. N. Findlay has shown, the *Tractatus* contains an elaborate Kantian subtext, a "governing slant" that "may be called 'transcendental,' in one of the many senses of that obscure, somewhat tendentious term."[4]

Wittgenstein's obsessive restrictions on verbalizing transcendental strategies demonstrate the strength of adversarial responses to neo-Kantian exploits.[5] If references to strategic foundations are considered nonsense, they must be such valuable nonsense that mere talk could cheapen them immeasurably. Only our feelings can register the fundamental importance of what cannot be captured by linguistic categories: "We feel that even when *all possible* scientific questions have been answered, the problems of life remain completely untouched."[6] Here, finally, is the powerful adversary that Rickert only belatedly acknowledged: the *Lebensphilosophie* that asserted its own transcendental claims through the strategic dichotomy of knowledge (here represented by language) and life.[7]

241

For Wittgenstein, Kant's tribunal remains in session, operating with full authority; but it is now entirely hidden from view. Like the secret tribunal that pursues Kafka's fictional Joseph K., this Kantian token of transcendental authority leads a fugitive existence. For decades it formed the nucleus of intense philosophical deliberation; but then, with a sudden shift, it simply vanished, along with the conceptual tools for comprehending its continuing jurisdiction. Our closest interpretive aid comes from jurisprudential analogies, like those used throughout this study, to whatever extent they can detect the tacit functions of transcendental authority within contemporary discourse.

As a matter of everyday practice, every nonmetaphorical tribunal performs this same functional shift. Before our eyes, it changes from a human process with its own elaborate procedures, rituals, and history into the timeless oracle of an unconditioned, higher legality. The paradox was summed up nicely for a skeptical age by United States Supreme Court Justice Robert Jackson: "We are not final because we are infallible; but we are infallible only because we are final."[8]

Like appellate courts, modern philosophical theories and public policies that aspire to final authority raise irreducible paradoxes, produced by strategic shifts that can never be fully articulated. These conceptual blind spots are at once more elusive and fundamental than the theories and policies they support. An observer can sometimes see into this vanishing point by the cumbersome maneuver of changing perspectives, often by going back in time and circumstance. But soon enough, every new standpoint must itself be changed; for it, too, presumes its own particular null-point. By analogy, one can always criticize an appellate court from the imagined position of a court of higher appeal. Eventually the presumptive authority of that imagined court comes under equally strong suspicion.

The plurality of juridical claims has turned twentieth-century discourse into an adversarial arena, filled with suits and countersuits among a vast army of litigants. These conflicts can sometimes be mediated by historical analysis, by locating the source of new doctrines in particular confrontations with adversaries that have long been forgotten (and whose positions have been distorted by the revisionist logic of victorious parties). But something more than history is needed: a synoptic grasp of oppositions, suitable for reconnecting the scattered fragments of shifting viewpoints.

Hegel's dialectical logic holds some promise for providing this more systematic, reconstructive method. Considering their contentious history, Hegel's views require some rescuing from opponents and defenders alike. Moreover, one's expectations must stay rather modest in a rhetorical era where victory is usually defined in zero-sum terms. By its own account, Hegelian dialectic establishes no final normative standpoint or absolute criterion for adjudicating controversies of the moment.

The conceptual blind spot at the core of transcendental reasoning is scarcely limited to recent philosophical movements. In a highly original study, Paul Diesing has argued that most social theories of the past century can be scrutinized for what they posit as self-acting, unconditional, autonomous forces behind social events. His analysis of neo-classical economic theory, for example, divides this durable conceptual framework into two parts: the market phenomena explained by the theory and the unanalyzable social forces presumed by the theory.[9] As even its critics have acknowledged, the neo-classical model provides a powerful explanation of market exchange (the laws of supply and demand, price theory, principles for efficient resource allocation), emphasizing long-term equilibrium results. At the core of this approach stands a series of presumptions: notably "the postulate of individual rationality," along with a series of acknowledged "exogenous" factors such as the prevailing state of technology, the initial distribution of income and property rights, and individual psychological qualities.

As for the exogenous variables, according to Diesing, the postulate of rationality can be pushed further to explain all future changes, just as prevailing social conditions are assumed to follow from past decisions by individual rational agents.[10] But neo-classical theory can never explain its core assumption of individual rationality. Here is the postulate that makes all subsequent explanation possible, and it cannot logically be extended to prove itself. Precisely this transcendental remove gives the model its extraordinary power: its a priori, analytical standpoint avoids the limitations of mere inductive generalizations about markets and prices, based on past observations. "Everyone thinks in terms of models, since the complexities of concrete reality are unknowable and knowledge necessarily involves abstraction from the concrete."[11]

Although Diesing never quite identifies the reasoning patterns behind these important postulates, his path follows the trail of transcendental arguments-from-ignorance.[12] The process begins with projecting a higher reality for individual rationality at the strategic foundations of the neo-classical model. Once invested with juridical authority, this central postulate lends normative force to artfully designed theorems about market phenomena, which display a fixity and certainty that stand in marked contrast to the chaos of unanalyzed economic reality. By making it possible to attribute lawlike patterns to concrete events, the neo-classical postulate performs the essential functions of Kant's tribunal. Diesing describes the next step in ideological terms: by default, the neo-classicist comes to believe "that the rational individual is real and knowable, while the outward manifestations of rationality are complex, shifting, and indeterminate and therefore knowable only derivatively."[13]

243

Diesing's analysis proceeds in similar ways through some dozen separate standpoints of social theory. Of special interest are the systematic connections he finds among theories, based on two common threads. First is the predictable emergence of paradoxes, as the critical authority of postulates remains outside the growing explanatory power of their respective theorems. In generating theorems of collective welfare, for instance, the neo-classical model encountered a formidable series of paradoxes, later catalogued by Kenneth Arrow.[14]

Second, according to Diesing, new social theories emerge to resolve the specific anomalies of their predecessors. Different explanatory principles arise that reverse the prior logical relationship, converting earlier postulates into current theorems. Diesing explores a wide range of theories that posit higher-order explanations for the neo-classical postulate of individual rationality. Keynesian theory hypothesized certain constraints on individual choice, flowing from organized, structured markets. Parsonian systems theory connected the individual decision-maker to a series of independent social structures. Schumpeterian "elite" theory treated most individual decisions as determined responses, in contrast to the rare creative force of entrepreneurial decisions. In every case, theorists follow a pattern of strategic reversal: old postulates become the dependent variables for new schools of thought, whereas new postulates play the role of independent, normative forces. According to Diesing, it is a process without apparent end.[15]

Unlike countless other analyses that use the descriptive terminology of Mannheimian ideologies, Kuhnian paradigms, or Goffmanesque frames, Diesing's standpoints were not differentiated solely by their historical, social, or psychological genesis. To be sure, every social theory is firmly rooted in complex background conditions, which can provide useful if controversial explanations of ideological positions.[16] But such explanatory exposés soon confront their own limitations, inherent in the selection of independent variables from an infinitely complex natural environment.

Diesing was clearly searching for a more comprehensive approach, one that could treat competing perspectives as complementary. But his linear analysis leads to an infinite regress of social theories, leaving no real hope that future integration will replace continued fragmentation. His Kantian conceptual terminology provides no clear direction, although it prepares the way for the more powerful logic of Hegelian dialectic. Hegel provides an exhaustive vocabulary for describing conceptual dichotomies and an ingenious procedure for reconnecting them within a mutually supporting structure.

The Hegelian Response to Kantian Antinomies

So long as adversarial debate can be dominated by one party, transcendental argumentation sweeps naturally to its inevitable conclusion. But the results are far less predictable when additional parties assert rival transcendental claims, splitting the rhetorical universe into competing jurisdictions. As discussed in the last chapter, the Baden School saw its enlightened pluralism torn apart by the centrifugal force of neo-Kantian projection, which has left our century pondering the recurring tensions of incommensurable conceptual schemes. With rhetorical dominance goes the power to assign the burden of proof to one's adversaries: the prize sought by all parties in true polemical debate. But once neo-Kantian methods have demonstrated their peculiar energy, transcendental victories rarely go uncontested. Polemics arise swiftly in this arena, requiring little more than a timely shift in the burden of proof. And when the issue has been joined at a transcendental level, no single tribunal can hold onto final power. The parties are free to assert opposing postulates, each defended by arguments-from-ignorance that aspire to exclusive authority.

Kant's antinomies provide an appropriate starting point for analyzing such disputes. No theme in all Kant's writings offers higher drama than his startling conclusion that human reason is torn by inevitable and irresolvable conflicts. From the opening sentence of the *Critique of Pure Reason*, he leaves no doubt as to the supreme importance of the problem: "Human reason has this peculiar fate that in one species of its knowledge it is burdened by questions which, as prescribed by the very nature of reason itself, it is not able to ignore, but which, as transcending all its powers, it is also not able to answer." [17] Most philosophers treat Kant's assessment with unusual caution. Whatever its implications for other doctrines, it raises disturbing questions about the conceptual stability of transcendental reasoning. At the very least, it foreshadows the spectacular fragmentation of Kant's own philosophical presumptions over the past two centuries. The antinomies rehearse the adversarial future awaiting all philosophical postulates that come before the bar of transcendental authority.

By contrast with most other philosophers, Hegel greeted the antinomies as a momentous discovery, and he expanded Kant's approach into a broader theory of conceptual dynamics.[18] According to Hegel, the antinomies point toward a more balanced rhetorical exchange by shifting the structure of transcendental argument from one-sided advocacy to reciprocal polemics. In standard transcendental reasoning, dichotomies polarize debate for the separate advantage of competing parties. When both sides learn to play the same game, the strategic forces are immediately equalized. Although this change leads first to polemical stalemate, it eventually throws the whole dispute into a broader arena.

Hegel's innovation was to force the recognition of conceptual antinomies within every transcendental argument and thus to reach beyond the limited ambitions of individual parties. Seen from a different angle, transcendental polemics move from symmetry to unity, as the exchange of proof burdens opens up a conceptual bridge across an otherwise impassable gulf. The original parties trapped in partisan polemics have no sense of this inchoate unity, which they would likely find unwelcome in any case. An observer, by contrast, can see how these inevitable extremes might eventually be rejoined, by shifting the entire antinomy into a broader conceptual context. This new standpoint should not be confused with that of a neutral arbiter or a court of final appeal. Indeed, it plays its own partisan role in yet another dispute, from which still further role-shifts must eventually unfold. The ingenious structure of Hegel's dynamic system allows him to treat the strategic roles of both partisan and observer as mutually complementary. How this process works in detail, and how it finds any resolution, will be discussed later in this chapter.

Kant's own reaction to the antinomies revealed his customary ambivalence on strategic matters. Kant acknowledged that transcendental polemics were unavoidable, even natural expressions of a human compulsion to explore fundamental issues. Questions such as how the world began, what its basic elements consist of, whether it is fully controlled by natural causes, and whether it could have come about without divine guidance—all these questions are impossible to ignore according to Kant. The same human reason that comprehends the rational order in mathematics and natural science reaches for comparable insights about the whole of experience, down to the presumptive unconditioned forces of self, nature, and God. But Kant also believed that any intimations of these higher conditions must remain tantalizing mysteries. We can never fulfill these deep-seated ambitions; our reason is strong enough to project the endpoints of inquiry but too weak ever to reach them. Human capacities are unalterably constrained by transcendental boundaries, laid down by unappealable authority. Although more inclined than Wittgenstein to articulate both sides of this dilemma, Kant delivers similar strictures against speculation on matters of highest importance.[19]

The mystery surrounding the antinomies confirms the unsettled status of transcendental reasoning in Kant's own writings. Kant uses transcendental argumentation freely for defending his own philosophical conclusions—from the deductions of his epistemological models to his postulates of practical reason. He was always more concerned with the specific products of these distinctive arguments than with the process that creates them; his accounts of transcendental proof are (at best) obscure, punctuated by metaphorical references to the legal tribunal. From time to time he issued special dispensations for critical philosophy (his own transcendental conclusions), exempting it from the strict prohibitions that awaited all other efforts in higher speculation.[20] Kant's successors, however, quickly saw the paradox of asserting limits to knowledge, based on normative standards that presuppose a capacity to think beyond those limits.[21]

The exposition of specific antinomies in the First *Critique* created a sensation when Kant argued both sides of the polemical debate, which appeared in parallel columns on the printed page. To silence charges of special pleading, Kant invited his readers to scrutinize both arguments carefully, to determine if he had failed to make the best possible case for either party. Although his earliest interpreters noticed the consistent pattern of indirect arguments on both sides of the antinomies,[22] they failed to see any broader connection with Kant's own peculiar style

246

of philosophical reasoning. It was left to Hegel to find similarities between argument patterns in the antinomies and a generic style of transcendental argument.

The four antinomies acknowledged by Kant are tokens of a larger problem that has plagued transcendental philosophy to the present day: the relations between transcendental postulates and the nontranscendental (or immanent) data or events they presume to explain. This whole style of reasoning starts by presuming a discontinuous universe, where transcendental space is utterly separate from immanent experience. The two realms must later be rejoined, however, after transcendental reasoning has produced a set of operational principles for restructuring everyday experience. Except for the rhetorical thread, there is no clear way to explain precisely how the transcendental and immanent worlds come together. In the spirit of Kant's antinomies, this relationship may be interpreted through two equally sound but contrary models: either the link between worlds is just another immanent datum or it remains completely outside the field of immanent experience. Both these approaches and their attendant paradoxes were investigated in the respective summaries of the Baden and Marburg schools of neo-Kantianism in chapter 7.

Kant's antinomies reduce this broader problem to four classic metaphysical debates. The first antinomy, for instance, deals with the question of whether the world "has a beginning in time, and is also limited as regards space." The "thesis" says it does; the "antithesis" says it does not. The proof for each position, in Kant's treatment, follows the strategic pattern of transcendental arguments-from-ignorance. Each side claims victory by default, based on the opponent's inability to establish a credible case. Thus, to show that the world has a beginning in time, Kant submits the following proof:

247

> If we assume that the world has no beginning in time, then up to every given moment an eternity has elapsed, and there has passed away in the world an infinite series of successive states of things. Now the infinity of a series consists in the fact that it can never be completed through successive synthesis. It thus follows that it is impossible for an infinite world-series to have passed away, and that a beginning of the world is therefore a necessary condition of the world's existence.

Would it be possible to prove, in some more direct fashion, that the world really did have a beginning? Kant's argument for the antithesis tries to show why not:

> Let us assume that it has a beginning. Since the beginning is an existence which is preceded by a time in which the thing is not, there must have been a preceding time in which the world was not, i.e., empty time. Now no coming to be of a thing is possible in an empty time, because no part of such a time

possesses, as compared with any other, a distinguishing condition of existence rather than of non-existence. . . . In the world many series of things can, indeed, begin; but the world itself cannot have a beginning, and is therefore infinite in respect of past time.[23]

Kant's exposition directs attention to the symmetry of both passages, without noting their strategic resemblance to all transcendental arguments, including his own philosophical proofs. Removed from its polemical context, either side of the antinomy could easily be modified to show how it is possible that the world really does have a beginning (or, alternatively, that it could have no beginning). Instead of coming so abruptly to categorical conclusions, any creative Kantian knows how to posit new principles for explaining how any temporal series can be interpreted as discrete (or continuous). Among the many who tried were Hegel and Hermann Cohen.[24]

Indeed, Kant himself manages to find suitable postulates to supplement the thesis half of his last two antinomies. With obvious similarities to his postulates of practical reason, Kant projected rational Ideas of human freedom and God, notwithstanding their violation of empirical limits imposed by the standard of experience.[25] This is not the only place Kant introduces ad hoc terminology to disguise sudden shifts in his serpentine narrative. The Ideas of reason are nominal illusions, but they are obviously important illusions that perform useful regulative functions in our practical lives. We may treat them "as if" they were the genuine article, Kant concluded, as long as we remember the difference.[26]

The parallel rhetoric found in antinomies and transcendental arguments deepens the mystery of Kant's philosophical strategy. If, with only a slight shift in mood, we can terminate the antinomy and convert each half into a self-standing transcendental argument, we should be able to put the same shift into reverse. In other words, we should be able to transform Kant's philosophical proofs into antinomies; all it takes is the imagination to construct an opposing transcendental argument by reversing the burden of proof.

Kant used uncontested arguments-from-ignorance to project his entire transcendental apparatus of categories, the forms of space and time, and the postulates of practical reason. These are the philosophical principles that explain, respectively, how synthetic a priori knowledge, mathematics, and ethical prescriptions are possible. Along with Hegel, one can try to construct an antithetical argument in every case, demonstrating (via arguments-from-ignorance) the impossibility of licensing human capacities for these distinctive modes of experience. Faced with such philosophical polemics, the Kantian tribunal would have found a much tougher jurisprudential challenge.

But Kant never went this far in the Hegelian direction. Amid the rich strategic

248

opportunities surrounding transcendental polemics, Kant drew mainly negative lessons from the antinomies. Most Kantians have followed his prohibitory route: indeed, it is one of the most heavily traveled roads leading modern philosophy "back to Kant." From a juridical perspective, Kant wanted to resolve polemical antinomies by sending them down to the lesser court of spatial-temporal evidence. Before that tribunal, neither the thesis nor the antithesis can present any credible evidence, and so the controversy is dismissed as lying beyond the capacity of the highest competent court. In one sense the slate is wiped clean.

Kant was careful to draw one further conclusion from this process: the change of venue is also a strategic maneuver within a broader controversy.

> Since the arguments on both sides are equally clear, it is impossible to decide between them. The parties may be commanded to keep the peace before the tribunal of reason; but the controversy nonetheless continues. There can therefore be no way of settling it once for all and to the satisfaction of both sides, save by their becoming convinced that the very fact of their being able so admirably to refute one another is evidence that they are really quarreling about nothing, and that a certain transcendental illusion has mocked them with a reality where none is to be found.[27]

Kant thus introduces the notion of concurrent jurisdictions. The first is transcendental (the "true tribunal"[28]), whose function is to certify philosophical proofs that can somehow avoid collapsing into antinomies, including Kant's own arguments and the postulates of practical reason. The second tribunal is Kant's heritage from the Enlightenment: a court of empirical standards, whose doctrines are shaped by the presumption that actual human experience extends no farther than natural science and mathematics can take it.[29] In this carefully balanced system, the transcendental tribunal serves primarily to validate decisions by the tribunal of experience.[30]

By the time of Wittgenstein's *Tractatus*, the higher tribunal had retreated into virtual obscurity. It had nearly vanished altogether from public view after vesting transcendental authority in a surrogate court (in this case, a linguistic analogue to the empiricist court of final appeal). It was thus from some mystical jurisdiction that we received Wittgenstein's mandate to pass no higher than the linguistic tribunal of the *Tractatus*.

Hegel's response to Kant began with a polemical shift and then moved on to a broader, systematic alternative.[31] In his earliest encounters with Kant's antinomies, Hegel noted that a slight change in emphasis might have taken Kant down an entirely different path. The stalemate of the antinomies can support more than one strategic inference: whereas one route leads by default to the juridical endorsement of empirical standards, a second route turns instead to broader issues of juridical authority. This second route leads to a critical investigation of the normative tribunal implied by Kant's and Wittgenstein's prohibitions.[32]

Kant's dialectical discoveries purport to establish the impossibility of reducing every expression of reason to precisely those questions that natural science and mathematics are prepared to answer. At times he seems to say, "so much the worse for reason." But one could just as well respond: "so much the worse for natural science and mathematics." Rather than limiting reason, Kant may have shown the inability of spatial-temporal experience to encompass reason's wider concerns. Most important, he has not established which of these reciprocal inabilities is the proper one to emphasize. Exactly where, in other words, should the burden of ignorance fall?

In a famous passage in the First *Critique*, Kant raises this very question: "Why have we not expressed ourselves in the opposite manner?" he asks. If the postulates that might rescue both sides of the antinomies do not happen to fit into the forms of space and time, perhaps it is these forms that should be faulted.

> For we can say of anything that it is too large or too small relatively to something else, only if the former is required for the sake of the latter, and has to be adapted to it. Among the puzzles propounded in the ancient dialectical Schools was the question, whether, if a ball cannot pass through a hole, we should say that the ball is too large or the hole too small. In such a case it is a matter of indifference how we choose to express ourselves, for we do not know which exists for the sake of the other.[33]

Kant insists, nonetheless, that we simply know the priority of empirical standards over the postulated Ideas of reason. Instead of the ball passing through the hole, he invokes a different image: "In the case . . . of a man and his coat, we do not say that a man is too tall for his coat, but that the coat is too short for the man."[34] Kant's figure of speech, which takes advantage of a linguistic convention, begs the source for our assurance that all such issues should be referred back to the court of empirical evidence. As John E. Smith has commented, "it is precisely the establishment of this priority which Hegel contests on the grounds that it represents a dogmatic preference for . . . empirical knowledge over the claims of reason."[35]

If, in contrast to Kant's conclusion, the antinomies open up a broader understanding of philosophical reasoning, they may explain certain mysteries in the transcendental style of argument. If, however, the antinomies are used to banish certain questions that reason "cannot ignore," they subject reason to the whims of an opaque, tyrannical norm.[36] The gap between what can be known (by empirical standards) and what can be thought will persist, but by definition we can never know anything about it. Into this breach, nonetheless, will flow a powerful stream of subjective musings, quasi-empirical hypotheses, and accompanying polemics. Hegel draws examples of these philosophical ciphers from the first generation of Kantian philosophers,[37] and doubtless he would have included Wittgenstein's call from *das Mystische* in the same category.

Hegel's mature philosophy explores systematically the option not followed by Kant: to clarify and reorient the procedures of philosophical reasoning. To the extent it was or remains successful, Hegel's dialectic provides a useful framework for interpreting the diverse strategies and standpoints explored throughout this book. Hegel was not troubled by the illusions that dissuaded Kant from advancing any farther down this path. If all Kant meant by illusion was that the concepts and methods of philosophy are different from those of science and mathematics, Hegel saw nothing to fear. For whatever reason, Kant never abandoned the presumption that spatial-temporal experience was the unappealable norm for reality. If this were simply a definition of terms, Hegel saw no reason to challenge it; but if it purported to carry normative authority, then it freezes the dichotomy of "is" and "ought" into a permanent, paradoxical absolute. Juridical authority becomes another reality cut off from all sensory appearance, and yet deeply implicated in ways that ordinary people dare not explore.

251

A General Model of Hegelian Dialectical Procedure

A schematic model of dialectical logic can be added to the basic model of transcendental reasoning, just as the Hegelian system emerged historically from the intellectual concerns of Kantian philosophy. The unusual conceptual dynamics of Hegel's logic take on new life in classifying the transcendental strategies that still guide public argument. This approach to Hegel differs in many respects from the commentaries of both friend and foe, which have tended to interpret his project in terms congenial to more restrictive philosophical aims. The precise pattern of dialectical reasoning has eluded even the best Hegelian critics up to the present day, and thus its potential applications to argumentation theory have remained unexplored. My contention is that Hegel adopted this peculiar serpentine logic as a tool for expanding the critical, reflexive, and creative implications of Kant's transcendental method. After first describing the basic conceptual pattern of Hegelian analysis, I will suggest its value as a comprehensive guide to argument strategies resting on transcendental presumptions.

Dialectical logic presupposes a relational and nonlinear structure of argumentation, in which specific conceptual conflicts (or transitions) are located simultaneously along two overlapping rhetorical dimensions. Dialectic recognizes and encourages adversarial conflict, but it projects a concurrent level of reasoning devoted to the specific presumptions that make such conflicts possible and manageable. Within this two-dimensional dialectical framework, transcendental dichotomies always presuppose a larger, strategic context. On the broader dimension, the postulates of transcendental reasoning are introduced functionally as a higher-order commentary on conflicts that cannot be fully resolved at their most immediate level of discourse.

In contrast to the later neo-Kantians, Hegel emphasized the reciprocal nature of concurrent argument levels. For Hegel, the higher-order commentary does not subsist independently but draws specific contextual meaning from its functional role in regulating subordinate arguments. In addition, all higher-order arguments must endure the same rhetorical conflicts as the dichotomies they presume to clarify. They, too, are susceptible to polarizing shifts, including strategic changes guided by yet higher levels of functional commentary.

Some of the mystery surrounding Hegel's triadic divisions (surely the most notorious feature of Hegel's dialectic) can be cleared away by reference to this two-dimensional structure. Hegel's triads do not move in a mere three-step pattern but are embedded in a structural matrix, an ordered series of triads-of-triads. It is this larger pattern (consisting of some twelve reference points) that can eventually be applied to the rhetorical dynamics of transcendental reasoning. The triad-of-triads model provides a schematic inventory of all the strategic functions that give life to dialectical logic.

The following diagram represents the smallest unit of reasoning within which these unusual functional relationships can emerge. For now, the numbers simply indicate generic positions in an argument framework that Hegel used throughout his mature writing, for structuring his own narrative as well as for expressing the nature of transcendental argument. The directional arrows indicate the dynamic flow connecting this core analytical unit with neighboring levels in a hierarchy of interlocking triads.

Table 1. Overlapping Triads

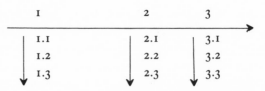

	1		2	3
	1.1		2.1	3.1
	1.2		2.2	3.2
	1.3		2.3	3.3

Within this structured unit of dialectical reasoning, Hegel eventually finds room for all the interactive standpoints, dichotomies, and conceptual shifts that figure in transcendental argument. The basic flow of concurrent argument levels can be monitored from a series of twelve distinct perspectives, represented by the numbered positions above, each of which has a specific rhetorical connection with all the others. The logical relations internal to each of the three columns overlap with an analogous three-part movement across the top row.[38]

Both within and beyond this two-dimensional framework, dialectical reasoning employs two distinct modes of conceptual development: *specification* and *enrichment.* In rhetorical terms, these two dynamic principles represent the transcendental strategies of positing new dichotomies and consolidating postulates with everyday experience, respectively. These two movements provide all the fluidity needed by Hegel's twelve-part scheme, even as it moves up or down the dialectical hierarchy to more distant levels of argument. The triad-of-triads model shows schematically why all of Hegel's conceptual transitions must fall into these two basic categories, as movements from either 1 to 2 or from 2 to 3.[39]

Movements of the first type, specification, lend systematic support to all the adversarial and polemical oppositions surveyed throughout this book. The strategic function of these oppositions, in transcendental terms, is represented by the broader level of advance along the horizontal axis in Hegel's schema: this is the path of projecting new postulates, based on a provisional distinction between immanent and transcendental realms. The purpose of projection is fulfilled in the complementary transcendental step of using new postulates to reinterpret the data of immanent experience. All dialectical transitions of the second type, enrichment, support this process of rhetorical closure by drawing out the conceptual implications of arguments-from-ignorance and their default solutions.

Hegel's' overlapping levels of argument unite substance and function, and they expand the very notion of logic to include the strategic context on which ordinary arguments typically rely. His model extends the central dynamics of transcendental reasoning by requiring all triumphant postulates to acknowledge their strategic genesis in particular controversies. In Hegel's scheme, transcendental postulates assert absolute differences for specific functional reasons, whereas the functional dimension of argument provides a higher-order context for reestablishing unity. As the dialectic moves all the way across the horizontal axis, it recasts the original postulates in instrumental rather than absolute terms, guided by the presumption that transcendental projection serves the larger task of conceptual integration.[40]

Dialectical reasoning always reaches closure within specific conceptual boundaries defined by the basic two-dimensional procedure. For any single level of argument, however, dialectical closure is also a preliminary step in some further argument process, shaped by different conceptual boundaries. Concurrent

253

levels of argument are systematically linked through the hierarchical ordering of triads.

Hegel's logic was designed to ensure that explanatory principles and postulates would not be left hanging as unconditioned abstractions—whether as philosophical postulates or axioms, as first-person intuitions or professions of faith, or as naturalistic descriptions of alleged fundamental realities. The overlapping triadic levels in Hegel's logic are thus expandable along both axes of the triadic matrix. Moving one step up the hierarchy, the same triad displayed along the horizontal axis in the framework of table 1 will now appear as a subordinate triad within another schematic framework. Despite the shift in specific reference (which is much like any shift to a metalevel of description), these two frameworks remain structurally and strategically identical.

Table 2. A Shift in Triadic Levels

	1	2	3
	1.1 (1 from table 1)	2.1	3.1
	1.2 (2 from table 1)	2.2	3.2
	1.3 (3 from table 1)	2.3	3.3

In this purely schematic treatment, such shifts up or down the triadic hierarchy would seem to fall into an infinite regress. Despite its systematic concern with rhetorical closure, dialectical reasoning will always shift to new proximate levels of discourse, for which closure still lies in the future. In strategic terms, every specific transcendental dichotomy brings a provisional solution to some specific antinomy, and yet every dichotomy gives rise to a further antinomy. At no point do we reach a quiet summit; there is always some further peak waiting to connect us with whatever lies on the other side of the mountain. Similarly, if we reverse the flow and analyze each antinomy as the product of some prior transcendental strategy, we will never uncover a truly foundational premise.[41]

Hegel would not have disputed these formal implications, but he would surely have discounted their practical and philosophical significance.[42] Dialectical reasoning brings a highly fluid, situational orientation to all the rhetorical patterns discussed in this book. Wherever adversarial controversies exist, Hegel's logic pushes both parties to move one or two steps farther than their immediate strategic interests would otherwise carry them. If the dialectic reminds us that the work of argument is never done, it also requires us to become more systematic in whatever arguments we may pursue. Hegel's own reconstructions of intellectual controversies, both historical and contemporary, manage to cover enormous conceptual ground while staying within a fairly narrow band of triadic levels. His critiques start in medias res and ordinarily move only two or three levels in either direction.

Within the formal structure of overlapping triads, all the relationships displayed in these tables (including further shifts up and down the triadic hierarchy) are governed by the two dynamic principles of specification and enrichment. In schematic terms, each of the triadic positions connects with all the others through some combination of relations between 1 and 2 and 2 and 3. These two transitions appear directly along the horizontal axis in Hegel's schema. Moving down each of the vertical axes, the same two connections occur in microcosm: 1.1 and 1.2, 1.2 and 1.3; 2.1 and 2.2, 2.2 and 2.3; 3.1 and 3.2, 3.2 and 3.3.

It should be noted that Hegel has no occasion for engineering a transition from 3 to 1, a step that was often awkwardly characterized by early commentators as a conceptual "synthesis" turning into a new "thesis."[43] As dialectic reaches periodic closures at positions 1.3, 2.3, 3.3, its dynamic pulse is always regulated by the horizontal advance. When the horizontal triad closes in the completed transition from 2 to 3, the level of triadic advance has already shifted, such that the closure at 3 (as in table 1) becomes the more limited closure of 1.3 (table 2).

Hegel realized early in his career that dialectical procedures could not be formally diagrammed or verbally described with notations or terminology taken from nondialectical frameworks. His later works succeeded in developing a special language for explaining the principles of dialectical method, along with a narrative structure that could accommodate the concurrent dimensions of argument. I have so far ignored this self-referential side of Hegel's method, which is the source of its notorious challenge to readers across many generations. In this summary, I have clung to the schematic features of dialectical logic in order to suggest its applications to rhetorical strategies of post-Kantian discourse. So precisely what do all these numbers mean in rhetorical terms?

The triadic connections made through specification (all the relations of 1 and 2) refer to conflicts of various kinds: adversarial polemics (1.1 and 1.2), transcendental dichotomies (2.1 and 2.2), and the special antinomies that emerge from applying transcendental postulates to immanent experience (3.1 and 3.2). Looking along the horizontal axis, the basic idea of conflict appears in its strategic guise of transcendental projections.

The overlap of triadic levels in Hegel's system provides an intriguing commentary on the strategic relation between Kantian-style antinomies and the method of transcendental arguments. Both these rhetorical forms are built on dichotomous relationships, and yet both contain the promise of strategic unity. The two-dimensional diagram in table 1 captures the specific rhetorical context in which today's transcendental shift (the relation between 1 and 2, including the entire vertical column under 2) is a provisional response to today's polemics (the opposition of 1.1 and 1.2 under column 1). Within this schematic framework, transcendental reasoning can be said to project higher-order postulates for the purpose of resolving a pendent conceptual dilemma. The general movement from 1 to 2 can be illustrated in Kant's shift to transcendental concepts in the First *Critique*, with which he hoped to resolve the Humean dualism of synthetic and a priori relations of ideas.

The same basic schema, interpreted now according to table 2, shows how yesterday's transcendental shift sets the stage for today's polemics—after the two higher-order terms (1 and 2 in table 1) have moved into a symmetrical relationship, from which each tries to dominate the other (1.1 and 1.2 in table 2). Here we may discern the likes of Kant's famous antinomies of pure reason, which grew "naturally" out of the very presumption that allowed Kant to respond so effectively to Hume's dilemma. These antinomies arose from a profound dichotomy that Kant was forced to posit for his immediate strategic purposes: the dichotomy of separation and unity in the boundary between transcendental reflection and the world of immanent experience.

Once transcendental controversies achieve polemical symmetry, they settle into a permanent stalemate if there are no further shifts in strategic levels. (For Hegel, this kind of conflict reaches possible stalling points at both 1.3 and 2.3, with distinct but equally paradoxical consequences.) Alternatively, the polemics of today can yield to still another transcendental shift, with the projection of new metapostulates (represented in table 2 in the movement from 1 to 2, including the vertical column under 2). According to this pattern, today's transcendental shift is always the prelude to tomorrow's polemics.

The movement from 1 to 2 is the general rhetorical pattern associated with Kant's Copernican revolution—his turn to transcendental concepts, in response to Hume's skeptical treatment of relations of ideas. It was only after making this shift, of course, that Kant could draw out its implications, especially his doctrine that "synthetic" and "a priori" are complementary aspects of a unitary human knowledge. But Kant had difficulty facing up to still further implications of transcendental strategy. He tried to interpret this postulated unity in either quasi-naturalistic or phenomenological terms, rather than focusing on its important strategic dimensions.

While Kant was busy constructing paradoxical emblems of unity that were forever marooned in transcendental space (the unity of apperception, the things-in-themselves), he neglected to explore the rhetorical bridges that connect transcendental projection and the immanent world it was supposed to clarify. The futility of Kant's approach has shaped the gnarled controversies associated with later neo-Kantian movements, including the standard critiques by their twentieth-century successors. By contrast, Hegelian dialectic dwells on the rhetorical function of Kant's transcendental surmise, which becomes the chief topic of philosophical study.

In dialectic, as a result, triadic positions that relate through enrichment (all the relations of 2 and 3) can be interpreted as strategic unities of various kinds. Unfortunately, there is no Kantian or neo-Kantian terminology to label this complementary dynamic principle. As in all transcendental reasoning, the dialectical shift from 2 to 3 means projecting new postulates; but these are now presumptions of unity, rather than the more familiar transcendental dualities. As it moves across the horizontal axis, dialectic seeks to explore the presumptive unity behind all transcendental reasoning, which can never reach full expression within its dualistic categories. This unity is not the undifferentiated One of Parmenides,[44] but a contextually defined relation that supports the precise distinctions contained within the particular boundaries of a two-dimensional schema. The movement to complete the horizontal triad opens a new rhetorical chapter, in which transcendent and immanent worlds are presumed to flow together.

Looking down the vertical axis, all triadic positions at the bottom (those with the suffix .3) reflect diverse aspects of rhetorical closure, governed by the broader strategic context of the horizontal triad. The first example of closure (1.3) abstracts from the transcendental shift (the shift from 1 to 2 in the horizontal triad), and thus it demands (and receives) no higher-order conceptual support. This position suggests the kind of argument that accepts—by default—the paradoxical disjunction between assertions and their justifications, just as Wittgenstein and Kant embraced normative conceptual boundaries that they would not (and could not) express.

The second variety of closure (2.3) specifically accepts the strategic shift to transcendental postulates, but it presumes an eternal disjunction between transcendental and immanent realms. This rhetorical position is the favorite resting place for contemporary deconstruction, among other schools that generate relativist paradoxes. Both varieties of closure can be contrasted with Hegel's reconstructive approach (the horizontal movement from 2 to 3), which includes the vertical triad of 3.1, 3.2, and 3.3.

As the whole neo-Kantian legacy has demonstrated, the peculiar conceptual unity at the far end of transcendental argument encounters its own special antinomy, according to whether it begins from the direction of immanence (the Baden School) or transcendence (the Marburg School). In dialectic, this vestige of the broader duality between 1 and 2 is reflected within the structured unity of 3, in the dialectical positions 3.1 and 3.2. The broad presumption of unity is

257

never sufficient to adjudicate this specific antinomy, either side of which is fully and equally capable of bridging the separable worlds defined within the same two-dimensional schema. Any further inquiry into the source of this oscillating unity (3.3) must shift to another dialectical level, just as the horizontal triad in table 1 shifts to a new triadic level in table 2. What appears collectively as 3 within the schematic context of table 1 reverts to the different strategic role of 1.3 in table 2.

This formal reciprocity between 3 and 1.3 contains some broad clues for interpreting the twentieth-century philosophical response to neo-Kantian transcendentalism. The deeper unity of Kant's two worlds—immanent (for Kant, "empirical") and transcendental (for Kant, "critical")—was faithfully presumed by all neo-Kantians, who disagreed among themselves only about "how it was possible." The rising opposition to neo-Kantian formalism, which grew increasingly powerful in the decades after World War I, curtailed further experimentation with transcendental strategies. Neo-Kantian texts were attacked as empty rationalization, and philosophers developed new prohibitory theories about things that could not (and therefore should not) be said. The presumptive unity behind transcendental reasoning was thus banished from the only level of discourse on which open discussion was to be permitted. Not surprisingly, the dualistic projections of transcendental reasoning quickly became unfit topics for direct expression, even though their strategic presence remained vital to twentieth-century philosophy.[45]

258

Given the historical weight of this strategic shift, however, tacit transcendental presumptions could not be utterly ignored. They were preserved in normative prohibitions like those delivered by Wittgenstein, redolent with Kantian juridical authority. These prohibitions recall Kant's negative solution to the antinomies: they set firm limits to philosophical reflection, often associated with putative limits to the world itself (or, as in Kant, limits to "our" knowledge of it). In this preclusive retreat from neo-Kantian speculation, the entire dichotomous rhetoric of transcendental philosophy came down to a distinction between "our" side of the boundary (1.1) versus the "other" side (1.2), for which no one was entitled to speak.

The paradoxical notion of a limit (1.3) represents the sole point of contact between these two disconnected worlds.[46] Everything beyond the limit was presumed to be unknowable, but the very task of mapping the limit brings both worlds back together—however briefly. The rhetorical vehicle for this task is the argument-from-ignorance, which twentieth-century philosophers began using to block the neo-Kantian move to transcendental projection.[47] As the price for this moratorium on further transcendental advances (condemned as forays into a world that can never, and therefore shall never, be entered),[48] the exponent of the schematic position 1.3 must learn to coexist with a formidable number of unexplainable assertions. Like Kafka's mythical juridical forces, normative paradoxes become permanent features of human life in a default universe—the universe defined by its militant exclusion of everything transcendental.

Even if these dark prohibitions are somehow evaded, yet another moment of closure can interrupt our dialectical progress at 2.3. For dialectic, the final passage from transcendental dichotomy to presumptive unity (the move from 2 to 3) is the natural complement of transcendental projection, but it comes at the strategic moment of greatest peril. To abandon this second phase of argument is to interrupt the horizontal advance halfway down the road, before it has reached the destination that gives the whole journey its particular meaning. Instead of the anticipated reconstruction, this decision leaves discourse stranded in a realm of deconstruction—in the broadest sense in which that term is used in contemporary criticism. The rhetoric of deconstruction participates in the skepticism that brought dialectic to its first pause at position 1.3. However, rather than directing prohibitions against the transcendental shift (the move from 1 to 2), this variety of closure denies the expression of dialectical unity (the move from 2 to 3). It accepts the provisional, strategic division between immanent and transcendental worlds and converts it, by default, into a permanent condition of the universe.

259

Hegel's complex theory of argument seems to court its own set of paradoxes, which critics have always found especially bewildering. This schematic description leaves unexplored many curious features of dialectical procedure, including its restless, continuous movement, its seemingly infinite boundaries, and the normative question of whether dialectic commands the same rhetorical authority as Kant's durable tribunal. These problems can be addressed only by considering Hegel's idiosyncratic presentation of dialectic, in addition to this schematic model.

The strategic requirements of Hegel's basic enterprise are easy to misread. His calculated ambivalence on dichotomies, for example, can be variously interpreted as yet more transcendental rhetoric or as a scandalous disregard of fixed distinctions. Hegel's refusal to construe dichotomies as absolute presumptions narrowed his own expository options. It left him without the usual stock of question-begging explanatory principles, protected from critical attack in some impregnable, transcendental fortress. Worse yet, Hegel would actively cultivate such principles (especially rival postulates) only to disregard their supposed immunity from further higher-order scrutiny. To this day, Hegel is taken to task for his willful failure to defend, in unqualified terms, one or more of the critic's presumptive dichotomies: content and form, thesis and postulate, reality and appearance, being and thought, consciousness and its object, intuition and explanation, the "natural attitude" and philosophy.[49]

When it came time to present his dialectical method in rigorous fashion, Hegel realized that the philosophical lexicon of his day was already preempted by Kantian postulates; and thus he was forced to craft his own descriptive and explanatory language. All the elements in this self-descriptive language were designed to conform to the reflexive patterns of dialectical procedure. In particular, logical concepts and strategic movements had to be interchangeable; the dialectical positions and their connecting functions had to circulate positions and functions among themselves. There was, in short, no ultimate division between *explicans* and *explicandum* in a dialectical description of dialectical procedure. In my schematic summary, I avoided these narrative problems by borrowing an explanatory language from the everyday notions of rhetoric. My allusions to strategies, standpoints, and conceptual shifts assumed that the reader was already familiar with these rhetorical practices, based on the analyses of previous chapters.

Hegel's exposition follows a very different path. Rather than formally separating ideas from their strategic underpinnings, Hegel joined ideas and strategies in a special set of functional—indeed, willful—concepts. These hybrid "concepts" (no English word can capture the dual meaning of Hegel's term, *Begriffe*) are the unique entities that occupy his triadic positions. Within these reflexively structured schemata of dialectic, the Begriffe are both agents and recipients of strategic action. The narrative challenges of dialectical self-description forced Hegel into a most perilous grammatical experiment, in which traditional-sounding philosophical categories were allowed to disport themselves as active subjects, transitive verbs, and direct objects—simultaneously and interchangeably.

Hegel certainly understood the linguistic and conceptual confusion this experiment would inevitably cause, as it challenged all juristic boundaries associated with powerful and popular dichotomies. One still hears complaints, for example, that Hegel's procedure violates the distinction between "use" and "mention." Similar objections come from critics wielding the various dualisms of thought and being, logic and history, analytic and synthetic, nomothetic and ideographic. A valuable history of Hegel-reception remains to be written: the chronicle of how these entrenched dichotomies have, over time, stubbornly resisted Hegel's threat to expose and reverse all transcendental strategies.

This is not the occasion to pursue any farther the narrative peculiarities of Hegel's dialectical defense of dialectic.[50] The schematic picture of dialectical procedure can, however, be supplemented with some important Hegelian terminology. For, despite his rigorously contextual use of language, Hegel also offered a set of paradigmatic terms that unify the expressive and functional aspects of dialectical procedure. Hegel let his system of logic generate these special Begriffe, which integrate meaning and use and thereby capture all the reciprocal connections between ideas and rhetorical strategies. Table 3 places this terminology alongside the triadic numbers from earlier tables.

Table 3. Hegelian Terms for Dialectical Relations

1 Universality (U)	2 Specificity (S)	3 Individuality (I)
1.1 Uu	2.1 Su	3.1 Iu
1.2 Us	2.2 Ss	3.2 Is
1.3 Ui	2.3 Si	3.3 Ii

Hegel's text reveals the linguistic consequences of integrating meaning and use within his explanatory Begriffe. Hegel introduces these paradigmatic terms at a critical point in the dialectical flow of his dialectically structured logic: the turn from 2 to 3, taken at the broadest triadic level covered by the entire narrative.[51] At this point in his narrative, Hegel's terms furnish their own self-commentary.

> At first the Begriff is the pure Begriff or the determination of universality. The pure or universal Begriff is, however, also merely a determined or specific Begriff that places itself on one side over against other Begriffe. Because the Begriff is a totality—hence essentially determining and differentiating within its universality or purely identical relation to itself—the Begriff possess within itself the standard whereby this form of its self-identity, as permeating and holding within itself all its moments, determines itself no less immediately as merely the universal in opposition to the differentiation of its moments [52]

261

By the time this passage occurs in Hegel's text, every explanatory noun in it has already appeared (or will soon appear) somewhere within the triadic matrices. The same is true for every verb, leading up to a subtle analysis of "is" in the subchapter on judgment. If one reads every term contextually, this passage contains a literal self-description of generic dialectical patterns, focusing on the dynamics in column 1 (see table 3). Once Hegel has given the entire field of explanatory language its strategic as well as expressive meanings, the self-exposition of his logic requires no further upward shift along the triadic hierarchy.[53]

At this highly embedded level of discourse, Hegel defines the term *universality* as that concept (Begriff) that contains both its own contrasting element and the impulse to posit it as something contrasting.[54] He then lays out dialectical implications in the conceptual domains of *specificity* and *individuality:*

> Individuality is, as it has shown itself, posited by specificity; it is determinate universality; hence the determinateness that relates itself to itself, the determined determinate.
>
> Individuality first appears as the reflection of the Begriff out of determinateness back into itself. It is the mediation of the Begriff through itself, inasmuch as the Begriff's otherness [specificity] has made itself into an other through which the Begriff is restored as equal to itself, only now in the form of absolute negativity.
>
> Universality and specificity appear on one side as the moments of the becoming of individuality.[55]

Out of the complex narrative structure of Hegel's logic, this paradigmatic triad of self-differenting and self-unifying Begriffe embodies all the strategic dynamics of specification and enrichment. Together with its distinguishable parts, Hegel's Begriff is the irreducible notion of a self-defining process. It supports the projections of transcendental reasoning as necessary but provisional shifts, complementary to the reconstructive strategies that mark the distinctive rhetorical contributions of dialectic. Hegel thus supplies a rigorous (if esoteric) account of transcendental and dialectical reasoning as the generic activity of these unique dialectical concepts, which are on full display throughout the logic.

Despite the notorious difficulties of excerpting Hegel's language from its self-defining context, his comprehensive analysis lends valuable support to the more eclectic method I have been following throughout this book. My basic approach, organized somewhat like a survey, has been to analyze a series of rhetorical performances by prominent arguers under a variety of historical conditions. But this survey has also been guided by Hegel's more systematic approach, which purports to chart the entire universe of presumptions that can enter into diverse styles of argument, including dialectic. To whatever extent Hegel's ambitious project may be judged successful, it provides a unique critical perspective on both adversarial and transcendental polemics. In this book, at least, dialectic has been used all along as a standard for interpreting rhetorical performance.

Dialectic in the Public Sphere: Institutional Presumptions

Unlike Kant's transcendental tribunal, dialectical logic was never meant to serve as a higher source of authority, let alone a court of final appeal. Hegel presumes, rather, that authorities of all kinds—political, religious, scientific, ethical—reveal themselves through rhetorical procedures that conform to the broader dialectical framework. Whatever Hegel's reputation in the textbooks, his approach stays firmly rooted in the everyday reality of human reasoning about real events and real objects. And unlike contrived forms of realism, it includes the common reality of rhetorical strategies, including transcendental projection.

Dialectic searches out these thoroughly human behaviors in all arguments, including arguments that specifically disavow the use of mere rhetoric and those that reject the very possibility of transcendental argument. From a dialectical perspective, the divergence between express and implied messages reflects the distinct levels of argumentation that converge in particular utterances. Even where conceptual content and strategic function meet in close harmony, all arguments presume much more than they can openly express through any single aspect. A willingness to explore these rhetorical gaps and shifts can enrich public reflection on past discourse and expand the scope of future expression. The warrant for all these benign conclusions about human reasoning comes not from some hidden tribunal, but rather from Hegel's self-justifying—if narratively peculiar—principles of dialectical logic.

Dialectical criticism upholds no privileged position or particular authority of its own. It is, rather, a comprehensive procedure, under which all authorities passing across the public stage are invited to display their specific intentions, their most likely contributions to human understanding, and their inevitable presumptions and limitations. To whatever extent these performers invoke the higher authority of Kantian tribunals, the harsh lights of dialectical scrutiny will eventually reveal their strategic supports and props. At such times, this otherwise tolerant and balanced procedure may seem every bit as threatening to the rhetorical performers as their strongest adversary. Dialectic exposes any gap between expressive posture and strategic practice; it spotlights the inevitable presumptions in order to see through pretense and illusion, and it exalts the claims of rival authorities. Yet dialectical procedure is no ordinary adversary, open to equally strong counterattack. It adds insult to opposition by attributing all these deficits to the self-presentation of every putative authority, forced by dialectic to remain on stage long enough to expose its entire strategic repertoire to public view.

To stay true to its own principles, dialectical criticism can never relax its systematic procedures—its functions of specifying and enriching the strategic elements of all perspectives that come within its range (including, in due course, its own self-presentation). The unyielding pace makes this procedure both a doubtful ally and an elusive enemy. To the legal defense team representing each adversarial position, the half-hearted support from dialectic is little better than outright opposition; the dialectical critic might just as well join the deconstructionist in the category of professional nay-sayers. Dialectical reconstruction always tells us too little, too late to enter directly into the partisan battles of public life.[56]

From a dialectical point of view, public discourse has grown increasingly opportunistic in its selective use of strategic argument. These days, rhetorical success in the public sphere depends on using the argument-from-ignorance once to shift strategic burdens against a specific opponent, only to resist further changes that would undermine the default outcome. An adversarial mode of argumentation strikes a single rhetorical posture and then stubbornly refuses to shift any farther, either down the vertical axis (to meet its adversary on level ground) or across the horizontal axis (to encounter its own presumptions). The major alternative, under the continuing glare of dialectical scrutiny, is for each figure to find a determinate role within larger rhetorical tableaux, complementary to other positions. Hegel's dialectical logic sketches the broadest possible strategic pattern, which includes the very principles of its own design. In this unique tableau vivant, the figures themselves are in constant motion, and the only fixed element is the schematic pattern of dialectical movement.[57]

By looking beyond the isolated strategic shift, in all its momentary drama for the entangled parties, dialectic invites erstwhile adversaries to join together in further movements down a common strategic path. Not everyone is ready or able to accept this unusual invitation, and certainly not at every opportunity. A normal life demands its periods of respite, its stable perspectives, its established interests. For the public sphere these moments of repose can be compared to conceptual presumptions, which bid for relative autonomy by suspending further dialectical movements, at least temporarily. To borrow a common sociological term, these contextually bounded presumptions may be thought of as rhetorical institutions,[58] which influence our lives through social organizations and through diverse schools of thought. These organizations include the major forms of publicly administered rhetoric: bureaucracies, legislatures, markets, and the courts.

Organizations play a powerful strategic role in any post-Kantian public sphere, where empirical facts are ritually distinguished from a more elusive realm of values. Organizations separate their social environments into normative and evidentiary elements and then operate like tribunals in construing and combining both realms. Their capacity to generate collective normative judgments becomes increasingly important, by default, in a culture that divides cognitive authority among its individual members. As collective values from past eras vanish into the haze of transcendental ignorance, they leave to public discourse the daunting task of constructing public presumptions from residual sources: the emotional, aesthetic, or transcendental judgments of sovereign persons.[59] Social organizations are indispensable, if problematic, devices for assigning legitimacy to public action.

In their rhetorical aspect, public institutions are defined by internal goals and operating rules, which together provide the default procedures for reaching

264

institutional judgments. Organizational decisions are presumed legitimate to the extent they flow from established principles that lie beyond internal challenge. To be sure, all modern organizations feature special norms that freely encourage changes in particular rules: within limits, public bureaucracies may change their policies, just as corporations change their marketing plans; legislatures can revise past decisions and even amend the constitution; markets can alter their structural underpinnings; and courts can overrule precedent or otherwise break new legal ground. The rapid spread of self-modifying formal procedures within organizational boundaries may be interpreted as self-preservation in the face of external challenges. Perhaps the purest example of these reflexive elements is the self-justifying authority of judicial procedure, which most other institutions have tried to adapt to their own circumstances.

Formal bureaucracies offer the simplest illustration of institutionalized default mechanisms in practice. Both public and private organizations fall somewhere within a broader hierarchy of social institutions, in that they must answer to the higher authorities of legislation, markets, and adjudication. Within these constraints, normative authority in administration typically presents itself in Weberian terms: bureaucracies are instrumental structures that administer a body of rules. No one expects bureaucrats to be moral philosophers; quite the contrary, under Weber's definition, the legitimacy of their judgments depends on rigorous fidelity to established rules, accepted as default standards of normative conduct. In strategic terms, unless it can be shown that administrators have deviated from their governing rules, their actions are presumptively correct.[60] Thus the legitimacy of bureaucratic action is always a conclusion reached by default reasoning, based on the twin presumptions that clear and valid governing standards already exist and that they have been flawlessly applied to concrete situations.[61]

Over the past several decades, reigning theories of formal organizations have vigorously questioned these presumptions, compiling a long list of ills surrounding the whole bureaucratic mission. The microscopic empirical examination of organizational life reveals countless intrusions by factors other than the stated organizational norms—most notably the concurrent, private agendas of organizational personnel, from key executives to street-level workers.[62] These empirical studies make it plain that unwritten rules and informal procedures have a profound influence on organizational behavior, as do the more subtle conditions of leadership and management style. Whether or not one approves of these nonformal or discretionary conditions (and at least some critics, as a practical matter, clearly approve),[63] they conflict with the strict conditions under which bureaucratic organizations conserve their autonomy and normative authority.

Moving beyond the truism that private agendas compromise the purity of bureaucratic autonomy, another line of research has emphasized ambiguities in organizational rules—in both written and unwritten rules.[64] To whatever extent the established principles vary according to contextual interpretations, the whole notion of rule-governed decisions becomes much more fluid. Empirical studies of ambiguity frequently reach conclusions that would seem paradoxical under the Weberian presumption of fixed rules. They show how institutional decisions retroactively define their own governing principles and how workable solutions create the problems they are supposed to solve. In other words, the very criteria of decision are selected ex post facto by predestined or privileged outcomes, reversing the standard formula for administrative objectivity.[65]

From a dialectical standpoint, both perspectives on bureaucratic action raise important questions about institutional presumptions. The general theme that things are never what they seem is rich enough to launch a broader dialectical review. Academic theorists of formal organizations have carried this theme through countless variations, with extraordinary subtlety and even wit. Most of them purport to rely on nothing more than empirical observation, which disavows any prescriptive ambitions of its own; their job is simply to show whether factors other than Weberian instrumental rationality have entered into the bureaucratic vortex.[66]

But empirical studies alone cannot support the next step in dialectical analysis, which is to examine the presumptions of their own critique. From a strategic perspective, most studies of bureaucracy manage to draw normative conclusions from allegedly descriptive analysis, if only as default judgments. Since impersonal observation is ordinarily insufficient to derive "ought" from "is," there must be broader assumptions from which these critical judgments emerge. Most students of bureaucracy draw a distinctive criterion from Weber's definition, which converts it into a normative presumption in a contingent relation to empirical facts.[67] All at once, the presumption of administrative legitimacy becomes nothing more than an empirical hypothesis, now subject to strict counterfactual conditions. Whenever the observed facts fail to meet these prescribed conditions—and there will always be some facts that fail in this regard—the presumption of legitimacy may shift against the normative authority of organizations.

This response to Weber's definition matches closely the structure of strict scrutiny in constitutional law, which plays the identical role of shifting juridical presumptions against the pretensions of bureaucratic action. In both arenas—in the court of empirical evidence as well as in the federal courts—critics of social organizations may find a protected position from which to counter strong normative presumptions. In both forums the tacit assignment of evidentiary burdens is essential to the default outcome.

Whenever an organization is forced to demonstrate that every action follows with deductive force from its stated goals, a heavy burden of proof makes this task unsupportable. Any court that agrees to exercise strict scrutiny has little trouble finding gaps that separate particular actions from general or formal rules. By contrast, the scrutiny is usually much less demanding when organizations are allowed to judge their own performance. Most bureaucracies have developed elaborate internal procedures for validating the transfer between goals and action; indeed, in many respects these procedural devices dominate substantive goals as default mechanisms for validating administrative behavior.[68] Needless to say, there is frequently a wide difference between the negative judgments of external tribunals (whether empirical sociology or the federal courts) and laudatory judgments by the internal tribunals of administrative procedure.

This antinomy—which affects all public institutions and not just bureaucracies—turns on the choice of presumptions about how general rules relate to particular events. Hegelian logic anticipates the many forms such presumptions may take, guided by the central principles of specification and enrichment. Rules and events lend themselves to fundamentally different patterns of analysis, but it should also be possible to reconstruct the conceptual point at which these two paths start to diverge. One path presupposes the absolute difference between universality and particularity; its customary metaphor is the the gulf between abstract ideals and their nominal realization. The other path presupposes their absolute unity; here the dominant image is the identity of the whole and the sum of its parts. Dialectical logic recognizes both models applied to social institutions but permits neither one to preempt the conceptual stage.[69]

In scrutinizing public bureaucracies, external tribunals often lean toward the presumption of fundamental gaps between stated goals and observed actions.[70] The guilt or innocence of an institution depends on the level of scrutiny used to measure these gaps. It all depends, in the end, on who bears the burden of proof. The strategic advantages are reversed when it comes to internal procedures, which generally presuppose the harmony of word and deed. To whatever extent these internal mechanisms mimic judicial procedures, the flow of evidence and even due process creates the impression that organizational presumptions are being put to some risk. (And occasionally, these mechanisms take on a life of their own, exposing internal tensions within the organization.) For the most part, external and internal tribunals begin from different extremes in their treatment of institutional presumptions. The message of dialectic is not that the truth

267

lies somewhere between these two extremes; both extremes are true relative to their respective strategic positions. Dialectic can never dictate which adversarial position deserves support on any particular occasion. The reconstructive forces of dialectic do not guarantee brokered solutions to specific polemical conflicts, but they do point in some new critical directions.

A dialectical analysis of social institutions suggests, for example, that external tribunals always constitute their own organizations by presiding over a distinctive set of presumptions. These presumptions may be summed up in the procedures of law courts, in legislative or market-based procedures, or in the investigatory procedures of social science. As bureaucracies in their own right, these structures themselves are subject to both internal and external scrutiny. For courts, legislatures, and markets, these self-monitoring devices are exceedingly elaborate. Not only can they insulate presumptions from outside critics, but they generally provide implicit standards for launching critical investigations of other institutions.

The same degree of authority and autonomy is profoundly desired by intellectual institutions as well, and above all by established schools of natural and social science. Seen as organizations—as distinctive embodiments of rhetorical presumptions—scientific procedures can be judged from internal or external points of view. To the practicing scientist, internal goals are met by following standard research procedures with the utmost care. Historians of science often divide scientific schools into categories, according to these self-fulfilling procedures. As Kuhn pointed out, anyone who stands outside a particular school or method will probably be using different standards for assessing what the rules should be and whether they are being appropriately followed. Philosophers have long noted the wide gulf between the most powerful hypotheses of empirical science and the observations that are expected to confirm them. In relation to the available evidence, scientific theories are always overbroad and underinclusive; they are both overdetermined and underdetermined by their own stock of evidence, let alone by the evidence gathered by rival schools.[71]

Popper's famous critique of scientific method illustrates the rhetorical advantages held by external critics of institutions. By assuming a wide gap between universal hypotheses and particularized evidence (the scientific analogue to the gap between juridical norm and factual event), Popper placed all claims of verification under the strictest possible scrutiny. From this heavy burden of proof on all defenders of scientific hypotheses, he drew the appropriate conclusion that none could ever amass enough evidence to sustain their affirmative scientific claims. In a rhetorical gesture that initially outraged defenders of scientific orthodoxy, Popper declared falsehood as the default judgment awaiting all serious hypotheses. At most, scientific evidence could confirm the postulated gap that separated it from general hypotheses, which Popper treated as transcendental norms.

Despite the diverse agendas that distinguish external judges of social institutions, each tribunal construes the Weberian definition according to the same logical model, with its uncrossable divisions between universals and particulars. But Weber himself had presupposed a different logical construction, following his neo-Kantian associates Rickert and Lask. For the Baden School, the link between established values and value judgments was much like the union of terms within the classic Aristotelian judgment.[72] However, as part of the strategic turn against neo-Kantian value theory, most twentieth-century social theorists have now abandoned this organic model. In retrospect, it seems like one more case of neo-Kantian formalism, which fails to acknowledge the presumed dichotomy between mere thought and true reality.

Critics thus reinterpret the organic judgment of the Kantian tradition as a set of Aristotelian abstractions; in real life, according to this view, universals and particulars never coincide. In operational terms, universals (including norms and values) are simply the labels we attach to events in order to suit our private or public purposes. They are a natural residue from everyday decisions, an official history of how we have actively classified (and simplified) our diverse experiences.

It is difficult today to raise objections to this powerful approach, such has been the success of antiformalist presumptions in social science. From a dialectical standpoint, moreover, the strategic relations between universals and particulars are complex enough to bring this modern shift within the circle of natural oppositions: the dialectical universal exhibits both patterns and enters into both internal and external relations.[73] For all dichotomies, in effect, Hegelian dialectic presumes both an inside and an outside perspective; the first type of relation will always seem formalistic to the latter, whereas the external relation will always seem shallow and accidental from an inside perspective. The reciprocity of these critiques sets the stage for polemical battles, in which extensional critics unmask the pretenses of the intensionalists, who in turn accuse their critics of reducing an organic bond to mere analytic conjunction.[74]

Dialectical analysis suggests that such interpretive conflicts are unavoidable, but it also suggests further moves for reducing their intensity. For certain historical periods, to be sure, extensional critics seize the strategic advantage; in a philosophical climate that has turned against neo-Kantian value theory, Weber's theory of bureaucracy becomes a self-refuting idealization, an impression that was only strengthened by Weber's own terminology of "ideal types." But the antiformalist critique is not the end of the story. Indeed, it imports a new set

269

of presumptions associated with a dominant strategic move in twentieth-century philosophy, based on the transcendental dichotomy of thought and being. Dialectical logic reminds us that all transcendental moves of this sort contain their own anomalies and presumptions.

Positing the distinction between thought and reality (and, in this context, their analogues of value judgments and values) is a useful strategy for clarifying the complex normative procedures of modern institutions. Beyond this practical application, however, the dichotomy produces its own set of puzzles. If values alone do not determine institutional judgments, then what does? Are these supplementary causal forces entirely self-explanatory, or do they not contain strategic presumptions of their own? And finally, what normative lessons should be drawn, after this wedge has been driven between organizational values (exposed as formal pretensions) and value judgments (put forward as the true efficient causes of organizational behavior)? Have we discovered something wrong or shameful about bureaucracies, as many critics manage to imply?

In short, once we confess our profound ignorance about the true relation between norms and normative judgments in organizational settings, what conclusions are we entitled to draw? The most convenient default conclusions are postulated theories of psychological, political, or economic causation. Once the façade of impartial administration has been exposed, bureaucracies can thus be variously assumed to operate on the basis of personal manipulation by those in authority, or political intervention by outside institutions, or economic determination from broad historical forces. A well-formed argument-from-ignorance can convert these or other hypotheses into default explanations via the standard practices of transcendental reasoning.

Behind the common reliance on arguments-from-ignorance, these residual explanations are all hypotheses competing for intellectual authority. Ironically, they need to project their own normative backing once they come under direct scrutiny, as eventually they must under sustained dialectical procedures. As judgments in need of backing from authority, these hypotheses must find their own brand of institutional support, whether from a socially powerful organization or from some conceptual institution or school of thought. And when this new authority steps onto the dialectical stage, it, too, will have to bridge the connection between norms and normative judgments. The critique of bureaucratic organizations must therefore defer to other organizational forces like the political system, the economic market, and the judiciary or to various conceptual institutions (self-interest theories of behavior, interest-group politics, Marxist economics). Dialectical criticism would eventually expose conflicts within these powerful institutions that shield the default presumptions of external critique.

Observing the ironies of strategic reversals is not the final preoccupation of dialectic. It returns to a model of universality, out of which both conflict and specificity arise; it reformulates the initial term as the kind of entity that both specifies and reintegrates its own conflict. By extrapolating this unfamiliar way of speaking to the problem of bureaucratic organizations, we develop the concept of organizations as self-enclosed procedures through which conflicts are routinely managed. Procedures imply both a set of rules that must be operationalized and an active process of implementation that must, in turn, conform to reflexive elements within the rules.

This procedural model of organizations restores the central aspect of bureaucratic autonomy in accordance with Weber's definition.[75] More important, it also supplements Weber's theory with more complex elements of autonomy, such that organizations (over time, at least) become responsible for generating their own rules and also serve as judges of their own success in the procedural matching of rules and decisions. The spread of procedural regularity within formal organizations can thus be considered a strategic rejoinder to the pervasive twentieth-century skepticism about institutional authority. Assuming that modern communities must have such forms of authority, in an age where postulated ignorance can always put institutions on the defensive, it seems likely that Weber's procedural rationality will continue growing at the expense of an earlier ideal of substantive rationality.

271

Let me conclude these dialectical reflections on social institutions with two observations. First, as overlapping rhetorical streams converge in public action, they produce practical dilemmas that demonstrate all the complexities of Hegel's Begriffe. Hegel's patient descriptions of important dualisms—inside-outside, appearance-reality, whole-part, and (above all) universality-specificity—forecast the dynamic tensions that all institutions struggle to suppress. By carving highly situational presumptions into structures built to resist strategic change, societies erect monuments to their transitory desires. Organizational life must therefore accept a permanent element of hypocrisy in the struggle to maintain internal autonomy and in the parallel campaign to discredit rival institutions.[76]

Second, the spectacle of institutions is played out on the larger political stage, where not just single organizations but entire social structures may compete for the power to control public argument through default presumptions. The interplay of bureaucracies, legislatures, markets, and courts contains the same antinomy of adversarial attack and self-protection that haunts organized public action. The ideal market is thus put up against the chaos of legislative regulation; the ideal court is presented as the necessary corrective for endemic bureaucratic failure. In the polemics of social debate, these presumptions can easily be reversed. Over time they will inevitably shift back, and new genera-tions will rediscover the problems of market failure and judicial discretion, for which the institutional solutions may (once again) be political regulation and bureaucratic rationality. The argument-from-ignorance is both the instrument of radical change and the last refuge of all reactionaries.

Notes

1   Gottfried Wilhelm Leibniz to M. Jaquelot, November 20, 1702, in C. I. Gerhardt, ed., *Philosophische Schriften*, vol. 3 (Berlin: Weidmannsche Buchhundlung, 1887), 444.
2   Sigmund Freud, *The Future of an Illusion* (New York: Norton, 1975), 66.
3   The grounds for reversal were elaborated well before Freud's case was ever uttered. See, e.g., William James, *The Will to Believe and Other Essays in Popular Philosophy* (New York: Longmans, Green, 1897). Many popular movements at the turn of the century imagined this higher tribunal as reconciling the diverse claims of science and religion. See Charles S. Braden, *Spirits in Rebellion: The Rise and Development of New Thought* (Dallas: Southern Methodist University Press, 1963).
4   The statutory burden of proof in employment discrimination cases became the subject of heated Congressional debate after the U.S. Supreme Court's decision in Wards Cove Packing Co. v. Atonio, 490 U.S.642 (1989). In the Civil Rights Act of 1991 (Pub. L. No. 102-166, 105 Stat. 1071), Congress reversed the Court's interpretation, restoring the burden-of-proof standard from prior caselaw.

Chapter 1. The Burden of Proof

1   Justice Oliver Wendell Holmes, Jr., submitted the initial epigram for this trend in his declaration that "the life of the law has not been logic: it has been experi-

ence" (*The Common Law* [Boston: Little, Brown, 1881], 1). The ensuing move-ment was summed up in Max Radin's lectures, published as *Law as Logic and Experience* (New Haven: Yale University Press, 1940). For more contemporary perspectives on the dynamic elements in legal logic, see, e.g., William Twining and David Miers, *How to Do Things with Rules*, 2d ed. (London: Weidenfeld & Nicolson, 1982).

2 Judge Learned Hand provided the classic statement of this dilemma facing the modern judge: "His authority and immunity depend upon the assumption that he speaks with the mouth of others. . . . He must pose as a kind of oracle, voicing the dictates of a vague divinity. . . . Yet the customary law of English-speaking peoples stands, a structure indubitably made by the hands of generations of judges, each professing to be a pupil, yet each in fact a builder who has contrib-uted his few bricks and a little mortar, often indeed under the illusion that he has added nothing. A judge must manage to escape both horns of this dilemma: he must preserve his authority by cloaking himself in the majesty of an overshadow-ing past; but he must discover some composition with the dominant trends of his time" ("Mr. Justice Cardozo," *Harvard Law Review* 52 [1939]: 361).

3 Very few writers have emerged from this search with much confidence in the results—perhaps none since Edward H. Levi's *An Introduction to Legal Reason-ing* (Chicago: University of Chicago Press, 1948). Levi borrowed his confidence from the "experimental logic" of John Dewey, which has since fallen into ne-glect. Dewey's contributions are discussed below in chap. 5.

4 Stephen Toulmin, *The Uses of Argument* (Cambridge: Cambridge University Press, 1958).

5 For some extensions of Toulmin's work to normative issues, see Robert J. Fogelin, *Evidence and Meaning* (London: Routledge, 1967). Applications of arti-ficial intelligence to argumentation theory are still quite preliminary. For early examples, see, Raymond Reiter, "On Reasoning By Default," in David L. Waltz, ed., *TINLAP-2: Theoretical Issues in Natural Language Processing-2* (New York: Association for Computing Machinery, 1978), 210–18; Lawrence Birnbaum, Margot Flowers, and Rod McGuire, "Towards an AI Model of Argumenta-tion," in American Association for Artificial Intelligence, *Proceedings of the First National Conference* (Stanford: American Association for Artificial Intelligence, 1980), 313–15. For a basic introduction to related issues in artificial intelligence, see Gerhard Brewka, *Nonmonotonic Reasoning: Logical Foundations of Common-sense* (Cambridge: Cambridge University Press, 1991). A more formal analysis appears in Robert Ernest Mercer, *A Default Logic Approach to Natural Language Presuppositions* (Vancouver: University of British Columbia Department of Com-puter Science, 1987). I am grateful to James Kilbury for bringing this last refer-ence to my attention.

6 See, e.g., Richard A. Posner, *The Problems of Jurisprudence* (Cambridge: Harvard University Press, 1990). The classic case is Levi's *Introduction to Legal Reasoning*, which invoked pragmatist models of logic to dissolve the mysteries of judicial reasoning.

7 Toulmin, *Uses of Argument*, 7 (emphasis in original).

8 Ibid., 7–8.

9 Ibid., 105, 98. As Charles B. Schaefer points out, Toulmin's initial examples are far more abstract than practical legal questions. "It is unlikely that a judge would be asked to decide merely whether Harry is a citizen. Rather Harry may ask a court to prevent his deportation, to recover his income taxes, to allow him to sue in federal court, or to compel the state department to grant him a passport. In the course of deciding the court might be asked to pass on Harry's citizenship. But that abstract issue of categorization arises in the context of a practical problem. The real issue before a court is not what it shall say but what it shall do" ("Think Like A Lawyer," in George Ziegelmueller and Jack Rhodes, eds., *Dimensions of Argument: Proceedings of the Second Summer Conference on Argumentation* [Annandale, Va.: Speech Communication Association, 1981], 244 [hereafter cited as *Second Summer Conference*]). For additional criticisms, see Peter T. Manicus, "On Toulmin's Contributions to Logic and Argument," *Journal of the American Forensic Association* 3 (1966): 83–94.

10 Toulmin, *Uses of Argument*, 98.

11 Ibid., 241 (emphasis added by Toulmin). The quotation is from P. G. Wodehouse, *The Code of the Woosters*. (No page number is supplied, but Bertie says much the same thing on every page of several dozen stories and books.)

12 Toulmin, *Uses of Argument*, 234.

13 It should perhaps be noted that Toulmin was Wittgenstein's student at Cambridge and that ordinary-language philosophy developed somewhat differently at the two British universities. The lines of influence are admirably sorted out in John Passmore, *A Hundred Years of Philosophy* (London: Duckworth, 1957), chap. 18.

14 The ultimate purpose of correct logical form was to arrange knowledge claims in a fashion suitable for direct empirical verification. A popular treatment of this school can be found in A. J. Ayer, *Language, Truth and Logic* (1936; 2d ed. rpt., New York: Dover, 1952). A more rigorous presentation is J. R. Weinberg, *An Examination of Logical Positivism* (London: Routledge, 1936).

15 This view was sanctified by Wittgenstein's dictum in the *Philosophical Investigations* that "every sentence in our language 'is in order as it is'" (2d ed., [New York: Macmillan, 1958], §98).

16 The same strategy was used in the influential works on philosophy of law by H. L. A. Hart. See William Twining, "Academic Law and Legal Philosophy: The Significance of Herbart Hart," *Law Quarterly Review* 95 (1979): 557–80; Michael Martin, *The Legal Philosophy of H. L. A. Hart: A Critical Appraisal* (Philadelphia: Temple University Press, 1987), 276; Peter Goodrich, *Legal Discourse: Studies in Linguistics, Rhetoric, and Legal Analysis* (New York: St. Martin's, 1987), 54–62.

17 The leading arguments came from the American legal realist school. For an overview of that movement and one of its leading figures, see William Twining, *Karl Llewellyn and the Realist Movement* (Norman: University of Oklahoma Press, 1985).

18 Toulmin, *Uses of Argument*, 255, 251 (emphasis in original), 248. Put in more

275

subjunctive terms, Toulmin acknowledges that, "to the extent that there are common and understood interpersonal procedures for testing warrants in any particular field, a judicial approach to our problems will be possible" (175–76).

19 Compare ibid., 216. Toulmin's later works have added numerous refinements to his theory of fields of inquiry. Most important, "fields" are not expected to deal thematically with their own limits (in contrast to how courts are continually called on to define their own jurisdictional boundaries). See also his popular textbook, written with Richard Rieke and Allan Janik, *An Introduction to Reasoning*, 2d ed. (New York: Macmillan, 1984). For critical discussions see Charles Arthur Willard, *Argumentation and the Social Grounds of Knowledge* (University, Ala.: University of Alabama Press, 1983), chap. 3; Paul A. Bové, "The Rationality of Disciplines: The Abstract Understanding of Stephen Toulmin," in Jonathan Arac, ed., *After Foucault* (New Brunswick, N.J.: Rutgers University Press, 1988), 42–70.

20 Toulmin, *Uses of Argument*, 257. Toulmin takes issue with J. L. Austin's suggestion that human fallibility may introduce systematic mistakes into the content of specific fields (237). For criticisms of Toulmin's empiricist faith in the growth of argument fields, see Harald Wohlrapp, "Toulmin's Theory and the Dynamics of Argumentation," in Frans H. van Eemeren et al., eds., *Argumentation: Perspectives and Approaches*, vol. 3A (Dordrecht: Foris, 1987), 333–34.

21 Toulmin, *Uses of Argument*, 255, 7.

22 Toulmin's critics have not pressed their criticisms to this degree. They have emphasized the need to highlight the context in which arguments occur, and even the process, but not the procedure. See (on context) Brant R. Burleson, "On the Analysis and Criticism of Arguments: Some Theoretical and Methodological Considerations," *Journal of the American Forensic Association* 15 (1979): 137–47; and (on process) Willard, *Argumentation*. On the distinction between "process" and "procedure," see Joseph W. Wenzel, "Perspectives on Argument," in Jack Rhodes and Sara Newell, eds., *Proceedings of the Summer Conference on Argumentation* (Annandale, Va.: Speech Communication Association, 1980), 112–33 (hereafter cited as *First Summer Conference*).

23 See references in note 5.

24 Argumentation theorists have given surprisingly little attention to strategies of burden-shifting. A typical treatment is the quick summary in George W. Ziegelmueller and Charles A. Dause, *Argumentation: Inquiry and Advocacy* (Englewood Cliffs, N.J.: Prentice-Hall, 1985), 19–20. Among current theorists, Charles Arthur Willard has provided the clearest perspective for analyzing such shifts (*A Theory of Argumentation* [Tuscaloosa: University of Alabama Press, 1981], 117–18). See also Robert Alexy, *A Theory of Legal Argumentation* (Oxford: Clarendon Press, 1989), 195–97 (trans. of *Theorie der juristischen Argumentation*, 1978). Some empirical studies have documented the appearance of burden-shifting in ordinary conversation. See, e.g., Richard D. Rieke, "Adult Reasons in Supplication," and Mary Louise Willbrand, "Child Reasoning in Supplicatory Discourse: Rules to be Refined," in *Second Summer Conference*, 579–608. James W. Paulson and Jack Rhodes have augmented Toulmin's terminology with a related

concept: "The Counter-Warrant as a Negative Strategy," *Journal of the American Forensic Association* 15 (1979): 205–10.

25 For standard legal treatments, see John Henry Wigmore, *Evidence in Trials at Common Law*, Chadbourn revision (Boston: Little, Brown, 1981), §§2485–89; Charles T. McCormick, *McCormick on Evidence*, 4th ed. (St. Paul: West, 1992), chap. 36. For a nontechnical discussion see Daniel M. Rohrer, "Jurisprudential Origins and Applications of Presumption and the Burden of Proof," in *Second Summer Conference*, 159–78.

26 See William Holdsworth, *A History of English Law*, 7th ed., vol. 1 (London: Methuen, 1956), 301–02; Loretta B. DeLoggio, "Beyond a Reasonable Doubt —An Historical Analysis," *New York State Bar Journal* 58, no. 3 (1986): 19–25.

27 For a standard survey of the term near the height of its popularity, see Note, "The Presumption of Constitutionality," *Columbia Law Review* 31 (1931): 1136–48.

28 A well-known example is the Delaney clause, added in 1958 to the federal Food, Drug, and Cosmetic Act, which bars food additives found to have any carcinogenic effects (21 U.S.C. §348[c][3][A]). See Debra M. Strauss, "Reaffirming the Delaney Clause," *Food Drug Cosmetic Law Journal* 42 (1987): 393–428. For a comparative survey of evidentiary standards in environmental legislation, see Devra Lee Davis, "The 'Shotgun Wedding' of Science and Law: Risk Assessment and Judicial Review," *Columbia Journal of Environmental Law* 10 (1985): 67–109.

29 In recent years, the Supreme Court has extended a relatively generous presumption of constitutionality to federal environmental standards, although not without internal dissent. Two cases of particular note involved the standards for benzene (Industrial Union Department, AFL-CIO v. American Petroleum Institute, 448 U.S. 607 [1980]), and for cotton dust (American Textile Manufacturers Institute, Inc. v. Donovan, 452 U.S. 490 [1981]).

30 The same set of questions can be asked in the context of artificial intelligence research, where the default frameworks of logical inference take the place of the institutionalized structures of the law. In addition to sources cited in note 5, see Raymond Reiter, "A Logic for Default Reasoning," *Artificial Intelligence* 13 (1980): 81–132. For a more popular summary see Kent Bach, "Default Reasoning," *Pacific Philosophical Quarterly* 65 (1984): 37–58.

31 William Twining, *Theories of Evidence: Bentham and Wigmore* (London: Weidenfeld & Nicolson, 1985), 177. Twining earlier explains that this special sense of "rationality" "found its classic expression in English empirical philosophy in the writings of Bacon, Locke, and John Stuart Mill" (16).

32 Robert Hutchins's early work on legal evidence raised many of these issues. See, e.g., "The Law and the Psychologists," *Yale Review* 16 (July 1927): 678–90; "Some Observations on the Law of Evidence," *Columbia Law Review* 28 (1928): 432–40. For recent empirical discussions, see Kay Neal, "The Effects of Evidence on the Perceived Outcome in Superior-Subordinate Decision-Making Situations," in J. Robert Cox, Malcolm O. Sillars, and Gregg B. Walker, eds., *Argument and Social Practice: Proceedings of the Fourth SCA/AFA Confer-*

ence on Argumentation (Annandale, Va.: Speech Communication Association, 1985), 782–806; Dennis S. Gouran, "Cognitive Sources of Inferential Error and the Contributing Influence of Interaction Characteristics in Decision-Making Groups," in *Second Summer Conference,* 728–48.

33 Holdsworth traces the presumption of innocence in criminal trials to thirteenth century borrowings from Roman law (*History of English Law* 1:302). Wigmore notes that placing the risk of non-persuasion on plaintiffs in civil cases is simply "the situation common to all cases of attempted persuasion, whether in the market, the home, or the forum. . . . In the affairs of life there is a penalty for not sustaining the burden of proof." (*Evidence in Trials,* §2485).

34 See John Stuart Mill's remarks on the general conditions for induction, *A System of Logic,* 1843, in J. M. Robson, ed. *Collected Works* (Toronto: University of Toronto Press, 1973), vols. 7–8, bk. 3, chaps. 1–4. For a recent reevaluation of Mill's theory of induction, see Geoffrey Scarre, *Logic and Reality in the Philosophy of John Stuart Mill* (Dordrecht: Kluwer, 1989). Karl Popper's philosophy of science seeks to shift this basic presupposition of empiricism, turning scientific inquiry into a process of falsification rather than verification. For Popper, theories are not innocent until proven guilty. See *The Logic of Scientific Discovery* (London: Hutchinson, 1959) (trans. of *Logik der Forschung,* 1934). Popper's views are analyzed below in chap. 5.

35 Twining, *Theories of Evidence,* 1, 3.

36 See, James Bradley Thayer, *A Preliminary Treatise on Evidence at the Common Law* (Boston: Little, Brown, 1898), 2.

37 Twining, *Theories of Evidence,* 12, 7, citing Thayer, *Preliminary Treatise,* 535. Twining's reference to "policy" anticipates the later political critique of the judicial process identified with American legal realism. Thayer's turn-of-the-century confidence in self-regulating judicial procedures led him to conclude that wise judges and sagacious lawyers could bring sufficient order into the "motley and undiscriminated character" of the law as he described it. He also assumed "a properly qualified tribunal, one that knows an evidential thing when it sees it" (Thayer, 527; see also 509).

38 Wigmore, *Evidence in Trials,* §2486.

39 Mill, *System of Logic,* bk. 3, chap. 4. See Scarre, *Logic and Reality,* chap. 4.

40 For an overview of these standards from the perspective of probability theory, see V. C. Ball, "The Moment of Truth: Probability Theory and Standards of Proof," *Vanderbilt Law Review* 14 (1961): 807–30.

41 For an extended discussion, see W. Lance Bennett and Martha S. Feldman, *Reconstructing Reality in the Courtroom: Justice and Judgment in American Culture* (New Brunswick, N.J.: Rutgers University Press, 1981).

42 In the United States, these framework conditions received special attention during the 1950s and 1960s, in the context of public debate over the legitimacy of judicial review. Perhaps the fullest account came in the unpublished but widely circulated teaching materials assembled by Herbert M. Hart, Jr., and Albert M. Sacks, *The Legal Process,* tentative ed. (Cambridge: Harvard Law School, 1958). According to some accounts, wise judicial administration of procedural rules was the necessary counterweight to democratic impulses in postwar society. See,

e.g., Alexander M. Bickel, *The Least Dangerous Branch* (Indianapolis: Bobbs-Merrill, 1962; 2d ed., New Haven: Yale University Press, 1986), whose discussion of the "passive virtues" still commands much attention. Richard A. Epstein has discussed the allocation of proof burdens at the level of pretrial motions and pleadings. His analysis focuses on formal allocation rules and says little about the dynamic sources of those rules ("Pleadings and Presumptions," *University of Chicago Law Review* 40 [1973]: 556–82).

43 Peirce's concept of the scientific community and Dewey's procedural treatment of scientific inquiry are discussed in chap. 5. For a sympathetic summary see Charles Morris, *The Pragmatic Movement in American Philosophy* (New York: George Braziller, 1970). The social implications of pragmatism were forcefully argued in Morton White, *Social Thought in America: The Revolt Against Formalism* (New York: Viking, 1949).

44 See Bennett and Feldman, *Reconstructing Reality*, chap. 4.

45 David A. Binder and Paul Bergman, *Fact Investigation: From Hypothesis to Proof* (St. Paul: West, 1984), 5–6 (emphasis in original).

46 For a full description, see Fowler V. Harper, Fleming James, Jr., and Oscar S. Gray, *The Law of Torts*, 2d ed., vol. 4 (Boston: Little, Brown, 1986), §§19.5–.12.

47 Ibid., 25. See also Rohrer, "Jurisprudential Origins," 168–69.

48 "[S]ince juries incline heavily towards plaintiffs . . . the net practical effect of the doctrine is to shift the substantive burden of loss from unexplained accidents . . . from plaintiffs to defendants" (Harper, James, and Gray, *Law of Torts*, 4:30).

49 Arguments of this sort frequently appear in trade journals of the organized bar. See, e.g., "Dare We Trust the Jury?" *The Brief* 18, no. 1 (1988): 6–15.

50 Harper, James, and Gray, *Law of Torts*, 4:11.

51 See Bennett and Feldman, *Reconstructing Reality*, chaps. 7–8. For empirical data on group dynamics and persuasion, see the essays in Michael E. Roloff and Gerald R. Miller, eds., *Persuasion: New Directions in Theory and Research* (Beverly Hills, Calif.: Sage, 1980).

52 Harper, James, and Gray, *Law of Torts*, 4:11–13.

53 This is in fact an important trend in American accident law. See ibid., vol. 3, chap. 14.

54 Epstein emphasizes this formal structure ("Pleadings and Presumptions," 571–78).

55 For an interpretation of the broader intellectual strategy, see Arthur Lovejoy's classic treatment, *The Revolt against Dualism* (New York: Norton, 1930).

56 For an overview of the rhetoric movement, see Joseph Schwartz and John A. Rycenga, eds., *The Province of Rhetoric* (New York: Ronald Press, 1965). The aspirations of the movement were summed up in Lloyd F. Bitzer and Edwin Black, eds., *The Prospect of Rhetoric: Report of the National Development Project* (Englewood Cliffs, N.J.: Prentice-Hall, 1971). Contemporary developments are reviewed in Herbert W. Simons, ed., *The Rhetorical Turn: Invention and Persuasion in the Conduct of Inquiry* (Chicago: University of Chicago Press, 1990). Further consideration of modern rhetorical theory will be found below in chap. 4, in an assessment of practical reasoning.

57 In addition to Morris, *Pragmatic Movement*, see John E. Smith, *Purpose and*

Thought: The Meaning of Pragmatism (Chicago: University of Chicago Press, 1984).

58 Some early essays are translated in Chaïm Perelman, *The Idea of Justice and the Problem of Argument* (London: Routledge, 1963). Kelsen's *Reine Rechtslehre* (1st ed., 1934) is translated as *The Pure Theory of Law* (Berkeley: University of California Press, 1967).

59 In addition to the later essays in *Idea of Justice*, see Chaïm Perelman and L. Olbrechts-Tyteca, *The New Rhetoric: A Treatise on Argumentation* (Notre Dame, Ind.: University of Notre Dame Press, 1969). This is a translation of *La nouvelle rhétorique: Traité de l'argumentation* (1958). A further collection of essays appears in Perelman, *Justice, Law, and Argument* (Dordrecht: Reidel, 1980).

60 Perelman and Olbrechts-Tyteca, *New Rhetoric*, 514. Despite the intervening influence of post-modern styles of reasoning, contemporary rhetoricians still define their distinctive mission as the search for an informal logic that transcends both hard facts and cold logic. The recurring dilemmas of this search are summarized by Simons in "The Rhetoric of Inquiry as an Intellectual Movement," which introduces his edited volume, *Rhetorical Turn* (1–31).

61 For a range of scholarly reactions, see James L. Golden and Joseph J. Pilotta, eds., *Practical Reasoning in Human Affairs: Studies in Honor of Chaïm Perelman* (Dordrecht: Reidel, 1986). Favorable reviews predominate in Ray D. Dearin, ed., *The New Rhetoric of Chaim Perelman: Statement and Response* (Lanham, Md.: University Press of America, 1989). Within contemporary rhetorical discussions, subdisciplines appear to be developing, based on critical responses to the University of Iowa Project on Rhetoric of Inquiry. For an overview, see John S. Nelson, Allan Megill, and Donald N. McCloskey, eds., *The Rhetoric of the Human Sciences* (Madison: University of Wisconsin Press, 1987).

62 Aristotle, *Analytica Posteriora*, 99b15–100b18; *Analytica Priora*, 46a3–30. The corresponding advantages of dialectic are noted by Aristotle in the *Topica* (see, e.g., 101a36–b4).

63 In more recent works, the foundations of rhetoric have been interpreted as analogous to the founding myths of political communities (John S. Nelson, "Political Foundations for the Rhetoric of Inquiry," in Simons, ed., *Rhetorical Turn*, 258–89).

64 Perelman and Olbrechts-Tyteca, *New Rhetoric*, 103. Perelman's description of inertial tendencies in audience expectations follows conventional wisdom.

65 Ibid.

66 Richard Whately, *Elements of Rhetoric* [1827], ed. Douglas Ehninger (Carbondale: Southern Illinois University Press, 1963). For a discussion of alternative interpretations of Whately's work, see J. Michael Sproule, "The Psychological Burden of Proof: On the Evolutionary Development of Richard Whately's Theory of Presumption," *Communication Monographs* 43 (1976): 115–29.

67 For a perceptive discussion of these opposing rhetorical possibilities, see G. Thomas Goodnight, "The Liberal and the Conservative Presumptions: On Political Philosophy and the Foundation of Public Argument," in *First Summer Conference*, 304–37.

68 Whately, *Elements*, pt. 1, chap. 3, §2.

69 See Ray E. McKerrow, "Richard Whately's Theory of Rhetoric," in Ray E. McKerrow, ed., *Explorations in Rhetoric* (Glenview, Ill.: Scott, Foresman, 1982), 137–56.

70 "Our concern is not for an identification of philosophic methods with legal methods because the role of authority in law does not have its counterpart in philosophy and the authority of *res judicata*, which is necessary in law in order to end controversy, is, in no way, recognized in philosophy. In fact, in philosophy where the controversies are such that each attempts to justify his own position, to convince his interlocutor, the controversies may continue indefinitely, and the decision of a third party cannot put an end to them" (Perelman, *Justice, Law, and Argument*, 158). This open-ended search adds critical appeal to Jürgen Habermas's influential notion of the ideal speech community, which will be discussed below in chap. 4.

71 Anxiety over this possibility figures prominently in the anthologies edited by Simons (*Rhetorical Turn*) and by Nelson, Megill, and McCloskey (*Rhetoric of the Human Sciences*).

72 See Michael Calvin McGee, "A Materialist's Conception of Rhetoric," in McKerrow, ed., *Explorations in Rhetoric*, 23–48.

73 This is the theme of bk. 1 of the *Topica*. On dialectic as a procedure for qualifying the principles of demonstration, see 101a36–b4. On practical conflict as the source of dialectical problems, see 104b1–17, 158a31–159a14. For commentary, see J. D. G. Evans, *Aristotle's Concept of Dialectic* (Cambridge: Cambridge University Press, 1977); G. E. L. Owen, ed., *Aristotle on Dialectic* (Oxford: Clarendon Press, 1968).

74 The term has a complex history, both in Greek thought and in later times. For an overview of ancient uses, see Richard McKeon, "Greek Dialectics: Dialectic and Dialogue, Dialectic and Rhetoric," in Chaïm Perelman, ed., *Dialectics* (The Hague: Nijhoff, 1975), 1–25. Kenneth Burke catalogued still other uses in *A Grammar of Motives* (Berkeley: University of California Press, 1969), pt. 3.

75 Maurice Natanson outlined a similar role for dialectic as a supplement to rhetoric. See his 1955 essay, "The Limits of Rhetoric," reprinted in Maurice Natanson and Henry W. Johnstone, Jr., eds., *Philosophy, Rhetoric and Argumentation* (University Park: Pennsylvania State University Press, 1965), 93–101. For a related treatment of dialectic as "an established methodology of probative assessment," or "machinery for the evaluation of arguments," see Nicholas Rescher, *Dialectics* (Albany: SUNY Press, 1977), 45. Rescher's analysis does not, however, associate its logical functions with cultural, social, or organizational elements. R. C. Pinto has pointed some of Rescher's ideas in broader directions. See "Dialectic and the Structure of Argument," *Informal Logic* 1 (1984): 16–20. Kenneth Burke's discussion of the "dialectic of constitutions" brings the cultural dimension of dialectic within a jurisprudential metaphor (*Grammar of Motives*, 323–401).

76 The legal context of Aristotle's rhetoric was discussed by Robert Johnson Bonner, *Lawyers and Litigants in Ancient Athens* (Chicago: University of Chicago Press, 1927). See also G. E. R. Lloyd, *Demystifying Mentalities* (Cambridge: Cambridge University Press, 1990), chap. 3.

281

77 See Goodnight, "Liberal and Conservative Presumptions."

78 See, e.g., the anthology edited by Mary Douglas, *Rules and Meanings* (Harmondsworth, England: Penguin Books, 1973).

79 See in particular Harold Garfinkel's *Studies in Ethnomethodology* (Englewood Cliffs, N.J.: Prentice-Hall, 1967). For critical discussions see John C. Heritage, "Ethnomethodology," in Anthony Giddens and Jonathan Turner, eds., *Social Theory Today* (Stanford: Stanford University Press, 1987), 224–272; Graham Button, ed., *Ethnomethodology and the Human Sciences* (Cambridge: Cambridge University Press, 1991).

80 These structural rules in law were conveniently labeled "secondary rules" by H. L. A. Hart in his influential *Concept of Law* (Oxford: Clarendon Press, 1961), chap. 5. Hart did not, however, explore the dialectical preconditions for secondary rules. Recent analytic treatments have acknowledged this omission but have done little to remedy it. See Frederick Schauer, *Playing by the Rules* (Oxford: Clarendon Press, 1991), epilogue.

81 G. P. Baker and P. M. S. Hacker, *Language, Sense and Nonsense* (Oxford: Blackwell, 1984), 265–66.

82 Nor is there much gained from adding some components of Rescher's version of dialectic to Toulmin's model. See Paul Healy, "Critical Reasoning and Dialectical Argument: An Extension of Toulmin's Approach," *Informal Logic* 9 (1987): 1–12.

83 Toulmin cites at length the celebrated passage from Hume's *Treatise* expressing gratitude that the cure for philosophical puzzlement is to try some other activity. ("I dine, I play a game of back-gammon, I converse, and am merry with my friends; and when after three or four hours' amusement, I wou'd return to these speculations, they appear so cold, and strain'd, and ridiculous, that I cannot find in my heart to enter into them any farther" [*Uses of Argument*, 164–65].)

84 In addition to works cited earlier in this chapter, see Jerome Frank, *Courts on Trial: Myth and Reality in American Justice* (Princeton: Princeton University Press, 1949).

85 An especially rich source among periodicals is the *Law and Society Review.*

86 For a discussion of related trends in American political thinking, see Judith N. Shklar, "Decisionism," in Carl J. Friedrich, ed., *Rational Decision* (New York: Atherton Press, 1964), 3–17.

87 Rescher, for example, sees dialectic as a kind of inertial force accompanying the evolution of dominant perspectives and thus as protection against the "all-too-destructive weapons of the skeptic" (*Dialectic*, 100–109). See also Wayne C. Booth, *Modern Dogma and the Rhetoric of Assent* (Notre Dame, Ind.: University of Notre Dame Press, 1974).

88 This movement is too diverse to summarize here. One of the central manifestoes is Roberto Mangabeira Unger, *The Critical Legal Studies Movement* (Cambridge: Harvard University Press, 1986). For a useful anthology, see Allan C. Hutchinson, ed., *Critical Legal Studies* (Totowa, N.J.: Rowman & Littlefield, 1989).

89 Mark Kelman summarizes the CLS indictment of these liberal ideals in his *Guide to Critical Legal Studies* (Cambridge: Harvard University Press, 1987), chaps. 1–3.

90 See, e.g., David Couzens Hoy, "Interpreting the Law: Hermeneutical and Post-Structuralist Perspectives," *Southern California Law Review* 58 (1985): 135–76.

91 The contrast with an assumed Athenian unity is emphasized by writers of both conservative and liberal persuasions, from Allan Bloom to Alasdair Mac-Intyre. For useful commentary on these works, see Ian Shapiro, *Political Criticism* (Berkeley: University of California Press, 1989).

92 See, e.g., Alasdair MacIntyre, *After Virtue,* 2d ed. (Notre Dame, Ind.: University of Notre Dame Press, 1984); Theodore J. Lowi, *The End of Liberalism,* 2d ed. (New York: Norton, 1979).

93 For the rhetorical aspects of this condition, see Michael Calvin McGee, "The 'Ideograph': A Link Between Rhetoric and Ideology," *Quarterly Journal of Speech* 66 (1980): 1–16.

94 Goodnight deals with these reactionary and radical extensions in his essay, "Liberal and Conservative Presumptions," 309–11.

Chapter 2. Shifting the Presumptions of Social Order

1 See, e.g., Archibald Cox, *The Warren Court: Constitutional Decision as an Instrument of Reform* (Cambridge: Harvard University Press, 1968); see also the textbook by Harold W. Horowitz and Kenneth L. Karst, *Law, Lawyers, and Social Change* (Indianapolis: Bobbs-Merrill, 1969). For a descriptive study see Joel F. Handler, *Social Movements and the Legal System* (New York: Academic Press, 1978). A more critical perspective on the movement appeared in Jerold S. Auerbach, *Unequal Justice* (New York: Oxford University Press, 1976), chap. 9.

2 For influential programmatic statements, see Edgar S. Cahn and Jean Camper Cahn, "Power to the People or the Profession? The Public Interest in Public Interest Law," *Yale Law Journal* 79 (1970): 1005–48; Gordon Harrison and Sanford M. Jaffe, "Public Interest Law Firms: New Voices for New Constituencies," *American Bar Association Journal* 58 (1972): 459–67. The general characteristics of public-interest law were summarized in Joel F. Handler, Ellen Jane Hollingsworth, and Howard S. Erlanger, *Lawyers and the Pursuit of Legal Rights* (New York: Academic Press, 1978); Burton A. Weisbrod, *Public Interest Law: An Economic and Institutional Analysis* (Berkeley: University of California Press, 1978). For parallel reactions within legal education, see Robert Stevens, *Law School* (Chapel Hill: University of North Carolina Press, 1983), chap. 13.

3 The vast literature includes Ronald M. Dworkin's influential writings, beginning with *Taking Rights Seriously* (Cambridge: Harvard University Press, 1977). Another philosophical haven for activist judges can be found in the work of Owen Fiss. See, e.g., "The Forms of Justice," *Harvard Law Review* 93 (1979): 1–58. On the turn to "faith" within the legal professoriate, see Stevens, *Law School,* chap. 14.

4 See, e.g., David Kairys, ed., *The Politics of Law: A Progressive Critique,* 1st ed. (New York: Pantheon, 1982).

5 The reduction of judicial regimes to politics has been a popular theme in radical academic circles. See, e.g., Paul Brest, "The Fundamental Rights Controversy: The Essential Contradictions of Normative Constitutional Scholarship," *Yale*

283

Law Journal 90 (1981): 1063–109; Mark Tushnet, *Red, White, and Blue: A Critical Analysis of Constitutional Law* (Cambridge: Harvard University Press, 1988).

6 For empirical evidence on lay attitudes, see Tom R. Tyler, *Why People Obey the Law* (New Haven: Yale University Press, 1990).

7 See Senate Committee on the Judiciary, *Nomination of Robert H. Bork to Be an Associate Justice of the United States Supreme Court,* 100th Cong., 1st sess., 1987, Exec. Rept. 100–7. For a rhetorical analysis of the Bork hearings, see Stephen M. Griffin, "Politics and the Supreme Court: The Case of the Bork Nomination," *Journal of Law and Politics* 5 (1989): 551–604.

8 The story is recorded in a great many sources, including Robert H. Jackson, *The Struggle for Judicial Supremacy: A Study of a Crisis in American Power Politics* (New York: Knopf, 1941); Alpheus Thomas Mason, *The Supreme Court from Taft to Warren* (Baton Rouge: Louisiana State University Press, 1958); William F. Swindler, *Court and Constitution in the 20th Century,* vol. 2 (Indianapolis: Bobbs-Merrill, 1970).

9 A typical statement of this position can be found in Cox, *Warren Court,* 9. The underlying reasons were elegantly summarized in Alexander M. Bickel, *The Least Dangerous Branch* (Indianapolis: Bobbs-Merrill, 1962; 2d ed., New Haven: Yale University Press, 1986).

10 For a description of legal realism and its impact, see Wilfred Rumble, Jr., *American Legal Realism: Skepticism, Reform, and the Judicial Process* (Ithaca, N.Y.: Cornell University Press, 1968); William Twining, *Karl Llewellyn and the Realist Movement* (Norman: University of Oklahoma Press, 1985).

11 For a broad interpretation of legal realism in the context of American democratic thinking, see Edward A. Purcell, Jr., *The Crisis of Democratic Theory: Scientific Naturalism and the Problem of Value* (Lexington: University Press of Kentucky, 1973), 74–94.

12 Oliver Wendell Holmes, Jr., *The Common Law* (Boston: Little, Brown, 1881), 1. See Max Radin, *Law as Logic and Experience* (New Haven: Yale University Press, 1940).

13 For a contemporary sense of the meaning of this term, see Note, "The Presumption of Constitutionality," *Columbia Law Review* 31 (1931): 1136–48.

14 On the general concept of equality, see Bernard Williams, "The Idea of Equality," in Peter Laslett and W. G. Runciman, eds., *Philosophy, Politics and Society,* 2d series (Oxford: Blackwell, 1972), 110–31. The philosophical framework for legal equality was reviewed by Amy Gutmann, *Liberal Equality* (Cambridge: Cambridge University Press, 1980).

15 On the distinction between formal and substantive equality, see Albert Weale, *Equality and Social Policy* (London: Routledge, 1978), 11–44.

16 For the full realist attack on judicial objectivity, see Jerome Frank, *Courts on Trial: Myth and Reality in American Justice* (Princeton: Princeton University Press, 1949). A more optimistic picture of judicial creativity can be found in Benjamin N. Cardozo's influential lectures, *The Nature of the Judicial Process* (New Haven: Yale University Press, 1921).

17 This case, Lochner v. New York, 198 U.S. 45, will be fully analyzed later in this chapter.

18 For a discussion of the progressive critique of the early due process cases, see

Robert G. McCloskey, "Economic Due Process and the Supreme Court: An Exhumation and Reburial," *Supreme Court Review* (1962): 34–62.

19 See, e.g., Robert Bork, "Neutral Principles and Some First Amendment Problems," *Indiana Law Journal* 47 (1971): 1–35. Supreme Court decisions concerning personal privacy and abortion were especially vulnerable to this kind of attack. See Richard A. Epstein, "Substantive Due Process by Any Other Name," *Supreme Court Review* (1973): 159–85.

20 Cox, *Warren Court*, 4–5.

21 See G. Edward White, "The Evolution of Reasoned Elaboration: Jurisprudential Criticism and Social Change," *Virginia Law Review* 59 (1973): 279–302. This approach was deftly explored in Bickel, *Least Dangerous Branch*. For a critical discussion of Bickel's position, along with a cultural assessment of reasoned elaboration, see Edward A. Purcell, Jr., "Alexander M. Bickel and the Post-Realist Constitution," *Harvard Civil Rights-Civil Liberties Law Review* 11 (1976): 521–64.

22 See Purcell, *Crisis of Democratic Theory*, 235–66, for a discussion of comparable directions taken by "relativist democratic theory" after World War II.

23 See Purcell, "Alexander M. Bickel," 539.

24 Cox, *Warren Court*, 25–27.

25 See Alexander M. Bickel, *The Supreme Court and the Idea of Progress* (New York: Harper & Row, 1970; rev. ed. 1978).

26 See John Hart Ely, *Democracy and Distrust* (Cambridge: Harvard University Press, 1980).

27 The doctrine of judicial restraint was thus not interpreted as insulating legislation from review under core provisions of the Bill of Rights, such as the First Amendment right of free speech. In 1938, Chief Justice Stone made the distinction that was later used as a retrospective defense for Warren Court activism. "There may be narrower scope," he said, "for operation of the presumption of constitutionality when legislation appears on its face to be within a specific prohibition of the Constitution, such as those of the first ten amendments, which are deemed equally specific when held to be embraced within the Fourteenth" (United States v. Carolene Products Co., 304 U.S. 144, 152 n.4 [1938]).

28 This was the constitutional issue presented in Lochner v. New York, 198 U.S. 45 (1905), to be discussed below.

29 347 U.S. 483 (1954).

30 For background on the Brown litigation, see Richard Kluger, *Simple Justice* (New York: Knopf, 1976). For a rhetorical analysis of Warren's decision, see Nancy Dunbar and Martha Cooper, "A Situational Perspective for the Study of Legal Argument: A Case Study of Brown v. Board of Education," in George Ziegelmueller and Jack Rhodes, eds., *Dimensions of Argument: Proceedings of the Second Summer Conference on Argumentation* (Annandale, Va.: Speech Communication Association, 1981), 213–41.

31 347 U.S. at 489. Soon after the Brown decision, Alexander Bickel published an essay on this topic, based on his research as a Supreme Court clerk for Justice Frankfurter in 1953. "The Original Understanding and the Segregation Decision," *Harvard Law Review* 69 (1955): 1–65.

32 Plessy v. Ferguson, 163 U.S. 537 (1896). For an examination of the unusual

facts in this case, see Charles A. Lofgren, *The Plessy Case: A Legal-Historical Interpretation* (New York: Oxford University Press, 1987).

33 347 U.S. at 492.

34 347 U.S. at 495.

35 Cited in the Brown opinion, 347 U.S. at 494. For background on this testimony, see Kluger, *Simple Justice*, 315–45, 400–24.

36 347 U.S. at 494.

37 Indeed, the Kansas court had found the Topeka school district to be in compliance with the separate but equal doctrine and thus did not see any special constitutional implications in the testimony on psychological impact.

38 Compare Cox, *Warren Court*, 26 with Herbert Wechsler, "Toward Neutral Principles of Constitutional Law," *Harvard Law Review* 73 (1959): 1–35. Most commentators eventually adopted the balanced assessment of Bickel, *Least Dangerous Branch*, chap. 6.

39 Dunbar and Cooper reach four conclusions: "The Court makes indeterminate situations determinate by issuing statements which are factual and absolute; legal statements by the Court reflect and create a cloak of authoritative power; legal statements of the Court embody relevant social conditions; the Court's discursive practice alters discourse across discursive domains" ("Situational Perspective," 234).

40 347 U.S. 497, 500 (emphasis added).

41 347 U.S. at 499. The essential parts of this argument, including the strict-scrutiny metaphor, had already been assembled by Justice William O. Douglas in Skinner v. Oklahoma, 316 U.S. 535, 541 (1942).

42 Gerald Gunther, "In Search of Evolving Doctrine on a Changing Court: A Model for a Newer Equal Protection," *Harvard Law Review* 86 (1972): 8.

43 In the aftermath of its Brown decision, the Supreme Court proceeded to strike down legally mandated segregation in public facilities (parks, golf courses, beaches, and the like) and pointedly omitted factual inquiry into the empirical effects of such segregation. See "Developments in the Law—Equal Protection," *Harvard Law Review* 82 (1969): 1089. The Court issued only two significant equal protection decisions in which race discrimination was not directly at issue: Griffin v. Illinois, 351 U.S. 12 (1956), involving criminal justice procedures, and Harper v. State Board of Elections, 383 U.S. 663 (1966), dealing with voting rights in state elections. In both cases the Court used a form of heightened scrutiny based on compelling due process interests and the Court's controversial reapportionment philosophy, respectively. The Harper case, a 6–3 decision that drew withering assessments of the majority's craftsmanship, comes as close as any Warren Court opinion to the formal model of equal protection that has been retrospectively imposed on its judicial practice. See the discussion in Bickel, *Supreme Court*, 59–61.

44 It would also have meant overruling Supreme Court precedents from the late nineteenth century. As it was, those precedents were at least severely eroded, adding to the contemporary debate on whether the Warren decisions could be explained according to neutral principles.

45 Loving v. Virginia, 388 U.S. 1 (1969).

46   In his pivotal article, Gunther concedes that the Warren legacy was one of "anticipation," based on "tantalizing statements" and "dicta." His position that "the Warren Court embraced a rigid two-tier attitude" leaves ambiguous the relation between "attitude" and "doctrine," although the surrounding text acknowledges that, "in the extraordinary amount of commentary that followed [the Warren Court's decisions], analysts searching for justifications . . . were understandably tempted to ponder analogous spheres." It was thus the Court's largely ad hoc practice, rather than rigid doctrine, that "especially invited the spinning of analogies to justify strict scrutiny in one area after another" ("In Search of Evolving Doctrine," 8–10).

47   A prime example of such inventive advocacy and lower court judging was the Washington, D.C., school-funding case, Hobsen v. Hansen, 269 F.Supp. 401 (D.D.C. 1967), 327 F.Supp. 844 (D.D.C. 1971), which was eventually stalled by the Supreme Court's 1973 decision that a right to education could not be used to shift the presumption of constitutionality in cases involving systemwide school funding (San Antonio Independent School District v. Rodriguez, 411 U.S. 1). For an extended discussion of the Hobsen case, with careful attention to how Judge J. Skelly Wright handled burdens of proof, see Donald L. Horowitz, *Courts and Social Policy* (Washington: Brookings Institution, 1977), 106–70.

48   The inspiration for this portion of the doctrine was the 1963 opinion by Justice Brennan in a case with important racial implications, NAACP v. Button, 371 U.S. 415. In that case the state of Virginia (soon after the Supreme Court's decision in Brown v. Board of Education) enacted several laws purporting to protect "legal ethics" but with the likely motive of limiting further litigation activities of the NAACP. See Bernard Schwartz, *Super Chief: Earl Warren and His Supreme Court* (New York: New York University Press, 1983), 684, 450–53.

49   394 U.S. 618 (1969).

50   See, e.g., briefs filed on behalf of the appellee in the Shapiro case, 1967 Term (filed April 12, 1968) and 1968 Term (filed September 19, 1968). For contemporary analysis reflecting the terms of Harlan's critique, see Frank I. Michelman, "On Protecting the Poor through the Fourteenth Amendment," *Harvard Law Review* 83 (1969): 7–59.

51   394 U.S. at 662.

52   Even the most careful commentators have sometimes lost track of this chronology. Laurence H. Tribe, after noting that Shapiro is "widely considered the classic case" illustrating the strict-scrutiny doctrine, reports that "In Shapiro, the Warren Court made its *earliest* major statement of the 'fundamental rights' strand of equal protection strict scrutiny" (*American Constitutional Law*, 2d ed. [Mineola, N.Y.: Foundation Press, 1988], 1455 [emphasis added]). Ironically, this earliest case was decided in April 1969, well after Warren had announced his resignation from the Court and just two months before Warren Burger became the new Chief Justice. Far from anticipating the doctrinal system now misleadingly attributed to Warren, the Shapiro case provided Warren with a painful occasion for dissenting from this extension of his own strategy, transplanted from the race discrimination cases.

53   This intent is clearly formulated in the briefs cited in note 50. On the litigation

287

agenda of the welfare rights movement, see Edward V. Sparer, "Social Welfare Law Testing," *Practical Lawyer* 12, no. 4 (1966): 13–31; Nick Kotz and Mary Lynn Kotz, *Passion for Equality: George A. Wiley and the Movement* (New York: Norton, 1977).

54 This is what some commentators called the "break the bank strategy." See Frances Fox Piven and Richard A. Cloward, *Poor People's Movements: Why They Succeed, How They Fail* (New York: Pantheon, 1977).

55 394 U.S. at 644. For background on Warren's position in Shapiro, see Schwartz, *Super Chief,* 725–32.

56 The leading cases included Dandridge v. Williams, 397 U.S. 471 (1970); Lindsey v. Normet, 405 U.S. 56 (1972); Jefferson v. Hackney, 406 U.S. 535 (1972); and San Antonio Independent School District v. Rodriguez, 411 U.S. 1 (1973).

57 Justice Brennan pointed out that this allocation of proof burdens reversed the states' own presumption that residency requirements did not penalize interstate travel, 394 U.S. at 631. In later years, the Court flirted with the theory that state legislatures deny constitutional due process by incorporating such statutory presumptions—bureaucratic shortcuts that were virtually impossible for individual citizens to challenge. The formalism of this argument eventually made it unattractive to liberal reformers, who soon realized that most of the legislative policies they favored could thus be challenged by conservative opponents. Tribe notes that "most commentators have regarded the Court's invocation of the irrebuttable presumption doctrine as analytically confused and ultimately unhelpful" (*American Constitutional Law,* 1622), although Tribe himself did not always share those doubts (see "Childhood, Suspect Classifications, and Conclusive Presumptions: Three Linked Riddles," *Law and Contemporary Problems* 39, no. 3 [1975]: 8–37).

58 See Samuel Krislov, "The OEO Lawyers Fail to Constitutionalize a Right to Welfare: A Study in the Uses and Limits of the Judicial Process," *Minnesota Law Review* 58 (1973): 211–45.

59 These obvious strategic factors were all pointed out in Gunther's 1972 article "In Search of Evolving Doctrine."

60 In retrospect, Gunther's article can also be read as anticipating these defensive uses of doctrine ("In Search of Evolving Doctrine"). See also Frank I. Michelman, "Welfare Rights in a Constitutional Democracy," *Washington University Law Quarterly* (1979): 659–93.

61 A statute must still have a "reasonable basis" but under the post-1937 presumption of constitutionality "a statutory discrimination will not be set aside if any state of facts reasonably may be conceived to justify it." McGowan v. Maryland, 366 U.S. 420, 426 (1961) (cited in Dandridge v. Williams, 397 U.S. at 485).

62 Tribe and other progressive commentators expressed great frustration with this craftsmanship. In *American Constitutional Law* Tribe criticized the Burger Court for "lapses of logic, disregard or distortion of relevant precedent, and other indications that . . . decisions are impelled by considerations that never quite surface in the opinions" (1665; this language is unchanged from the first edition). Similarly, Gunther found "grounds to doubt that the new [cases] rest on a carefully considered, fully elaborated rationale. Expediency may have influ-

enced some of the votes" ("In Search of Evolving Doctrine," 19). The rhetoric of neutral principles seems to be irresistible for the critics of Court decisions, whether conservative or liberal.

63 397 U.S. at 476–77.

64 397 U.S. at 485.

65 394 U.S. at 627.

66 397 U.S. at 484 n.16.

67 397 U.S. at 520–21. Marshall expanded on this approach in his dissent in San Antonio Independent School District v. Rodriguez, 411 U.S. 1, 70 (1973).

68 See references in note 62.

69 For the inevitable competing views on this aspect of the adversary process, see Monroe H. Freedman, *Lawyers' Ethics in an Adversary System* (Indianapolis: Bobbs-Merrill, 1975); David Luban, *Lawyers and Justice: An Ethical Study* (Princeton: Princeton University Press, 1988), 50–66.

70 Frontiero v. Richardson, 411 U.S. 677. See Ruth Bader Ginsberg, "Gender and the Constitution," *University of Cincinnati Law Review* 44 (1975): 1–42.

71 The case usually credited with establishing this standard is Craig v. Boren, 429 U.S. 190 (1976). For a discussion see Nancy S. Erickson, "Equality between the Sexes in the 1980s," *Cleveland State Law Review* 28 (1979): 591–610.

72 For a survey of Supreme Court cases touching on problems of pregnancy, protective employment legislation, domestic relations, and other decisions, see Christine A. Littleton, "Reconstructing Sexual Equality," *California Law Review* 75 (1987): 1279–1338; Sylvia A. Law, "Rethinking Sex and the Constitution," *University of Pennsylvania Law Review* 132 (1984): 955–1040. For comprehensive treatments, see Deborah L. Rhode, *Justice and Gender* (Cambridge: Harvard University Press, 1989); Martha Minow, *Making All the Difference: Inclusion, Exclusion and American Law* (Ithaca, N.Y.: Cornell University Press, 1990).

73 See Barbara A. Brown, Thomas I. Emerson, Gail Falk, and Ann E. Freedman, "The Equal Rights Amendment: A Constitutional Basis for Equal Rights for Women," *Yale Law Journal* 80 (1971): 871–985.

74 There are numerous conflicting assessments on the failure of the ERA. For the argument that the ERA was the victim of its excessive formalism and thus allowed a political burden of proof to fall on its defenders, see Jane J. Mansbridge, *Why We Lost the ERA* (Chicago: University of Chicago Press, 1986). See also Gilbert Y. Steiner, *Constitutional Inequality: The Political Fortunes of the Equal Rights Amendment* (Washington: Brookings Institution, 1985).

75 In addition to Minow, *Making All the Difference*, see, Catherine MacKinnon, *Feminism Unmodified* (Cambridge: Harvard University Press, 1987).

76 Mary E. Becker, "Prince Charming: Abstract Equality," *Supreme Court Review* (1987): 215.

77 Ibid., 235. See also 214–24. Against the reform ideology of the 1960s, based on expectations for social change through constitutional law, Becker believes that "many women would have been better off if feminists had argued for needed economic rights and greater economic security for women (in recognition of their domestic production and reproduction) rather than for strict formal equality in family law matters" (222).

289

78 See, e.g., John Hart Ely, "The Constitutionality of Reverse Racial Discrimination," *University of Chicago Law Review* 41 (1974): 723–41. For arguments backed by moral philosophy, see Alan H. Goldman, *Justice and Reverse Discrimination* (Princeton: Princeton University Press, 1979).

79 See, e.g., the unanimous school-busing decision, Swann v. Charlotte-Mecklenburg Board of Education, 402 U.S. 1 (1971), and the decision upholding federal requirements for minority participation in federally financed construction projects, Fullilove v. Klutznick, 448 U.S. 448 (1980).

80 Deference to Congressional findings was central in the Fullilove decision but was not extended to affirmative action plans drawn up by municipalities in the case of Richmond v. J. A. Croson Co., 488 U.S. 469 (1989). The presumption that widespread inequalities can be assumed to result from documented instances of past discrimination was used in the Swann case, justifying the broad remedial response from federal courts. The inference from statistical patterns has been carefully regulated by the Court since 1971, especially as it affects the burden of proof. The 1989 decision in Wards Cove Packing Co. v. Atonio, 490 U.S. 642, angered many civil rights advocates by holding that the risk of non-persuasion remains with the plaintiff in employment discrimination suits, no matter what kind of statistical disparities can be shown.

81 488 U.S. at 493.

82 See the concurring opinions by Justice Kennedy, 488 U.S. at 518, and Justice Scalia, 488 U.S. at 520. Justice Scalia's opinion provides a textbook demonstration of judicial declaratory power. On a matter that had been heavily disputed by justices and litigants for many years, Scalia was prepared to treat the "color-blind" interpretation of the the Fourteenth Amendment as a strict deduction from "American principles," from prior caselaw, and from such experts on public morality as Alexander Bickel.

83 488 U.S. at 552, Justice Marshall dissenting (quoting from his opinion in University of California Regents v. Bakke).

84 The 101st Congress had originally included this case in its sweeping review of recent Supreme Court civil rights decisions, but the Civil Rights Act of 1991 (Pub. L. No. 102–166, 105 Stat. 1071) does not address those issues.

85 Pub. L. No. 88–352, Title VII; 78 Stat. 253; 42 U.S.C. §2000e.

86 For a political history, see Paul Burstein, *Discrimination, Jobs, and Politics: The Struggle for Equal Employment Opportunity in the United States since the New Deal* (Chicago: University of Chicago Press, 1985).

87 This was the Tower Amendment, which appears as §703(h) of the act.

88 401 U.S. 424, 429, 431 (1970).

89 His opinion cited approvingly the EEOC guideline that required employers using tests to have available "data demonstrating that the test is predictive of or significantly correlated with important elements of work behavior which comprise or are relevant to the job or jobs for which candidates are being evaluated" (401 U.S. at 433 n.9, quoting from 29 C.F.R. §1607.4[c], 35 Fed. Reg. 12333 [Aug. 1, 1970]).

90 In addition to the Griggs case, two other early cases further defined the burden-shifting consequences of prima facie evidence: McDonnell Douglas Corp. v.

Green, 411 U.S. 792 (1973) and Albemarle Paper Co. v. Moody, 422 U.S. 405 (1975).

91 Wards Cove Packing Co. v. Atonio, 490 U.S. 642, 659 (1989) (the latter quote is cited by the Court, with emphasis added, from its prior opinion in Watson v. Fort Worth Bank & Trust Co.). Some commentators had noted the Court's previous mixed signals on this point. See Charles A. Sullivan, Michael J. Zimmer, and Richard F. Richards, *Employment Discrimination*, 2d ed. (Boston: Little, Brown, 1988 and 1990 supplement), §4.3.

92 The familiar terms of twentieth-century debate over judicial review can already be found in the writings of James B. Thayer, including "The Origin and Scope of the American Doctrine of Constitutional Law," *Harvard Law Review* 7 (1893): 129–56. Thayer acknowledges that "the constitution often admits of different interpretations," and that "a court cannot always . . . say that there is but one right and permissible way of construing the constitution" (144, 150). In comparing legislation to constitutional language, Thayer argues, a court will often not be in a position to make a definitive judgment of similarity or difference. Legislation must be deemed to issue from a reasonable body of democratic servants, and courts are generally limited to saying that the law is "not unconstitutional beyond a reasonable doubt." The default judgment is that the legislature has acted properly, unless the court can somehow form a contrary judgment that is "very plain and clear, clear beyond a reasonable doubt." In sum, "the ultimate question is not what is the true meaning of the constitution, but whether legislation is sustainable or not" (151, 150).

93 198 U.S. 45 (1905).

94 Libertarian theorists have campaigned to reverse this common interpretation. See, e.g., Richard A. Epstein, "The Mistakes of 1937," *George Mason University Law Review* 11 (1988): 5–20.

95 198 U.S. at 53, 74–76.

96 198 U.S. at 53–56. This aspect of the opinion is heavily emphasized by modern libertarian champions of constitutional protection for property rights. See Bernard H. Siegan, *Economic Liberties and the Constitution* (Chicago: University of Chicago Press, 1980), 113–20.

97 198 U.S. at 57.

98 Ibid.

99 198 U.S. at 58.

100 198 U.S. at 59.

101 198 U.S. at 62.

102 198 U.S. at 68.

103 198 U.S. at 69–70 (citations omitted). Note the rhetorical "therefore" in the last sentence.

104 198 U.S. at 75–76.

105 On Holmes's skepticism, see G. Edward White, *The American Judicial Tradition: Profiles of Leading American Judges* (New York: Oxford University Press, 1976), chap. 8.

106 198 U.S. at 75.

Chapter 3. Institutionalizing the Challenge to Authority

1 For a political and institutional survey of this trend, see Joel F. Handler, Ellen Jane Hollingsworth, and Howard S. Erlanger, *Lawyers and the Pursuit of Legal Rights* (New York: Academic Press, 1978).

2 For a description of these doctrines prior to the Warren Court's innovations, see Robert G. McCloskey, "Economic Due Process and the Supreme Court: An Exhumation and Reburial," *Supreme Court Review* (1962): 34–62.

3 These developments in constitutional law are widely chronicled. See, e.g., Henry J. Abraham, *Freedom and the Court*, 5th ed. (New York: Oxford University Press, 1988), chap. 3. The Warren Court had to operate under the handicap of the 1947 decision in Adamson v. California, 332 U.S. 46, in which only four votes were mustered to support the position that the Fourteenth Amendment due process clause incorporated all of the Bill of Rights. Without directly overruling the majority argument in that case, however, the Warren Court eventually wore it down through an incremental approach to incorporation.

4 Gideon v. Wainwright, 372 U.S. 335 (1963). The federal rule was adopted in Johnson v. Zerbst, 304 U.S. 458 (1938). The Gideon decision had to overrule the 1942 decision in Betts v. Brady, 316 U.S. 455, which had declined to extend the right to counsel in state cases involving noncapital felonies.

5 Mapp v. Ohio, 367 U.S. 643 (1961). The comparable decision affecting federal courts was Weeks v. United States, 232 U.S. 383 (1914).

6 For a historical overview, see Charles A. Miller, "The Forest of Due Process of Law: The American Constitutional Tradition," in J. Roland Pennock and John W. Chapman, eds., *Due Process* (New York: New York University Press, 1977), 3–68.

7 See James M. Landis, *The Administrative Process* (New Haven: Yale University Press, 1938).

8 Herbert L. Packer, *The Limits of the Criminal Sanction* (Stanford: Stanford University Press, 1968), 166.

9 Ibid., 167.

10 Ibid., 163.

11 In re Gault, 387 U.S. 1 (1967). Several of these requirements had only recently been constitutionally imposed on state criminal court proceedings: the right to legal representation, in Gideon v. Wainwright, 372 U.S. 335 (1963); the right to confront witnesses, in Pointer v. Texas, 380 U.S. 400 (1965); and the right against self-incrimination, in Malloy v. Hogan, 378 U.S. 1 (1964). It was only after such decisions that the Court made its famous ruling in Miranda v. Arizona, 384 U.S. 436 (1966), which required procedural safeguards for criminal suspects at the moment of arrest. The reasonable doubt standard in criminal trials became a constitutional requirement only in 1970, after In re Winship, 397 U.S. 358.

12 The abstract idealism of the due process model has doubtless contributed to a lack of critical attention to the specific effects of procedural innovations. The primary exception is Donald L. Horowitz, *Courts and Social Policy* (Washington: Brookings Institution, 1977). See also Sanford H. Kadish, "Methodology

and Criteria in Due Process Adjudication—A Survey and Criticism," *Yale Law Journal* 66 (1957): 319–63.

13   Erving Goffman's influential work, *Asylums* (Garden City, N.Y.: Anchor Books, 1961), was a contemporary reflection of the same kind of shift.

14   For a legal summary see Laurence A. Tribe, *American Constitutional Law*, 2d ed., (Mineola, N.Y.: Foundation Press, 1988), chap. 10.

15   The quotation is from Blackstone's *Commentaries on the Laws of England*, vol. 4 (Chicago: University of Chicago Press, 1979 [facsimile of 1st ed., 1765–69]), 352. The law review literature has been filled with arguments for extending criminal procedures to other forms of adjudication. See, e.g., Edward L. Rubin, "Generalizing the Trial Model of Procedural Due Process: A New Basis for the Right to Treatment," *Harvard Civil Rights—Civil Liberties Law Review* 17 (1982): 61–132. Rubin concludes his article with the disarmingly frank hope that his argument can "protect these rights from the vicissitudes of political change" and can "fix these rights more firmly in our constitutional doctrine, so that they are perceived as genuine interpretations of acceptable constitutional principles. A procedural due process derivation for these rights would achieve this purpose, and it is for this reason that such a derivation has been sought."

16   On the progressive reforms and their ambiguous results, see David J. Rothman, *Conscience and Convenience: The Asylum and Its Alternatives in Progressive America* (Boston: Little, Brown, 1980). For the standard due process critique of progressive institutions, see Nicholas N. Kittrie, *The Right to Be Different: Deviance and Enforced Therapy* (Baltimore: Johns Hopkins University Press, 1971).

17   Packer, *Limits of the Criminal Sanction*, 170–71.

18   Horowitz, *Courts and Social Policy*, 173.

19   See, e.g., Ira Glasser, "Prisoners of Benevolence: Power Versus Liberty in the Welfare State," in Willard Gaylin et al., *Doing Good: The Limits of Benevolence* (New York: Pantheon, 1978), 99–168.

20   See, e.g., Charles A. Reich, "Individual Rights and Social Welfare: The Emerging Legal Issues," *Yale Law Journal* 74 (1965): 1245–57.

21   Parham v. J.R., 442 U.S. 584 (1979).

22   See Jeffrey L. Jowell, *Law and Bureaucracy: Administrative Discretion and the Limits of Legal Action* (Port Washington, N.Y.: Kennikat Press, 1975), chap. 1.

23   At least some members of the critical legal studies movement seem to have reached this advanced stage of skepticism. See Mark Tushnet, *Red, White, and Blue: A Critical Analysis of Constitutional Law* (Cambridge: Harvard University Press, 1988).

24   397 U.S. 254 (1970).

25   See, e.g., the discussion of due process challenges in civil suits against private employers in James N. Dertouzos et al., *Legal and Economic Consequences of Wrongful Termination* (Santa Monica: Rand Corporation, 1988).

26   Initially, the two school cases, Goss v. Lopez, 419 U.S. 565 (1975), and Wood v. Strickland, 420 U.S. 308 (1975), seemed to point toward further expansion of due process jurisprudence. But soon thereafter (Mathews v. Eldridge, 424 U.S. 319 [1976]) the Court began narrowing its approach.

27   397 U.S. at 259–60.

293

28 397 U.S. at 260 (emphasis in original).

29 397 U.S. at 263, 261.

30 Packer, *Limits of the Criminal Sanction*, 167.

31 Cited in 397 U.S. at 261. Justice Brennan had made a similar argument in a First Amendment case dating from 1958: "There is always in litigation a margin of error, representing error in factfinding, which both parties must take into account. Where one party has at stake an interest of transcending value—as a criminal defendant his liberty—this margin of error is reduced as to him by the process of placing on the party the burden . . . of persuading the factfinder at the conclusion of the trial of his guilt beyond a reasonable doubt" (Speiser v. Randall, 357 U.S. 513, 525–26).

32 Gerald Gunther, "In Search of Evolving Doctrine on a Changing Court: A Model for a Newer Equal Protection," *Harvard Law Review* 86 (1972): 8.

33 397 U.S. at 269.

34 397 U.S. at 270.

35 This point is echoed by Justice Black in his dissent, 397 U.S. at 278.

36 For a discussion of the balancing metaphor in the context of assumptions about evidence and proof, see R. S. Radford, "Statistical Error and Legal Error: Type One and Type Two Errors and the Law," *Loyola of Los Angeles Law Review* 21 (1988): 843–81.

37 Jerry L. Mashaw, *Bureaucratic Justice: Managing Social Security Disability Claims* (New Haven: Yale University Press, 1983), 2. For a survey of the law prior to the Warren Court's initiatives, see Louis L. Jaffe, *Judicial Control of Administrative Action* (Boston: Little, Brown, 1965).

38 This doctrinal invention—fully as artificial as the strict-scrutiny doctrine attributed to the Warren Court—was championed in the law review literature by Kenneth Culp Davis. See "An Approach to Problems of Evidence in the Administrative Process," *Harvard Law Review* 55 (1942): 364–425. The career of this doctrine can be followed in editions of Davis's widely used *Administrative Law Treatise* (St. Paul: West, 1971), §§7.02–.06, 15.00 [cf. §7.02 of 1958 ed.]).

39 FCC v. Pottsville Broadcasting Co., 309 U.S. 134, 143 (1940).

40 Mashaw, *Bureaucratic Justice*, 2.

41 Glasser, "Prisoners of Benevolence," 124.

42 Ibid., 107–08.

43 Ibid., 145–46.

44 Mashaw, *Bureaucratic Justice*, 3. See also William Van Alstyne, "Cracks in 'The New Property': Adjudicative Due Process in the Administrative State," *Cornell Law Review* 62 (1977): 445–93.

45 Mathews v. Eldridge, 424 U.S. 319, 334–35. Powell was bold enough to follow this declaration with a citation to Goldberg v. Kelly.

46 Philippe Nonet and Philip Selznick have argued that strategic initiatives in law have a tendency to degenerate into "ad hoc, unguided 'balancing' of competing goals and interests. . . . Ultimately the continuing affirmation of purpose requires energies and resources that cannot be called forth by legal invention alone. A point is soon reached where only larger resources will permit preserving the integrity of ends . . . while taking effective account of their costs" (*Law and*

Society in Transition: Toward Responsive Law [New York: Harper & Row, 1978], 85–86).

47 Henry J. Friendly, " 'Some Kind of Hearing,' " *University of Pennsylvania Law Review* 123 (1975): 1268, 1300.

48 Jerry L. Mashaw, *Due Process in the Administrative State* (New Haven: Yale University Press, 1985), 9–12. See also *Bureaucratic Justice*, 2.

49 See esp. David J. Rothman, "The State as Parent," in Gaylin, *Doing Good*, 69–96.

50 Mashaw reaches similar conclusions on the relation between recent legal trends and the broader social and political landscape. First, "a procedurally oriented judicial review seemed to have at its command a range of techniques for intruding without deciding." Second, the "contemporary notion, that disagreement with the outcome of administrative action should be reformulated as a disagreement with administrative decision processes, has a strong ideological foundation. It satisfies simultaneously a craving for direct democratic participation in an increasingly bureaucratic public life and the demand for equality before the law" (*Due Process*, 15, 26–27).

51 397 U.S. at 279.

52 Mashaw, *Bureaucratic Justice*, 4. See also Mashaw, *Due Process*, 32–36, 126.

53 424 U.S. at 340–41, 343. For good measure, Powell interpreted the basic SSDI statute as imposing a "continuing burden" on claimants to demonstrate their eligibility (at 336). Justice Brennan's dissent attacks these arguments as "speculative. . . . Indeed, in the present case, it is indicated that because disability benefits were terminated there was a foreclosure upon the Eldridge home and the family's furniture was repossessed, forcing Eldridge, his wife and children to sleep in one bed" (at 350). This is another instance when the liberal minority under the Burger Court indignantly rejects the formalism they so eagerly embraced when speaking for the majority. In Goldberg, Brennan relied on the presumption of overpowering need and would accept no evidence to counter that presumption, short of a formal hearing.

54 Mashaw, *Bureaucratic Justice*, chap. 3.

55 Ibid., chap. 10. See also Mashaw, *Due Process*, chap. 3, for an exhaustive treatment of the "incoherence" of the Mathews formula as a balancing device.

56 See Deborah A. Stone, *The Disabled State* (Philadelphia: Temple University Press, 1984); Robert H. Haveman, Victor Halberstadt, and Richard V. Burkhauser, *Public Policy toward Disabled Workers* (Ithaca, N.Y.: Cornell University Press, 1984).

57 Mashaw, *Bureaucratic Justice*, 55.

58 Ibid., 76.

59 Mashaw, *Due Process*, 36.

60 See Niklas Luhmann, *Legitimation durch Verfahren* (Darmstadt: Luchterhand, 1978); John W. Meyer and Brian Rowan, "Institutional Organizations: Formal Structure as Myth and Ceremony," *American Journal of Sociology* 83 (1977): 340–63. For illustrations in legal contexts, see Guido Calabresi and Philip Bobbitt, *Tragic Choices* (New York: Norton, 1978).

61 Partisans of the intrinsic value of procedural rights must face the likelihood

that personal participation in mass programs will become a mere ritual, diverting attention from the underlying structure of authority. For a discussion, see William Graebner, *The Engineering of Consent: Democracy and Authority in Twentieth-Century America* (Madison: University of Wisconsin Press, 1987).

62 See, e.g., John A. Robertson, "The Lower Court Problem," in John A. Robertson, ed., *Rough Justice: Perspectives on Lower Criminal Courts* (Boston: Little, Brown, 1974), xvii–xxix. Robertson argues that "The main obstacles to realizing due process in the lower courts are three: (1) the lack of judges with a strong commitment to due process values; (2) competing norms and interests; and (3) the lack of organizational support for due process values" (xxvii).

63 Abraham S. Blumberg, *Criminal Justice* (Chicago: Quadrangle Books, 1967), 169. See also Malcolm M. Feeley, *The Process Is the Punishment: Handling Cases in a Lower Criminal Court* (New York: Russell Sage Foundation, 1979); James Eisenstein and Herbert Jacob, *Felony Justice: An Organizational Analysis of Criminal Courts* (Boston: Little, Brown, 1977). Blumberg's distinction goes back to Packer's two models, which were introduced in a law review article. "Two Models of the Criminal Process," *University of Pennsylvania Law Review* 113 (1964): 1–68.

64 A less melancholic response was the movement toward informal procedures for criminal and civil dispute resolution, including proposals for neighborhood justice courts and other community-based procedures borrowed from other cultures, as reported on by academic anthropologists. For an overview, see Jerold S. Auerbach, *Justice without Law? Resolving Disputes without Lawyers* (New York: Oxford University Press, 1983), chap. 5. Despite Auerbach's evident sympathies for these trends, based on the view that formal "litigation expresses a chilling, Hobbesian vision of human nature" and a loss of "communitarian vision," he reluctantly concludes that "litigiousness more appropriately expresses the dominant values of our individualistic culture" (vii, viii). For a less troubled defense of formal procedures, see Richard Abel, "The Contradictions of Informal Justice," in Richard Abel, ed., *The Politics of Informal Justice* (New York: Academic Press, 1982), 267–320.

65 During this period, Donald Horowitz was virtually alone in challenging the inherent capacity of Supreme Court activism to impose organizational rationality on lower courts (*Courts and Social Policy*, chaps. 6–7). By the 1980s, the managerial limitations of appellate courts were more widely discussed (and often conceded) in response to a series of lower federal court cases involving the wholesale reform of mental hospitals, prisons, and similar institutions. For a review of cases and commentary, see Phillip J. Cooper, *Hard Judicial Choices: Federal District Court Judges and State and Local Officials* (New York: Oxford University Press, 1988). For an important case study, see David J. Rothman and Sheila M. Rothman, *The Willowbrook Wars* (New York: Harper & Row, 1984).

66 This movement is anticipated in Laurence Tribe's work, which advocated a doctrinal shift from procedural to substantive due process. See, in addition to his *American Constitutional Law*, "The Puzzling Persistence of Process-Based Constitutional Theories," *Yale Law Journal* 89 (1980): 1063–80.

67 Joseph Goldstein, Anna Freud, and Albert J. Solnit, *Beyond the Best Interests of*

the Child (New York: Free Press, 1973); *Before the Best Interests of the Child* (New York: Free Press, 1979). See also *In the Best Interests of the Child* (New York: Free Press, 1986). References in the text to "Goldstein" refer to the collective views expressed by these authors.

68 For the reception of the initial volume, see Richard Edelin Crouch, "An Essay on the Critical and Judicial Reception of *Beyond the Best Interests of the Child*," *Family Law Quarterly* 13 (1979): 49–103.

69 This theory—the notion that significant bonds between children and parents are the direct function of continuity of care, rather than biological relationship—has been heavily debated by professional and legal opinion. See Gary B. Melton, "Children's Rights: Where Are the Children?" *American Journal of Orthopsychiatry* 52 (1982): 530–38; Marsha Garrison, "Why Terminate Parental Rights?" *Stanford Law Review* 35 (1983): 423–96. Critics from the field of child development tend to find the Goldstein standard too restrictive on public intervention, while legal critics generally find it not restrictive enough.

70 See Robert H. Mnookin, "The Enigma of Children's Interests," in Robert H. Mnookin, ed., *In the Interest of Children: Advocacy, Law Reform, and Public Policy* (New York: W. H. Freeman, 1985), 16–24.

71 See, e.g., the early criticisms in Alan M. Oster, "Custody Proceeding: A Study of Vague and Indefinite Standards," *Journal of Family Law* 5 (1965): 21–38.

72 Goldstein, Freud, and Solnit, *Beyond the Best Interests*, chap. 3. The continuity-of-care theory was presented as "scientific" in form, although virtually untestable in fact. This appeal to authority seems especially paradoxical, given the suspicion with which Goldstein views other theories of clinical intervention. In *Before the Best Interests*, Goldstein does not hesitate to invoke "professional" insight in articulating his own standards, even though his theory of nonintervention is built largely on a critique of professional judgment. Furthermore, his footnotes read like the references in a polished legal brief, seldom citing titles beyond those works that reinforce his general conclusion (see, e.g., 201).

73 This corollary offended the natural-rights theories of some legal advocates and was also criticized by other child welfare specialists. See the discussion by David L. Chambers and Michael S. Wald of Goldstein's role in the Supreme Court litigation involving foster parents in Smith v. OFFER (431 U.S. 816 [1977]), "Smith v. OFFER," in Mnookin, *In the Interest of Children*, 101–110.

74 See Sheila B. Kamerman and Alfred J. Kahn, *Social Services in the United States: Policies and Programs* (Philadelphia: Temple University Press, 1976), chap. 3.

75 Goldstein, Freud, and Solnit, *Before the Best Interests*, 4–5.

76 Ibid., 13–14.

77 See the analysis of Michael S. Wald, "Thinking about Public Policy toward Abuse and Neglect of Children: A Review of *Before the Best Interests of the Child*," *Michigan Law Review* 78 (1980): 645–93.

78 Goldstein, Freud, and Solnit, *Before the Best Interests*, 25.

79 Ibid., 94–95.

80 Ibid., 92.

81 Ibid., 18: "It is important to place a heavy burden of proof upon those who are empowered to intrude."

82 Ibid., 64–65. Goldstein would also intervene in cases of acquittal by reason of insanity.

83 In its due process decisions regarding parental rights, the federal courts have steered a middle course. In Santosky v. Kramer (455 U.S. 745 [1982]), the Supreme Court interpreted the Constitution as requiring an intermediate standard of proof ("clear and convincing") in cases terminating parental rights.

84 For a sociological study, see Kathi V. Friedman, *Legitimation of Social Rights and the Western Welfare State: A Weberian Perspective* (Chapel Hill: University of North Carolina Press, 1981).

85 For a survey of current approaches see Charles Perrow, *Complex Organizations: A Critical Essay*, 3rd ed. (New York: Random House, 1986).

86 See, e.g., Charles E. Lindblom's familiar text, *The Intelligence of Democracy: Decision-Making through Mutual Adjustment* (New York: Free Press, 1965).

87 The empirical evidence is summarized in E. Allan Lind and Tom R. Tyler, *The Social Psychology of Procedural Justice* (New York: Plenum Press, 1988). Much of the research is associated with John Thibaut. See, e.g., two works written with Laurens Walker, *Procedural Justice: A Psychological Analysis* (Hillsdale, N.J.: Erlbaum, 1975); "A Theory of Procedure," *California Law Review* 66 (1978): 541–66.

88 *Protecting the Social Service Client* (New York: Academic Press, 1979), 7. Handler is aware that "discretion is inherent in all professional work," and may play a different role in organizational settings outside the special environment of the criminal trial (8).

Chapter 4. Antinomies of Interpretation

1 Immanuel Kant, *Critique of Pure Reason*, trans. Norman Kemp Smith (London: Macmillian, 1964), Axi-xii. For an interpretation of Kant's tribunal in relation to contemporary philosophy, see Gillian Rose, *Dialectic of Nihilism: Post-Structuralism and Law* (Oxford: Blackwell, 1984), chap. 1.

2 Max Weber, "Science as a Vocation," in H. H. Gerth and C. Wright Mills, eds., *From Max Weber: Essays in Sociology* (New York: Oxford University Press, 1946), 155. See also Peter Lassman and Irving Voeldy, eds., *Max Weber's "Science as a Vocation"* (London: Unwin Hyman, 1989).

3 Weber, "Science as a Vocation," 151.

4 See Herbert A. Simon, "A Behavioral Model of Rational Choice," *Quarterly Journal of Economics* 69 (1955): 99–118; and *Models of Man: Social and Rational* (New York: Wiley, 1957), 196–206.

5 James G. March and Herbert A. Simon, *Organizations* (New York: Wiley, 1958).

6 Charles Perrow, *Complex Organizations: A Critical Essay*, 3rd ed. (New York: Random House, 1986), 125. The quotation is from March and Simon, *Organizations*, 165.

7 Perrow, *Complex Organizations*, 127.

8 Philippe Nonet and Philip Selznick, *Law and Society in Transition: Toward Responsive Law* (New York: Harper & Row, 1978).

9 See Alasdair MacIntyre, *After Virtue*, 2d ed. (Notre Dame, Ind.: University

of Notre Dame Press, 1984); E. D. Hirsch, Jr., *Cultural Literacy: What Every American Needs to Know* (Boston: Houghton Mifflin, 1987).

10 Walter Lippmann, *An Inquiry into the Principles of the Good Society* (Boston: Little, Brown, 1937), 334, 346; cited in Edward A. Purcell, Jr., *The Crisis of Democratic Theory: Scientific Naturalism and the Problem of Value* (Lexington: University Press of Kentucky, 1973), 154.

11 A prominent recent example is Allan Bloom, *The Closing of the American Mind* (New York: Simon and Schuster, 1987). Earlier works would include Julien Benda, *The Betrayal of the Intellectuals* (Boston: Beacon Press, 1955) (trans. of *La trahison des clercs* [1929]).

12 See, e.g., the painfully qualified arguments of Leo Strauss in the recently published collection of essays, *The Rebirth of Classical Political Rationalism: Essays and Lectures by Leo Strauss* (Chicago: University of Chicago Press, 1989).

13 A major source for this notion can be found in works of the Marburg neo-Kantian Hermann Cohen. See, e.g., his *Ethik des reinen Willens*, 2d ed. (Berlin: B. Cassirer, 1907). According to Thomas L. Pangle, Cohen was the "great guide of [Leo Strauss's] youth" (Strauss, *Rebirth*, xxxv).

14 Purcell, *Crisis of Democratic Theory*, 156–57, based on Hutchins's speech, "What Shall We Defend? We Are Losing Our Moral Principles," printed in *Vital Speeches of the Day*, 6 (July 1, 1940): 546–49.

15 Ibid., 158. Purcell emphasizes the role of war-time pressures and international events in the 1930s as sources of the neo-Aristotelian counterattack on scientific naturalism.

16 See the discussion in C. L. Hamblin, *Fallacies* (London: Methuen, 1970), 43–44. See also Hamblin's related treatment of the burden of proof, 170–76, 294–95. The first reference to *ad ignorantiam* arguments appears in Locke's *Essay Concerning Human Understanding*, vol. 2 (Oxford: Clarendon Press, 1894), 410–11.

17 Among Mortimer J. Adler's numerous works, the most directly relevant is *Dialectic* (New York: Harcourt, Brace, 1927). The same themes continue into his later works; see, e.g., *Reforming Education: The Opening of the American Mind* (New York: Macmillan, 1988).

18 See, e.g., Donald C. Bryant, "Rhetoric: Its Function and Scope," *Quarterly Journal of Speech* 39 (1953): 401–24; Maurice Natanson, "The Limits of Rhetoric," *Quarterly Journal of Speech* 41 (1955): 133–39.

19 Richard Weaver, *The Ethics of Rhetoric* (Chicago: Regnery, 1953), 21, 53.

20 Ibid., 17. Adler's book speculates at length on the elusive structure of this Platonic realm, continually circling around the notion of an infinitely expandable set of terms representing potential uses of everyday discourse. "Dialectic may be defined metaphysically as the logical structure of the universe of discourse when that is considered as an infinite class of parts, all of which are internally related. The universe of discourse is, therefore, a whole, capable of infinite determinations. In this sense it is a realm of possibility, and dialectic becomes the class of all possible determinations in discourse" (*Dialectic*, 2014). Although it is customary to refer to this movement as neo-Aristotelian, its philosophical presumptions are neo-Kantian, combining elements of both Marburg and Baden schools (see chap. 7 for a discussion of these positions). As for Aristotle, recent

investigations by G. E. R. Lloyd have clarified the strategic elements underlying his notion of demonstration (*Demystifying Mentalities* [Cambridge: Cambridge University Press, 1990], chap. 3).

21 Weaver believed that rhetoric thus surpasses "mere scientific demonstration" (*Ethics of Rhetoric*, 21).

22 Charles Follette, "Deep Rhetoric," in George Ziegelmueller and Jack Rhodes, eds., *Dimensions of Argument: Proceedings of the Second Summer Conference on Argumentation* (Annandale, Va.: Speech Communication Association, 1981) (cited hereafter as *Second Summer Conference*), 993. Compare Adler's statement, that "there is one meaning common to all . . . uses of the truth ideal, and that is that thinking is to be judged in terms of something extrinsic to itself—an absolute of some kind" (*Dialectic*, 18).

23 Follette, "Deep Rhetoric," 997.

24 Ibid., 994. All these arguments mimic the more polished systems of the Baden neo-Kantians. One would need to look for strategic reasons why the Hutchins-Adler-Weaver school ignored this obvious philosophical source and preferred to find their roots in Aristotle.

25 The neo-Aristotelian approach stands in contrast to positions taken by Maurice Natanson and Henry W. Johnstone, Jr., who treat rhetoric as a form of self-assertion, echoing themes from European phenomenology and existentialism. See, e.g., the separate essays in Natanson and Johnstone, eds., *Philosophy, Rhetoric and Argumentation* (University Park: Pennsylvania State University Press, 1965); as well as Johnstone's *Philosophy and Argument* (University Park: Pennsylvania State University Press, 1959). Neo-Aristotelianism also differs from Chaïm Perelman's influential "new rhetoric," which emphasizes the speaker's orientation to an audience, rather than purely cognitive preconditions of communication. See Perelman and L. Olbrechts-Tyteca, *The New Rhetoric: A Treatise on Argumentation* (Notre Dame, Ind.: University of Notre Dame Press, 1969), which was discussed in chap. 1.

26 Owen M. Fiss, "The Forms of Justice," *Harvard Law Review* 93 (1979): 29 (meaning), 30 (proper meaning), 51 (true meaning). Dworkin's approach to adjudication assigns comparable prowess to idealized or transcendental judges; and thus he can protect his confidence that legal questions have "correct" answers without tying those answers to the vagaries of actual court opinions. See Ronald Dworkin, *Taking Rights Seriously* (Cambridge: Harvard University Press, 1977). Dworkin's theory is discussed in chap. 6.

27 Fiss, "Forms of Justice," 9.

28 Weaver, *Ethics of Rhetoric*, 112–13. A useful analysis of Weaver's basic argument can be found in G. Thomas Goodnight, "The Liberal and the Conservative Presumptions: On Political Philosophy and the Foundation of Public Argument," in Jack Rhodes and Sara Newell, eds., *Proceedings of the Summer Conference on Argumentation* (Annandale, Va.: Speech Communication Association, 1980) (hereafter cited as *First Summer Conference*), 304–37.

29 Joseph Vining, *The Authoritative and the Authoritarian* (Chicago: University of Chicago Press, 1986), 147.

30 Ibid., 40.

31 Fiss, "Forms of Justice," 16–17.

32 See Edwin Meese III, "The Attorney General's View of the Supreme Court: Toward a Jurisprudence of Original Intention," *Public Administration Review* 45 (1985): 701–04. Raoul Berger has supplemented the theory by placing the burden of proof on interpreters who would depart from his formula for discovering the original intent behind the Fourteenth Amendment (*Government by Judiciary* [Cambridge: Harvard University Press, 1977], 17, 153–55). For commentary, see Michael J. Perry, "The Authority of Text, Tradition, and Reason: A Theory of Constitutional 'Interpretation,'" *Southern California Law Review* 58 (1985): 551–602.

33 See Mark Tushnet, *Red, White, and Blue: A Critical Analysis of Constitutional Law* (Cambridge: Harvard University Press, 1988), 317–18.

34 Paul Brest, "The Fundamental Rights Controversy: The Essential Contradictions of Normative Constitutional Scholarship," *Yale Law Journal* 90 (1981): 1063.

35 In his somewhat selective *Guide to Critical Legal Studies* (Cambridge: Harvard University Press, 1987), Mark Kelman is often at a loss to explain what his more radical colleagues are hoping to accomplish. He has particular difficulties with Roberto Unger's psychological investigations and hasn't "got a clue as to why some Critics give such importance to this issue." As for the "deconstruction" of the self, "The point of this exercise escapes me" (112–13). No such reticence limits the scope of Roberto Mangabeira Unger's manifesto, *The Critical Legal Studies Movement*, (Cambridge: Harvard University Press, 1986).

36 To raise this point is not necessarily to dismiss post-structuralism as self-refuting. However, as Christopher Norris suggests, the tendency of post-structuralist critics to generalize on their specific arguments implies an idealist framework, even as the existence of such frameworks is systematically denied. "Deconstruction, in short, is a kind of abortive or half-hearted pragmatist venture. It is willing to dispense with most of the truth-claims and illusions of method which have so far served to prop up an ailing philosophical enterprise. But it still has this unfortunate (Kantian) tendency to take its own arguments seriously and—like Habermas—to 'go transcendental' at the drop of a hat" (*The Contest of Faculties: Philosophy and Theory After Deconstruction* [London: Methuen, 1985], 8).

37 Brest, "Fundamental Rights Controversy," 1109. Similarly, Tushnet wants to allow normative principles to emerge spontaneously through the cultivation of "consensus in decentralized intentional communities," where "face-to-face interactions may provide a model for an alternative way of resolving conflict" (*Red, White, and Blue*, 316). For both writers, the ideals of community participation have replaced due process in criminal trials as the self-justifying model of procedure.

38 Kelman, *Guide to Critical Legal Studies*, 4–6, 86–87.

39 Ibid., 4.

40 Ibid., 291

41 Ibid., 5.

42 Terry Eagleton, *Literary Theory: An Introduction* (Minneapolis: University of Minnesota Press, 1983), 144.

43 David Cratis Williams has offered a less flattering critique of a similar strategy,

which he labels "ideological." "Ideological criticism uses the analytic tools of criticism, but it uses them perversely and in a self-serving manner: deconstructive techniques become sublated by ideological commitments. They are preserved in their application against other ideological constructions, but they are repressed or 'destroyed' in relation to any inward turn. The ideological critic thus privileges his/her own epistemological presuppositions about the way the world is or ought to be but then employs universally applicable deconstructive strategies in dismantling the arguments of the opposition" ("The Assent of Rhetoric," in Joseph W. Wenzel, ed., *Argument and Critical Practices: Proceedings of the Fifth SCA/AFA Conference on Argumentation* [Annandale, Va.: Speech Communication Association, 1987] [hereafter cited as *Fifth Summer Conference*], 49).

44 Gerald E. Frug, "The Ideology of Bureaucracy in American Law," *Harvard Law Review* 97 (1984): 1386.

45 Frug leavens his realism with a dose of transcendental argument: "The argument for freedom constantly threatens to overcome the argument for necessity and make even the 'hard realities' of modern life available to human reconstruction. If so, we can reject the supposedly immutable characteristics of bureaucracy and act instead on the belief that the quest for democracy is possible even within modern structures. Of course, we need energy and courage to overcome the pervasive presence of the status quo in our thoughts, hopes, and actions. To gain this determination, it seems helpful to undermine the incessant assurances that there is no need to revise the status quo" (ibid., 1388). For Kelman, see *Guide to Critical Legal Studies*, 290–91.

46 For a historical and conceptual deconstruction of group process, see William Graebner, *The Engineering of Consent: Democracy and Authority in Twentieth-Century America* (Madison: University of Wisconsin Press, 1987).

47 For a contrasting treatment of jurisprudential analogies, see Rose, *Dialectic of Nihilism.*

48 Paul De Man, *Allegories of Reading: Figural Language in Rousseau, Nietzsche, Rilke, and Proust* (New Haven: Yale University Press, 1979), 10.

49 Weaver, *Ethics of Rhetoric*, 17. On the dichotomy between post-structuralism and methods comparable to neo-Aristotelianism, see G. Thomas Goodnight, "Argumentation, Criticism, and Rhetoric: A Comparison of Modern and Post Modern Stances in Humanistic Inquiry," in *Fifth Summer Conference*, 61–67.

50 Edmund Husserl, *The Crisis of European Sciences and Transcendental Phenomenology* (Evanston, Ill.: Northwestern University Press, 1970) (trans. of the posthumously published work, *Die Krisis der europäischen Wissenschaften und die transzendentale Phänomenologie* (1936, 1954).

51 See, e.g., Art Berman, *From the New Criticism to Deconstruction* (Urbana: University of Illinois Press, 1988).

52 See, e.g., the works of Stanley Fish, including *Is There a Text in This Class? The Authority of Interpretive Communities* (Cambridge: Harvard University Press, 1980); Sanford Levinson, "Law as Literature," *Texas Law Review* 60 (1982): 373–403. Similar arguments filled countless anthologies throughout the 1980s.

53 Peter Dews, *Logics of Disintegration: Post-Structuralist Thought and the Claims of Critical Theory* (London: Verso, 1987), 96. Earlier, Dews provides a useful com-

parison between Derrida's *différance* and Schelling's principle of identity (22–27), drawing on the discussion in Manfred Frank, *Eine Einfühurung in Schellings Philosophie* (Frankfurt am Main: Suhrkamp, 1985).

54 Ibid., 37.

55 Psychoanalytic parallels to this conjecture can be found in Harold Bloom, *The Anxiety of Influence* (New York: Oxford University Press, 1973).

56 Dews, *Logics of Disintegration*, 44. Dews interprets Derrida's work historically as a specific response to French phenomenology's reception of philosophical ideas from both Husserl and Heidegger.

57 In this usage, the term *antinomy* is drawn from the *Critique of Pure Reason*, where Kant defines it as a "natural and unavoidable" conflict of contrary assertions, "in which no one assertion can establish superiority over another" (A421–22/B448–50). The metaphor of bounded rationality invites comparison with Kant's first antinomy on the universal limits of time and space.

58 According to Kant, although our "reason proceeds by one path in its empirical use, and by yet another path in its transcendental use," any nonempirical explanation of our concrete experience "transcends all the powers of our reason, indeed all its rights of questioning" (*Critique of Pure Reason*, A563/B591, A557/B585).

59 In continental Europe, the shift from static to dynamic fundamental categories was prefigured by various strands of *Lebensphilosophie* in Germany (see Herbert Schnädelbach, *Philosophy in Germany, 1831–1933* [Cambridge: Cambridge University Press, 1984]); and by the descendants of Bergsonism in France (see Vincent Descombes, *Modern French Philosophy* [Cambridge: Cambridge University Press, 1980]). The same shift took place early in American pragmatism (see John E. Smith, *Purpose and Thought: The Meaning of Pragmatism* [Chicago: University of Chicago Press, 1978]); and much later in the antiformalist themes emerging from Wittgenstein's later works and from the Oxford analytic school (see John Passmore, *A Hundred Years of Philosophy* [London: Duckworth, 1957]). In chap. 7 I will explore the neo-Kantian origins for all these burden-shifting movements.

60 J. R. Searle ("How to Derive 'Ought' from 'Is,' " *Philosophical Review* 73 [1964]: 43–58) develops one version of this idea.

61 Russell's essay, containing his "theory of descriptions," was "On Denoting," *Mind* 14 (1905): 479–93. P. F. Strawson's response, "On Referring," *Mind* 59 (1950): 320–44, retained the notion of presuppositions but shifted them from an idealized metaphysical space into a purely semantic realm. Both senses were anticipated by the Austrian logician Gottlob Frege in his famous essay, "Über Sinn und Bedeutung" (*Zeitschrift für Philosophie und philosophische Kritik* 100 [1892], 25–50), which spoke of "selbstverständliche Voraussetzungen." All of the above essays have been widely reprinted. By contrast, the Austrian philosopher Meinong's theory of *Annahmen*, dating from 1902, treated presuppositions as ontological rather than linguistic or epistemological. See the exposition by J. N. Findlay, along with Findlay's assessment of the British response to Meinong. *Meinong's Theory of Objects and Values*, 2d ed. (Oxford: Clarendon Press, 1963).

62 These themes were developed in parallel ways during the late 1930s by Witt-

genstein at Cambridge and Austin at Oxford, although neither version saw publication until the 1950s (see Mats Furberg, *Saying and Meaning* [Oxford: Blackwell, 1971]). These works broaden the concept of presupposition beyond earlier uses by Russell and Strawson to include implicit references to pragmatic or contextual conditions (see Edward L. Keenan, "Two Kinds of Presuppositions in Natural Language," in Charles J. Fillmore and D. Terence Langendoen, eds., *Studies in Linguistic Semantics* [New York: Holt, 1971], 45–54). The notion of "appropriateness" conditions in verbal behavior was systematically presented by J. R. Searle, *Speech Acts* (Cambridge: Cambridge University Press, 1969). For a formalized treatment of pragmatic presuppositions, see Gerald Gazdar, *Pragmatics: Implicature, Presupposition, and Logical Form* (New York: Academic Press, 1979).

63 Stephen Toulmin, *The Uses of Argument* (Cambridge: Cambridge University Press, 1958). Toulmin's reduction of validity to the everyday uses of argument parallels the pragmatic theory of meaning tied to the varied uses of speech. My criticisms of Toulmin (presented below and in chap. 1) could be extended to the wider programs of the late-Wittgenstein and the Oxford analysts. They are similar, for example, to objections raised in J. N. Findlay's article, "Use, Usage, and Meaning," published in *Proceedings of the Aristotelian Society* 35 (1961): 231–42. While Toulmin's book was welcomed by philosophers sympathetic to the pragmatic turn in the philosophy of language, it virtually transformed the academic field of speech communication. In light of Toulmin's views, every debate coach suddenly became a practicing epistemologist (see Robert L. Scott, "On Viewing Rhetoric as Epistemic," *Central States Speech Journal* 18 [1967]: 9–17), and the contextual conditions of argument have received far more searching examination in the literature of this group than in the formal idiom of ordinary-language philosophy (see esp. the papers delivered in the biannual *Summer Conferences* on argumentation, cited throughout this chapter). For a systematic critique of Toulmin, which incorporates much of the recent speech-communication research, see Charles Arthur Willard, *Argumentation and the Social Grounds of Knowledge* (University, Ala.: University of Alabama Press, 1983).

64 The most vivid critique—both philosophical and sociological—remains Ernest Gellner, *Words and Things* (London: Gollancz, 1959).

65 Unless Toulmin was prepared to generate new fiefdoms (new "fields") for every controversy within an existing field, his judicial model ignored all the centrifugal pressures impinging on public argument. Toulmin was apparently willing to freeze the traditional jurisdictions of established disciplines, shoring up their authority with powerful presumptions, including a Darwinian confidence in the progress of scientific advance (see his *Human Understanding*, vol. 1 [Princeton: Princeton University Press, 1972]). Charles Arthur Willard has argued that the "notion of argument fields . . . is sufficiently fuzzy and imprecise that it can be made to authorize entirely incompatible projects. It can be read as an extreme sociological relativism . . . or it can be more narrowly seen (à la Toulmin) as the anthropological face of philosophy which is to be transcended by philosophy's critical face. It can be defined in terms of logical types or in terms of real social entities bearing no clear relation to types. It can serve as a surro-

gate term for what ethnographers call 'speech communities' or as a label for 'rhetorical communities' " ("Field Theory: A Cartesian Meditation," in *Second Summer Conference*, 21). Willard's own discussion emphasizes the sociological aspects over Toulmin's elusive conceptual ecologies. In contrast to Toulmin, the philosopher L. Jonathan Cohen seems prepared to accept the evolutionary dispersion of fields, with an accompanying divergence of public discourses (*The Dialogue of Reason: An Analysis of Analytical Philosophy* [Oxford: Clarendon Press, 1986], 31).

66 Willard raises similar objections. "Fields are created and sustained by the ongoing defining activities of actors within them; they are not static entities to be equated with a history of ideas . . . ; people breathe life into fields, they animate them, as they deal with situations" ("Field Theory," 27).

67 For analytic philosophers who follow Toulmin, the assignment of proof burdens is one of the tacit conditions for argument within a specified field. See Robert Brown, "The Burden of Proof," *American Philosophical Quarterly* 7 (1970): 74–82. This silent role may explain the remarkable lack of contemporary philosophical interest in dialectical issues, as well as the idiosyncratic exceptions. Nicholas Rescher, for example, identifies a great many dialectical elements in argumentation but assigns them to the idealized tribunals of "conventional" or "natural" standards. "Without the existence of objective *standards of adequacy*, rational controversy is inherently impossible" (*Dialectics: A Controversy-Oriented Approach to the Theory of Knowledge* [Albany: State University of New York Press, 1977], 43). Similarly, Fred J. Kauffield resurrects the rhetorical theory of presumptions and proof burdens that originated with Whately but allocates these dialectical burdens in accordance with intuitive standards of "discursive responsibilities." Kauffield derives these responsibilities from a neo-Aristotelian rhetorical foundation, which he calls "practical necessity" ("Rhetoric and Practical Necessity: A View from the Study of Speech Acts," *Fifth Summer Conference*, 83–96). The best corrective to these idealized models is Charles Arthur Willard's social and interactive perspective on argument (*A Theory of Argumentation* [Tuscaloosa: University of Alabama Press, 1989]).

68 Toulmin's evolutionary theory of scientific progress disguises this narrowing effect of fields understood as a system of rules. His substitution of scientific authority for judicial dialectics—notwithstanding the jurisprudential analogy— allows him to ignore the boundary issues that haunt the notion of progress in any field of knowledge.

69 In criticizing this aspect of Toulmin's jurisprudential analogy, Willard adds that "fields are not reducible to their written artifacts . . . ; the old sociological notion of 'informal structures' of groups applies here; and as far as I can see, it is devastating for those who would equate fields with their documents" ("Field Theory," 27).

70 Edward H. Levi, *An Introduction to Legal Reasoning* (Chicago: University of Chicago Press, 1948), 1.

71 This is the approach suggested by John Rawls's influential essay, "Two Concepts of Rules" (*Philosophical Review* 64 [1955]: 3–32) and by H. L. A. Hart in his distinction between primary and secondary rules (*The Concept of Law* [Oxford:

305

Clarendon Press, 1961], chap. 5). Both writers were borrowing from Russell's theory of types, which was originally held out as a solution to certain verbal and mathematical paradoxes ("Logical Atomism," in J. H. Muirhead, ed., *Contemporary British Philosophy* [New York: Macmillan, 1924], 357–83). The classic objection to the theory of types—that it cannot itself be stated without incurring the very paradoxes it was designed to solve—should make us question the function of secondary or "constitutive" rules (see Max Black, "Russell's Philosophy of Language," in Paul Arthur Schilpp, ed., *The Philosophy of Bertrand Russell* [Evanston, Ill.: Library of Living Philosophers, 1944], 229–55).

In Hart, these "meta-rules" are posited to organize the indeterminate aspects of ordinary legal rules, but in turn they are denied similar pragmatic protection; Hart allows no meta-meta-rules. Accordingly, the dialectical aspects of primary rules are reduced to their own special rulelike form, where they are suspended in the same nondialectical vacuum occupied by Toulmin's warrants.

Like Toulmin, Hart entertains the possible "open texture" of secondary rules with some reluctance; he identifies this kind of indeterminacy not with standard dialectical application, but with the breakdown of existing systems. Commenting on the possibility of "aberrations" in officiating at the proverbial cricket match that runs throughout the writings of the Oxford school, Hart treats "games" with the same obscure relativity that Toulmin applies to fields. "The fact that isolated or exceptional official aberrations are tolerated does not mean that the game of cricket or baseball is no longer being played. On the other hand, if these aberrations are frequent, or if the scorer repudiates the scoring rule, there must come a point when either the players no longer accept the scorer's aberrant rulings or, if they do, the game has changed. It is no longer cricket or baseball but 'scorer's discretion'; for it is a defining feature of these other games that, in general, their results should be assessed in the way demanded by the plain meaning of the rule, whatever latitude its open texture may leave to the scorer" (*Concept of Law*, 141).

Hart ignores the dialectical problems of how "we" identify the aberrations in the first place (and just who we are), how we assess their gravity, and how we determine which game is actually being played. When a public wishes to reach authoritative final decisions on such questions, it must rely on unstated presumptions and burdens of proof applied by situated actors—all of which fall outside the scope of Hart's system.

72 The constitutional doctrines examined in chaps. 2 and 3 offered numerous examples of retrospective ordering of judicial history. The classic example is the virtually universal endorsement of Justice Holmes's dissent in the Lochner case, discussed in chap. 2. Other examples in those chapters include the attempts of progressive advocates during the 1970s to impute a formal doctrine of strict scrutiny to the remarkably fluid decisions of the Warren Court.

73 Even that ultimate pragmatist, Richard Rorty, seems to operate with some intuitive sense of who should be the relevant judges in assessing the "edifying" qualities in competing modern discourses (see, e.g., "Professionalized Philosophy and Transcendentalist Culture," in *Consequences of Pragmatism* [Minneapolis: University of Minnesota Press, 1982], 60–71).

74   This burden-of-proof argument fitted nicely with a pluralist definition of truth borrowed from American pragmatism. The break-up of this theory—the reversal of its presumption—has been the key move in neo-conservative social theory, which elevates market performance above political failure (reversing the assumption of progressive critics.) The weight of critical opinion can promote sudden shifts of this sort, in response to a perceived public need to ensure finality—to make binding social decisions. As Willard writes, "The history of the public sphere is one of *decisions,* not accomplishments. A decision is the fruit of a momentary working coalition. It takes its form from the tradeoffs and compromises sufficient to secure majority votes. It takes its urgency from time pressure, real or imagined. . . . In a bizarre reversal of *weltanschauungen* accounts, we might say that decision-makers select the decision they can get, the one they have the votes for, and then select the world view to rationalize their decision" ("Problems, Puzzles, and Progress," in David Zarefsky, Malcolm O. Sillars, and Jack Rhodes, eds., *Argument in Transition: Proceedings of the Third Summer Conference on Argumentation* [Annandale, Va.: Speech Communication Association, 1983], 93).

75   Some analytic philosophers now postulate the occurrence of fundamental "intuitions" against which individual actors may directly assess the validity of procedural norms of practical judgment. Although the basic metaphor of these assessments is one of empirical testing, the intuitions themselves are not publicly observable data. They are, as will be discussed in chap. 6, transcendental analogues of empirical data, strategically postulated to underwrite the legitimacy of everyday ethical speculation. These intuitions are prominently featured in John Rawls's references to the method of "reflective equilibrium" (*A Theory of Justice* [Cambridge: Harvard University Press, 1971]; "Kantian Constructivism in Moral Theory," *Journal of Philosophy* 77 [1980]: 515–72). See also Cohen, *Dialogue of Reason,* 73–82. It is especially ironic that this analogy with empirical perception follows the sense-data solipsism of Locke, which analytic writers have otherwise taken great pains to expel from their philosophical perspective.

76   These two options were actively debated between rival schools of neo-Kantian philosophy at the end of the nineteenth-century. To oversimplify a complex movement, the Marburg School embraced the paradoxes of foundationalism, whereas the Baden School explored the procedural approach to legitimacy. For a discussion, see Gillian Rose, *Hegel Contra Sociology* (London: Athlone Press, 1981), chap. 1. Both tendencies within the neo-Kantian movement have had a major impact on the way burdens of ignorance are treated in modern debate, and their contributions will be considered more fully in chap. 7.

77   This condition corresponds roughly to Kant's second antinomy.

78   Jürgen Habermas, *The Theory of Communicative Action,* vol. 1 (Boston: Beacon Press, 1984), chap. 1.1 (trans. of *Theorie des kommunikativen Handelns,* 1981).

79   See Daniel J. O'Keefe, "Two Concepts of Argument," *Journal of the American Forensic Association* 13 (1977): 121–28.

80   The best-known illustration of this pattern is the series of changes in American linguistic theory from syntax to semantics to pragmatics; see Frederick J. Newmeyer, *Linguistic Theory in America,* 2d ed. (San Diego: Academic Press,

1986). Following the jurisprudential analogy, rational reconstructions in practical reasoning are equivalent to the majority opinions issued by judges in contested legal cases. Habermas addresses the process of rational reconstruction, drawing heavily on Chomskian generative models, in "What Is Universal Pragmatics?" reprinted in Jürgen Habermas, *Communication and the Evolution of Society* (Boston: Beacon Press, 1979), 1–68.

81 Chomsky's model was presented in *Syntactic Structures* (The Hague: Mouton, 1957). For an historical overview see Newmeyer, *Linguistic Theory in America,* chaps. 2–3.

82 The retrospective rationalism of the generative model makes it the ideal companion to a variety of process-oriented philosophical viewpoints, which were thus relieved of meeting empirical standards of legitimacy. Thus Chomsky saw his formalism as a way to reconcile interests in scientific rigor with nondeterministic ideals of personal freedom. See Frederick J. Newmeyer, *The Politics of Linguistics* (Chicago: University of Chicago Press, 1986), chap. 5.

83 Searle, *Speech Acts.* For a summary and commentary, see Stephen C. Levinson, *Pragmatics* (Cambridge: Cambridge University Press, 1983), chap. 5. Grice's works are notoriously exiguous in relation to their impact. See, however, "Logic and Conversation," in Peter Cole and Jerry L. Morgan, eds., *Syntax and Semantics,* vol. 3 (New York: Academic Press, 1975), 41–58; "Presupposition and Conversational Implicature," in Peter Cole, ed., *Radical Pragmatics* (New York: Academic Press, 1981), 183–98. Grice's leading essays were reprinted in H. Paul Grice, *Studies in the Way of Words* (Cambridge: Harvard University Press, 1989). For extended commentary on Grice, see Richard E. Grandy and Richard Warner, *Philosophical Grounds of Rationality: Intentions, Categories, Ends* (Oxford: Clarendon Press, 1986).

84 It would seem that, for Grice and his followers, the sociolinguists have the task of filling in the empirical details of exactly when and how speakers actually comply with conversational maxims. This leaves us with a virtual truism, that when people really do follow the maxims, then real communication has in fact occurred. For Grice, the normative aspects of this theory supersede the empirical concerns of the sociologist, and the actual participants in any speech encounter are rarely in doubt about when they have scored a success. Here Grice seems to fall back on the linguistic intuitionism of the Oxford school, reinforced to some degree by a model of linguistic competence borrowed from Chomsky. See Grice, "Reply to Richards," in Grandy and Warner, *Philosophical Grounds of Rationality,* 46–73.

85 For Grice's works, see references in note 83. In the vast literature on semantic presumptions, the most revealing studies (for our purposes) concern the paradoxes that result from trying to specify a complete set of preconditions for determinate meaning. See Bas C. van Fraassen, "Presupposition, Implication, and Self-Reference," in János S. Petöfi and Dorothea Franck, eds., *Präsuppositionen in Philosophie und Linguistik* (Frankfurt am Main: Athenäum, 1973), 97–116.

86 "Method in Philosophical Psychology (From the Banal to the Bizarre)," *Proceedings and Addresses of the American Philosophical Association* 48 (1975): 52.

87 The leading work is Frans H. van Eemeren and Rob Grootendorst, *Speech Acts in Argumentative Discussions* (Dordrecht: Foris, 1984). These authors extend the same criticisms to the works of Chaïm Perelman (13).

88 Ibid., 23. Van Eemeren and Grootendorst distinguish their efforts from those of other speech-act theorists by referring back to J. L. Austin's distinction between perlocution and illocution.

89 Ibid., 18. This definition has been criticized as overly rationalistic, in that it abstracts from "mundane" arguments, in which participants may not set out "self-consciously and deliberately to cooperatively test an idea" (Sally Jackson, "What Can Speech Acts Do for Argumentation Theory?" in J. Robert Cox, Malcolm O. Sillars, and Gregg B. Walker, eds., *Argument and Social Practice: Proceedings of the Fourth SCA/AFA Conference on Argumentation* [Annandale, Va.: *Speech Communication Association,* 1985] [hereafter cited as Fourth Summer Conference], 136).

90 Van Eemeren and Grootendorst, *Speech Acts,* 17.

91 Ibid., 7. For a brief discussion of empirical approaches to argument practices in adversarial groups, see Steven Alderton, "A Processual Analysis of Argumentation in Polarizing Groups," *Second Summer Conference,* 693–703. See also Gregg B. Walker, "Argument and Negotiation," *Fourth Summer Conference,* 747–69. Willard's interactionist theory supplies most of the missing social dimensions in the Amsterdam School's approach (*Theory of Argumentation*).

92 Van Eemeren and Grootendorst, *Speech Acts,* 151–52.

93 Ibid., 161. Echoing a standard move in Oxford language analysis, this approach reduces the problems surrounding burden of proof to a matter of definitions: argumentation is defined as a process in which dialectical issues are intuitively handled by mutual agreement. See also the essay by Fred J. Kauffield, cited in note 67.

94 In analytic philosophy itself, the prospect is for apparently interminable scrutiny of mundane questions, which, nonetheless, are discussed as though definitive answers are possible. See Cohen, *Dialogue of Reason,* 107–17. Reporting on his collaborations with J. L. Austin at Oxford, Grice concedes that the yield was often very modest. "We once spent five weeks in an effort to explain why sometimes the word 'very' allows, with little or no change of meaning, the substitution of the word 'highly' (as in 'very unusual') and sometimes does not (as in 'very depressed' or 'very wicked'); and we reached no conclusion" ("Reply to Richards," in Grandy and Warner, *Philosophical Grounds of Rationality,* 57). Grice's defensive postscript to this comment seems even more revealing—in both its content and prolixity. "Our discussion was directed, in response to a worry from me, towards an examination, in the first instance, of a conceptual question which was generally agreed among us to be a strong candidate for being a question which had no philosophical importance, with a view to using the results of this examination in finding a distinction between philosophically important and philosophically unimportant enquiries. Unfortunately the desired results were not forthcoming" (57–58). Nor have they emerged in the intervening years.

95 Joseph W. Wenzel recommends blending this normative theory with the existing

descriptive literature on argumentation. See "Toward a Normative Theory of Argumentation: Van Eemeren and Grootendorst's Code of Conduct of Rational Discussions," *Fourth Summer Conference*, 139–53.

96 Penelope Brown and Stephen C. Levinson, *Politeness: Some Universals in Language Usage* (Cambridge: Cambridge University Press, 1987). A growing number of linguistically oriented studies of interpersonal discourse have begun to document the contextual importance of participant strategies other than rational agreement. Variously labeled "conversation analysis," "discourse analysis," and "strategic analysis," these approaches add so much complexity to the felicity conditions of speech acts that formalism can scarcely keep pace. It seems reasonable to conclude that the next pragmatic turn in linguistics will move the field even further from its formal study of phonology and syntax: this time from pragmatics to strategics (or perhaps even dialectics). See Levinson, *Pragmatics,* chap. 6; Teun A. van Dijk and Walter Kintsch, *Strategies of Discourse Comprehension* (New York: Academic Press, 1983). For a review of more experimental approaches, see Frank E. Millar, "Control and Intent Profiles of Interpersonal Conflict," *Third Summer Conference*, 707–24; Richard Nisbett and Lee Ross, *Human Inference: Strategies and Shortcomings of Social Judgment* (Englewood Cliffs, N.J.: Prentice-Hall, 1980).

97 Goffman's works can be included in the broader research program of symbolic interactionism. For recent critical surveys on that subject, as well as on ethnomethodology, see Anthony Giddens and Jonathan H. Turner, *Social Theory Today* (Stanford: Stanford University Press, 1987), 82–115, 224–72.

98 See Toulmin, *Uses of Argument*, 10; for a critique, see Habermas, *Theory of Communicative Action*, 1:34–35.

99 Joseph W. Wenzel, "Perspectives on Argument," *First Summer Conference*, 112–33. See also Randy Y. Hirokawa and Dirk R. Scheerhorn, "The Functions of Argumentation in Group Deliberation," *Fourth Summer Conference*, 737–46.

100 The latest systematic statement appears in Habermas, *Theory of Communicative Action*. For basically sympathetic expositions see Thomas McCarthy, *The Critical Theory of Jürgen Habermas* (Cambridge: MIT Press, 1978); Stephen K. White, *The Recent Work of Jürgen Habermas* (Cambridge: Cambridge University Press, 1988). For additional commentary, see John B. Thompson and David Held, eds., *Habermas: Critical Debates* (Cambridge: MIT Press, 1982).

101 The transcendental conditions of ideal speech were presented by Habermas in the essay translated as "What Is Universal Pragmatics," reprinted in Habermas, *Communication and the Evolution of Society*. See John B. Thompson's critical summary, "Universal Pragmatics," in Thompson and Held, eds., *Habermas*, 116–33; McCarthy, *Critical Theory of Jürgen Habermas*, chap. 4.

102 Habermas, *Theory of Communicative Action*, 1:17–18 (emphases added and removed).

103 This aspect of Habermas's theory was emphasized in the essay translated as "Toward a Theory of Communicative Competence," reprinted in Hans Peter Dreitzel, ed., *Recent Sociology No. 2* (New York: Macmillan, 1970), 114–48.

104 Habermas, *Theory of Communicative Action*, 1:42.

105 Habermas's running dispute with Hans-Georg Gadamer highlights the ambi-

guities in Habermas's transcendental move beyond the cultural sphere. Gadamer is concerned with straddling the antinomy of relativism and objectivism; his defense of a hermeneutic pragmatism presupposes the rejection of either extreme. By contrast, Habermas's model of the ideal speech situation wants to straddle the dichotomy of finality and legitimacy. His transcendental pragmatics specifically rejects what he sees as Gadamer's unwillingness to look beyond the historical horizons of contemporary culture. The controversy seems destined to continue, so long as each assigns the other to one extreme within his own particular antinomy. Central positions in the debate are featured in Karl-Otto Apel et al., *Hermeneutik und Ideologiekritik* (Frankfurt am Main: Suhrkamp, 1971).

106　The infectious optimism of Richard J. Bernstein's works seems to draw much of its strength from Habermas's transcendentalism. See, e.g., *Beyond Objectivism and Relativism: Science, Hermeneutics, and Praxis* (Philadelphia: University of Pennsylvania Press, 1983). "Like . . . Habermas . . . , I want to stress the danger of the type of 'totalizing' critique that seduces us into thinking that the forces at work in contemporary society are so powerful and devious that there is no possibility of achieving a communal life based on undistorted communication, dialogue, communal judgment, and rational persuasion. What we desperately need today is . . . to seize upon those experiences and struggles in which there are still the glimmerings of solidarity and the promise of dialogical communities in which there can be genuine mutual participation and where reciprocal wooing and persuasion can prevail" (227–28).

107　Thomas B. Farrell refers to Habermas's vision as a "procedural dialectical fiction" ("The Ideality of Meaning of Argument: A Revision of Habermas," *Second Summer Conference*, 925, n.34).

108　See Steven Lukes, "Of Gods and Demons: Habermas and Practical Reason," in Thompson and Held, *Habermas*, 134–48; Joseph W. Wenzel, "Habermas's Ideal Speech Situation: Some Critical Questions," *Second Summer Conference*, 940–54.

109　See Bob Pryor, "Saving the Public Sphere Through Rational Discourse," *Second Summer Conference*, 848–64.

110　Willard, *Argumentation*, 229.

111　Charles Arthur Willard, "Problems, Puzzles, and Progress: A Microsketch Toward a Philosophy of the Public Sphere," *Third Summer Conference*, 87–88.

311

Chapter 5. The Erosion of Scientific Authority

1　The critique of science from a higher cognitive plane can be found in numerous writings of the Frankfurt School. See Max Horkheimer and Theodor W. Adorno, *The Dialectic of Enlightenment* (New York: Seabury, 1972) (trans. of *Dialektik der Aufklärung*, 1947). See also Alvin W. Gouldner, *The Dialectic of Ideology and Technology* (New York: Seabury, 1976).

2　The Durkheimian perspective on meta-scientific systems as social facts was further advanced by Lucien Lévy-Bruhl and Karl Mannheim, among other leading figures in the sociology of knowledge. For an assessment of the scientific ideal within contemporary social theory, see Anthony Giddens and Jonathan Turner, eds., *Social Theory Today* (Stanford: Stanford University Press, 1987) (see, e.g., 1–4 on the "dramatic change" during the past two decades, based on trends in the philosophy of science).

3   Judicial fundamentalism was described in chap. 4. The role of ethical authority is discussed in chap. 6.

4   Toulmin hides these implications behind a residual scientism in *The Uses of Argument* (Cambridge: Cambridge University Press, 1958). See, e.g., his conclusion that his method of investigating arguments is "confessedly empirical" (257). The transcendental turn is described in Karl-Otto Apel, *Towards a Transformation of Philosophy* (London: Routledge, 1980) (trans. of *Transformation der Philosophie*, 1973) and in works by Jürgen Habermas discussed in chap. 4.

5   See Robert Merton's classic essay, "The Normative Structure of Science," in Robert K. Merton, *The Sociology of Science* (Chicago: University of Chicago Press, 1973), chap. 13. Joseph Ben-David has argued that seventeenth-century scientific movements were identified with certain institutionalized procedures of dispute resolution, whose authority was derived by analogy from juridical norms. *The Scientist's Role in Society: A Comparative Study* (Chicago: University of Chicago Press, 1984).

6   This nonperspectival ideal of authority has guided the ongoing opposition to "psychologism" in both philosophy and the social sciences. For a summary of European trends, see Marvin Farber, *The Foundations of Phenomenology* (Cambridge: Harvard University Press, 1943), 4–8, chap. 4. For Anglo-American developments, see John Passmore, *A Hundred Years of Philosophy* (London: Duckworth, 1957), chap. 8. For a historical treatment of changing standards of disciplinary authority, see Thomas L. Haskell, *The Emergence of Professional Social Science* (Urbana: University of Illinois Press, 1977).

7   Merton cites Max Weber's comment that "the belief in the value of scientific truth is not derived from nature, but is a product of particular cultures" (Robert K. Merton and Jerry Gaston, eds., *The Sociology of Science in Europe* [Carbondale: Southern Illinois University Press, 1977], 109). See also Peter T. Manicas, *A History and Philosophy of the Social Sciences* (Oxford: Blackwell, 1987), 259–65.

8   Well-documented case studies of boundary conflicts can be found, e.g., in Dorothy Nelkin, ed., *Controversy: Politics of Technical Decisions,* 2d ed. (Beverly Hills: Sage, 1984). For theoretical reflections on these boundaries, see Thomas F. Gieryn, "Boundary-Work and the Demarcation of Science from Non-Science," *American Sociological Review* 48 (1983): 781–95.

9   For current perspectives on critical realism, see Bas C. van Fraassen, *The Scientific Image* (Oxford: Clarendon Press, 1980); Mary Hesse, *Revolutions and Reconstructions in the Philosophy of Science* (Bloomington: Indiana University Press, 1980).

10 H. A. Prichard, *Kant's Theory of Knowledge* (Oxford: Clarendon Press, 1909), 118. Prichard's antipsychologism anticipates the growing reaction against imagined excesses of British neo-idealism; nearly all subsequent Anglo-American developments in philosophy were shaped by efforts to deny that we can somehow create our experience. In this reaction (shared also by Prichard's Oxford

colleague Cook Wilson), Passmore has traced the metaphysical presumptions of recent Oxford linguistic philosophy (*Hundred Years of Philosophy,* chap. 10).

11 For standard treatments, see Carl Hempel, *Aspects of Scientific Explanation* (New York: Free Press, 1965); Ernest Nagel, *The Structure of Science,* 2d ed. (Indianapolis: Hackett, 1979).

12 See Warren O. Hagstrom, *The Scientific Community* (New York: Basic Books, 1965). As mentioned in earlier chapters, both Toulmin and Kuhn offer somewhat hazy sociological descriptions of scientific communities. Manicas has emphasized the idealized nature of social preconditions assumed by current defenders of scientific inquiry. "Theoretical, fundamental, explanatory, classical science is just that set of practices in which the social conditions of free inquiry are realized and whose practitioners are socialized and guided by the [prescribed] criteria for theory choice." When the social conditions for science are satisfied, "we have the (idealized) analogy of a jury trial in which all the relevant evidence is produced, in which the jurors then negotiate from their respective postures, and from which a collective judgment eventually emerges" (*History and Philosophy of the Social Sciences,* 265). As Manicas further notes, "the social conditions for scientific knowledge have never been fully realized, and it may well be the case that the ideal of scientific practice sketched above is now beyond recovery" (ibid.). Similar conclusions were drawn by Charles Sanders Peirce in "Consequences of Four Incapacities," in *Collected Papers* (Cambridge: Harvard University Press, 1965), 5.311.

13 For a sympathetic overview see John E. Smith, *Purpose and Thought: The Meaning of Pragmatism* (Chicago: University of Chicago Press, 1984), chap. 4.

14 John Dewey, "Logical Method and Law," in John Dewey, *The Middle Works, 1899–1924* (1924; rpt., Carbondale: Southern Illinois University Press, 1983), 76.

15 Ibid., 71, 71–72.

16 See Dewey's *Essays in Experimental Logic* (Chicago: University of Chicago Press, 1916), esp., 335–442; *Logic: the Theory of Inquiry* (New York: Holt, 1938). In *Experience and Nature* (Chicago: University of Chicago Press, 1925), Dewey tried to deal with the metaphysical implications of making indeterminate or "problematic" situations the initial data of experience.

17 See Dewey's Gifford Lectures, *The Quest for Certainty: A Study of the Relation of Knowledge and Action* (New York: Minton, Balch, 1929).

18 For a review of linguistic models and their role in recent academic debates, see Frederick J. Newmeyer, *The Politics of Linguistics* (Chicago: University of Chicago Press, 1986).

19 Compare Peirce, "Consequences of Four Incapacities," 5.316.

20 John Dewey, *The Public and Its Problems* (New York: Holt, 1927). For an interpretation of Dewey's argument that emphasizes rhetorical deficiencies in public discourse, see Lloyd Bitzer, "Rhetoric and Public Knowledge," in Don M. Burks, ed., *Rhetoric, Philosophy, and Literature: An Exploration* (West Lafayette, Ind.: Purdue University Press, 1978), 67–93.

21 Charles Arthur Willard, "The Science of Values and the Values of Science," in J. Robert Cox, Malcolm O. Sillars, and Gregg B. Walker, eds., *Argument*

313

and *Social Practice: Proceedings of the Fourth Summer Conference on Argumentation* (Annandale, Va.: Speech Communication Association, 1985), 439

22 This was the message of Karl Popper's influential work, *The Open Society and Its Enemies* (London: Routledge, 1945). For the influence on social science of Popper's proceduralized version of scientific method, see David M. Ricci, *The Tragedy of Political Science: Politics, Scholarship, and Democracy* (New Haven: Yale University Press, 1984), 114–32. Earlier versions of Popper's theme can be found, e.g., in C. K. Ogden's and I. A. Richard's distinction between denotation and connotation (*The Meaning of Meaning* [New York: Harcourt, Brace, 1923]). On the cultural underpinnings of the objectivist defense of science, see David A. Hollinger, "Inquiry and Uplift: Late Nineteenth-Century American Academics and the Moral Efficacy of Scientific Practice," in Thomas L. Haskell, ed., *The Authority of Experts* (Bloomington: Indiana University Press, 1984), 142–56; Frank M. Turner, "Public Science in Britain, 1880–1919," *Isis* 71 (1980): 589–608.

23 See generally Edward A. Purcell, Jr., *The Crisis of Democratic Theory: Scientific Naturalism and the Problem of Value* (Lexington: University Press of Kentucky, 1973).

24 This legalistic turn was explored by Rudolf Stammler, a disciple of the Marburg neo-Kantian Hermann Cohen. See Stammler's *Theory of Justice* (New York: Macmillan, 1925) (trans. of *Die Lehre von dem richtigen Rechte*, 1902).

25 David Dickson, *The New Politics of Science* (Chicago: University of Chicago Press, 1988), 3, 264.

26 Richard Ice, "Presumption as Problematic in Group Decision-Making: The Case of the Space Shuttle," in Joseph W. Wenzel, ed., *Argument and Critical Practices: Proceedings of the Fifth SCA/AFA Conference on Argumentation* (Annandale, Va.: Speech Communication Association, 1987), 411–17. Similar to my procedure at the beginning of chap. 4, Ice provides a rhetorical application of concepts from organizational theory. Compare his analysis to that of James G. March and Herbert A. Simon, *Organizations* (New York: Wiley, 1958).

27 *Report of the Presidential Commission on the Space Shuttle Challenger Accident*, vol. 4, (Washington: Government Printing Office, 1986), 632; cited in Ice, "Presumptions," 414. As Ice notes, the presumption of flight readiness was not some recent development but was rather part of NASA's technique of Success Oriented Management (SOM). According to one popular account of this approach, SOM "assumes that everything will go right. As one official put it, 'It means you design everything to cost and then pray'" (Thomas J. Peters and Robert H. Waterman, Jr., *In Search of Excellence* [New York: Harper & Row, 1982], 135).

28 Ice, "Presumption," 415. Although we cannot rule out possible strategic motivations for these self-serving recollections in later testimony, it does not matter for our discussion whether such burdens of proof were explicitly recognized during the actual incident.

29 In the history of scientific method, the model of Baconian induction became problematic as soon as bits of evidence were measured by a standard of logical universality rather than by their capacity to stimulate human belief. This distinction emerged clearly in the eighteenth century with Hume, although it has had remarkably little impact on Anglo-American approaches to legal evidence,

which rest on psychologistic metaphors. Concerning the hypothetical-deductive model of science, which stresses the formal articulation of general theories and controlled testing of hypotheses, see Nagel, *Structure of Science.*

30   For theoretical analyses of termination in scientific debates, along with a series of practical examples, see H. Tristram Engelhardt, Jr., and Arthur L. Caplan, eds., *Scientific Controversies: Case Studies in the Resolution and Closure of Disputes in Science and Technology* (Cambridge: Cambridge University Press, 1987).

31   For several case studies of epidemiological argument, see the essays in Sol Levine and Abraham M. Lilienfeld, eds., *Epidemiology and Health Policy* (London: Tavistock, 1987).

32   G. Thomas Goodnight, "The Liberal and the Conservative Presumptions: On Political Philosophy and the Foundation of Public Argument," in Jack Rhodes and Sara Newell, eds., *Proceedings of the Summer Conference on Argumentation* (Annandale, Va.: Speech Communication Association, 1980), 304–37. Goodnight concentrates on liberal and conservative presumptions as relatively moderate examples of a wide range of responses to the relation between objective evidence and the social status quo. "The revolutionary stands at the far left of a continuum of feeling about social action. He is a 'fanatic,' for no proof is necessary to defend the self-evident proposition that all must be changed. He is a skeptic also. No amount of proof can possibly make a conclusive case for standing still. . . . At the far right stands the reactionary. He, too, is a fanatic, for no evidence is necessary to defend the self-evident proposition that the essential must be preserved. He is also a skeptic because no proof is possible to conclusively demonstrate a case for substantial change" (309–10). These extreme reactions to arguments based on objective proof will become relevant to the discussion (in the next section) of Thomas Kuhn's theory of scientific revolutions.

33   Ibid., 312, 317. Goodnight's notion of presumption provides a useful supplement to the theory of offsetting types of error in both law and social research. Although he fails to draw connections with rhetorical uses of presumption, R. S. Radford's article usefully compares the legal analogues of statistical concepts ("Statistical Error and Legal Error: Type One and Type Two Errors and the Law," *Loyola of Los Angeles Law Review* 21 [1988]: 843–82).

34   The Delaney clause was added in 1958 to the Food, Drug, and Cosmetic Act of 1938. See 21 U.S.C. §348(c)(3)(A). This rule was not specifically based on epidemiological theories, but it created a presumption in favor of extrapolation to humans from laboratory studies involving animals.

35   David M. O'Brien, *What Process Is Due? Courts and Science-Policy Disputes* (New York: Russell Sage Foundation, 1987), 31. (O'Brien's book is not always careful in distinguishing between two kinds of conflicts: those between rival versions of science, on the one hand, and those between science and politics, on the other. Of course, both kinds may exist simultaneously in the same controversy.) Two recent studies offer mutually offsetting examples of arguments that present themselves as scientific and dismiss the opposition as political: see Samuel Epstein, *The Politics of Cancer* (Garden City, N.Y.: Anchor Books, 1979) and Edith Efron, *The Apocalyptics: Cancer and the Big Lie* (New York: Simon and Schuster, 1984).

36   Jane C. Kronick, "Values as They Inform the Use of Scientific Evidence:

315

Contextual Analysis of Congressional Hearings on Hazardous and Radioactive Waste," Final Report to the National Science Foundation, Grant No. RII-8408980 (1988), 301, 293.

37　Ibid., 296, 290.

38　O'Brien, *What Process Is Due?*, 80–102.

39　Ibid., 90.

40　Cited in ibid., 94.

41　O'Brien, *What Process Is Due?*, 95.

42　Reserve Mining Company v. EPA, 514 F.2d 492, 519 (8th Cir. 1975).

43　Along the way, U.S. Supreme Court Justice William O. Douglas had an opportunity to castigate the initial Court of Appeals ruling: "If, as the Court of Appeals indicates, there is doubt, it should be resolved in favor of humanity, lest in the end our judicial system be part and parcel of a regime that makes people . . . the victims of the great God Progress which is behind the stay permitting this vast pollution of Lake Superior and its environs" (Minnesota v. Reserve Mining Company, 419 U.S. 802, 804 [1974]).

44　See, e.g., Manicas, *History and Philosophy of the Social Sciences*, chap. 12; Ernan McMullin, ed., *Construction and Constraint: The Shaping of Scientific Rationality* (Notre Dame, Ind.: University of Notre Dame Press, 1988), 1–47.

45　Karl Popper, *The Logic of Scientific Discovery* (London: Hutchinson, 1959). (The original Austrian edition was published in 1934 under the title *Logik der Forschung*.) At the close of the main body of the book, Popper concludes that "science never pursues the illusory aim of making its answers final, or even probable. Its advance is, rather, towards the infinite yet attainable aim of ever discovering new, deeper, and more general problems, and of subjecting its ever tentative answers to ever renewed and ever more rigorous tests" (281). As numerous critics have pointed out, Popper's definition of science leaves in doubt the scientific status of his own theory. This final statement on the infinite revisability of science was itself a kind of dogma for Popper, which he jealously guarded against all foes.

46　Thomas S. Kuhn, *The Structure of Scientific Revolutions*, 2d ed. (Chicago: University of Chicago Press, 1970). The first edition appeared in 1962. Although Popper and Kuhn often adopted the role of adversaries, in many ways their contributions to philosophy of science are closely related. See their exchange and the interpretive essays in Imre Lakatos and Alan Musgrave, eds., *Criticism and the Growth of Knowledge* (Cambridge: Cambridge University Press, 1970).

47　See esp. Barry Barnes, *Scientific Knowledge and Sociological Theory* (London: Routledge, 1974) and David Bloor, *Knowledge and Social Imagery*, 2d ed. (Chicago: University of Chicago Press, 1991). Similar perspectives on science have a close affinity with phenomenological schools of philosophy. See, e.g., Paul A. Komesaroff, *Objectivity, Science and Society: Interpreting Nature and Society in the Age of the Crisis of Science* (London: Routledge, 1986).

48　Popper and his followers served up a number of central themes previously explored by American pragmatism, but with a more highly formalized conception of scientific theory and a less concrete sense of social context. On the relation to American pragmatism, see Charles W. Morris, *Logical Positivism, Pragmatism and Scientific Empiricism,* (Paris: Hermann, 1937) and Charles W. Morris, "Scientific Empiricism," in Otto Neurath, Rudolf Carnap, and Charles W. Morris, eds., *Foundations of the Unity of Science* (Chicago: University of Chicago Press, 1955), 63–75. Popper's work did not become well known in Britain and the United States until after the pragmatic turn in analytic philosophy, occasioned by the circulation of Wittgenstein's later works. As British philosophy exorcised the spirit of metaphysical realism that haunted earlier analytical schools, Popper's attacks on similar doctrines in Viennese positivism proved highly attractive. But Popper himself seemed skeptical of efforts to reduce metaphysical problems to the misuse of ordinary language (see *Logic of Scientific Discovery,* 18–20). His confidence that the procedures of science offered a privileged view of an unknowable but "real" universe seems entirely compatible with the position taken by Stephen Toulmin, discussed in chaps. 1 and 4. As Popper declared in a 1960 lecture, "I propose to replace . . . the question of sources of our knowledge by the entirely different question: 'How can we hope to detect and eliminate error?'" (*Conjectures and Refutations* [London: Routledge, 1962], 25). According to Herbert Schnädelbach, the neo-Kantian Bruno Bauch "was the first to allow the idea of system to recede into the background in favour of the procedural characterization of science; science, according to him, is 'founded knowledge'; in science it is a matter of 'how in general it is necessary to proceed, in order that scientific knowledge should be attained, so that science should be the foundation of science and in the founded knowledge truth should be achieved'" (Herbert Schnädelbach, *Philosophy in Germany, 1831–1933* [Cambridge: Cambridge University Press, 1984], 245n54).

317

49 See Popper, *Logic of Scientific Discovery,* 86–87, for his distinction between falsification and falsifiability.

50 Ibid., 278–81. "Once put forward, none of our [scientific hypotheses] are dogmatically upheld. Our method of research is not to defend them, in order to prove how right we were. On the contrary, we try to overthrow them. Using all the weapons of our logical, mathematical, and technical armoury we try to prove that our [hypotheses] were false—in order to put forward, in their stead, new unjustified and unjustifiable [hypotheses], new 'rash and premature prejudices,' as Bacon derisively called them" (279).

51 See Popper's comments in *Conjectures and Refutations,* 28.

52 In *Logic of Scientific Discovery,* Popper treats corroboration as a relativistic term—a kind of pragmatic fiction if measured against the timeless objectivity of his scientific ideal. Although he treats that ideal as an idol that must be dethroned (280), it remains the implicit standard by which Popper condemns the unwelcome, radical extensions of his own skeptical theory. "I am not a relativist," he insists, but "I do believe in 'absolute' or 'objective' truth . . . (although I am, of course, not an 'absolutist' in the sense of thinking that I, or anybody else, has the truth in his pocket)." In an attempt to strike a judicious tone, Popper turned increasingly to paradoxical formulations that parallel those of the moderate-liberal proponents of American judicial review in the 1960s (see my discussion of "reasoned elaboration" in chap. 2). "I believe that science is essentially critical; that it consists of bold conjectures, controlled by criticism, and that it may,

therefore, be described as revolutionary. But I have always stressed the need for some dogmatism: the dogmatic scientist has an important role to play. If we give in to criticism too easily, we shall never find out where the real power of our theories lies" ("Normal Science and Its Dangers," in Lakatos and Musgrave, *Criticism and the Growth of Knowledge*, 56, 55).

53 Karl Popper, *The Open Society and Its Enemies* (London: Routledge, 1945). For comparable rhetoric of suspicion, see Ira Glasser's critique of public welfare bureaucracies, "Prisoners of Benevolence," in Willard Gaylin, et al., *Doing Good: The Limits of Benevolence* (New York: Pantheon, 1978), 99–168. The social and religious overtones of Popper's universal skepticism toward authority are manifest in his speech "On the Sources of Knowledge and Ignorance," printed in *Conjectures and Refutations*, 3–30.

54 Popper was fully aware of this idealism: "Our motives and even our purely scientific ideals, including the ideal of a disinterested search for truth, are deeply anchored in extra-scientific and, in part, in religious evaluations. Thus the 'objective' or the 'value-free' scientist is hardly the ideal scientist. Without passion we can achieve nothing—certainly not in pure science. The phrase 'the passion for truth' is no mere metaphor" ("The Logic of the Social Sciences," rpt. in Theodor W. Adorno et al., *The Positivist Dispute in German Sociology* [New York: Harper & Row, 1976], 97 [trans. of *Der Positivismusstreit in der deutschen Soziologie*, 1969]).

55 See Popper, *Conjectures and Refutations*, 253–92. Earlier in this volume, Popper gave his endorsement to a "reality" that interacts with scientific theories: "Theories are our own inventions, our own ideas; they are not forced upon us, but are our self-made instruments of thought: this has been clearly seen by the idealist. But some of these theories of ours can clash with reality; and when they do, we know that there is a reality; that there is something to remind us of the fact that our ideas may be mistaken. And this is why the realist is right" (117).

56 See the symposium edited by Adorno, *Positivist Dispute*. As the contributions by Adorno and Habermas make clear, Popper's willingness to accept "truth" as the "regulative ideal" approached through the interaction of logic and scientific procedure separated him from the hermeneutic tradition. Habermas's response was to postulate a separate hermeneutic reason as the appropriate procedure for reaching interpersonal consensus on value issues; this theory eventually expanded into his transcendental quest for the ideal speech community. Under the influence of Heidegger, however, other hermeneutic writers have resisted any reunion of truth and procedure as an inevitable reversion to the sort of instrumental logic endorsed by Popper (see, e.g., Hans-Georg Gadamer, *Wahrheit und Methode*, 3rd ed. [Tübingen: J. C. B. Mohr, 1972], 432–49).

57 Popper, *Logic of Scientific Discovery*, 104.

58 This concept was originally defended by Moritz Schlick and most notably by Rudolf Carnap in *The Logical Structure of the World* (Berkeley: University of California Press, 1967) (trans. of *Der logische Aufbau der Welt*, 1928); but it was eventually abandoned under the influence of Otto Neurath (see "Protokollsätze," *Erkenntnis*, 3 [1933]: 204–14) in favor of what has been described as the "linguistic Kantian" view that primitive linguistic categories supply the "conditions

of significant discourse" (George D. Romanos, *Quine and Analytic Philosophy: The Language of Language* [Cambridge: MIT Press, 1983], 21–31). The positivists' problems with basic sentences were similar to those surrounding the sense data in Russell's theory of logical atomism, and the *Tatsachen* in Wittgenstein's *Tractatus*. For Wittgenstein, too, the pragmatic turn against metaphysical realism eventually provided a welcome solution, and the influence of Wittgenstein's later linguistic behaviorism doubtless set the stage for the favorable reception of Popper's work in Britain in the late 1950s. An even longer delay occurred in Germany, where Popper's popularity came only in the 1960s by way of England. See Rüdiger Bubner, *Modern German Philosophy* (Cambridge: Cambridge University Press, 1981), 106.

59 Popper, *Logic of Scientific Discovery*, 108–09. In introducing this judicial analogy, Popper emphasizes the behavioristic reference in the etymology of *verdict*, ("vere dictum = spoken truly"). His definition of *verdict* corresponds to the *quid facti* of Roman law ("The verdict of the jury . . . , like that of the experimenter, is an answer to a question of fact." [109]).

60 Ibid., 109–10.

61 Ibid., 110. Popper's view of law as a system of logically connected rules was formulated in its most uncompromising form by his Viennese contemporary, Hans Kelsen, whose *Reine Rechtslehre* appeared the same year as Popper's *Logik der Forschung*. Kelsen's work was translated as *The Pure Theory of Law* (Berkeley: University of California Press, 1967).

62 Popper, *Logic of Scientific Discovery*, 111.

63 These common terms from American legal realism are discussed by Jerome Frank in *Courts on Trial: Myth and Reality in American Justice* (Princeton: Princeton University Press, 1949), 73–77.

64 Popper, *Logic of Scientific Discovery*, 53–56. In line with the positivist theory of law, Popper imagined these rules as hierarchically ordered under a single *Grundnorm*, "which serves as a kind of norm for deciding upon the remaining rules, and which is thus a rule of a higher type. It is the rule which says that the other rules of scientific procedure must be designed in such a way that they do not protect any statement in science against falsification" (54). This was precisely the sort of legal formalism that drove the American realists to look for sociological and dialectical elements in adjudication, to which Kuhn's strategy is the scientific analogue. For alternative approaches that were available in contemporary German jurisprudence, see Josef Esser, *Grundsatz und Norm in der richterlichen Fortbildung des Privatrechts*, 4th ed., (Tübingen: J. C. B. Mohr, 1990). Habermas criticizes Popper for confining his judicial analogy to the determination of facts. "The *quaestio facti* must be determined with reference to a given *quaestio juris*, that is, one understood in its immanent claims. In legal proceedings, this question is prominent in everyone's mind. The whole affair here revolves around the question of an offence against general prohibitive norms, positively set down and sanctioned by the state. Correspondingly, the empirical validity of basic statements is measured against a behavioural expectation governed by social norms. But, what does the *quaestio juris* look like in the research process, and how is the empirical validity of basic statements measured in this case?" (in Adorno,

Positivist Dispute, 153). Habermas is concerned specifically with the social origin of rules and not with other dialectical aspects of rule-articulation.

65 The starting point for such debates is Margaret Masterman, "The Nature of a Paradigm," in Lakatos and Musgrave, *Criticism and the Growth of Knowledge,* 59–89.

66 See ibid., 65.

67 Kuhn, *Structure of Scientific Revolutions,* 46.

68 Ibid., 23.

69 Similarly, Kuhn notes that "often a paradigm developed for one set of phenomena is ambiguous in its application to other closely related ones. Then experiments are necessary to choose among the alternative ways of applying the paradigm to the new area of interest." His example is the extension of caloric theory, which was first developed for substances that were either mixed together or underwent a change of physical state. The caloric theory then had to be applied to cases involving chemical reactions, friction, and compression or absorption of a gas, "and to each of these other phenomena the theory could be applied in several ways" (ibid.).

70 The legal system can thus thrive over long periods with constant dissension. Provided the community as a whole appears generally satisfied with the outcomes, such controversy may be greeted as a sign of healthy debate—a source of pride and self-confidence. (Indeed, the true Popperian scientist should probably encourage a similarly combative science, including a formally adversarial structure for scientific discussion.) In either setting, however, the difference between normality and crisis depends on preserving the jurisdictional framework within which a community can satisfy its needs for finality and legitimacy. A Popperian call for more critical debate presupposes that this dialectical framework will not itself be called into question.

71 Kuhn, *Structure of Scientific Revolutions,* 46. The analogous point about the judicial system was made in chaps. 1–3; legal rules are always suspended within an active judicial process, which institutionalizes the elusive critical functions of dialectic.

72 Ibid., 47.

73 Ibid., 47–48.

74 Ibid., 148.

75 Ibid., 155–56.

76 Ibid., 150, 121–22.

77 For representative impressions from the early 1970s, see Joel Primack and Frank von Hippel, *Advice and Dissent: Scientists in the Political Arena* (New York: Basic Books, 1974). See also Don K. Price, *The Scientific Estate* (Cambridge: Harvard University Press, 1965).

78 For an extensive collection of case studies on the termination of scientific debates, see Engelhardt and Caplan, eds., *Scientific Controversies.*

79 For a restatement of the pragmatist notion of a scientific community, see Hagstrom, *Scientific Community.* For political and sociological implications of this concept, in light of recent experience, see Everett Mendelsohn, "The Politi-

cal Anatomy of Controversy in the Sciences," in Engelhardt and Caplan, eds., *Scientific Controversies*, 93–124.

80 For an overview and critique of the main positions, see Albert R. Matheny and Bruce A. Williams, "Scientific Disputes and Adversary Procedures in Policy-Making: An Evaluation of the Science Court," *Law and Policy Quarterly* 3 (1981): 341–64, to which is appended a reply by Arthur Kantrowitz and a rejoinder by the authors. Kantrowitz's views are discussed below. See also Sheila Jasanoff and Dorothy Nelkin, "Science, Technology, and the Limits of Judicial Competence," *Science* 214 (1981): 1211–15.

81 A. Hunter Dupree, *Science in the Federal Government: A History of Policies and Activities to 1940* (Cambridge: Harvard University Press, 1957).

82 In addition to Haskell, *Emergence of Professional Social Science*, see Dorothy Ross, *The Origins of American Social Science* (Cambridge: Cambridge University Press, 1991).

83 For similar perspectives, sometimes at odds with pragmatism, see David A. Hollinger, *Morris R. Cohen and the Scientific Ideal* (Cambridge: MIT Press, 1975).

84 On the subtleties of this postwar ambivalence, see Purcell, *Crisis of Democratic Theory*, chap. 13.

85 Task Force of the President's Advisory Group on Anticipated Advances in Science and Technology, "The Science Court Experiment: An Interim Report," *Science* 193 (1976): 653. Kantrowitz was one of three members of this task force.

86 Matheny and Williams summarize the main objections ("Scientific Disputes"). O'Brien also raises objections, but at times his own analysis seems to define politics as the set of all limits to professional objectivity (see *What Process Is Due?*, chap. 1).

87 Arthur Kantrowitz, "Proposal for an Institution for Scientific Judgment," *Science* 156 (1967): 763. Kantrowitz's reference to "unanimity" should be interpreted in the Kuhnian sense of unity-within-a-paradigm. The identical proposal appeared in slightly expanded form eight years later, "Controlling Technology Democratically," *American Scientist* 63 (1975): 505–09.

88 Kantrowitz, "Proposal," 763.

89 Ibid., 764.

90 Ibid. Kantrowitz also worried that science was too conservative at the level of drawing inferences from experimental results. He hoped that science court judges would be less inclined to make "negative judgments" about "novel approaches" to scientific issues. "It is actually very difficult to offer rigorous proof that something cannot be done," he reminds us, and science court judges should be held accountable for resorting to negative inferences (ibid.). In short, Kantrowitz was clearly interested in using the science court to move the burden of proof away from the Popperian presumption.

91 See U.S. Department of Commerce, *Proceedings of the Colloquium on the Science Court*, (Washington: Commerce Technical Advisory Board, 1977) (available through National Technical Information Service, #PB-261 305). The colloquium, held on September 19–21, 1976, was jointly sponsored by the Commerce Department, the National Science Foundation, and the American Association

for the Advancement of Science. Among the notables invited to speak were Margaret Mead and Elliot Richardson. Prior to the meeting, the Presidential Task Force "Interim Report" (cited in note 85) had issued its qualified endorsement of the idea. As already mentioned, Kantrowitz (still the entrepreneur) was one of three members of that body.

92 U.S. Department of Commerce, *Proceedings*, 38. A number of participants pointed out that federal agencies were already weighed down with cadres of scientific consultants, advisory committees (more than 600 strong), and connections with powerful scientific associations—all of which had previously been proposed as methods for ensuring more objectivity in political decision-making. Indeed, the very creation of specialized federal agencies was intended to promote the use of expert judgment in the regulatory process. Other procedural innovations were dedicated to the same purpose, including the requirement of professionally prepared "impact statements" and mandatory cost-benefit calculations prior to regulatory decisions (see ibid., 32, 36, 43, 65). All of these methods for protecting the scientific integrity of public decisions, it seems, suffered at least some loss of neutral authority soon after their implementation. Scientists at the colloquium were especially cynical about the manipulation of advisory committees (see 144). On the federal advisory apparatus, see Primack and von Hippel, *Advice and Dissent;* David Collingridge and Colin Reeve, *Science Speaks to Power: The Role of Experts in Policy Making* (New York: St Martin's, 1986).

93 The lawyer's position: "I do not believe truth and justice are the same thing, and in fact I believe that the legal system is structured specifically to put the emphasis on justice, often to minimizing the quest for truth" (James S. Turner, in U.S. Department of Commerce, *Proceedings*, 162). The scientist's position: "We don't want a process where all the motivation is to win. We want a process where the motivation is to seek the truth about scientific facts only" (Richard O. Simpson, ibid., 43).

94 See also Task Force, "Interim Report," 655.

95 U.S. Department of Commerce, *Proceedings*, 143. Stever was President Ford's science advisor, former director of the National Science Foundation, and former president of Carnegie-Mellon University.

96 Ibid., 115 (Alan McGowan, president of Scientists for Public Information).

97 Matheny and Williams, "Scientific Disputes," 350. Kantrowitz and other proponents responded by insisting that scientific inquiry would continue unchallenged, that court decisions were only advisory, and that prudent judges would refrain from endorsing positions that were not fully justified by evidence (see Arthur Kantrowitz, "A Response to Methany and Williams," *Law and Policy Quarterly* 3 [1981]: 365–68). Perhaps so; both sides of this dispute imagined the particular future that agreed with their respective assumptions. But Kantrowitz apparently forgot his own warnings that powerful social and economic pressures already push toward limiting inquiry, abandoning new hypotheses, and stifling the creativity of the individual scientist. His confidence seems to ignore the ability of courts (and adversarial parties) to thrive on appearances of neutrality.

98 Roy Bhaskar, *The Possibility of Naturalism*, 2d ed. (Hemel Hempstead, Eng.: Har-

vester, 1989), 8. See also his *A Realist Theory of Science*, 2d ed. (Sussex, Eng.: Harvester, 1978).
99 Bhaskar, *Possibility of Naturalism*, 8.
100 Ibid., 169. Sean Sayers has presented a somewhat different picture of this postulated reality, but he endorses Bhaskar's transcendental reversal as "the only basis upon which freedom can properly be understood" (*Reality and Reason* [Oxford: Blackwell, 1985], 208).
101 Ian Shapiro, *Political Criticism* (Berkeley: University of California Press, 1990), 274.

Chapter 6. The Rise of Ethical Authority

1 George Orwell, *Collected Essays, Journalism, and Letters*, vol. 4 (New York: Harcourt, Brace, 1968), 463.
2 Ibid., 466–67. Orwell nonetheless measures Gandhi's life favorably by political standards. "One may . . . reject sainthood as an ideal and therefore feel that Gandhi's basic aims were anti-human and reactionary: but regarded simply as a politician, and compared with the other leading political figures of our time, how clean a smell he has managed to leave behind!" (470).
3 "Ethics has replaced mom, the flag and apple pie as something one must not only be for these days, but appear to be doing something about. We may not be able to define it. We aren't sure whether the word is singular or plural, but we know it when we see it" (former New York Congressman Otis G. Pike, quoted in connection with the sudden resignation of Congressman Tony Coelho), "New Fallout Over Ethics," *New York Times*, May 27, 1989, 9.
4 The phrase "transcendental ethics" (my own label) does not correspond to any particular term in the highly specialized vocabulary of current ethical theory. Throughout this book, the term *transcendental* is used in a broad Kantian sense, which is fully analyzed in chap. 7. It designates a philosophical strategy of projecting a realm of objects or concepts beyond the reach of human experience, which is allegedly necessary for justifying certain conclusions about our immediate experience. Rather than designating any particular contemporary school of ethical theory, my term refers to an overarching strategy shared by theorists who may well differ in mapping the contents of the transcendental realm and in describing its accessibility. In philosophical circles, this transcendental strategy is a durable Kantian procedure that has experienced its own cycles of acceptance and rejection over two hundred years. It has never required direct guidance from the Supreme Court, but its sudden rise to public prominence in the 1960s and 1970s may well have been encouraged by developments in the legal realm.
5 Dworkin's essays were collected in Ronald Dworkin, *Taking Rights Seriously* (Cambridge: Harvard University Press, 1977). The other works are John Rawls, *A Theory of Justice* (Cambridge: Harvard University Press, 1971) and Robert Nozick, *Anarchy, State, and Utopia* (New York: Basic Books, 1974). Since my purpose in this chapter is historical as well as analytical, my discussion will

323

remain centered on these seminal texts. Philosophers evolve, but I shall not attempt to trace their full development in this chapter.

6 It should be noted that Dworkin would reject the term *transcendental* as a description of his ethical cosmology. See, however, Thomas D. Perry, "Dworkin's Transcendental Idea," in Peter A. French, Theodore E. Uehling, Jr., and Howard K. Wettstein, eds., *Social and Political Philosophy*, (Minneapolis: University of Minnesota Press, 1982), 255–69, which draws some appropriate Kantian parallels.

7 It is important to remember that this line of critique, descended from legal realism, held presumptions that made it virtually impossible for the courts to establish correctness by standards other than pure deductive logic. Holmes's dissent in the Lochner case, discussed in chap. 2, is the *locus classicus* for this highly restrictive approach. Dworkin's essay, "The Model of Rules," (in *Taking Rights Seriously*, 14–45) appeared in 1967 as these critical controversies reached their peak (see ibid., 14). In a later essay, Dworkin allowed that his theory of adjudication "supports the constitutional philosophy, if not the particular decisions, of the Warren Court." It did so mainly by showing that "there is in fact no coherent philosophy to which [critics] may consistently appeal" (ibid., 132).

8 Ibid., 81. Dworkin repeats the identical argument, in virtually the same words, in his introduction (xiv).

9 As with the Supreme Court's initiatives, Dworkin's new approach helped to sustain a large cadre of supporting forces. See, e.g., the essays collected in Marshall Cohen, ed., *Ronald Dworkin and Contemporary Jurisprudence* (Totowa, N.J.: Rowman & Allanheld, 1984).

10 Dworking, *Taking Rights Seriously*, 22–28, 185.

11 Dworkin generally acknowledges the hypothetical status of his transcendental theory. In the words of one critic, his argument that "hard cases" have correct answers "is perhaps best viewed, as far as its theoretical validity is concerned, as a sketch of the hypothetical framework implied by judicial opinions that are written *as if* the decision in a hard case were uniquely required, much as Kelsen's theory may be viewed as an attempt to describe what must be hypothesized if one is to explain the normative aspect of law" (E. Philip Soper, "Legal Theory and the Obligation of a Judge," in Cohen, ed., *Ronald Dworkin*, 12). At the same time, Dworkin periodically seeks to justify his practice by a completely independent appeal to linguistic intuitions. His rights thesis, for example, provides merely "a new way of describing what we all know [judges] do," making it "less radical than it might first have seemed" (*Taking Rights Seriously*, 90). Commentators have also responded to this line of justification: "Dworkin's argument for the existence of right answers has never amounted to much more than assertions about the way we think and talk. (His recent essays focusing on the 'right answer' problem consist primarily of rebuttals to various possible arguments for the claim that there are not right answers)" (Donald H. Regan, "Glosses on Dworkin," in Cohen, ed., *Ronald Dworkin*, 142). This supplementary line of argument will be examined closely in the next section.

12 *Taking Rights Seriously*, 37. As the passage continues, Dworkin adds that judicial decisions "could not depend on the judge's own preferences . . . , because if that were the case we could not say that any rules were binding." The references

to "what we can say" are not to be taken lightly but are meant as confirming evidence for Dworkin's postulated theory.

13 Ibid., 36.

14 Ibid., 40.

15 Ibid., 41.

16 "An argument of principle fixes on some interest presented by the proponent of the right it describes, an interest alleged to be of such a character as to make irrelevant the fine discriminations of any argument of policy that might oppose it" (ibid., 85). See also 191–92 for something equivalent to the compelling-state-interest branch of strict-scrutiny. The major components of strict-scrutiny doctrine were discussed in chap. 2, including its reliance on burden-shifting strategies.

17 "Those Constitutional rights that we call fundamental like the right of free speech, are supposed to represent rights against the Government in the strong sense" (ibid., 191). See also chap. 7.

18 See, e.g., David L. Shapiro's prominent assessment covering Rehnquist's first four terms on the Court, which complained about his deficient craftsmanship and excessive reliance on ideology ("Mr. Justice Rehnquist: A Preliminary View," *Harvard Law Review* 90 [1976]: 293–357).

19 Dworkin's essay "Civil Disobedience" (in *Taking Rights Seriously*, 206–22) was originally published in the *New York Review of Books* in 1968. Dworkin's plea for extending some presumptive legality to acts of conscience was yet another occasion for skillfully shifting the burden of proof. How do we know, after all, that the individual is not correct in forming a judgment at variance with the declared law? "It is one thing to say that an individual must sometimes violate his conscience when he knows that the law commands him to do it. It is quite another to say that he must violate his conscience even when he reasonably believes that the law does not require it, because it would inconvenience his fellow citizens if he took the most direct, and perhaps the only, method of attempting to show that he is right and they are wrong" (*Taking Rights Seriously*, 214). Dworkin specifically states that, at least for him, "the balance of fairness and utility" argued against the highly publicized prosecution of the Boston draft resisters (219).

20 Ibid., 212–13. Dworkin's operational test for legal uncertainty seems to be met whenever "lawyers can reasonably disagree on what a court ought to decide" (212). Elsewhere Dworkin seems to say that lawyers and political philosophers are the persons best equipped technically to perform a conscientious analysis (215).

21 Ibid., 214–15 (emphasis added). Dworkin's conclusions are carefully worded in negative statements, which appropriately reflect his inference that no one is in a position to prove that conscientious civil disobedience was not closer to the law than were the decisions by actual courts.

22 Ibid., 211. Thomas D. Perry notes the trouble created by Dworkin's stipulation that judges themselves cannot know when they have properly carried out their procedural obligations. As a result, he says, even easy cases become undecidable, if a judge cannot rest secure in standard interpretations of precedents, like those available to "any competent lawyer. . . . This is because the judge

cannot know that the 'settled rule' which he or she is about to apply in such a case has *not* lost all its legal authority" ("Dworkin's Transcendental Idea," 261). Dworkin reaches divergent conclusions that illustrate the unlimited power of the argument-from-ignorance. He establishes, for example, that "no judicial decision is necessarily the right decision," that "a reasonable and competent lawyer might well think" that the Supreme Court was wrong on a constitutional matter, and that "there will be no way of proving that he is wrong" (*Taking Rights Seriously*, 185, 209–10). But a later essay concludes that "It is necessary also to be satisfied that, though the decision of any particular group of judges is fallible, and may never be proved right to the satisfaction of all other lawyers, it is nevertheless better to let that decision stand than to assign the decision to some other institution, or to ask judges to decide on grounds of policy, or in some other way that does not require their best judgment about the rights of the parties" (281). As for his own prescriptions on how fundamental rights should be recognized through institutional structures, Dworkin believes that they "therefore must count" as long as they "have not yet been shown to be misguided" (217).

23 Ibid., 215.

24 Ibid., 105, 115. The phrase "taken to be" is yet another vestige of Dworkin's tendency to find normative standards in ordinary speech.

25 Ibid., 115.

26 This set of abilities bears an uncanny resemblance to qualities of organizational leadership described in Philip Selznick's classic work, *Leadership in Administration* (New York: Harper & Row, 1957). Like Hercules, the leaders of modern organizations (according to Selznick) are responsible for continually creating the system within which rule-governed behavior can become an operational reality.

27 Dworkin, *Taking Rights Seriously*, 130 (emphasis added). As quoted earlier in note 22, Dworkin elsewhere advises us that, despite the fallibility of judges, it is better to let their decisions stand than "to assign the decision to some other institution" (281). The ambiguity of Dworkin's position is captured by Soper's comment that Dworkin's approach "appears at times to be making a somewhat quibbling point about the inherent limits of language and human foresight. When language and purpose fail to guide unequivocally, one must fall back on something else, and that something else might just as well be (or 'must be,' depending on the particular variation of the theory) the judge's sense of what best 'coheres' with the aim of the entire legal system" ("Legal Theory and the Obligation of a Judge," 21).

28 In its combination of intuitionism and respect for ordinary language, this movement had its proximate sources in G. E. Moore (*Principia Ethica* [Cambridge: Cambridge University Press, 1903]) and W. D. Ross (*The Right and the Good* [Oxford: Clarendon Press, 1930]). See also Kurt Baier, *The Moral Point of View* (Ithaca, N.Y.: Cornell University Press, 1958). For general background, see Mary Warnock, *Ethics Since 1900* (Oxford: Clarendon Press, 1960). Major debates within this movement, including the controversy between moral realists and constructivists, occur within a common framework of strategy. (For a summary see David O. Brink, *Moral Realism and the Foundations of Ethics* [Cambridge: Cambridge University Press, 1989]). I shall be focusing mainly on the constructivist approach in view of its influential development by Dworkin and Rawls.

29 Brink, *Moral Realism*, 23, 24, 36.

30 Rawls, *Theory of Justice*. For references and commentary on Rawls's writings through 1988, see "Symposium on Rawlsian Theory of Justice: Recent Developments," *Ethics* 99 (1989): 695–944. Reflective equilibrium will be discussed in the next section of this chapter.

31 For a representative collection of philosophical commentary, see Douglas Odegard, ed., *Ethics and Justification* (Edmonton, Alberta: Academic Printing & Publishing, 1988).

32 John Rawls, "Justice as Fairness," *Philosophical Review* 67 (1958): 164–94. For a contemporary assessment, see John W. Chapman, "Justice and Fairness," in Carl J. Friedrich and John W. Chapman, eds., *Justice* (New York: Atherton Press, 1963), 147–69.

33 Rawls's notion of "pure procedural justice" rests on "the intuitive idea" of designing the social system "so that the outcome is just whatever it happens to be" (*Theory of Justice*, 85). The deliberate neutrality built into this theory is similar to the posture adopted by the U.S. Supreme Court in its doctrine of procedural due process. Both formulations seemed to satisfy the anti-ideological and avowedly secular orientation of philosophy and culture preceding the sharp judicial conflicts of the late 1960s.

34 Rawls also wanted to provide an approach to ethical authority different from the "economic-man" reductivism of James M. Buchanan and Gordon Tullock, as expressed in their influential work, *The Calculus of Consent* (Ann Arbor: University of Michigan Press, 1962). See Rawls, "Constitutional Liberty and the Concept of Justice," in Friedrich and Chapman, eds., *Justice*, 100n1.

35 *Theory of Justice*, §24.

36 The original position was another version of the Hercules story but with an entirely different agent representing ethical authority: instead of the unified jurisdiction presided over by the Herculean judge, Rawls gave us a convocation of Kantian noumenal selves. Their authority is not earned by any virtuoso sweep of legal precedents, political events, cultural history, and social philosophy—all of which came under review by Hercules in his act of applying legal rights to concrete situations (and particularly to hard cases). But their authority is nonetheless expressed in the form of a decision, which occurs at a much higher level of generality. In an unusually frank statement of his strategic purposes, Rawls acknowledges that reasons for devices like the "veil of ignorance go beyond mere simplicity. We want to define the original position so that we get the desired solutions" (ibid., 141).

37 Richard Dien Winfield, *Reason and Justice* (Albany: State University of New York Press, 1988), 110.

38 Perhaps the leading example was the Austrian neo-Kantian Hans Kelsen, in his *Pure Theory of Law* (Berkeley: University of California Press, 1967) [trans. of *Reine Rechtslehre* (1934)]. Except for its neo-Hegelian episode, British moral philosophy has been more comfortable with nominalism and inductivism—greatly stimulated by G. E. Moore and evident in writers like Stephen Toulmin.

39 Winfield, *Reason and Justice*, 110. Winfield's initial rejoinder is to shift the burden of proof back onto Rawls: "Of itself, the bankruptcy of the teleological appeal to privileged givens provides *no compelling reason* to embrace pure procedural jus-

327

tice" (111, emphasis added). Whether this response is decisive, its implications are clear enough: "Merely constructing a coherent system of moral sentiments is *in*sufficient. It can *neither ex*clude the possibility of other competing coherent systems *nor* establish that ethical theory has *no* other alternative to resigning itself to the doxology of coherence. And even if these problems could be solved, there would still be *no* defense against the nihilist objection that our ultimate entrapment within a unique framework of coherent ethical claims is *no compelling reason* to accept its authority" (116, emphasis added). Note that Winfield's earlier comment echoes the language of his postulated nihilist objection.

40 Rawls derived two major "principles of justice" from his decision procedure: commonly referred to as the "liberty principle" and the "difference principle" (*Theory of Justice*, chaps. 4–5). For contemporary commentary, see Brian Barry, *The Liberal Theory of Justice* (Oxford: Clarendon Press, 1973), chaps. 4–5.

41 For representative early commentary, see the collection edited by Norman Daniels, *Reading Rawls: Critical Studies on Rawls's A Theory of Justice* (New York: Basic Books, 1975). For more recent references see the symposium cited earlier in note 30.

42 Dworkin, *Taking Rights Seriously*, 152 (emphasis added). The transition represented by Dworkin's "therefore" recalls the similar shift in Chief Justice Warren's opinion in Brown v. Board of Education, discussed in chap. 2.

43 Ibid., 183.

44 See esp. John Rawls, "Kantian Constructivism in Moral Theory," a set of three lectures reprinted in *Journal of Philosophy* 77 (1980): 515–72. For still later works, see Thomas E. Hill, Jr., "Kantian Constructivism in Ethics," *Ethics* 99 (1989): 752–70.

45 Rawls, "Kantian Constructivism," 533.

46 Ibid., 554 (emphasis added). Note that the conceptual premises for the original position theory (and for its companion ideal, the well-ordered society) are treated as given or presumed.

47 Ibid., 565, 571. For criticism from the moral realist standpoint, see Brink, *Moral Realism*, 303–21.

48 Rawls, "Kantian Constructivism," 533.

49 Ibid., 563 (emphasis added).

50 Nothing prevents us, that is, from assigning a broad presumption of innocence to constructivist arguments. Rudolf Carnap endorsed a similar notion for discussions of logic, which he approached through a "principle of tolerance" (*Logical Syntax of Language* [London: Routledge, 1937], 51–52) (trans. of *Logische Syntax der Sprache* [1934]).

51 Rawls, "Kantian Constructivism," 564. Rawls usually tries to avoid flat statements denying the existence of moral facts but emphasizes that we cannot know them. Either way, we are free to construct the normative world in a functional manner. As Rawls acknowledges in *Theory of Justice*, "We want to define the original position so that we get the desired solution" (141).

52 Rawls, "Kantian Constructivism," 570.

53 See Rawls's essay, "The Idea of an Overlapping Consensus," *Oxford Journal of Legal Studies* 7 (1987): 1–25. Fred D'Agostino has shown how such a contingency

would help rescue Rawls's argument from problems of relativism ("Relativism and Reflective Equilibrium," *Monist* 71 [1988]: 420–36).

54 Rawls, "Kantian Constructivism," 534. Rawls entered the same plea in *Theory of Justice:* "We should view a theory of justice as a guiding framework designed to focus our moral sensibilities and to put before our intuitive capacities more limited and manageable questions for judgment. The principles of justice identify certain considerations as morally relevant and the priority rules indicate the appropriate precedence when these conflict, while the conception of the original position defines the underlying idea which is to inform our deliberations. If the scheme as a whole seems on reflection to clarify and to order our thoughts, and if it tends to reduce disagreements and to bring divergent convictions more in line, then it has done all that one may reasonably ask. Understood as parts of a framework that does indeed seem to help, the numerous simplifications may be regarded as provisionally justified" (53).

55 L. Jonathan Cohen, *The Dialogue of Reason: An Analysis of Analytical Philosophy* (Oxford: Clarendon Press, 1986), 49–148. "What is claimed here . . . is that the unifying force in analytical philosophy is its engagement with the reasoned investigation of reasons at that level of generality . . . where no conclusions can be taken as universally granted. Not that this investigation, whether conservatively or reformatively oriented, has been a widely declared aim in the present century, or an acknowledged masterplan. But it nevertheless turns out to be the objective that has in effect been systematically fostered and promoted by analytical philosophers. *The importance of this objective is the underlying, though unrecognized, presupposition of the movement* (57, emphasis added).

56 Rawls used this analogy in an early essay, "Outline of a Decision Procedure for Ethics," *Philosophical Review* 60 (1951): 177–97. He also mentions it in *Theory of Justice* (579) and makes particular reference to Quine's pragmatic (or "coherentist") view of scientific verification, as opposed to the realist assumption that hypotheses must accord with a self-standing reality.

57 As discussed in chap. 1, dialectical aspects of the judicial process include all the rule-interpreting, -defining, and -creating behavior of the judiciary.

58 See John Passmore, *A Hundred Years of Philosophy* (London: Duckworth, 1957), chap. 18. As Passmore indicates, congenial interpretations of Aristotle were common among the forerunners of this movement, notably Cook Wilson and Austin.

59 In both cases, a new presumption is strategically introduced to close off a form of analysis deemed to exceed human capacities: metaphysics in the philosophical context, substantive due process in the constitutional context. Once the new presumption is frozen into doctrine, its proponents no longer need to make an argument in its behalf. By treating its own presumptions as a default solution, each of these skeptical movements could afford to base its reputation on the neutral virtues of prudence and restraint. Just as judges clung to the rhetoric of neutrality, Cohen notes the claim by early analysts to remain "above the ordinary mêlée of conflicting schools. Indeed, some of them even used the term 'philosophers' to refer only to those allegedly confused thinkers from whom they wished to distance themselves, with the implication that the analytical method was so

different from traditional philosophical methods that its practitioners should not be expected to pass under the same professional label" (*Dialogue of Reason*, 27).

60 Cohen, *Dialogue of Reason*, 57. Cohen introduces his study as "a way of reinforcing [analytical philosophy] from within by an updating of its sense of identity. In the earlier phase of the analytical movement a considerable variety of metaphilosophical theories about therapeutic analysis, conceptual clarification, linguistic geography, rational reconstruction, logical formalization, regimentation into canonical symbolism, etc. were actively discussed. These discussions tended gradually to fade out in the 1950s and early 1960s, giving way to an enormous expansion of substantive philosophical analysis. So now, with the products of this expansion before us, we are in a decidedly better position to discuss its implicit, underlying programme" (9).

61 As Cohen notes, the quoted phrase comes from W. V. O. Quine, *Word and Object* (Cambridge: MIT Press, 1960), 270–76.

62 Cohen, *Dialogue of Reason*, 26.

63 The shift from a linguistic analogy to an intuitionist foundationalism has significant philosophical consequences. Most important, it means the loss of the presumed public nature of language, and it thus favors the quick return to a solipsism of individual experience. One of the great attractions of the linguistic formulation was its equivocal relationship to traditional epistemology. In analyzing the norms of linguistic usage, analytical philosophers did not have to decide whether these norms were derived from possible deep structures of thought, from social conventions, or from personal intuition.

64 Rawls, *Theory of Justice*, 47.

65 See references in notes 51 and 54.

66 Cohen, *Dialogue of Reason*, 73.

67 Ibid., 77 (emphasis added).

68 As mentioned earlier, Rawls was prepared to acknowledge that "the practical task of political philosophy" could be "doomed to failure," if individuals (within themselves and among each other) are unable to find the harmony postulated by reflective equilibrium.

69 See Richard H. Deane, "Ethical Considerations in Frequent Flyer Programs," *Journal of Business Ethics* 7 (1988): 755–62.

70 Nozick, *Anarchy, State, and Utopia*, 4.

71 Early in the text, Nozick reveals his argument (or a series of assertions) for treating individual consent as the only legitimate source of social obligation. "Moral philosophy sets the background for, and boundaries of, political philosophy. What persons may and may not do to one another limits what they may do through the apparatus of a state. . . . The moral prohibitions it is permissible to enforce are the source of whatever legitimacy the state's fundamental coercive power has. (Fundamental coercive power is power not resting upon any consent of the person to whom it is applied)" (ibid., 6). As a constructivist, Nozick was free to speak as though moral philosophy provided an unequivocal source of categorical norms, which dictated constraints on what anyone else could (justifiably) do. If no one could carry the burden of proving the state's right to enforce moral prohibitions, then the default principle for social relationships has already been defined by some residual notion of individual consent.

72 Ibid., 33.

73 One catches glimpses of arguments-from-ignorance in the early chapters, often in the interstices of rhetorical questions. For example, Nozick asks: "Why not . . . hold that some persons have to bear some costs that benefit other persons more, for the sake of the overall social good? But there is no *social entity* with a good that undergoes some sacrifice for its own good. There are only individual people, different individual people, with their own individual lives. . . . Talk of an overall social good covers this up. (Intentionally?) To use a person in this way does not sufficiently respect and take account of the fact that he is a separate person, that his is the only life he has" (ibid., 32–33). Here the postulated (intuited?) lack of a social entity is used as evidence for the fact that separate individuals have the sort of moral autonomy Nozick wants them to have.

74 Richard Dien Winfield (among others) identifies liberalism with "the repudiation of the appeal to privileged givens defining teleological ethics" (*Reason and Justice*, 110)

75 Ibid., 49.

76 Ibid., 50. In a well-known passage from *On Liberty*, John Stuart Mill reaches a similar stage in his argument about the limits of state interference with personal rights. "There is no reason that all human existence should be constructed on some one or some small number of patterns. If a person possesses any tolerable amount of common sense and experience, his own mode of laying out his existence is the best, not because it is the best in itself, but because it is his own mode" (New York: Norton, 1975, 64).

77 Ibid., 51.

78 Ibid., 35–36.

79 "My purpose here in presenting these examples is to pursue the notion of moral side constraints, not the issue of eating animals. Though I should say that in my view the extra benefits Americans today can gain from eating animals do *not* justify doing it. So we shouldn't" (ibid., 38). The shift from singular to plural in this first-person narrative is a common grammatical device used by analytical philosophers on the path toward reflective equilibrium. Judges use the same grammatical shift, which can often be found in majority opinions.

80 Mary Midgley, *Animals and Why They Matter* (Athens: University of Georgia Press, 1983), 101. The literature is now too extensive even to summarize. For an overview, see Tom Regan and Peter Singer, eds., *Animal Rights and Human Obligations*, 2d ed. (Englewood Cliffs, N.J.: Prentice-Hall, 1989).

81 Midgley, *Animals*, 95.

82 See in particular Midgley's chapter, "Women, Animals and Other Awkward Cases." Although she does not pretend that facts about animals can make an affirmative case for protecting their rights, Midgley does place great emphasis on ethological evidence to dispel assumptions that animals do not have such characteristics as social attachments and problem-solving capacities (see, e.g., 59–61). This strategic use of facts is identical to the role of factual evidence in appellate judicial review. It corresponds, for example, to Chief Justice Warren's controversial footnote reference in Brown v. Board of Education to social-psychological studies on segregation.

83 For the sake of brevity, I have not considered commentators who adopt the gen-

331

eral orientation of transcendental ethics but demur on granting specific axioms or postulates (often pleading that their intuitions can take them only so far, but no farther). These writers provide a significant skeptical counterpoint to the works cited here, although their criticism remains internal to the transcendental method. Bernard Williams has taken this internal critique about as far as it can go, with his systematic doubts that people's intuitions about ethical principles will ever line up in the orderly ways known to scientific inquiry. See his *Ethics and the Limits of Philosophy* (Cambridge: Harvard University Press, 1985). Such skeptical works have remarkably little impact on the field, since they stand on the same jurisdictional level with more activist ethical tribunals.

84 Philip Pettit, *Judging Justice* (London: Routledge, 1980), 40. Pettit notes that reflective equilibrium can also be understood strategically, "as a tool for pre-empting particular acts of judgment"—in short, a decision method for resolving the inevitable uncertainties and ambiguities of one's personal experience (39–41). This is the sense in which reflective equilibrium operates like a tribunal. Pettit decides to leave unresolved the question of which perspective (transcendental or strategic) should be adopted.

85 Cohen, *Dialogue of Reason*, 3. Popper's optimism was perhaps the more remarkable, in that he found progress in science notwithstanding his insistence that scientific theories labored under a presumption of guilt.

86 Ibid., 30–31.

87 Ibid., 18, 29.

88 Ibid., 61.

89 Ibid.

90 Ibid., 12, 11, 46, 1. Cohen appropriately distinguishes his aspirations for analytical philosophy from the essentially descriptive practice of a philosopher like Toulmin. "What the epistemologist has to investigate is not how beliefs come in practice to be thought well-attested. He is concerned instead with how beliefs *ought* to attain that status and what criteria they *ought* to satisfy" (44–45, emphasis in original).

91 Ronald Dworkin, *A Matter of Principle* (Cambridge: Harvard University Press, 1985), 172. (Here as elsewhere in Dworkin, the interplay of "I" and "we" reflects the unresolved struggle for jurisdictional supremacy between transcendental and temporal perspectives.)

92 See, e.g., David Luban, *Lawyers and Justice: An Ethical Study* (Princeton: Princeton University Press, 1988).

93 For an historical discussion, see David J. Rothman, *Strangers at the Bedside: A History of How Law and Bioethics Transformed Medical Decision Making* (New York: Basic Books, 1991).

94 See, e.g., Ruth Macklin, *Mortal Choices: Bioethics in Today's World* (New York: Pantheon, 1987).

95 H. Tristram Engelhardt, Jr., *The Foundations of Bioethics* (New York: Oxford University Press, 1986).

96 "Thinking about blaming or praising with justification presupposes a framework in terms of which there can be a criterion or authority for evaluation" (ibid., 79).

97 Ibid., 42.

98 Ibid., 43. Engelhardt repeats essentially the same argument several pages later (and, indeed, throughout the initial chapters). "Since this view of public authority will appear to some to be a radical suggestion, it is worthwhile remembering why one is driven to accept it. One accepts this view because of the difficulty of giving a general secular argument to justify a particular concrete view of the good life, and therefore of any public endeavor fashioned to support it" (48).

99 Ibid., 46. There is a potential conflict between this skeptical view of professional expertise and Stephen Toulmin's theory locating epistemic authority in diverse knowledge "fields." (See the earlier discussions of Toulmin's *Uses of Argument*, in chaps. 1 and 4). By construing argumentation as a type of behavior, Toulmin neatly avoided the measurement of common inferences (both popular and academic) by the uncompromising standards of logical deduction. According to Toulmin, argumentation behavior within individual fields can maintain its own pragmatic unity (and, thus, its situational validity) under the guidance of professional expertise. But Toulmin does not seem to consider the possibility that expert influence in argument fields may become epistemologically coercive (in Engelhardt's sense) and thus may raise moral objections to the ordinary uses of argument.

100 "The use of persuasion, inducements, and market forces is rendered rational as a means of making it worthwhile for individual persons to will to join in particular communal undertakings. Such manipulations, as long as they are peaceable, as long as they do not involve threats of force or unconsented-to interventions that make free choice impossible . . . form part of the proper fabric of a peaceable community. . . . Mutual peaceable negotiation emerges as the lynchpin of public authority in general" (ibid., 44). For skepticism about the consensual basis of economic markets, see, among other sources, Nicholas Abercrombie, Stephen Hill, and Bryan S. Turner, *Sovereign Individuals of Capitalism* (London: Allen & Unwin, 1986); Amartya Sen, *On Ethics and Economics* (Oxford: Blackwell, 1987).

101 Engelhardt, *Foundations of Bioethics*, 12.

102 Ibid., 13.

103 Bioethicists disagree among themselves on appropriate middle-level principles, and even more on the unstated presumptions that accompany any set of operational rules for promoting individual autonomy. For procedural recommendations that contrast with those of Engelhardt, see, e.g., Alan A. Stone, *Mental Health and Law: A System in Transition* (New York: Jason Aronson, 1976); Paul S. Appelbaum, Charles W. Lidz, and Alan Meisel, *Informed Consent: Legal Theory and Clinical Practice* (New York: Oxford University Press, 1987). The literature on particular case examples is, of course, quite vast.

104 On the growth of bioethical review committees, see, in addition to Rothman, *Strangers at the Bedside*, the overview in Bowen Hosford, *Bioethics Committees: The Health Care Provider's Guide* (Rockville, Md.: Aspen Systems, 1986).

333

Chapter 7. Transcendental Foundations

1 An unusually broad interpretation of these struggles can be found in Hans Blumenberg, *The Legitimacy of the Modern Age* (Cambridge: MIT Press, 1983) (trans. of *Die Legitimität der Neuzeit*, 1976 edition). In contemporary academic debate, phrases like "the problem of modernity" and "post-modernism" often suggest that the speaker has found a critical standpoint for surveying the leading presumptions of our era—a point of critical repose not unlike the ideal of juridical impartiality. See, e.g., Jürgen Habermas, *Der philosophische Diskurs der Moderne* (Frankfurt am Main: Suhrkamp, 1985).

2 Comparable themes can of course be found within classical philosophy, especially in such later movements as stoicism and gnosticism. More relevant for our purposes here, however, is the current interest in postulating a radical split between classic and modern value systems, which are then interpreted as competing sources of authority. Many contemporary appeals to classical learning presume this Kantian framework, according to which the authority of the ancients—partly or wholly inaccessible to us moderns—supports a postulated vantage point for challenging dominant ideas. For a range of examples, see Leo Strauss, *Natural Right and History* (Chicago: University of Chicago Press, 1953); Alasdair MacIntyre, *After Virtue*, 2d ed. (Notre Dame, Ind.: University of Notre Dame Press, 1984); Stanley Rosen, *The Ancients and the Moderns* (New Haven: Yale University Press, 1989); David Lachterman, *The Ethics of Geometry: A Genealogy of Modernity* (New York: Routledge, 1989).

3 See Norbert Hinske, *Kants Weg zur Transzendentalphilosophie* (Stuttgart: Kohlhammer, 1970), and "Kant's Begriff des transzendentalen und die Problematik seiner Begriffsgeschichte," *Kant-Studien* 64 (1973): 56–62; Ignacio Angelelli, "On the Origins of Kant's 'Transcendental'," *Kant-Studien* 63 (1972): 117–22. Hinske's views are spelled out more completely in his *Kant als Herausforderung an die Gegenwart* (Freiburg: Karl Alber, 1980). The word *transcendental* will be used in this chapter in a less technical sense than one finds in numerous post-Kantian philosophies and in commentaries on Kant. Many of Kant's successors and interpreters, hoping to avoid paradoxes associated with his strategic method, have introduced intricate verbal distinctions, often rejecting altogether the term *transcendental.*

4 Stephen Palmquist has shown how the word *perspective* can be used to distinguish the radically distinct levels within human experience that are presupposed by Kant's philosophical system. See the discussion in Palmquist, "Knowledge and Experience: An Examination of the Four Reflective 'Perspectives' in Kant's Critical Philosophy," *Kant-Studien* 78 (1987): 170–200. To clarify the epistemological status of all these perspectives, one must inevitably borrow terms from current philosophical frameworks, most of which derive from Kant's system.

This circularity might be mitigated by looking also to pre-Kantian philosophers. Leibniz and his followers, for example, explored the strategy of separating contingent and timeless principles into alternative levels of reality, distinguished in terms of their completeness. As J. N. Findlay sympathetically noted, Kant's accomplishment was to move the whole Leibnizian apparatus out of its postulated metaphysical sphere and to reposition it within an enriched human sphere. Kant thus replaced the metaphysical concept of "transcendence" with a problematic notion of the "transcendental." "Certainly, a great light dawned when Kant began to formulate his critical philosophy, but it was not a light that dissolved the old German metaphysics, nor one that based all certainties on the self-active, pure ego. It was rather a light that relegated the structures of the old German metaphysics to regions where they could only be thought but not known, and where one had to find a directly experienced, phenomenal surrogate for what so transcended experience and knowledge. . . . What Kant was to do . . . was to suspend transcendent affirmations in order fully to understand the complex experiential and cogitative mechanisms which alone give them a working reality. The transcendental note of the 'as if' can, however, not be eliminated . . . , for, in default of it, the whole structure of intentional reference will crumble and the self-active subject will become a plant torn from the rude soil in which alone it can flourish." (*Kant and the Transcendental Object* [Oxford: Clarendon Press, 1981], 68). Even this comparison, however, presupposes a rich stock of post-Kantian idioms for describing elusive transcendental strategies.

5 The tribunal passage occurs in the preface to the first edition of Immanuel Kant's *Critique of Pure Reason* (referred to hereafter as *CPR*), Axi–xii. All references to this work will include customary citations to "A" and "B" versions as they appear in the Prussian Academy edition, and translations will be adapted from Norman Kemp Smith's edition (London: Macmillan, 1964). For an original (if sometimes elusive) meditation on Kant's tribunal, see Gillian Rose, *Dialectic of Nihilism: Post-Structuralism and Law* (Oxford: Blackwell, 1984), chap. 1. See also Eve W. Stoddard, "Reason on Trial: Legal Metaphors in the *Critique of Pure Reason*," *Philosophy and Literature* 12 (1988): 245–60.

6 "Back to Kant" was the refrain in Otto Liebmann's contentious work, *Kant und die Epigonen* (1865; rpt., Berlin: Reuther und Reichard, 1912). For an historical overview see Thomas R. Willey, *Back to Kant: The Revival of Kantianism in German Social and Historical Thought, 1860–1914* (Detroit: Wayne State University Press, 1978).

7 See the chapters on "Science" and "Values" in Herbert Schnädelbach, *Philosophy in Germany, 1831–1933* (Cambridge: Cambridge University Press, 1984). Parallels with English thought are suggested by Willey, *Back to Kant*. For developments in France, see William Logue, *From Philosophy to Sociology: The Evolution of French Liberalism, 1870–1914* (DeKalb: Northern Illinois University Press, 1983).

8 See, e.g., Georg Simmel's "Der Begriff und die Tragödie der Kultur," in *Philosophische Kultur* (Leipzig: Kröner, 1911), 245–77 (trans. in Georg Simmel, *The Conflict in Modern Culture and Other Essays* [New York: Teacher's College Press, 1968], 27–46). For a survey essay see Kurt Lenk, "The Tragic Consciousness of German Sociology," in Volker Meja, Dieter Misgeld, and Nico Stehr, eds., *Modern German Sociology* (New York: Columbia University Press, 1987), 57–75. The inversion of this pessimistic streak can be found, e.g., in Ernst Bloch's *Geist der Utopie* (Munich: Duncker & Humblot, 1918) and *Das Prinzip Hoffnung* (Berlin: Aufbau, 1954).

9 Edward Caird, *The Critical Philosophy of Immanuel Kant*, 2 vols. (Glasgow: James Maclehose, 1889), 1:42–43.

10 Ibid., 1:26.

11 Ibid., 1:41.

12 Ibid., 1:39.

13 Ibid., 1:7.

14 Ibid., 1:8.

15 Ibid., 1:7.

16 Ibid., 1:43.

17 See Palmquist, "Knowledge and Experience."

18 Ibid. See also Stephen Palmquist, "The Architectonic Form of Kant's Copernican Logic," *Metaphilosophy* 17 (1986): 266–88.

19 After 1830, what Schnädelbach calls the "realist movement in culture" was sustained by increasingly successful battles against surviving exponents of Hegelian philosophy (*Philosophy in Germany*, 76–81). On critical realism and naturalism, see John Passmore, *A Hundred Years of Philosophy* (London: Duckworth, 1957), chap. 12.

20 The influential contrast between "nomothetic" inquiry (concerned with general, objective laws) and "ideographic" inquiry (concerned with singular, subjective experience) was formulated by the Baden neo-Kantian Wilhelm Windelband with the strategic aim of challenging the dominance of nomothetic methods. See Windelband's *Präludien: Aufsätze und Reden zur Philosophie und ihrer Geschichte*, 5th ed., 2 vols. (Tübingen: J. C. B. Mohr, 1915), 2:145.

21 This implication of Kantian philosophy was forcefully restated in the nineteenth century by Rudolf Hermann Lotze, whom Willey aptly describes as "a leader in the search for independent humanistic values in a culture captivated by scientific method" (*Back to Kant*, 47). On Lotze's influence, see Hajo Holborn, "Die deutsche Idealismus in sozialgeschichtlicher Beleuchtung," *Historische Zeitschrift* 174 (1952): 359–384.

22 *CPR*, Bxxiv–xxv. This famous passage clarifies the strategic relations embedded in Kant's larger philosophical system, in which the claims of speculative reason are restrained by the conditions of experience (or rule-governed spatial-temporal knowledge), but the claims of experience are themselves restrained by the postulated terms of practical reason. Both kinds of restraints, in turn, must be juridically approved by philosophical reason, which operates on the authority of transcendental deductions.

23 Perhaps the most-quoted evidence comes from the preface to the second edition of the *CPR:* "Morality does not, indeed, require that freedom should be understood, but only that it should not contradict itself. . . . The doctrine of morality and the doctrine of nature may each, therefore, make good its position. This, however, is only possible in so far as criticism has previously established our unavoidable ignorance of things in themselves, and has limited all that we can theoretically know to mere appearances. . . . I have therefore found it necessary to deny *knowledge,* in order to make room for *faith*" *CPR*, Bxxix–xxx).

24 *CPR*, Axi–xii.

25 This feature of Kant's work has been discussed by Dieter Henrich, among many

others, who notes that "Kant always had the tendency to make his theory convincing by virtue of its theoretical consequences and, as far as possible, to reduce analysis of its foundations to a minimum" ("The Proof-Structure of Kant's Transcendental Deduction," *Review of Metaphysics* 22 [1969], 650).

26 *CPR*, A787/B815.

27 Kant explicitly relates deductions to juristic practices and not to the formal syllogistic model that most of his interpreters have assumed (*CPR*, A84–85/B116–17). For a brief explanation of what Kant probably understood by juridical deductions, see Dieter Henrich, "Kant's Notion of a Deduction and the Methodological Background of the First *Critique*," in Eckart Förster, ed., *Kant's Transcendental Deductions* (Stanford: Stanford University Press, 1989), 29–46. According to Henrich, the term originally covered learned arguments used "to justify controversial legal claims between the numerous rulers of the independent territories, city republics, and other constituents of the Holy Roman Empire." Typically, the problem was to justify an acquired title or claim by tracing it back to some original act of possession or creation; but "the very notion of a deduction is compatible with any kind of argument suitable for reaching the goal [of justifying] our claims." And the peculiar structure of Kant's philosophical deductions, Henrich notes, allows the "court of reason" to resolve philosophical disputes in the absence of conclusive evidence: "Where conflicting claims cannot be settled . . . in favor of one of the parties," the tribunal's job is to issue "an order to keep the peace" (32, 39, 38).

28 See *CPR*, A84/B116; for commentary, see Klaus Hartman, "On Taking the Transcendental Turn," *Review of Metaphysics* 20 (1966), 225.

29 See, e.g., *CPR*, A794/B822. If these ostensive arguments in fact occur anywhere in Kant, it should be in the section on transcendental deduction, to be discussed below. Palmquist clarifies the distinction between the transcendental ambitions of Kant's own method and his somewhat conventional views about the logic of argumentation ("Knowledge and Experience," 188–90).

30 These arguments are intriguing primarily because of Kant's firm strictures against the apogogic method of proof, which he calls "the real deluding influence by which those who reason dogmatically have always held their admirers. It may be compared to a champion who seeks to uphold the honour and incontestable rights of his adopted party by offering battle to all who would question them. Such boasting proves nothing, however, in regard to the merits of the issue but only in regard to the respective strength of the combatants, and this indeed only in respect of those who take the offensive" (*CPR*, A793/B821).

31 This is surely the condition, reflected through numerous neo-Kantian lenses, that was so masterfully explored by Franz Kafka. Among many examples, see esp. the intricate discussion of "ostensible acquittal" ("scheinbare Freisprechung") in *The Trial* (New York, Schocken Books, 1988), 153–62 (trans. of *Der Prozeß*, published 1925).

32 *CPR*, A739/B767.

33 *CPR*, A739–40/B767–68.

34 *CPR*, A794/B822.

35 *CPR*, A756/B784.

36 *CPR*, A776/B804.

37 For Kant's careful distinction between ordinary ignorance and "ignorance in regard to all possible questions of a certain kind," see *CPR*, A761/B789. Additional remarks on ignorance occur at A758/B786.

38 *CPR*, A776–77/B804–05. (In Norman Kemp Smith's translation, the second sentence reads, "The burden of proof accordingly rests upon the opponent.") The entire quote continues, "These [hypotheses] are not intended to strengthen the proof of his position, but only to show that the opposing party has much too little understanding of the matter in dispute to allow of his flattering himself that he has the advantage in respect of speculative insight." Caird rightly notes that this negative argument "is of the highest importance both speculatively and practically" (*Critical Philosophy of Kant*, 2:157).

39 *CPR*, A776/B804.

40 "It is . . . apodeictically certain that there will never be anyone who will be able to assert the opposite with the least show [of proof], much less, dogmatically. . . . We may therefore be so completely assured that no one will ever prove the opposite, that there is no need for us to concern ourselves with formal arguments. . . . As against our opponent, . . . we are equipped with our *non liquet* . . . and under its protection we can look upon all his vain attacks with a tranquil indifference" (*CPR*, A742–43/B770–71).

41 As mentioned earlier, Kant denounced apogogic proof as "the real deluding influence by which those who reason dogmatically have always held their admirers" (*CPR*, A793/B821).

42 *CPR*, A752/B780.

43 *CPR*, A794/B822.

44 *CPR*, A751–52/B779–80.

45 See Förster, *Kant's Transcendental Deductions*, for critical summaries of Kant's various attempts at deduction throughout his writings. But critics cannot agree on whether such an argument is possible, even in the limited contexts where Kant tries to deploy it. Moreover, his interpreters (including his most ardent defenders) appear to import their evaluative criteria from outside Kant's system. Ironically, this method of argument, which is supposed to certify the highest tribunal of intellectual authority, is itself subjected to a variety of presumptive standards: verification principles, phenomenological reflection, and semantic analysis, among others. If, for instance, we take the common presumption that ordinary logical deduction and empirical induction exhaust the means of valid proof, we still find contrary assessments of Kant's efforts: among many examples, compare Humphrey Palmer, *Presupposition and Transcendental Inference* (New York: St. Martin's, 1985), 137–47, and W. H. Walsh, *Kant's Criticism of Metaphysics* (Edinburgh: Edinburgh University Press, 1975), 100–06.

46 See, e.g., the polemical struggle over criteria, between Stephan Körner ("The Impossibility of Transcendental Deductions," *Monist* 51 [1967]: 317–31) and Eva Schaper ("Arguing Transcendentally," *Kant-Studien* 63 [1972]: 101–16). These polemical exchanges have continued in a stream of anthologies: Stephan Körner, ed., *Zur Zukunft der Transzendentalphilosophie, Neue Hefte für Philosophie* #14 (Göttingen: Vandenhoeck & Ruprecht, 1978); Peter Bieri, Rolf-P. Horstmann, and

Lorenz Krüger, eds., *Transcendental Arguments and Science* (Dordrecht: Reidel, 1979); Eva Schaper and Wilhelm Vossenkuhl, eds., *Bedingungen der Möglichkeit: 'Transcendental Arguments' und transzendentales Denken* (Stuttgart: Klett-Cotta, 1984); Eva Schaper and Wilhelm Vossenkuhl, *Reading Kant: New Perspectives on Transcendental Arguments and Critical Philosophy* (Oxford: Blackwell, 1989); Förster, *Kant's Transcendental Deductions.*

47   Kant notes this circularity in his comment that the transcendental deduction "has the peculiar character that it makes possible the very experience which is its own ground of proof, and that in this experience it must always be presupposed" (*CPR*, A737/B765). For a useful discussion of this point, see Rüdiger Bubner, "Kant, Transcendental Arguments and the Problem of Deduction," *Review of Metaphysics* 28 (1975): 453–67.

48   In this light, Kant's commitment to philosophical reflection is similar to the faith he openly embraced in the practical sphere. As Stephen Palmquist has argued, "The whole realm of transcendental reflection is closed to the philosopher who is unwilling to adopt faith at this point" ("Faith as Kant's Key to the Justification of Transcendental Reflection," *Heythrop Journal* 25 [1984], 454). According to Palmquist, "Kant never intends his comments to provide anything but *good reasons* for adopting his transcendental perspective" (450). The transcendental perspective shares with the practical sphere a radical indifference to empirical evidence; both are immune from empirical or purely logical critique, but then both are prevented from basing their own credentials solely on empirical or logical criteria. Kant's own arguments on behalf of his transcendental tribunal come closer to a "good reasons" strategy, according to Palmquist, than to apodeictic proofs.

49   Ibid., 454. Bubner stresses the elements of indirect reasoning that surround this strategic move ("Kant, Transcendental Arguments and the Problem of Deduction," 463–66).

50   *CPR*, A829/B857.

51   "The holding of a thing to be true is an occurrence in our understanding which, though it may rest on objective grounds, also requires subjective causes in the mind of the individual who makes the judgment" (*CPR*, A820/B848). See also Bubner, "Kant, Transcendental Arguments and the Problem of Deduction," 464.

52   *CPR*, A738–39/B706–07.

53   In another image of rhetorical anarchy, Kant recommends his own philosophical constructions as an alternative to the "babel of tongues, which inevitably gives rise to disputes among the workers in regard to the plan to be followed, and which must end by scattering them over all the world, leaving each to erect a separate building for himself, according to his own design" (*CPR*, A707/B735).

54   See references in note 46.

55   Kant suggested that these Humean consequences are the only alternatives to transcendentalism, even though Hume would have entertained other options.

56   This deontological formulation appears frequently in the writings of contemporary philosophers. Ronald Dworkin, for example, consolidates his postulate of judicial principles by reminding us what they must mean if they are to fulfill

their intended function (*Taking Rights Seriously* [Cambridge: Harvard University Press, 1977], 115).

57   In this respect, schools of thought practice what Thomas Kuhn called "normal science" (see *Structure of Scientific Revolutions,* 2d ed. [Chicago: University of Chicago Press, 1970], chap. 3).

58   Dworkin, *Taking Rights Seriously,* 130. Other essays in this volume suggest that individuals form their own sovereign jurisdictions—or, at least, that no one can prove that they do not (see chap. 8).

59   The traditional view is admirably summarized in Richard A. Wasserstrom, *The Judicial Decision* (Stanford: Stanford University Press, 1961).

60   The term *neo-Kantian* is unusually elastic, covering diverse and often conflicting points of view dating from the 1850s up to World War I. For the initial phases of this movement, see Klaus Christian Köhnke, *Entstehung und Aufstieg des Neukantianismus* (Frankfurt am Main: Suhrkamp, 1986). A brief overview of major figures and disciples can be found in Hans-Ludwig Ollig, *Der Neukantianismus* (Stuttgart: Metzler, 1979). For an intellectual history of the movement, stressing its influence on social and political philosophy, see Willey, *Back to Kant.*

61   Neo-Kantian influences on current thought have been obscured by the partisan opposition of intervening thinkers (Schlick, Carnap, Wittgenstein, Husserl, Heidegger, Lukács, among many others), who "defined their new positions primarily by differentiating them from that once dominant tendency in academic philosophy" (Herbert Schnädelbach, *Philosophy in Germany, 1831–1933* [Cambridge: Cambridge University Press, 1984], 1). The post–World War I generation of philosophers tended to build their respective claims to originality on strategic overstatement: many of their works announce sharp, revolutionary alternatives to allegedly monolithic traditions of metaphysics, epistemology, psychologism, and (in negative terms) the almost conspiratorial neglect of deeper truths. Adversarial interpretations of one's predecessors were scarcely new, however. Strident polemics against Hegel, from the time of Schopenhauer to Otto Liebmann, helped prepare the way for the whole neo-Kantian revival (see Köhnke, *Entstehung und Aufstieg,* esp. 168–230).

62   The most famous critique was Friedrich Albert Lange's *Geschichte des Materialismus,* which went through numerous editions after its original publication in 1866. For a balanced description of the intense battles over materialism in the 1850s see Köhnke, *Entstehung und Aufstieg,* pt. 2. The success of neo-Kantian movements depended heavily on the strategy of distorting or oversimplifying the materialist adversary, thus clearing the path for various default alternatives.

63   For a balanced assessment of these movements, see Herbert Schnädelbach, *Geschichtsphilosophie nach Hegel* (Freiburg: Alber, 1974). On the historical school, see Georg G. Iggers, *The German Conception of History,* rev. ed., (Middletown, Conn.: Wesleyan University Press, 1983), chaps. 4–5. On Hegelian movements following Hegel's death, see John Edward Toews, *Hegelianism* (Cambridge: Cambridge University Press, 1980). Among the whole range of neo-Kantians, the case against historical analysis was less monolithic than the opposition to materialism. Historical determinism was seen as threatening the neo-Kantian postulates of human freedom and autonomy, but it was questionable whether all temporal elements should be excluded from the transcendental sphere. Most

neo-Kantians rejected the broad historical forces of the Hegelian schools and settled (by default) on postulated transcendental dynamics compatible with their respective political programs, which ranged from classical liberalism to democratic socialism. This meant, however, maintaining constant vigilance against relativism. See Willey, *Back to Kant,* chap. 7. For Marxist applications of the neo-Kantian model, see Gillian Rose, *Hegel Contra Sociology* (London: Athlone Press, 1981), 24–39.

64 Willey, *Back to Kant,* 26.

65 Ibid., 41, citing Paul Grimley Kuntz, introduction to George Santayana's study, *Lotze's System of Philosophy* (Bloomington: Indiana University Press, 1971), 48.

66 Kant always distinguished the juridical process of deduction from the putative authority of practical reason, and he never abandoned the conviction that transcendental authority must be apodeictic to provide a solid foundation for the apogogic defense of practical reason. In Palmquist's terms, Kant treated his transcendental perspective as the logical ground for his practical perspective. Nonetheless, Kant's most famous example of transcendental deduction borrowed the strategies of indirect argument that gave practical reason its smashing victory in the polemical struggle with scientific authority. The neo-Kantians collapsed these two Kantian perspectives; unlike Kant, they accepted the circular logic of grounding transcendental authority on transcendental arguments-from-ignorance.

67 The phenomenologists eventually posited a distinctive type of inspection, which gave the philosopher intuitive access to these various postulates. In later Husserlian phenomenology (signaled first in his *Ideen zu einer reinen phänomenologischen Philosophie* of 1913), this access was treated as an esoteric form of perception, defined as the default activity of consciousness after the "reduction," "suspension," or "bracketing" of what Husserl called the "natural attitude"—leaving behind a "phenomenological residue." (This last phrase comes from Herbert Spiegelberg, *The Phenomenological Movement,* 2 vols., 2d ed. [The Hague: Nijhoff, 1976], 1:140). Exploiting this new duality between natural and phenomenological awareness, Husserl could then project, as the major postulate of his own transcendental argument, the activity of constructing transcendental postulates ("konstituieren," in his vocabulary). This move brought revolutionary changes in idiom to the whole neo-Kantian enterprise. Spiegelberg's historical analysis of this movement provides excellent raw material for documenting strategic moves in the creation, evolution, and fragmentation of philosophical phenomenology. Nearly all the founding phenomenologists were reacting against specific doctrines advanced by their neo-Kantian teachers, and their adversarial criticisms still dominate current understanding of neo-Kantianism. Nonetheless, the phenomenological turn fits securely within the broader pattern of neo-Kantian (and, of course, Kantian) rhetorical strategies, including reliance on transcendental arguments-from-ignorance.

68 The Baden neo-Kantian Heinrich Rickert spoke of this location both as "unreal" and as a mediating world ("Zwischenreich," "Mittelgebiet"). See the discussion below, in the text surrounding notes 98 and 99. See also Schnädelbach, *Philosophy in Germany,* 184.

69 These distinctions between the two major neo-Kantian schools are often simply

a matter of interpretive emphasis. They are rooted in a specific tension in Kant's philosophy, between the legalistic rulings of the tribunal and the more pragmatic spirit of Kant's "regulative" interests of reason.

70 Kant's treatment of antinomies appears in the *CPR* section entitled "Transcendental Dialectic." His provocative account of these intellectual puzzles anticipated the modern fragmentation of transcendental reasoning: the inevitability of irresolvable disputes, the binary oppositions that structure these disputes, and the role of arguments-from-ignorance in their rhetorical development. Early on, Schopenhauer (among others) pointed out that Kant used indirect arguments to develop both sides of the antinomies. (A fuller discussion of antinomies, along with references, can be found in chap. 8.)

71 Gillian Rose places similar historical emphasis on the divergent movements within neo-Kantianism, although her argument leads to different conclusions from those presented in this book (see *Hegel Contra Sociology*, chap. 1).

72 Hermann Cohen formulated this jurisprudential analogy in his main ethical treatise, *Ethik des reinen Willens*, 2d ed. (Berlin: B. Cassirer, 1907). According to Cohen, jurisprudential concepts play the same structural role in the cultural sciences and ethics that mathematics plays in the physical sciences (66).

73 Hermann Cohen, *Logik der reinen Erkenntnis* (Berlin: B. Cassirer, 1902), 40.

74 See, e.g., William Kluback, *The Legacy of Hermann Cohen* (Atlanta: Scholars Press, 1989).

75 On the distinction between "process" and "procedure," see Joseph W. Wenzel, "Perspectives on Argument," in Jack Rhodes and Sara Newell, eds., *Proceedings of the Summer Conference on Argumentation* (Annandale, Va.: Speech Communication Association, 1980), 112–33. This distinction was discussed in chap. 4.

76 Cohen's approach to this problem may have stretched the neo-Kantian strategy beyond its capacity. While critics attacked his juridical postulates as empty abstractions, Cohen sought to show how they might actively produce their own contextual field of application. (His case was argued in terms of mathematical physics, however, rather than law. See the first work in his philosophical system, *Logik der reinen Erkenntnis*.) Cohen came to deny that any true contingencies remained outside the creative power of transcendental principles, and he appeared finally to abandon the entire dualistic framework upon which neo-Kantianism was founded. This Fichtean turn brought Cohen dangerously close to the Hegelian traditions condemned by Cohen's famous teacher, Friedrich Adolf Trendelenburg, and by the other neo-Kantians. In the field of social philosophy, Cohen used more conventional Kantian strategies to support his political commitments to democratic socialism (see Willey, *Back to Kant*, 112–16).

77 Rudolf Stammler, *The Theory of Justice* (New York: Macmillan, 1925), 89–90 (trans. of *Die Lehre von dem richtigen Recht*, 1st ed. 1902). Stammler's rhetorical strategy followed the basic Kantian pattern of transcendental separation by (1) overruling all conceivable empirical efforts to qualify the universal scope of the "rule of right law" and (2) limiting the power of that rule to sanctify any particular set of existing laws. In addition, he followed the Marburg line by assigning juristic functions to the transcendental postulate; his rule was explic-

itly defined as having the power—through the proper exercise of a method or process—to designate the right law in fluid historical situations. This was not a mere abstraction, Stammler insisted, because it was postulated as something much more powerful. Only with such a postulate, he concluded, "do we really get a universal legal standard. . . . Only in this way is it at all possible to have a proper definition and determination of particular facts" (92). Like other transcendental postulates, Stammler's rule was thus projected as a default principle, as the only way left open after dismissing the twin evils of relativism and abstract determinism.

78 Carl J. Friedrich has placed Stammler in the context of European legal philosophy, noting that "Stammler succeeded in showing clearly what the logical premises of all legal thinking are." To counter skeptical challenges to the formalism of his rule, according to Friedrich, Stammler attempted to impose the burden of proof on his critics, by characterizing the regulative power of right law as a method whose "validity is absolute until an error has been proved" (*The Philosophy of Law in Historical Perspective*, 2d ed. [Chicago: University of Chicago Press, 1963], 164, 160). It might be added to Friedrich's analysis that Stammler did not address the dialectical presumptions of this strategy: who is responsible for guiding the method, under which conditions must it be applied, and which parties are asked to bear the risk of non-persuasion? For the standard critique of Stammler's uncompromising formalism see Erich Kaufmann, "Kritik der neukantianischen Rechtsphilosophie" [1921], in *Rechtsidee und Recht* (Göttingen: Otto Schwartz, 1960), 187–93. Franz Wieacker has shown how Stammler's formula led to divergent critical responses: from skeptical attacks on the whole idea of "richtiges Recht" to the revival of natural law doctrines (*Privatrechtsgeschichte der Neuzeit*, 2d ed. [Göttingen: Vandenhoeck & Ruprecht, 1967], 586–98).

79 For guidance along this important path, see Karl Larenz, *Richtiges Recht: Grundzüge einer Rechtsethik* (Munich: Beck, 1979).

80 Critics who unmask the foundationalism of these arguments usually expose little more than the universalists already concede: that universal norms are esoteric, elusive, and inconsistently represented in everyday situations. From virtually the same stipulations, contrary conclusions may be drawn, depending on where the rhetorical burden of proof has been placed. This symmetry was discussed with examples in chap. 4.

81 This is the major theme in the first work in Cohen's philosophical system, *Logik der reinen Erkenntnis.*

82 Chomsky heightened the audacity of his theoretical revolution by announcing he was going back even farther than Kant, to Kant's illustrious predecessor Leibniz. This claim underscored the sudden shift away from a prevailing climate of genial empiricism, with a provocative return to metaphysics—that bête noire of the most adversarial of empiricists, the logical positivists. But Chomsky's concern with universal human capacities, postulated as the structural underpinning of everyday experience, seems more like a variation on Kant's categories. Chomsky's metaphorical assignment of these deep structures to a biological substratum was reminiscent of the physiological neo-Kantianism of Lange and Riehl.

343

83 This story is well told in Frederick J. Newmeyer, *Linguistic Theory in America*, 2d ed. (San Diego: Academic Press, 1986), chap. 2. Chomsky's notion of grammatical competence seems to parallel Cohen's juridical model of transcendental space.

84 Roy Harris, *The Language Makers* (Ithaca, N.Y.: Cornell University Press, 1980), 186–87.

85 Ibid., 187.

86 Ibid.

87 See Willey, *Back to Kant*, 112–16. Similar traces of neo-Kantian humanism can be found in England (see Michael Freeden, *The New Liberalism: An Ideology of Social Reform* [New York: Oxford University Press, 1978]) and in France (see Logue, *From Philosophy to Sociology*, chaps. 7–8).

88 See Willey, *Back to Kant*, chap. 7.

89 The Baden School's distinction between historical inquiry and the natural sciences goes back to Wilhelm Windelband's 1894 speech, "Geschichte und Naturwissenschaft," rpt. in *Präludien* 2:136–60. For Heinrich Rickert's notion of "cultural sciences," based on the distinction between "the individualizing method of history" and "the generalizing method of natural science," see *Kulturwissenschaft und Naturwissenschaft*, 6th and 7th eds. (Tübingen: J. C. B. Mohr, 1926), esp. 55–56. It is important to note that the Baden School never abandoned scientific aspirations for social or humanistic study and never conceded a monopoly on rigorous methodology to the sciences of spatial-temporal experience. Rickert's attack on *Lebensphilosophie* condemned the transcendental dichotomy of knowledge and life, which he attributed to the line of thought running from Schopenhauer to Nietzsche, Dilthey, and Bergson (*Die Philosophie des Lebens*, 2d ed. [Tübingen: J. C. B. Mohr, 1922]; see also Rickert, "Lebenswerte und Kulturwerte," *Logos* 2 [1911–12]: 131–66).

90 For a similar view, see Schnädelbach, *Philosophy in Germany*, 196–98. For the early development of critical realism in Britain and the United States, emphasizing its Kantian origins, see Passmore, *Hundred Years of Philosophy*, chaps. 11–12.

91 On the academic environment, see Fritz K. Ringer, *The Decline of the German Mandarins: The German Academic Community, 1890–1933* (Cambridge: Harvard University Press, 1969), chap. 6.

92 In opposing relativism, the Baden School sought to avoid investing empirical inquiry (or any other procedure premised on realist foundations) with definitive authority. Its development of transcendental philosophy as *Erkenntnistheorie* was meant to project a sphere beyond the recurrent philosophical antinomy between realism (especially empirical realism) and idealism—a sphere from which the respective claims of both empirical truth and value determinacy could be secured. See Wilhelm Windelband, "Was ist Philosophie," rpt. in *Präludien* 1:1–54; Heinrich Rickert, "Vom Begriff der Philosophie," *Logos* 1 (1910): 1–34, and *Die Grenzen der naturwissenschaftlichen Begriffsbildung* (Tübingen: J. C. B. Mohr, 1902), 1–30 (these and other important programmatic passages are omitted from the abridged English translation).

Just as Kant's philosophy left itself open to adversarial interpretations, the

Baden School's delicately balanced position was subjected to merciless opposition from logical positivism (which dismissed *Erkenntnistheorie* as antiscientific metaphysics), and from new ontological philosophies asserting higher forms of realism (including Husserlian phenomenology, Heideggerian existentialism, and Bergsonian vitalism, which derided *Erkenntnistheorie* as bloodless idealism). Finally, the Baden School is still being attacked as the prime source of relativist assumptions in social sciences. Arnold Brecht resurrected this critique, which faults Windelband and Rickert (among others) for acquiescing in the de facto demotion of social sciences to an inferior level of truth (*Political Theory: The Foundations of Twentieth-Century Political Thought* [Princeton: Princeton University Press, 1959], 207–58 [denouncing what Brecht calls "scientific value relativism"]). Rather than falling back on the Marburg-style postulates of Leo Strauss and other revivalists of classical natural law, Brecht followed contemporary positivism in presuming the higher standing of scientific authority. But he reversed the usual inference from positivist presumptions, ending up with what might be called "scientific value realism." At critical junctures, his argument falls back entirely on jurisprudential analogies (159–60; 359–63).

93 "Intuition and concepts constitute, therefore, the elements of all our knowledge, so that neither concepts without an intuition in some way corresponding to them, nor intuition without concepts, can yield knowledge" (*CPR*, A50/B74).

94 Compare *CPR,* B127–28. What Kant called "synthetic a priori" experience was possible only if we embrace this higher theory (higher, at least, than the knowledge it certified). Kant's rescue of universally valid science was thus an exercise of transcendental authority, which overruled the skeptic but also stifled the advocate of pure a priori speculation. Without the signifying influence of spatial-temporal perceptions, according to Kant, the pure understanding was likely to extend its universal powers indiscriminately: rushing to conclusions about the world, the soul, and the divine that superseded the more restricted knowledge produced by science. Kant explored these "transcendental illusions" in his chapters in "Transcendental Dialectic," in which he treats illusions as "natural" and "inevitable" (A293–98/B349–55).

95 *CPR*, A51/B75.

96 Just as the Marburg School could not investigate sources of the content of experience, the Baden School could not speculate on the origins of ideographic reality. Windelband, for example, spoke of a "residuum of incomprehensibility" (*Präludien* 2:159). Kant's *CPR* contains many similar references: the sensory content of experience "must be given prior to the synthesis of understanding, and independently of it. How this takes place, remains here undetermined" (B145). Kant elsewhere identified the content of knowledge with his jurisprudential concept of *quaestio facti* (A87/B119). This connection was exploited by the Baden School's leading legal philosopher, Emil Lask, who eventually questioned the neo-Kantian priority of the *quaestio juris* (see Rudolf Malter, "Heinrich Rickert und Emil Lask," *Zeitschrift für philosophische Forschung* 23 (1969), 88–90.

97 The larger landscape, for Windelband, assumed the presence of a "universal normative consciousness," as well as object-like norms ("Normen und Naturgesetze," *Präludien* 2:59–98. Rickert also favored the language of independent

345

objects (see *System der Philosophie* [Tübingen: J. C. B. Mohr, 1921], 112–21). On judgments, see Heinrich Rickert, 6th ed., *Der Gegenstand der Erkenntnis* (Tübingen: J. C. B. Mohr, 1928), chap. 3 , and "Urteil und Urteilen," *Logos* 3 (1912): 230–45. (Kant's philosophical treatment of judgment appears in the *Kritik der Urteilskraft* of 1790, trans. as *Critique of Judgment*, [Oxford: Oxford University Press, 1952].)

98 Rickert uses both "unwirklich" and "irreal" (see, e.g., *System der Philosophie*, 132–37).

99 Rickert assigns the validity of judgments to a postulated mediating region of transcendental space, variously described as a "Zwischenreich," "Mittelgebiet," and even "das dritte Reich" (see *System der Philosophie*, chap. 5).

100 These distinctions were developed in jurisprudential terms by Rickert's student Emil Lask in his brief but powerful essay, "Rechtsphilosophie," in *Gesammelte Schriften*, 3 vols. (Tübingen: J. C. B. Mohr, 1923), 1:311–18). See esp. Lask's description of the "judicial attitude towards reality," which creates the connection between concrete events and cultural values through the balancing force of transcendental judgments (317). It was in this context that Lask seemed to move away from the Marburg School's emphasis on the *quaestio juris* and to reassert the importance of the judicialized *quaestio facti* (316–17).

101 Gillian Rose has explored similar shifts within the neo-Kantian movement using the metaphor of multiple lawsuits brought before Kant's tribunal (*Dialectic of Nihilism*, chap. 2).

102 On truth as a value, see Rickert, *Gegenstand der Erkenntnis*, 309–12.

103 Schnädelbach has analyzed this shift in normative weight, from form to content in the basic polarity of Kant's epistemology, in the line of thought running from Lotze to the Baden School (*Philosophy in Germany*, 168–89). As Rickert's theory of individualization made clear, however, this "content" is not the sheer contingency of history, but rather the conceptualized content in scientifically formed Begriffe, according to his theory in *Die Grenzen der naturwissenschaftlichen Begriffsbildung* (one of the sources for Max Weber's notion of the "ideal type").

104 These values were reminiscent of Kant's "kingdom of ends," except that they were assigned to a postulated "transpersonal" jurisdiction (Lask, "Rechtsphilosophie," 292–93), in contrast to Kant's juridical individualism, in which "each individual is his own judge" (*Die Religion innerhalb der Grenzen der blossen Vernunft, Gesammelte Werke*, vol. 6 [Berlin: Georg Reimer, 1907], 95).

105 The postulated irrationality of values comes from this identification with the blindness of content, in accordance with Kant's epistemological dualism. This technical meaning of irrationality as something unmediated by formal concepts has survived in Max Weber's works. It seems possible that Weber adopted the term from Lask's 1902 work on Fichte (see *Fichtes Idealismus und die Geschichte*, rpt. in *Gesammelte Schriften*, vol. 1, esp. 127–38).

106 For this dichotomy, see Windelband, *Präludien* 2:145.

107 See Guy Oakes, *Weber and Rickert* (Cambridge: MIT Press, 1988) for analysis and a review of the controversial literature on this relationship. However one reads the circumstantial evidence of Rickert's influence on Weber, their arguments show parallel applications of transcendental strategy.

108 See Lask's discussion of the "realm of pure meanings," *Rechtsphilosophie*, 317–20.

109 The customary reference for Weber's theory is the chapter on bureaucracy from *Wirtschaft und Gesellschaft*, which appears in translation in H. H. Gerth and C. Wright Mills, *From Max Weber* (New York: Oxford University Press, 1946), 196–244.

110 Max Weber, *The Protestant Ethic and the Spirit of Capitalism* (London: Allen & Unwin, 1976) (trans. of *Die protestantische Ethik und der Geist der Kapitalismus*, 1904–05).

111 Weber, *Protestant Ethic*, 182.

112 This strategic move can be found throughout the writings of the Frankfurt School. See, e.g., Herbert Marcuse, "Some Social Implications of Modern Technology," *Studies in Philosophy and Social Science* 9 (1941): 414–39.

113 Weber, *Protestant Ethic*, 105 (the German term *Entzauberung* appears in this translation as "the elimination of magic").

114 This is a recurrent theme in the Frankfurt School; see, e.g., Max Horkheimer's essays collected in *Critique of Instrumental Reason* (New York: Seabury Press, 1974) (trans. of *Zur Kritik der instrumentellen Vernunft*, 1967). Heidegger's turn away from epistemology to fundamental ontology has also influenced critics of instrumental thinking, including Hans-Georg Gadamer; see also Hans Jonas, *The Imperative of Responsibility* (Chicago: University of Chicago Press, 1984) (trans. of *Das Prinzip Verantwortung*, 1979). In a move borrowed from Windelband, Habermas posits a distinct human interest in the noninstrumental deliberation of values, which he calls "hermeneutics." See his published lecture, "Erkenntnis und Interesse," in *Technik und Wissenschaft als Ideologie* (Frankfurt am Main: Suhrkamp, 1968), 146–68 (trans. as "A Postscript" in *Knowledge and Human Interests* [Boston: Beacon Press, 1971]). His attack on the dichotomy of facts and values, as with similar arguments from earlier representatives of the Frankfurt School, is not so much a rejection of dichotomies as a challenge to the juridical authority of facts. Habermas posits his hermeneutic human interest in order to draw instrumental reason into a Kantian polemic, in which values would reclaim the privileges of Kant's practical reason. As was noted in chap. 4, Habermas foresees the end of this polemic with the achievement of his transcendental discourse community.

347

115 In addition to other material cited in chaps. 4 and 6, see esp. Edward A. Purcell, Jr., *The Crisis of Democratic Theory: Scientific Naturalism and the Problem of Value* (Lexington: University of Kentucky Press, 1973).

116 Karl Mannheim, *Ideology and Utopia* (London: Kegan Paul, 1936), 57–62 (trans., with additional materials, of *Ideologie und Utopie*, 1929). Mannheim credits Kant for developing the "noological" perspective, from which value systems can be seen as "total" or autonomous (59).

117 Noting that transcendental projections of reality cast uncertainty on everyday judgments, Mannheim stresses that "it is precisely our uncertainty which brings us a good deal closer to reality than was possible in former periods which had faith in the absolute" (ibid., 75).

118 Mannheim criticizes the "philosophy of formal validity" in his 1925 essay, "The Problem of a Sociology of Knowledge," in *Essays on the Sociology of Knowledge* (London: Routledge, 1952), 134–90.

119 In the years following World War I, thought and being emerged as perhaps

the major dichotomy that was used to project philosophical alternatives to neo-Kantianism. Ironically, the subtle argument strategy perfected by neo-Kantianism was used to bury it in adversarial contumely, and most twentieth-century philosophers have been content to label the entire movement as empty formalism, idealist metaphysics, or lifeless essentialism. For Husserlian phenomenology, logical positivism, existentialism, ontological realism, and linguistic analysis, polemical origins have long obscured their strategic foundations, which presupposed the neo-Kantian rhetorical framework. When transcendental postulates were suddenly raised in opposition to abstract thought, the whole process of argumentation was separated from higher reality: true being left no room for mere rhetoric.

120 Mannheim, "Problem of a Sociology of Knowledge," 137.

121 Ibid., 138.

122 Ibid., 137.

123 See Mannheim, *Ideology and Utopia*, 84–108. Mannheim was fully aware of his neo-Kantian philosophical roots and had already written an astute analysis of alternative idioms for expressing transcendental postulates based on tensions within Kant's system. See his long essay, "Die Strukturanalyse der Erkenntnistheorie," in *Kant-Studien*, Ergänzungsband 57 (Berlin: Reuther & Reichard, 1922).

124 Mannheim, "Problem of a Sociology of Knowledge," 144. See also *Ideology and Utopia*, pt. 2.

125 Mannheim put his endorsement in idealized, qualified terms, nominating the "relativ freischwebende Intelligenz" as the most probable point of contact between political events and normative social reality (see *Ideology and Utopia*, 136–46). For an assessment of this controversy, see Brian Longhurst, *Karl Mannheim and the Contemporary Sociology of Knowledge* (New York: St. Martin's Press, 1989), chap. 3.

126 For a balanced review of these constructions, see G. E. R. Lloyd, *Demystifying Mentalities* (Cambridge: Cambridge University Press, 1990).

127 Donald Davidson, "On the Very Idea of a Conceptual Scheme," *Proceedings and Addresses of the American Philosophical Association* 47 (1974): 5–20. Elsewhere Davidson has proposed a quasi-legal presumption, his principle of charity, to institutionalize the practice of leaving proof burdens on the proponents of discontinuity (see his essay "Mental Events," in *Essays on Actions and Events* [Oxford: Clarendon Press, 1980], 221). Rather than quietly implementing this shift, Davidson has been remarkably open to using transcendental strategies to attack the transcendental postulates of other philosophers. Thus, in opposition to the presumption of cultural discontinuity, Davidson builds a default argument on the intolerable consequences of that presumption ("On the Very Idea"). He uses similar arguments in other essays to establish, for example, the presumption that individuals hold sovereign authority over labeling their own intentions ("Hume's Cognitive Theory of Pride," in *Essays on Action and Events*, 290). Hilary Putnam uses many of the same rhetorical moves and has proposed his own version of the presumption against transcendental dichotomies: his Principle of Benefit of the Doubt ("What Is 'Realism'?", *Proceedings of the Aristotelian Society*, n.s., 76 [1975–76]: 183–84).

128   One especially popular anthology devoted to this theme is Bryan Wilson, ed., *Rationality* (Oxford: Blackwell, 1970). By now, a classic polemic has developed around the attribution of fundamentally separate mentalities to non-Western, traditional societies. See, e.g., Peter Winch, "Understanding a Primitive Society," *American Philosophical Quarterly* 1 (1964): 307–24; and I. C. Jarvie, "Understanding and Explanation in Sociology and Social Anthropology," in Robert Borger and Frank Cioffi, eds., *Explanation in the Behavioral Sciences* (Cambridge: Cambridge University Press, 1970), 231–48. These debates revolve around certain Kantian tensions in classic works by Durkheim and Lévy-Bruhl. (The Kantian themes in both these sociologists are clearly acknowledged in Durkheim's review essay on Lévy-Bruhl, rpt. in Anthony Giddens, ed., *Emile Durkheim: Selected Writings* [Cambridge: Cambridge University Press, 1972], 246–49). For an overview of broader implications for other branches of social theory, see Martin Hollis and Steven Lukes, eds., *Rationality and Relativism* (Cambridge: MIT Press, 1982), 1–20.

129   The witchcraft controversies are anthologized in materials cited above in note 128. On the sagas, see M. I. Steblin-Kamenskij,, *The Saga Mind* (Odense: University of Odense Press, 1973) (trans. of *Mir sagi,* 1971). In all these cases, authors seem much less concerned with asserting the truth of their radical postulates than with challenging the narrowness of prevailing cultural presumptions.

130   Barney G. Glaser and Anselm L. Strauss, *The Discovery of Grounded Theory: Strategies for Qualitative Research* (Chicago: Aldine, 1967); Clifford Geertz, *The Interpretation of Cultures* (New York: Basic Books, 1973). See also Theodore Abel, "The Operation Called *Verstehen,*" *The American Journal of Sociology* 54 (1948): 211–18, an early essay (preceding the major reassessment of the 1960s), which stresses the continuity of "verstehen" with prevailing views of scientific procedure.

131   The distinction between social investigatory methods of "verstehen" and "erklären" has been rediscovered in Weber, and its roots traced to Dilthey and (sometimes) Windelband. See, e.g., Charles Taylor's frequently reprinted essay, "Interpretation and the Sciences of Man," *Review of Metaphysics* 25 (1971): 3–51, which reestablishes neo-Kantian "verstehen" as the default method of social analysis, after "erklären" has reached its limits.

132   Discrete jurisdictions of meaning were treated as naturalistic domains by Stephen Toulmin, as discussed in chap. 1. In the Anglo-American tradition, the linguistic turn helped to disguise the transcendental functions freely imposed on more ordinary experience. In much recent analytic philosophy, language takes the place occupied by judgments in the Baden School's value theory. In Wittgenstein's language games, Strawson's "descriptive metaphysics," Austin's "57 varieties" approach to word definitions, and Hart's "linguistic sociology," we are taken back to Rickert's *Zwischenreich,* that middle zone between blind data and empty rules. The normative authority of linguistic patterns faces the same pressures toward fragmentation that are found in the Baden philosophy: it oscillates between the universal ideal (reflected in Wittgenstein's argument against a private language) and the particularized jurisdictions of individual speech communities—if not individual persons (represented in the theory of reflective

349

equilibrium, which was discussed in chap. 6). The consistent opposition of linguistic analysis to anything transcendental (see, e.g., P. F. Strawson's dismissal of metaphysical and psychological interpretations of Kant in *The Bounds of Sense* [London: Methuen, 1966]) can be compared to the Baden School's critique of Marburg formalism. As with Windelband and Rickert (and Kant himself), this critical perspective has scarcely inhibited all these philosophers from using transcendental reasoning in creative ways.

Chapter 8. Dialectical Alternatives

1 Ludwig Wittgenstein, *Tractatus Logico-Philosophicus* (London: Routledge, 1961), §6.54 (the Pears and McGuinness translation uses "transcend" for Wittgenstein's nontechnical "überwinden"). Wittgenstein's word for "propositions" is "Sätze," which carries the connotation of something "posited," the outcome of "setzen" ("positing") in Kantian terminology. ("Satz" is defined internally to the *Tractatus* at §3.1, and Wittgenstein's related theory of "projizieren" [§3.13] has strong parallels with the "constituting" metaphors of Baden neo-Kantianism.)

2 Just before the quoted passage, Wittgenstein invokes "das Mystische," which he defines as "the feeling of the world as a limited whole" (ibid., §6.45).

3 Hence the unappealable mandate with which the *Tractatus* ends: "Wovon man nicht sprechen kann, darüber muß man schweigen" (ibid. §7). Less categorical injunctions appear in later forms of linguistic analysis, where we are warned against careless "category mistakes"; in therapeutic offshoots of linguistic analysis, where the student is comforted at moments of linguistic indecision ("we simply don't know what to say"); and in even more permissive environments, where we are admonished to be edifying in our rare moments of creative discourse.

4 J. N. Findlay, *Wittgenstein: A Critique* (London: Routledge, 1984), 3. Findlay uses the entire study to support his comparisons with Kantian reasoning but does not deal with intervening neo-Kantian positions.

5 A consistent feature in much twentieth-century philosophy is its adversarial opposition to neo-Kantian transcendental speculation. Using its own transcendental dualism of thought and some projected reality-beyond-thought, this philosophical era employs transcendental strategies to oppose transcendental self-reflection. Notwithstanding its common strategic aims, academic philosophy has moved in separate ways, taking variable paths toward projected forms of reality. Rejuvenated positivism, for example, postulates a quasi-sensual materialism suited to scientific endeavors; phenomenology and existentialism postulate a nonmaterial (and often dynamic) reality by analogy with transcendental subjects or objects; and pragmatism postulates a self-constructing reality based on idealized procedures. A composite of all three movements has been provided by Richard Rorty in his widely read *Philosophy and the Mirror of Nature* (Princeton: Princeton University Press, 1979). This work combines a skeptical attack on neo-Kantian epistemology (presented as a generic, monolithic adversary) modeled on earlier attacks by the linguistic heirs of logical positivism; a plea

for a protected (transcendental) sphere of nonmaterialist, "abnormal" discourse adapted from Heideggerian themes; and a postulated method for resolving conflicts between these potentially warring presumptions under the guidance of an informed, benign, Mannheimian community.

6 Wittgenstein, *Tractatus*, §6.52 (emphasis in original). Later, in a stunning reversal, Wittgenstein declared that the problems of life were, indeed, always resolved through the correct practice of linguistic behavior. In a series of writings, culminating in his *Philosophical Investigations* (published posthumously in 1953), Wittgenstein shifted the putative location of the tribunal from the transcendent, Marburgian utopia to an immanent, Baden-style linguistic a priori.

7 Heinrich Rickert, *Die Philosophie des Lebens*, 2d ed. (Tübingen: J. C. B. Mohr, 1922).

8 Brown v. Allen, 344 U.S. 443, 540 (1953) (concurring opinion). This famous acknowledgment came precisely at the beginning of an historic shift in the Court's basic constitutional presumptions, as discussed in chap. 2.

9 Paul Diesing, *Science and Ideology in the Policy Sciences* (New York: Aldine, 1982), chap. 2.

10 Representatives of the Chicago School have shown how to import these exogenous variables into the domain of rationality (Gary S. Becker, *The Economic Approach to Human Behavior* [Chicago: University of Chicago Press, 1976]). James Buchanan and his colleagues have applied neo-classical presumptions to non-market events (James Buchanan and Gordon Tullock, *The Calculus of Consent* [Ann Arbor: University of Michigan Press, 1962]), including the choice of fundamental social presumptions (H. Geoffrey Brennan and James M. Buchanan, *The Reason of Rules: Constitutional Political Economy* [New York: Cambridge University Press, 1985]).

11 Diesing, *Science and Ideology*, 29. The a priori foundation of economics was forcefully asserted by Lionel Robbins and Ludwig von Mises, among others. For a review and discussion of a priorism in relation to empiricist views of science, see Mark Blaug, *The Methodology of Economics* (Cambridge: Cambridge University Press, 1980), pts. 1–2. The explicit rejection of a priorism by Paul Samuelson and Milton Friedman has dominated postwar economic theory. But Lawrence A. Boland, among others, has shown the rhetorical limits of this position (see *The Methodology of Economic Model Building* [London: Routledge, 1989]).

12 Diesing's terminology leads in a Kantian direction. By classifying the unconditioned postulates as "subject" and the explanatory field as the "object," he has borrowed terms from Kant's paralogisms of pure reason.

13 Diesing, *Science and Ideology*, 29.

14 See Kenneth Arrow, *Social Choice and Individual Values* (New York: Wiley, 1951). Similar issues emerged when these postulates were extended to noneconomic problems (see Dennis C. Mueller, *Public Choice II* [Cambridge: Cambridge University Press, 1989]).

15 See Diesing, *Science and Ideology*, chaps. 4–6. In chaps. 12–14, Diesing summarizes this process from historical, ethical, and logical perspectives.

16 Such accounts seek to unmask the suppressed foundations of the targeted object, but they eventually encounter their own suppressed presumptions. Karl

351

Mannheim's *Ideology and Utopia* (London: Kegan Paul, 1936) is still the classic description of these paradoxes (see pt. 2).

17 Immanuel Kant, *Critique of Pure Reason*, trans. Norman Kemp Smith (London: Macmillan, 1964) (referred to hereafter as *CPR*), Avii.

18 For comparison between Hegel's reactions and other philosophical positions, see Arend Kulenkampff, *Antinomie und Dialektik: Zur Funktion des Widerspruchs in der Philosophie* (Stuttgart: J. B. Metzlersche, 1970).

19 A typical formulation occurs in this well-known passage: "There exists, then, a natural and unavoidable dialectic of pure reason—not one in which a bungler might entangle himself through lack of knowledge, or one which some sophist has artificially invented to confuse thinking people, but one inseparable from human reason, and which, even after its deceptiveness has been exposed, will not cease to play tricks with reason and continually entrap it into momentary aberrations ever and again calling for correction" (*CPR*, A298/B354–55).

20 "Now I maintain that transcendental philosophy is unique in the whole field of speculative knowledge, in that no question which concerns an object given to pure reason can be insoluble for this same human reason, and that no excuse of an unavoidable ignorance, or the problem's unfathomable depth, can release us from the obligation to answer it thoroughly and completely" (*CPR*, A477/B505).

21 Among the first generation of Kantians, F. H. Jacobi, K. F. Reinhardt, and J. G. Fichte tried to strengthen the legitimacy of Kant's philosophical procedures. To explain how the critical method could be possible, they posited sources of authority in direct intuition or in the dynamic behavior of transcendental subjects. See generally Richard Kroner, *Von Kant bis Hegel*, 2d ed. (Tübingen: J. C. B. Mohr, 1961).

22 See, e.g., Arthur Schopenhauer's criticisms in *The World and Will and Representation*, 2 vols. (Indian Hills, Colo.: Falcon's Wing Press, 1958), 1:494 (trans. of *Die Welt als Wille und Vorstellung* [1819]).

23 *CPR*, A426–27/B454–55.

24 Hegel's effort appears in the *Wissenschaft der Logik*, ed. G. Lasson (Hamburg: Meiner, 1952), trans. by A. V. Miller as *Hegel's Science of Logic* (London: Allen & Unwin, 1969). This work will hereafter be cited as *WdL* followed by volume and page numbers. Hermann Cohen's attempt can be found in his *Logik der reinen Erkenntnis* (Berlin: B. Cassirer, 1902).

25 Kant acknowledges that these Ideas conform with the "practical interests" of human beings, as well as following from the somewhat cryptic "architectonic interest of reason" (*CPR*, A475/B503).

26 See, e.g., *CPR*, A619/B647, A671/B699, A678/B706. Hans Vaihinger's *Philosophie des "Als Ob"* (Berlin: Reuther & Reichard, 1911) returned to this figure of speech and applied it to the whole of Kant's transcendental speculations. In the appendix to "Transcendental Dialectic" in *CPR*, Kant developed an extensive terminology for meeting the paradoxes that result from presuming an absolute separation between the sensory and transcendental orders.

27 *CPR*, A501/B529.

28 *CPR*, A751/B779.

29 "Possible experience is that which can alone give reality to our concepts; in its absence a concept is a mere idea, without truth, that is, without relation to any object. The possible empirical concept is therefore the standard by which we must judge whether the idea is a mere idea and thought-entity, or whether it finds its object in the world" (*CPR*, A489/B517).

30 The outcome can also be characterized as a transcendental argument-from-ignorance used successfully on behalf of the defendant whose demurrer is sustained by the higher tribunal. (In civil lawsuits, when a defendant files a "demurrer" to the complaint brought by the plaintiff, the court must determine whether the plaintiff has stated valid legal arguments *[quid juris]*, taken in abstraction from any evidence *[quid facti]*. If the demurrer is sustained, the defendant wins by default.)

31 See Hegel's early essay, "Über das Wesen der philosophischen Kritik," reprinted in *Jenaer Kritische Schriften*, vol. 4 of *Gesammelte Werke* (Hamburg: Meiner, 1968), 117–28. For the intellectual context of Hegel's Jena writings, see H. S. Harris, *Hegel's Development: Night Thoughts (Jena, 1801–1806)* (Oxford: Clarendon Press, 1983). John H. Smith has examined some rhetorical techniques in Hegel's writings from this period (*The Spirit and Its Letter: Traces of Rhetoric in Hegel's Philosophy of Bildung* [Ithaca: Cornell University Press, 1988], chap. 3). For a comparison between Hegel's response to Kant and Greek skepticism, see Michael N. Forster, *Hegel and Skepticism* (Cambridge: Harvard University Press, 1989). Forster's analysis is more convincing for Hegel's early period than for his mature philosophical system.

32 Kant seems to start down this second path on more than one occasion. See, e.g., *CPR* A650/B678 (despite the criterion of sensory experience, "we yet presuppose . . . a systematic unity of reason" as well as a "transcendental principle whereby such a systematic unity is *a priori* assumed to be necessarily inherent in the objects"); A697/B725 (we "must" presuppose "a wise and omnipotent Author of the world").

33 *CPR*, A489–90/B517–18.

34 Ibid.

35 John E. Smith, "Hegel's Critique of Kant," *Review of Metaphysics* 26 (1973): 455. Smith points out that Kant was obviously willing to keep certain issues from being sent down to the tribunals of spatial-temporal evidence—most notably the a priori synthetic relations of sense objects (447). The whole transcendental apparatus of the *CPR* was intended to show how synthetic a priori judgments could be possible, even though they were not reducible to sensations. Kant's treatment of the Ideas of reason, by contrast, adopts the same approach Hume used for the idea of necessary connection.

36 This is one of Hegel's main points in the Jena-period essay, *Glauben und Wissen* (Hamburg: Meiner, 1962), 13–40.

37 In addition to the whole of *Glauben und Wissen*, which considers Jacobi and Fichte, Hegel's Jena-period views were developed in *Differenz des Fichteschen und Schellingschen Systems der Philosophie* (Hamburg: Meiner, 1962).

38 Needless to say, this nonlinear pattern of argument makes the surface of Hegel's narrative far more turbulent than the ordinary reader would expect. For a variety

of perspectives on these interpretive challenges, see the collection of essays edited by Dieter Henrich, *Die Wissenschaft der Logik und die Logik der Reflexion*, in *Hegel-Studien*, supp. 18 (Bonn: Bouvier, 1978).

39 In Hegel's methodological discussions, the distinction between these two principles is not as rigid as this formal schema suggests. At times he emphasizes their difference: specification is associated with "negation" and enrichment with "negation of the negation," terms that have baffled most interpreters. But Hegel also provides a completely different style of explanation, inseparable from the substantive content of the *Wissenschaft der Logik*, which emphasizes the unity of these diverse functions.

40 The shift of proof burdens represents the narrowest point at which both conceptual strategies come together.

41 This open-textured aspect of dialectic conflicts with many popular interpretations of Hegel's philosophy, based on his grandiose allusions to the "Absolute Idea" at the end of the system of logic, not to mention his opaque references to "the end of history" in the lectures on philosophy of history. Hegel's version of conceptual closure is always embedded in a strategic framework, from which new conceptual advances can (and must) be made, by way of further strategic shifts. The dynamic structure of dialectical reasoning (always a puzzle, even for Hegel's best commentators) requires that its own highest principles be associated with motion and change. Thus the Absolute Idea, in the final sections of his system of logic, is nothing more than the ordered evolution of shifting perspectives, the enrichment of separate ideas through their mutual reflection. "To speak of the Absolute Idea may suggest the conception that we are at length reaching the right thing and the sum of the whole matter. It is certainly possible to indulge in a vast amount of senseless declamation about the idea absolute. But its true content is only the whole system of which we have been hitherto studying the development. . . . It may in this respect be compared to the old man who utters the same creed as the child, but for whom it is pregnant with the significance of a lifetime" (*Enzyklopädie der philosophischen Wissenschaften*, ed. F. Nicolin and O. Pöggeler [Hamburg: Meiner, 1959] , §237 *Zusatz*). For an interpretation of Hegel's political and historical writings that acknowledges this interplay of context and closure, see Shlomo Avineri, *Hegel's Theory of the Modern State* (Cambridge: Cambridge University Press, 1972).

42 Hegel associates this regress with the "bad infinite," which could never be eliminated from formal schemata. See *WdL*, 1:128–30; 2:466–68.

43 For discussion, see Hans Friedrich Fulda, "Hegels Dialektik als Begriffsbewegung und Darstellungsweise," in Rolf-Peter Horstmann, ed., *Seminar: Dialektik in der Philosophie Hegels* (Frankfurt am Main: Suhrkamp, 1978), 124–74. Fulda found no solution to the problem of transitions from 3 to 1, other than to invoke Kuhn's notion of paradigm change (163).

44 At the very outset of the logic, Hegel explores the limitations of classical and post-Kantian treatments of philosophical unities (*WdL*, 1:67–92). In his famous image from the preface to the *Phenomenology of Spirit*, Hegel dismisses this vision of philosophical absolutes as "the night in which all cows are black" (*Phänomenologie des Geistes*, ed. J. Hoffmeister [Hamburg: Meiner, 1952], 19).

45 The discussion of neo-Kantian constructions survived in various theories of "fictional" discourse, which was imported from neo-Kantianism through C. K. Ogden's translation of Hans Vaihinger's *Philosophy of "As-If"* (London: Kegan Paul, 1924).

46 These paradoxes are fully developed in Hegel's dialectical treatment of Grenze in the first division of the Logic ("Sein").

47 Among the most militant obstructionists were the Viennese positivists, whose successive principles of verification sought to enforce juridical barriers against "meaningless" utterances. As the quote from Wittgenstein suggests, however, there was more than empiricist skepticism that prevented twentieth-century philosophers from gazing too far beyond the limited horizon. Both phenomenological philosophy and *Lebensphilosophie* posited a transcendental realm of being that had been liberated from the illusory influences of mere thought.

48 For Richard Rorty, at least, this is "The World Well Lost," *Journal of Philosophy* 69 (1972): 649–65.

49 Interpreters can back up almost any position by extracting passages from their dialectical context in Hegel's systematic works. For Hegel's critics, this practice is perhaps irresistible and has a distinguished history going back to Schopenhauer and Trendelenburg. For friendly interpreters, especially for those who overlook the systematic reversals of dialectical rhetoric, selective interpretation is the traditional way of extracting the secret core from its self-refuting context. J. N. Findlay was somewhat less generous in his assessment: "Hegel is a philosopher whose misfortune it has been to fascinate philosophers of a wholly different and much less subtle cast of mind, who have then created a one-sided image of his thought to fit their rather limited horizons, and who have involved Hegel in the discrediting reaction which their own views ultimately provoked" ("The Contemporary Relevance of Hegel" [1959], rpt. in *Language Mind and Value* [London: Allen & Unwin, 1963], 217).

50 I have explored some of these points more extensively in "The Structure of Self-Commentary in Hegel's Dialectical Logic," *International Philosophical Quarterly* 30 (1990): 403–17.

51 We thus have consistent, dialectical reasons for discovering paradigmatic language at precisely this point of Hegel's narrative. Dieter Henrich has made an argument for adopting paradigmatic terms from a different portion of the Logic ("Hegels Logik der Reflexion," in *Hegel im Kontext* [Frankfurt am Main: Suhrkamp, 1967], 95–156).

52 Hegel, *WdL*, 2:239. All the words in this passage (including the pivotal term *determinate*) are Begriffe that appear within the triadic matrix of the logic.

53 As Rüdiger Bubner explains, it is at this point that "the Science of Logic may . . . be called the theory to which there is no further metatheory, because it furnishes its own metatheory" (*Modern German Philosophy* [Cambridge: Cambridge University Press, 1981], 165).

54 "It is precisely the nature of Universality to be the kind of simple entity which contains . . . in itself the greatest difference and determinateness" (Hegel, *WdL* 2:240–41).

55 *WdL* 2:239. Findlay's paraphrase is useful here: "The going forth of Univer-

sality into the specific and the individual can, however, be seen, by a shift of the dialectic, as an inherent reference of the individual instance to the species and genera present in it. The individual becomes a specimen, a concrete embodiment of organizing universality, and lives together with other similar specimens in a world organized by the same Universal" (foreword to William Wallace's trans. of the first third of Hegel's *Enzyklopädie*, published as *Hegel's Logic* [Oxford: Clarendon Press, 1975], xxiv).

56 This is the famous (if cryptic) message in the preface to Hegel's *Philosophy of Right:* "One word more about giving instruction as to what the world ought to be. Philosophy in any case always comes on the scene too late to give it. . . . When philosophy paints its grey in grey, then has a shape of life grown old. By philosophy's grey in grey it cannot be rejuvenated but only understood. The owl of Minerva spreads its wings only with the falling of the dusk" (*Grundlinien der Philosophie des Rechts*, ed. J. Hoffmeister, [Hamburg: Meiner, 1955], 17).

57 Images of this dynamic equilibrium abound in Hegel's writings, including the famous "bacchanalian revel" in the preface to the *Phänomenologie des Geistes* (39). That passage continues with a rare legal metaphor: "As this movement passes before the tribunal, the individual forms of the spirit do not endure as determinate thoughts, but rather they are at once affirmative, necessary moments, but equally negative and evanescent."

58 Stephen Toulmin used this term in his notion that "law-suits are just a special kind of rational dispute, for which the procedures and rules of argument have hardened into institutions" (*The Uses of Argument* [Cambridge: Cambridge University Press, 1958], 7–8).

59 For emotivism—that ethical adjunct of logical positivism—see Charles L. Stevenson, *Ethics and Language* (New Haven: Yale University Press, 1944). The aesthetic response to naturalism was classically restated by G. E. Moore in *Principia Ethica* (1903; rpt. Cambridge: Cambridge University Press, 1966), and the transcendental turn has led to the diverse deontological movements discussed in chap. 6.

60 The neo-Kantian context of Weber's theory was discussed in chap. 7. For a summary of how sociological theory has responded to Weber, see Charles Perrow, *Complex Organizations: A Critical Essay*, 3d ed. (New York: Random House, 1986).

61 The question of who is entitled to make this judgment accounts for further strain between nominally autonomous organizations and public procedures for legislative or judicial review. Market tests of bureaucratic effectiveness are also quite common, and almost uniformly critical.

62 See Perrow, *Complex Organizations*, chap. 2; Michael Lipsky, *Street-Level Bureaucracy* (New York: Russell Sage, 1980).

63 The advocates of muddling through have construed these departures from strict formal rationality as a presumptive virtue. See Charles E. Lindblom and David Braybrooke, *A Strategy of Decision* (New York: Free Press, 1970).

64 An important collection of this work is James G. March and Johan P. Olsen, *Ambiguity and Choice in Organizations*, 2d ed. (Bergen: Universitetsforlaget, 1979).

65 This paradoxical theory was whimsically named the "garbage can model" (Michael D. Cohen, James G. March, and Johan P. Olsen, "A Garbage Can Model of Organizational Choice," *Administrative Science Quarterly* 17 [1972]: 1–25).

66 James G. March and Johan P. Olsen dutifully repeat this empiricist premise in their recent work (*Rediscovering Institutions* [New York: Free Press, 1989], 2) with apparently no inclination to look for ambiguity at the heart of empiricism.

67 This strategic construction of Weber's definition depends on raising it to the level of a normative ideal, which can rarely (if ever) satisfy the strictest evidentiary demands of an empirical court. Bureaucracies are thus assumed to proclaim their normative authority in terms that beg for disproof under empirical scrutiny. Although empirical methods alone cannot deduce "ought" from "is," they can do so easily in combination with skillfully laid presumptions. By default reasoning, if organizations cannot supply enough empirical evidence to match their normative pretensions, their claim to authority will be immediately overturned. This technique can be used to bring all normative assertions under the full jurisdiction of a court where they will never carry their burden of proof. (It is important to note that Weber never intended his "ideal types" to be treated either as prescriptive norms or testable empirical hypotheses, despite the connotations of his language. Borrowing from a neo-Kantian logic that has long since fallen victim to adversarial ridicule, Weber was building on the Baden School's analogy with judgments, in which norm and context fit together the way universal and particular terms merge in the classical syllogism. Whatever the difficulties with this formulation, any neo-Kantian would concede in advance that ideal types are always underdetermined by factual evidence.) The popularity of empirical arguments-from-ignorance matches the general spirit of disillusionment that pervades most twentieth-century scholarship on socially organized authority. By contrast, neo-Kantian social theory (like Kant himself) often used its commitment to transcendental value theory to insulate social institutions (at least, selected ones) from empirical critique.

68 See Niklas Luhmann, *Legitimation durch Verfahren* (Darmstadt: Luchterhand, 1978).

69 Hegel deals extensively with these dualities in the middle triad ("Wesen") of the system of logic.

70 The rhetorical implications of this presumption are summarized by G. Thomas Goodnight, "The Liberal and the Conservative Presumptions: On Political Philosophy and the Foundation of Public Argument," in Jack Rhodes and Sara Newell, eds., *Summer Conference on Argumentation* (Annandale, Va.: Speech Communication Association, 1980), 304–37.

71 These theories were discussed in chap. 5.

72 Commentators have not been notably successful in restating Weber's theory of ideal types in terms external to the neo-Kantian lexicon. For an interesting effort to reconstruct the neo-Kantian context of Weber's theory, see Thomas Burger, *Max Weber's Theory of Concept Formation*, expanded ed. (Durham, N.C.: Duke University Press, 1987).

357

73 Hegel explored the reciprocal dependencies of internal and external perspectives in the middle triad ("Wesen") of the logic.

74 This last response was Kant's answer to Hume's external critique of causal relations.

75 Niklas Luhmann has emphasized this autonomous dynamic within organizational structures. In addition to *Legitimation durch Verfahren*, see his *Soziale Systeme* (Frankfurt am Main: Suhrkamp, 1987).

76 This concept of organizational hypocrisy has been admirably developed by Nils Brunsson, *The Organization of Hypocrisy: Talk, Decisions and Actions in Organizations* (Chichester: Wiley, 1989).

Index

361